Cognition and Instruction

Cognition and Instruction

Edited by

Ronna F. Dillon

Departments of Educational Psychology and Psychology
Southern Illinois University
Carbondale, Illinois

Robert J. Sternberg

Department of Psychology
Yale University
New Haven, Connecticut

1986

ACADEMIC PRESS, INC.

Harcourt Brace Jovanovich, Publishers
Orlando   San Diego   New York   Austin
Boston   London   Sydney   Tokyo   Toronto

ACADEMIC PRESS, INC.
Orlando, Florida 32887

United Kingdom Edition published by
ACADEMIC PRESS INC. (LONDON) LTD.
24–28 Oval Road, London NW1 7DX

Library of Congress Cataloging in Publication Data

Cognition and instruction.

    Includes index.
    1. Cognition in children.   2. Learning.
3. Curriculum planning.   I. Dillon, Ronna F.
II. Sternberg, Robert J.
LB1062.C64   1986   370.15'2   86-10715
ISBN 0—12—216405—9 (alk. paper)

PRINTED IN THE UNITED STATES OF AMERICA

86 87 88 89   9 8 7 6 5 4 3 2 1

Contents

3 Writing

Marlene Scardamalia and Carl Bereiter

4 Second Language

John B. Carroll

5 Mathematics

Richard E. Mayer

6 Science

Marcia C. Linn

7 Social Studies

James F. Voss

8 Art

Susan C. Somerville and Jeffrey L. Hartley

9 Music

Mary Louise Serafine

10   Reasoning

Raymond S. Nickerson

Epilogue

**Cognition and Instruction: Why the Marriage
Sometimes Ends in Divorce**

Robert J. Sternberg

Preface

Cognitive psychologists in increasing numbers are becoming interested in the nature of knowledge and knowledge acquisition mechanisms. Instructional psychologists as well as educators and individuals working in other applied settings are concerned with how best to enhance learning. A growing awareness exists of the desirability of applying information gained by cognitive psychologists to issues of instruction. An area of study referred to as "cognitive instructional psychology" has been born out of this shared interest.

While individuals studying the relationship of knowledge acquisition processes to instruction are brought together by their common interest in knowledge acquisition, these investigators are at the same time kept apart because the processes are studied as they are manifested in a given academic discipline. In the past, individuals interested in knowledge acquisition and instruction in mathematics have not had a tremendous amount of contact with individuals studying science or writing.

This growing desire to inform instruction with principles, methods, and measures of cognitive psychology, coupled with our sense of the current lack of fertilization across academic disciplines, provided the impetus for the current volume. Our goal was to present in a single volume a body of work that centers on cognitive approaches to issues of curriculum design and instruction across a range of subject areas. Chapters include coverage of reading, writing, second language, mathematics, science, social studies, art, music, and reasoning.

We hope that, in addition to providing a sense of the common goal toward which a great deal of research in this area is directed, the material presented here will help spawn further communication on the part of researchers, educators, and diagnosticians working in different areas. Perhaps we may eventually develop and apply more unified subtheories or theories of learning from instruction. The material presented in this volume is appropriate for advanced undergraduate and graduate students as well as for professionals working in various fields of education and psychology.

1

Issues in Cognitive Psychology and Instruction

RONNA F. DILLON
Departments of Educational Psychology and Psychology
Southern Illinois University
Carbondale, Illinois 62901

I. INTRODUCTION

The chapters in this volume center on applications of principles of cognitive psychology to teaching and learning in different subject areas. The influence of cognitive psychology is felt in all academic disciplines. What to teach beginning learners, the nature of knowledge differences between experts and novices, and how best to accomplish the goals of instruction are key questions of central importance to facilitators of learning, regardless of subject area. The pervasive influence of cognitive psychology on curricular matters is underscored when one notes the existence of terms such as *process* and *problem solving* in the vernacular of facilitators of learning from widely differing fields. We no longer speak simply of verbal or quantitative learning; we speak at once of verbal cognition, spatial cognition, and music cognition.

The chapters in the present volume contain treatments of the application of principles of cognitive psychology to curriculum design and instruction in science, social studies, reading, writing, second language learning, mathematics, informal reasoning, art, and music. In the pages that follow, a number of issues that I believe are important will be highlighted. The manner in which these issues are relevant in the different academic disciplines will be noted.

1

II. NATURE OF RELEVANT KNOWLEDGE: WHAT IS ACQUIRED?

Perhaps the initial consideration that precedes the effective design and implementation of instructional experiences centers on the nature of knowledge within the discipline. What do experts know that novices do not? A common thread running through the subject areas presented in this volume is a distinction between types of requisite knowledge underlying successful problem solving.

A. Declarative Knowledge

A distinction is often made between declarative and procedural knowledge. The former type of knowledge refers to the content and facts of a discipline. The key role of declarative knowledge across subject areas is easy to see from the chapters in this volume. As Nickerson notes in his discussion of inferential skills involved in informal reasoning, even in subject areas that deal with the use of knowledge of "forms" of argument rather than of their content, intellectual problems encountered in school or everyday life have content in addition to form. The more an individual knows about the situation or topic for which a model is built, the better equipped he or she is to evaluate arguments about that topic.

Similarly, language-related disciplines involve considerable declarative knowledge; examples are the semantic and phonetic values of specific writing units, rules of grammar, and other language structures. In the fine arts, expert music ability involves not only temporal and abstract processes, but also considerable music knowledge of a declarative nature, comprising what Serafine refers to as a "music grammar." Serafine points out that a body of compositions having a particular grammar or style share similar features because a unitary set of rules or principles is used to compose and understand music of the particular style.

The central role of declarative knowledge in problem solving is demonstrated by the examples given, although illustrations could be given from other subject areas as well. The point is simply that our success at engaging in complex cognitive activities such as problem solving depends, in part, on our familiarity with the content or facts of the discipline.

B. Procedural Knowledge

Procedural knowledge also plays a key role in successful performance in all subject areas. I find it useful to conceptualize procedural knowledge along two continua. The first continuum pertains to the level of specificity or generality of the processes being explicated. Processes may range from being specific to a particular task or test item (such as figural analogical reasoning items having one transformation defined by the addition of pattern elements) to explaining a class of problems (such as all spatial rotation problems; examples of such processes include transformation and comparison) to being general to all cognitive problems (such as the ability to encode problem elements).

Perfetti and Curtis discuss the lexical processes (i.e., processes involving the encoding of words) and comprehension processes specific to reading. Sampling rate is an example of a lexical process. Comprehension processes include semantic encoding, proposition encoding (involving proposition assembly and integration), and text modeling. One can note the correspondence between declarative knowledge in reading and in writing as well as between procedural knowledge in reading and in writing. In this regard, van Dijk and Kintsch (1983) point out that language users probably have recourse to the same or similar levels, units, rules, or strategies during either receptive or productive discourse processing. Also relevant is Brown, Bransford, Ferrara, and Campione's report (1983) of a reading comprehension strategy that is very similar to the writing strategy of knowledge telling discussed by Scardamalia and Bereiter in this volume.

Serafine conceptualizes music knowledge as involving a set of temporal processes and a set of abstract processes that may be characterized as moderately general in nature. Such procedural knowledge includes temporal operations involving succession and simultaneity as well as abstract processes, including abstraction, transformation, hierarchical structuring, and closure. Temporal processes are important in reading and memory tasks also; similarly, abstract processes can be applied not only to musical material, but to other kinds of problems, including spatial rotation and various forms of reasoning.

Procedural knowledge that is general in nature includes memory processes and inferencing skills. For example, note the correspondence between the intralingual, interlingual, and extralingual inferencing skills involved in second language learning and the inferential processes involved in everyday reasoning.

The second dimension along which procedural knowledge can be usefully conceptualized concerns how molecular versus how aggregative the processes of interest are in a particular investigation. The level at which processes are studied is of interest in the present context because this level influences the nature of the suggested units of instruction. If a given model contains production systems of an aggregative nature, resulting components of instruction will be aggregative (see Posner & McLeod, 1982; Simon, 1979.) For example, the elementary processes of inductive reasoning (i.e., encoding, inference, mapping, application, confirmation) delineated by Sternberg (1983a, 1983b) are more molecular in nature than are components of Voss's model of problem solving in social studies.

C. Self-Knowledge

A third type of knowledge is of interest. Nickerson calls this "self-knowledge" and defines it as knowledge about our own strengths or limitations. Self-knowledge may pertain to the state of our declarative knowledge as well as to our procedural knowledge. At different levels of experience or skill, different degrees or types of self-knowledge may be reflected in performance in a given subject area. Scardamalia and Bereiter make an important distinction between knowledge-telling and knowledge-transforming (i.e., reprocessing, active reworking) cognitive strategies in writing. They propose that expert writers possess a structure for setting goals, monitoring progress, and identifying and solving problems, and that this is not among the executive structures that guide the composing processes of novice writers.

The importance of self-knowledge has been considered by other psychologists. For example, Sternberg (1983a, 1984) has delineated a set of executive processes that he calls metacomponents. These processes reflect the cognitive activities in which individuals engage as they prepare to perform intellectual tasks. Other investigators (e.g., Brown & Campione, 1977; Butterfield & Belmont, 1977) have studied the important role played by executive, or metacognitive, processes among subject groups manifesting retarded performance. With more specific reference to memory tasks, metamemory processes have been demonstrated to account for significant amounts of variation in performance on memory tasks among children (e.g., Pressley, Borkowski, & O'Sullivan, 1984).

III. DECISIONS REGARDING THE RELATIVE VALUE OF VARIOUS KINDS OF LEARNING EXPERIENCES

The accelerating rate of change, and the resulting information proliferation, coupled with limited time for instruction, necessitates careful setting of priorities for learning activities. Facilitators of learning must decide what sorts of declarative and procedural knowledge (a) have the greatest generalizable utility and (b) best equip students to learn on their own. When students make decisions about the relative value of specific materials or entire courses of study, they often attempt to evaluate the to-be-learned material in the context of their broader academic training. In this regard,

Linn contends, with respect to scientific knowledge, that existing curriculum materials are not suited to the present needs of learners. She proposes that science curricula must prepare individuals to deal with an increasing rate of change in scientific knowledge and inform students of options available for gathering their own information. With regard to helping students gain skills necessary to learn on their own, Scardamalia and Bereiter contend that the development of self-regulatory mechanisms is necessary for gaining higher-order abilities in writing. Furthermore, they believe that current schooling efforts, in large measure, lack school practices that encourage students to develop such self-regulatory mechanisms.

This emphasis on transferable knowledge is reflected in the problem-solving orientation of models guiding instruction in the academic disciplines considered in this volume, as well as in the inclusion of a separate chapter on the nontraditional subject area of teaching informal reasoning. The many information-acquisition, information-processing, and problem-solving skills delineated in the chapters of this book should have broad applicability in academic settings as well as in everyday life.

IV. PROCESSES OF KNOWLEDGE ACQUISITION:
HOW LEARNING OCCURS

A. Factors Affecting Knowledge Acquisition

A general goal of instruction is to alter a learner's knowledge in the particular subject area of interest. Models of learning cited or described in this volume implicitly or explicitly involve two broad categories of factors influencing learning. These categories of factors are (a) attributes of the learner and (b) characteristics of the learning situation.

How learning might be enhanced most effectively depends upon certain of the learner's attributes acting in concert with the type of knowledge one is trying to increase. With respect to learner characteristics, the researchers whose work is presented herein give at least tacit acknowledgment to the widely held notion that, as Carroll states with respect to second language learning, people with certain personality characteristics and certain motivations may perform better than individuals with different attributes. Also, certain attributes may be conducive to learning under certain conditions whereas other attributes may be conducive to learning under other conditions. (The vast aptitude-treatment interaction literature with its mixed findings is relevant but cannot be discussed here; see contributions in Wang & Walberg, 1985.) Carroll, Perfetti and Curtis, and Nickerson all note the influence of context on learning.

B. Processes of Knowledge Acquisition

The manner in which knowledge is acquired is of considerable interest to cognitive psychologists. In addition to the theoretical importance of understanding knowledge-acquisition processes, such understanding is important for effective instruction.

Differences in acquisition processes have been advanced not only for acquisition of different types of knowledge, but also for acquisition of a particular type of knowledge in different subject areas. Processes believed to underlie knowledge acquisition include structural elaboration (as in the elaboration of subject matter knowledge) and structural transformation, that is, transformation by a set of mental operations (Posner & McLeod, 1982). Examples of how different acquisition processes are believed to operate on representations of different types of knowledge follow.

1. Declarative Knowledge

All chapter authors consider the importance of increasing declarative knowledge. For example, Linn notes the importance of elaboration of subject matter knowledge, including the hierarchical organization of the material, for learning science content. A distinction can be made with respect to the learning agent: is the knowledge elaborated by an instructor or by the student himself or herself? Carroll notes the central role of the learner in language acquisition (i.e., informal learning wherein language is learned through its use in exchanging information). Of course, instruction is not limited to the written medium. Serafine notes the important role of oral transmission in imparting declarative knowledge.

2. Procedural Knowledge

Some investigators believe that procedural skill acquisition may be brought about by factors internal to the learner. Serafine proposes that, in music learning, the abstract processes of transformation, abstraction, hierarchic structuring, and closure versus movement depend upon general development of the cognitive system; that is, change in these processes depends upon structural transformation. Similarly, Somerville and Hartley link graphic productions among children to general symbolic skills of spatial relations, equivalence relations, and other forms of representational thinking.

Whereas procedural knowledge, such as the skills and processes discussed in the previous examples, is believed to be influenced by the general cognitive system, many psychologists also view the acquisition of these processes as subject to direct educational intervention. With respect to the type of procedural knowledge involved in making inferences during science learning, Linn proposes that we cue alternative solutions to change intuitive conceptions. The implication here is that instruction in such cuing should be effective in altering such inferencing skills. This suggestion clearly is relevant to Nickerson's query as to how we may best accomplish this goal in everyday reasoning. In addition, Mayer proposes techniques of direct instruction for enhancing skill at translating relational propositions.

It is possible, also, that the same type of knowledge (e.g., procedural knowledge) may be acquired through different specific mechanisms depending upon characteristics of the strategies guiding problem solving. For example, Scardamalia and Bereiter propose different external acquisition mechanisms for the qualitatively different and less complex knowledge-telling approach to writing that characterizes younger students and the more complex knowledge-transforming approach characteristic of more advanced (i.e., expert) writers. Although knowledge-telling skills are believed to be acquired through ordinary social experience, knowledge-transforming procedures are thought to be fostered by instruction. Thus, different kinds of mental activities having different mechanisms of acquisition may comprise the distinct strategies used by individuals at different levels of skill or experience, as these individuals approach a single writing goal.

3. Self-Knowledge

The importance of enhancing self-knowledge or metacognitive processing skills also is noted. Both Linn and Nickerson advocate increasing metareasoning about selection of problem solutions, whereas Carroll makes this point with specific reference to language by noting the importance of increasing metalinguistic knowledge about communicative responses. The possibility of enhancing metacognitive processing skills through educational intervention is considered.

The preceding discussion has centered on the nature of knowledge and knowledge-acquisition processes. The application of these psychological principles (i.e., the manner in which cognitive structures may be elaborated or transformed) in the form of prescriptions guiding teaching strategies and the development of curriculum materials is considered in the following section.

V. COGNITIVE PRESCRIPTIONS FOR TEACHING

A number of points of consensus exist across subject areas with respect to how best to accomplish the goals of instruction. In this final section, I offer a few brief comments regarding (a) teaching strategies and (b) the nature of curriculum materials.

A. Teaching Strategies

In this context I will consider issues relevant to the manner in which materials are presented. First, there is agreement that the teaching methods used should reflect the known mechanisms of conceptual change. If, for example, students must change the cues used to select problem solutions in order to alter what Linn calls the "hard core of their intuitive conceptions," teaching tactics such as guided discovery may be called for insofar as they may help the students become aware of the availability of alternatives. The point that methods should be theoretically motivated seems obvious but bears mentioning, because examination of programs (methods and materials) has revealed that they are not always theory based. (Sternberg, 1983a, makes this point with respect to programs designed to enhance intellectual skills, and Scardamalia and Bereiter note that both traditional and newer instructional procedures designed to enhance writing skills have not been based on explicit models of cognitive behavior.)

A second point on which there is considerable agreement is that optimal teaching method is partly a function of the type of knowledge being acquired. Direct instruction, discovery, and guided discovery are frequently used teaching strategies. In science education, direct (i.e., expository) instruction has been found to be effective for the purpose of teaching subject matter knowledge, knowledge of hierarchical relationships among bits of information, and knowledge of valid strategies.

Similarly, direct teaching is one approach that may be useful for increasing decoding skills in beginning reading. Further, summarizing, clarifying, questioning, and predicting are procedural skills that can be taught directly to beginning readers to improve comprehension. Nickerson used a form of direct instruction to teach skills such as analyzing, distinguishing, and evaluating as well. Mayer notes the importance of these types of procedural knowledge and advocates direct instruction aimed at problem representation in mathematics.

As Somerville and Hartley's work on art and Serafine's treatment of music make clear, a wider view of "the" curriculum may be warranted— a view that includes knowledge of the range of representational systems and modes that individuals use. The judgment and interpretive skills so important in science, mathematics, and everyday reasoning are central to understanding artistic material.

With respect to teaching executive processes, Mayer believes that such planning activities are crucial in mathematics learning and should be taught, although they are neglected in the traditional curriculum. Nickerson also advocates direct teaching of executive processes coupled with practice, whereas Linn doubts that such metacognitive skills can be taught most effectively by direct means. She recommends instead the use of discovery-learning techniques. Scardamalia and Bereiter note that advances in helping students acquire the knowledge-transforming strategies used by experts have been achieved through a student-directed instructional technique known as procedural facilitation. The technique involves identification of self-regulatory functions observable in expert performance, description of these functions in terms of mental operations, cuing procedures in a manner that minimizes demands on mental resources, and designing external supports for reducing information-processing burden. Thus, consensus exists that it may be possible to teach executive processes although somewhat different teaching tactics are advocated by different investigators working in different subject areas.

Irrespective of the type of desired learning outcome, there is consensus among authors that optimal teaching tactics may vary as a function of the learner's ability (see also Doyle, 1983; Gordon, DeStefano, & Shipman, 1985; Snow, 1976). A finding that is not uncommon in the instructional psychology literature is that low and average performers benefit from strategy instructions whereas such instructions impede performance for high-ability individuals. Performance for the latter group of learners is believed to be hindered by imposition of strategies that are incongruent with the learner's own (already efficient) tactics.

The point I am illustrating with respect to teaching methods and types of knowledge is simply that different instructional approaches may be appropriate for different types of knowledge. My comments should not be viewed as indicating that intact and distinct methods are advocated for enhancing various types of knowledge and skills. Indeed, several different teaching approaches often work equally well for the desired learning outome. Moreover, a single (i.e., "pure") approach rarely is used in a given instructional sequence. As Carroll notes, it may not be possible systematically to derive information about different teaching methods because their conceptual distinctiveness may be called into question.

B. Curriculum Materials

1. The Nature of Materials

What should be the nature of curriculum materials, and how should those materials be graduated and/or sequenced for optimal learning? I have already delineated three types of knowledge, and it seems reasonable for curriculum development efforts to reflect, to varying degrees, these types of knowledge. Clearly, procedural knowledge has received less attention by teachers and other curriculum developers than has declarative knowledge. This state of affairs exists despite the influence of cognitive-instructional psychologists, information-processing methods and measures, and widespread acknowledgment of the importance of understanding and mastering prerequisite skills and processes if complex learning is to be accomplished. For example, in mathematics learning students need practice in problem representation—sorting problems by type, selecting pictures corresponding to problems, and sorting relevant from irrelevant information. Computations are stressed heavily, with little attention to the skills just mentioned. Voss notes, also, that social studies instruction might benefit from a greater emphasis on developing reasoning and problem-solving skills. Knowledge of executive processes has received the least attention, despite the important role of these processes in cognitive problem solving. My sense is that the relative degree to which the various types of knowledge and processes are embodied in learning sequences reflects, inversely, the difficulty of conceptualizing these types of knowledge, rather than the relative importance of each type of knowledge with respect to gaining expertise in the particular discipline.

The desirability of teaching transferable skills and teaching students to learn on their own also has been mentioned, although few specific prescriptions for appropriate instruction have been given. When we consider the endless amount of information a student could be taught, instruction in procedures for locating information at times may be clearly preferable to instruction aimed at acquisition of a large number of facts, many of which will be irrelevant in the changed environment in which the student will be functioning upon completion of school. At any rate, the teaching of procedural knowledge and of executive processes merits consideration in integrated curriculum development efforts.

2. Sequencing Learning Materials

In sequencing learning materials, a few areas of common ground may be noted across subject areas. Sequencing of intermediate and target competencies, whether and how to graduate materials across competencies (i.e., task constraints), and graduating instruction on the basis of developmental considerations (i.e., developmental constraints) are issues of interest. First, en route to learning goals, target competencies may be identified. Instruction may be directed profitably toward these overlapping levels of skill, noting that different skill levels may necessitate using different curriculum materials and may yield qualitatively as well as quantitatively different learning outcomes. For example, lexical access requires fluent word recognition. A reasonable goal en route to fluent word recognition would be accurate word recognition. With increased skill achieved through practice, accuracy becomes fluency.

Whether or not instruction (across competencies) should be graduated and, if so, the most appropriate basis for making gradations (e.g., functionality, occurrence frequency, simplicity) is a more complex issue than that of helping learners achieve successive skill levels for a specific competency. Carroll notes, with reference to language, that the simpler aspects of the curriculum are not necessarily the most useful, nor is careful gradation necessarily likely to produce the most interesting curriculum packages. In addition, processing capacity may have implications for gradation of instruction, specifically with respect to the amount of information given or material covered in a particular instructional sequence. Clearly, a simple answer to the complex issue of gradation of instruction does not exist.

As mentioned, successive learning stages or levels of skill may be a function of the student's experience with the material being learned. In addition, the nature of performance may reflect more general development of the cognitive system. As noted earlier, Serafine illustrates this point with respect to the abstract processes involved in composing music. Similarly, Somerville and Hartley's work provides evidence that the development of skills necessary for representational thinking may be reflected in the nature of children's graphic productions. To the extent that these or other developmental constraints exist, sequencing of curriculum materials should be done in a manner consistent with the emergence of relevant logical operations.

In this chapter, I have attempted to highlight a few areas in which cognitive psychology helps elucidate curriculum and instruction in a variety of subject areas. Psychologists with interests in widely differing academic disciplines are directing their respective research efforts toward a similar body of issues. Some of these issues have been described here. I believe this similarity in conceptual underpinning reflects the pervasive influence of cognitive psychology on advances in curriculum and instruction.

ACKNOWLEDGMENT

Preparation of this chapter was supported by a Spencer Fellowship awarded by the National Academy of Education.

REFERENCES

Brown, A. L., Bransford, J. D., Ferrara, R. A., & Campione, J. C. (1983). Learning, remembering, and understanding. In J. H. Flavell & E. M. Markman (Eds.)., *Handbook of child psychology: Vol. 3. Cognitive development* (4th ed., pp. 77–166). New York: Wiley.

Brown, A. L., & Campione, J. C. (1977). Training strategic study time apportionment in educable retarded children. *Intelligence, 1,* 94–107.

Butterfield, E. C., & Belmont, J. M. (1977). Assessing and improving the executive cognitive functions of mentally retarded people. In I. Bialer & M. Sternlicht (Eds.), *The psychology of mental retardation: Issues and approaches* (pp. 277–318). New York: Psychological Dimensions.

Doyle, W. (1983). Academic work. *Review of Educational Research, 53,* 159–199.

Gordon, E. W., DeStefano, L., & Shipman, S. (1985). Characteristics of learning persons and the adaptation of learning environments. In M. C. Wang & H. J. Walberg (Eds.), *Adapting instruction to individual differences.* Berkeley: McCutchan.

Posner, M. I., & McLeod, P. (1982). Information processing models: In search of elementary operations. *Annual Review of Psychology, 33,* 477–514.

Pressley, M., Borkowski, J. G., & O'Sullivan, J. T. (1984). Memory strategy instruction is made of this: Metamemory and durable strategy use. *Educational Psychologist, 9*(2), 94–107.

Simon, H. A. (1979). Information-processing models of cognition. *Annual Review of Psychology, 30,* 363–396.

Snow, R. (1976). Research on aptitude for learning: a progress report. *Review of Research in Education, 4,* 50–105.

Sternberg, R. J. (1983a). Components of human intelligence. *Cognition, 15,* 1–48.

Sternberg, R. J. (1983b, February). Criteria for evaluating intellectual skills training programs. *Educational Researcher, 12*(2), 6–12 & 26.

Sternberg, R. J. (1984). Toward a triarchic theory of human intelligence. *Behavioral and Brain Sciences, 7,* 269–315.

van Dijk, T. A., & Kintsch, W. (1983). *Strategies of discourse comprehension.* New York: Academic Press.

Wang, M. C., & Walberg, H. J. (Eds.). (1985). *Adapting instruction to individual differences.* Berkeley: McCutchan.

2

Reading

CHARLES A. PERFETTI
Department of Psychology
Learning Research and Development Center
University of Pittsburgh
Pittsburgh, Pennsylvania 15260

MARY E. CURTIS
School of Education
Harvard University
Cambridge, Massachusetts 02138

I. INTRODUCTION

Reading occupies a central role in school curricula. First, learning to read is *the* object of beginning instruction. No other single activity occupies as much time in the school day of a first and second grade child. Second, reading is the primary means of acquiring skill and knowledge in other subject matters. Social studies, sciences, foreign languages, and even mathematics and art require reading. Thus reading is the *sine qua non* of the school curriculum from the first day through the end of a student's formal education.

We have to take account of this curricular pervasiveness of reading in trying to describe how it is taught and how it is learned. There are at least two different "levels" of reading as a curriculum problem: (1) reading as the object of instruction and (2) reading as the means of instruction. A narrow understanding of curriculum design permits a focus on the first of these. A broader perspective on the curriculum demands attention to the second as well.

In what follows, we try to take the broad perspective. That means we have to understand two aspects of reading processes as they relate to curriculum issues. One concerns the processes of initial reading acquisition, and the other has to do with the processes of skilled reading comprehension. As far as curriculum design issues are concerned, it is clear

13

that initial reading must be taught in the first grade and perhaps beyond. Whether there is or should be such a thing as a "reading comprehension" curriculum is less clear. It is possible, as we shall see, to appreciate the need for instruction in comprehension without necessarily advocating a comprehension curriculum. What is clear is that a student's progress in subject matter areas is affected by his skill in reading comprehension.

Before dealing with these issues of reading curriculum, we must address the prior issues of how reading skill is acquired and how it is used. We do this by considering the basic components of reading as they are seen in skilled performance and in acquisition. Following this, we address the question of how these reading components can be instructed.[1]

II. THE COGNITIVE COMPONENTS OF READING

There has been considerable work within cognitive psychology that can be applied to reading. Furthermore, there is a reasonable consensus concerning how to describe and understand the cognitive components of reading. Rather than evaluate different models that may differ only in detail, we shall describe what can be considered a reasonable consensus model, noting occasionally how some other model might be different.

The Cognitive Model of Reading (as we shall call our cognitive consensus model) has these salient features: reading is a cognitive activity to be described by component processes in interaction. The outcome of this activity at any given time is a mental representation, or mental model, of the text being read. The processes that comprise the activity of reading are classified, for convenience, as belonging to one of two classes: lexical access and comprehension. To allow clear understanding of the Cognitive Model of Reading we need a few definitions.

A. The Cognitive Model of Reading

1. Definitions and Features of the Model

Text model: The reader's mental representation of a text at any point during reading—the result of comprehension.

Proposition: The elementary meaning unit of a text. Its essential property is predication. A proposition predicates some state or action of some other text element. This element is typically a noun, but can be another prop-

---

[1] Because of length limitations, much of the manuscript for this chapter was deleted. The deleted sections discussed reading tests, including reading readiness, decoding, comprehension, and vocabulary, as tools to help obtain a clearer picture of the difficulties a student might encounter.

osition. Thus, propositions are self-embedding, and sentences can contain an indefinitely large number of propositions, but must contain at least one.

Schema: The organized knowledge a reader has about concepts, word meanings, and everyday events and actions. A schema has an invariant core content and variables or slots which depend on specific information. For example, a schema for opening a window has a core that can be expressed as causing a change of state in a window from not open to open. The variable slots include the manner of opening (lifting, pushing, or turning a handle) and the degree of opening (minimal to wide). Some schemata are encoded by single words. The schema for causing an object to transfer from person X to person Y by the exchange of money is encoded by the words *buy* and *sell.*

Lexical access: Contact with a word stored in permanent memory, given the word as a visual string of letters. In most research, lexical access is identified with a specific experimental operation—deciding whether a string of letters is or is not a word. Although this operational definition is rejected in our analysis, we retain the essence of the lexical access concept, which is its minimalness. Lexical access occurs when a reader recognizes a word. It allows semantic information and phonetic information stores with the word to be used, but access itself does not necessarily involve meaning or pronunciation.

Decoding: The process of converting a printed language form into a speech form. In contrast to lexical access, it is a process which can apply to nonwords as well as words. It does not entail the assumption that letter-phoneme coding rules are used. One can speak of decoding a nonorthographic script, such as Chinese, as well as an orthographic one.

Semantic encoding: The activation of a word's meaning attributes as a consequence of lexical access. In reading texts, semantic encodings are contextually appropriate, i.e., the reader encodes the word in a manner suitable for its context.

Interactive processes: Processes are interactive in one of two ways: (1) They exert mutual influence. (2) A higher level process influences a processing outcome for which a lower level process would be sufficient. Interactive processing models are strongly interactive if they assume (1) and weakly interactive if they assume (2). Whether the Cognitive Model of Reading should be strongly interactive or weakly interactive is not clear. (It is doubtful whether any curriculum issue hinges on this.)

2. Specifics of the Model

These descriptive tools allow a further elaboration of the description of reading. The skilled reader reads and understands a text through a process like the following: As individual words are encountered, they are recognized by the reader (lexical access), and their semantic attributes appropriate for the context are encoded (semantic encoding). Most words have multiple meanings, and more than one meaning may be activated for a brief time, perhaps a couple hundred milliseconds (Swinney, 1979). However, the meaning most appropriate for the context is quickly encoded as part of a proposition. In order for propositions to be encoded, a syntactic *parsing* process forms word groupings, or constituents. Two or more words are necessary for the reader to assemble propositions *(proposition assembly)* and to integrate them *(proposition integration)*. The integration process is facile to the extent that the reader has the propositions to be integrated simultaneously available in working memory. To the extent that he must search memory to find a linking proposition, the integration process will be effortful. As propositions are assembled and integrated, schemata appropriate for the text meaning are activated. These serve the reader's construction of a text model by providing larger meaning structures and by guiding subsequent processes of semantic encoding and proposition assembly. A text model is constructed by the reader as soon as possible, with the first encoded propositions. It is continually updated and, occasionally, significantly altered as new text information gets encoded.

This much is a general description of skilled reading. In the discussion that follows, we explain how some of these processes work together. First we look at processes of lexical access, then at processes of comprehension.

B. Lexical Processes

An important fact about reading is that it involves words. It has been tempting in some reading research and in some instructional prescriptions to ignore words as the uninteresting part of reading and to focus exclusively on comprehension. Such neglect is not warranted by our understanding of how reading works. It works only with the encoding of individual words.

One of the reasons, perhaps, that word reading is taken for granted in skilled reading is that we have the impression that we skip words when we read—that we "sample" the words in a text and use this sample to construct a text model. Certainly it is true that a skilled reader does not "read" every word, and there are occasions in which the reader samples the text very sparsely. The rate of sampling—whether the subject samples densely or sparsely—is a matter of the reader's strategy, at least in part. But what is the sampling rate when the reader wants to gain a rather full and accurate text model? In such a case, the rate of sampling is perhaps denser than one might suppose.

The evidence we have on this word sampling comes from eye-movement research. In eye-movement research, the reader's eye fixations and eye movements are recorded during reading. The measures of greatest interest are the number and durations of eye fixations. A fixation is the period, beyond a certain minimum, during which the eye is resting on a particular location within set spatial boundaries. Phrased differently, how often the eye fixates on a word and how long it does so are of interest for the question of word sampling.

Carpenter and Just (1981) used a measure that aggregates all fixations on a word over a certain minimum. This measure, called gaze duration, provided data that Carpenter and Just (1981; Just & Carpenter, 1980) used to construct a model of reading that takes account of both lexical access and comprehension factors. (It is not typical in eye camera research to summate over individual fixations. The processing conclusions that are drawn may depend to some extent on whether gazes or individual fixations are used [Kleigl, Olson, & Davidson, 1982], but the general conclusions we draw here are not affected.) The most important result for the sampling question is that readers fixated about 80% for the content words of a text (nouns, verbs, adjectives, adverbs). Function words (articles, prepositions) received fewer fixations, but the impression that readers skip lots of words is strongly disconfirmed.

Fixation (gaze) duration depends on the length of a word and the frequency of its use. An average gaze duration is about one quarter of a second. Just and Carpenter (1980) report that the average duration for subjects reading a variety of texts was 239 ms per word. In their model, a word of two syllables required 52 ms more than a word of one syllable. And there was a 53-ms reduction in gaze duration for each log unit of frequency increase; thus, in their model, the effects of word frequency are greater at the lower frequencies. The general conclusion to draw is that lexical factors known to affect lexical access and decoding for isolated words are also operative during text reading. Readers do not skip many words, and the time spent on a word reflects lexical properties of length and frequency.

The reader's purpose does affect sampling, however. Readers instructed to skim a text make fewer fixations than readers expecting to see true–false questions on the text (Just, Carpenter, & Masson, 1982). However, skimmers show a similar sensitivity to the lexical variables of length and frequency. Skimmers appear to modify their sampling rate in response to the difficulty of the text they are reading. As a text increases in difficulty, readers who are skimming sometimes increase their sampling rate so that it is close to the rate used in more exacting reading.

What about speed reading? People can be trained to read faster. What are their lexical access processes like? According to the research of Just et al. (1982), speed readers can reduce their sampling rate and their gaze durations. Interestingly, speed readers are not more selective with respect to lexical choice. They are not able to fixate more on "important" words than on unimportant words. The eye has to discover what is important by reading. There is, however, a cost to comprehension in speed reading, especially at the level of text detail. Overall, we can interpret the eye-fixation data for speed readers as showing that readers can be trained to modify their lexical sampling procedures by making fewer and shorter fixations with relatively uniform and unselective sampling. They reduce their comprehension by a considerable extent because of this sampling procedure.

1. The Perceptual Span

Normally, a comprehending reader may fixate up to 80% of the content words of a text, and readers who sample less frequently appear to miss some things needed for full comprehension. Why is so much text sampling required for reading?

Part of the explanation has to do with the perceptual span, that is, the spatial extent from the reader's central fixation to the point at which useful information is no longer obtained. The perceptual span is surprisingly narrow. Contrary to popular opinion, the reader does not pick up much information at the edge of the page when his fixation is in the middle of the page. In fact, the perceptual span for identifying specific letters is only a few letters, perhaps three or four letters to the right of the point of fixation (Rayner, 1975). On the other hand, some information about word shape and word length is available out to 12 spaces from the fixation (McConkie & Rayner, 1973).

The general principle seems to be that the eye obtains useful specific information—that is, information sufficient by itself to identify a word—only from within the word being fixated. Information not in the foveal area is only facilitative, not sufficient. We have mentioned length and shape cues that are picked up; in addition, Rayner, McConkie, and Zola (1980) found that when the first three letters of a word were presented parafoveally (to the right of the fixation area), recognition of the word was facilitated when it was encountered foveally on the next fixation. Thus, while the word could not be identified in the parafoveal region, the reader was picking up some information that could be used when the word was fixated. This facilitation can be described as a preactivation of letters in a word that may reduce the amount of processing the word requires. At the same time, it seems correct to say that lexical access itself occurs only for the word being fixated. This is why a reader's sampling rate is so high.

2. *Processes in Lexical Access*

Given that lexical access is so frequently necessary in reading, the processes by which access occurs are important. There are many models of lexical access or word recognition processes. Some emphasize the bottom-up nature of word recognition and some allow higher level influences on lexical access. The central issues in how lexical access works include these: (1) Is a word perceived as a whole, or is the recognition of a word built up solely through perception of individual letters? (2) Does a reader's knowledge of orthographic structure, i.e., constraints on letter patterns, play a part in the perception of a word? (3) Is the visually encoded grapheme string recoded into speech before lexical access is completed? These issues have been examined in studies of tachistoscopic word recognition and in studies of lexical decisions, and there has been plenty of room for different conclusions. For example, the *word superiority effect,* which refers to greater accuracy in perception of a letter when it is in a normal letter string, has been thoroughly examined. Although it appears that the bulk of the evidence supports the word superiority effect, there are a number of boundary conditions on it (Baron, 1979; Vellutino, 1982). Certainly the word superiority effect has important implications for reading. People's intuitions about their reading are that they see words more than letters, and the word superiority effect supports this intuition. We "see" a letter in a word better than a letter in exactly the same position in a nonword. Nevertheless, it seems equally clear that lexical access is possible only through the recognition of constituent letters.

So-called bottom-up theories of word perception make use of this last fact. The recognition of a word is described by assuming that each level of perceptual analysis uses the results of a lower level of analysis. Features such as lines and angles are detected, and this analysis triggers perception of a letter. As enough letters are recognized, the next level, recognition of a word, is achieved. This general account of word recognition, emphasizing the passing up of information from the sensory level through feature and letter and finally to word levels is a consensus of word recognition theories that differ in other ways (Gough, 1972; LaBerge & Samuels, 1974; Massaro, 1975).

One way to understand both salient facts about word recognition—i.e., both the superior perception of words and the necessity of letter perception for word recognition—is to look at the interactive model of Rumelhart and McClelland (McClelland & Rumelhart, 1981; Rumelhart & McClelland, 1981, 1982). This model includes bottom-up processes; information passes up from sensory input through feature detectors, letter identification, and word identification. However, as represented in Figure 1, the information process goes both ways, both up and down.

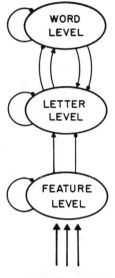

Fig. 1.   The interactive model of word representation, based on Rumelhart and McClelland (1981). The word level, letter level, and feature level communicate through activation that travels both upward from features and downward from words.

The circles in Figure 1 indicate levels of information in a memory representation. The arrows indicate activation between levels. The feature level represents simple lines and angles that make up letters, the letter level represents letters, etc. Activation of a word occurs because a letter it contains is activated from the feature level.

The model can be understood in terms of providing "evidence." Features provide evidence for letters, and letters provide evidence for words. The special feature of the model is that words also provide evidence for letters and letters also provide evidence for features. Information (activation) flows from the top down as well as from the bottom up. For example, assume that the system has evidence from the feature level that is consistent with an E, an F, or a T in the first position, that is, one vertical line with at least one right extending horizontal line. This means any word of a specified length that begins with E, F, or T gets some activation. At nearly the same time, evidence accumulates favoring an H in the second position. This increases activation of many words beginning with T (*this, that,* etc.) but few or no words beginning with F or E. Since activation spreads down to letters from words, the constituent letters of all TH words increase in their activation. Thus initial T gets activation from its links with all TH words. The evidence that was initially consistent with E, F, or T has by now been replaced by strong evidence for T without any further feature information to distinguish T from E or F. Of course, more feature information has become available, and evidence for additional letters has accumulated. So the up-and-down activation has allowed ample evidence for a particular word, e.g., *then,* and this word rather than *this, that,* and the last competitor, *them,* is the word accessed. Thus, out of many words that are activated because of lower level information, only one word is actually accessed.

The model is one of the strongly interactive type. There is a direct influence of higher level information on lower level information. Whether such a powerfully interactive model is necessary to explain the facts of word perception is not entirely clear, although it is clear that this model does well in accounting for a variety of such facts (Rumelhart & McClelland, 1981). Bottom-up models that are more strongly constrained by specific assumptions concerning processing may work as well. However, the interactive model is especially suitable for describing lexical access in skilled reading, and in our opinion, nothing crucial for curriculum hinges on which model is "best."

3. Orthographic Structure

A second major issue in lexical access is whether there is an intermediate level of analysis between the individual letter and the word. When the reader encounters the word *train* he has more than the knowledge that the letters *t, r, a, i, n* link with the word *train.* He knows that while *train* is a word in English, a possible but nonexistent word results from a minor rearrangement of letters. *Trian* is not a word in English, but it could be insofar as it is *orthographically* well formed. The same letters rearranged into *rtnai* clearly are othographically ill formed and could not be an English word. Every skilled reader of English has implicit knowledge of such orthographic rules, and knowledge of English orthography must play a role in lexical access. In fact, the patterns of allowable spelling have played an important role in the *perceptual discrimination* theory of reading (Gibson & Levin, 1975). The reader learns from experience patterns of letters that may occur. These thousands of permissible patterns can be summarized by the rules of English orthography (Venezky, 1970). It is implicit knowledge of those rules that we would like to impute to the skilled reader. Such knowledge helps explain part of the word superiority effect. Any well-formed orthographic string is recognized more readily than an ill-formed string. More importantly, it helps explain the reader's ability to read unfamiliar words—to recognize them as candidate words in his language and to pronounce them.

It is possible that a model of lexical access can get by without such an orthographic level. The interactive model of Rumelhart and McClelland does not have an orthographic level. In effect, however, the orthographic knowledge is represented in the model implicitly. This knowledge is the sum of all the letter level connections to specific word positions. Thus *tr* is a well-formed word-initial sequence and *rt* is an ill-formed word-initial sequence. (The reverse is true for the end of a word.) There are no word level nodes in the system that have links from both their first position to *r* and their second position to *t*. There are many links from first position *t* and second position *r*. Thus the system "knows" about orthography even though it cannot say much about what it knows. We could modify the system to have levels of letter patterns in between the letter level and the word level. However, it is not clear that this is necessary. It is clear that some implicit knowledge of orthography is part of what the reader has available to help with lexical access.

4. Speech Processes in Lexical Access

The third major issue in lexical access is whether the reader converts the graphemic input into a phonemic code as part of lexical access. In the usual formulation of this issue, the question is whether the visual input is recoded into a speech-based form before the word is accessed. It is clear that in many situations—e.g., reading a long and unfamiliar word—such recoding does occur. The reader can in fact notice his attempt to recode the word into a speech form and search memory for the speech form. However, it is far from clear that such recoding occurs routinely prior to lexical access. There is evidence against the assumption of routine speech recoding, especially in lexical decision tasks (Coltheart, 1978).

A proposal by Perfetti and McCutchen (1982) is that speech processes *do* accompany lexical access. However, they may or may not precede lexical access. Whether they do or not depends on whether evidence for a specific word accumulates rapidly enough. If it does, speech activation will not yet have occurred. If evidence for a word is more slowly accumulated, the speech activation will have had time to occur. The mechanism for this activation is provided by the kind of interactive model proposed by Rumelhart and McClelland (1981). In addition to the letter and word levels shown in Figure 1, we need a phoneme level. This level has links to both the letter level and the word level, but is not "in between" them. Thus phoneme activation is not necessary for lexical access, but it occurs nonetheless. As evidence for letters accumulates, phonemes that correspond to the letters also get activated. And as evidence for a word accumulates, the phonemes that compose it also get activated. Thus whether the reader's "inner speech" for a word is activated before he "accesses" the word depends on the exact time course of various activation functions. But activation of speech sounds will always occur. The activation of speech is important because it serves the reader's comprehension processes.

5. *Automaticity*

The principle of automaticity plays a central role in lexical access and is perhaps less controversial than the three major issues we have identified (word superiority, orthographic knowledge, and speech coding). LaBerge and Samuels (1974) developed this very important concept for reading. The basic idea is that some processes demand attention and some do not. Attention is a limited commodity. The reader can direct attention to one of the many elements available during the viewing of a word, but he cannot attend to all of them. LaBerge and Samuels demonstrated that the reader, with much practice, transfers some processing from attention demanding to automatic. For example, letter perception becomes automatic with practice; it requires none of the limited attention resources. The same principle extends to words, although to a more limited extent. Lexical access, with practice, may become automatic. There are ample demonstrations of this from various versions of the Stroop phenomenon: Skilled readers find it very difficult to name colors when an incorrect color name is printed on each color (e.g., the word *green* on a red stimulus). The word automatically activates its lexical entry in memory and interferes with the subject's main attention-demanding task.

6. *Lexical Access in Context*

A central question for reading is how lexical access works in context. That is, are the principles of lexical access modified when words occur in text? Our models of lexical access have been derived largely from research using single word paradigms, whether subthreshold tachistoscopic experiments that measure accuracy or suprathreshold experiments that measure speed. One model of lexical access that is developed within text itself is that of Carpenter and Just based on eye-movement research. We have already noted that their model allocates significant processing time during lexical access to words that are longer and less familiar. These factors are important in research on single words as well. It will not be the case that context dramatically alters processes of lexical access. That lexical access processes—either prior to access or following access—are facilitated by context is obvious and important. But we do not appear to need an entirely different theory to account for how lexical access works.

The fact that context facilitates word identification is well documented. The word *decision* is easier to identify when it follows *administrative* than when it occurs in isolation. The general principle is that text constrains its words on semantic, syntactic, and pragmatic grounds. *The president was faced with a difficult. . . .* The final word in such a context is more likely to be a noun than a verb, is likely to be semantically congruent with presidential activities that are difficult, and is (pragmatically) likely to be stylistically consistent with the rest of the text. Research has shown that the extent to which a word is predictable in context determines how quickly or accurately it is identified (Perfetti, Goldman, & Hogaboam, 1979; Stanovich & West, 1981; Tulving & Gold, 1963).

Is the facilitative effect of context great enough to allow the reader to skip words? We have already seen that most content words in a text are fixated by the reader. The impression that a reader skips words that are predictable from context may be false. Indeed, McConkie and Zola (1981) found that predictable words were not skipped any more than unpredictable words, although the reader spent about 15 fewer milliseconds on a word that was highly predictable. Ehrlich and Rayner (1981), using shorter words than McConkie and Zola, did find that highly predictable words were occasionally not fixated and when they were fixated, received about 30 milliseconds less fixation time than less predictable words. The overall conclusion is that context affects the probability of fixation only slightly, but has a more reliable influence on how long the reader views a word.

The effects of context are thus both profound and limited. Readers identify words more quickly in context, but they do not often skip them. It is possible that the effect of context on words could be explained within the interactive activation model. This would mean that prior to any activation from letters, semantic activation has spread to words in memory because of semantic processes of the reader. These processes would include especially automatic spreading activation (Collins & Loftus, 1975). However, we must acknowledge some uncertainty about this. It is possible that in normal reading situations, the main effect of context is not to provide prior activation that facilitates lexical access. It may instead primarily provide activation that facilitates semantic processes following lexical access.

By this latter account, lexical access itself (basic word recognition) is affected by context, but only minimally. Instead, what is affected are the comprehension processes that build upon lexical access. A word's semantic encoding is determined by context, and this encoding should take less time to the extent that one of the word's meanings is especially congruent with context. The assembly and integration of propositions, which depend on assigning relationships among word meanings, are also made more or less facile as a function of context. This view is quite compatible with an interactive model at the level of lexical access. It implies that prior activation of the word level node (Figure 1) is not likely to be very high in skilled, fluent reading. There may be too little time to allow activation for a specific word to build up, in a process in which four or five words are accessed in a second. Even more problematical is that the activation that could, in principle, arise from the text already read would have to be "spread" among too many words to give much access advantage to any one word.

Thus, we can suggest that in normal skilled reading lexical access is relatively autonomous with respect to context. In skilled reading, the access processes happen too rapidly to be very much affected by a word's predictability. A model described in Perfetti and Roth (1981) assumes that the level of word activation is affected by context in such a way that context affects a slower word-activation process more than a faster one. Contexts that make a given word more predictable decrease word-identification times. But the increase or decrease depends on the reader's basic word-identification time out of context. Consistent with this assumption is research showing that, among children, the word-identification times of less skilled readers are more affected by a word's predictability than those of skilled readers (Perfetti, Goldman, & Hogaboam, 1979; West & Stanovich, 1978).

This view of lexical access combines models which are strongly interactive (Rumelhart & McClelland, 1981) with those that assume processes such as lexical access are autonomous (Forster, 1979). The fast processes that enable lexical access, including prior content, can be interactive. However, there are limits placed on the contribution of any level of information by the speed with which access is accomplished. This explains both the limited effect of context and the limited occurrence of speech coding during reading. Depending on how fast execution of lexical access occurs, both context and speech coding may have early or late effects. Thus context has a powerful effect in reading, but not necesarily one that affects early processes of lexical access.

C. Comprehension

Comprehension processes occur at all times during reading. Even in discussing the effects of context on lexical access, it is clear that we have been talking about comprehension processes that go on during lexical access. In fact, the model of Just and Carpenter (1980) essentially distributes the time during which a reader fixates a word among several different processes of comprehension and lexical access. The Cognitive Model of Reading assumes that several different factors in comprehension occur in a more or less overlapping sequencing. These processes are semantic encoding, proposition assembly, integration, and text modeling.

1. Semantic Encoding

Semantic encoding is the link between lexical access and higher level comprehension processes. A reader encodes a word in a manner that fits the text model he has constructed to date. The encoding fits the context.

For example, in Sentence 1 below, the reader encodes the word *fair* differently from in Sentence 2:

1. The weather forecast calls for sunny and *fair.*
2. The weather was pleasant and sunny for the *fair.*

Obviously, a reader's mental dictionary must contain at least two entries under *fair* (actually more like five entries). Thus, a reader's "vocabulary knowledge" is part of the reading process even for commonplace words.

Equally important to semantic encoding is interpreting the referent of a word in the context. Compare Sentence 3 with 4:

3. The teacher's exam was *fair.*
4. The judge's sentence was *fair.*

There seems to be only one sense of fair, different from both Sentences 1 and 2, but the reader makes two rather different encodings. A fair exam must be understood in terms of classroom examination standards whereas a fair sentence must meet standards of punishments fitting crimes.

Thus, semantic encoding occurs when the reader's knowledge of concepts, i.e., word meanings, is applied to a text. The knowledge itself is the reader's "mental dictionary" and can be described in terms of a memory network; an example is the semantic memory model described in Lindsay and Norman (1977), which represents words as nodes in a network with labeled links between the nodes corresponding to basic semantic relationships. There are other models of semantic memory, but for our purposes their differences are unimportant (see Smith, 1978, for a review of semantic memory models). The essential ingredient of semantic representation models for reading is their description of the reader's abstract context-free knowledge of word meanings. They reflect the relational aspect of concept knowledge—for example, that *hot* is the opposite of *cold,* that the word *fish* is the name of a category of living things, and that *trout* is an example of this same category. It is this knowledge which constrains how a reader can interpret a text.

2. Proposition Encoding

As a reader encodes words in their contextually appropriate sense, propositions are assembled and integrated. To illustrate, the reader must encode six propositions to read Sentence 5:

5. The automatic reel was too expensive, so Fred bought the manual one.

(a) automatic	(The automatic reel)
(b) expensive (a)	(The reel was expensive)
(c) too (expensive)	(too expensive)
(d) so ((c), (e))	((e) happened because of (c))
(e) bought (Fred, (f))	(Fred bought a reel)
(f) manual (reel)	(a manual reel)

The major theory of propositional encoding comes from Kintsch (1974) and Kintsch and van Dijk (1978). The basic idea is obvious enough: Ideas expressed by sentences are not unitary. The elementary unit of meaning is a relationship between a predicate and one or more nouns (or arguments). This is the definition of a proposition. In our notation, the first element outside of the parentheses is the predicate. It "predicates" either an attribute of a single argument or a relationship between two or more arguments. Thus (a) is a single-attribution predicate: A certain reel is predicated to be automatic. And (e) predicates a *buy* relationship between *Fred* and *manual reel*. Since one proposition can be part of another proposition, the proposition system is embedding.

Thus Sentence 5 contains six discrete propositions. (It actually contains three additional existential propositions that predicate existence of one Fred and two different reel types.) So the reader is assembling either six or nine propositions, depending on how we count existential predicates, out of only eleven words. Thus the demands on the reader in terms of propositional encoding are potentially great. Nevertheless, the proposition appears to be a fairly good approximation to the reader's elementary unit of text meaning. It is a good predictor of reading rate when the number of words is held constant (Kintsch & Keenan, 1973).

In addition to the assembly of propositions, integration of propositions is also required. An elementary integration is required for Proposition (f). The word *one* must be encoded as anaphoric to the word *reel* in order to even assemble this proposition. Such integration is presumably easy when the antecedent and its anaphora are close together and likely to be in working memory at the same time. Another example of integration is Proposition (d), which links together two other propositions. The reader must await the end of the sentence before he can complete that proposition.

The major tool the reader has for some of these integration processes is syntax. In fact, the reader must be able to parse the sentence into constituents in order to encode propositions. In the Sentence 5 example, the word *so* is a syntactic trigger that instructs the reader to begin a new clause. Moreover, since *so* is associated with antecedent–consequence relationships, it may also instruct the reader to build a consequence proposition in that clause. Although syntactic parsing may generally proceed without semantic influence initially, it is possible that the reader can form a "frame" for the proposition without waiting for all the words. (For an illustration of how these proposition-encoding processes work together, see Perfetti, 1985.)

3. Text Modeling

The main goal of the reader is to construct a text model. Lexical and propositional processes are merely means to this end. They are not sufficient, however. The text model is in part a set of higher level propositions that summarize a larger number of text propositions. But this higher level summary is achieved only with a large contribution from the reader's knowledge. This knowledge goes beyond word meanings that are represented in the mental dictionary, but it does include them. It consists of large schemata (word meanings can be thought of as schemata also) based on richer and more specialized individual knowledge.

The evidence for the use of schemata in reading is fairly extensive. A few examples: Anderson, Spiro, and Anderson (1978) had some subjects read a passage about having dinner at a fancy restaurant. Another group read about a trip to a supermarket. Each passage contained reference to 18 food items which subjects later attempted to recall. Now the schema, the organization of knowledge, for restaurant dining is different in all sorts of ways from the schema for supermarket shopping. And, as Anderson et al. found, readers who could use their restaurant schema (or "script", Schank & Abelson, 1977) recalled more food items than readers who used their supermarket schema.

A second example demonstrating the role of schemata comes from situations in which subjects read vaguely worded or metaphorical passages with and without titles provided ahead of time. Subjects reading such passages without titles fail to comprehend and recall them, whereas subjects given titles ahead of time do much better (Dooling & Lachman, 1971; Bransford & Johnson, 1973).

Finally, because schemata are products of individual experience, they are important factors in individual differences in comprehension. Anderson, Reynolds, Schallert, and Goetz (1976) showed that a passage written to have two different interpretations was understood according to the background of the reader. Furthermore, research by Voss has demonstrated that the level of knowledge a person has about baseball affects his qualitative understanding about a baseball passage (Spilich, Vesonder, Chiesi, & Voss, 1979; Chiesi, Spilich, & Voss, 1979). Not only did subjects high in baseball knowledge recall more of an account of a fictitious game, but their recalls included more information about significant game events as opposed to incidental facts.

Thus schemata provide organization for the comprehension and recall of texts. And a person's comprehension will depend upon the particular knowledge he or she can bring to the service of a given text. In the Cognitive Model of Reading, we assume that these schemata are represented in the permanent memory of the reader. Some are highly specific and variable (e.g., baseball knowledge), and some are highly general and more universal (e.g., opening a window). Their service in reading is to guide the construction of a text model. The model constructed by a reader can be described as the updated high-level summary of the text propositions, supplemented by inferences and organized around appropriate schemata.

The inferences themselves are guided by schemata. In the baseball research of Voss and colleagues, for example, high-knowledge subjects show more appropriate inferring when reading an account of a baseball game. To illustrate, suppose the subject reads, "The ball was hit to Chase at third. The batter was out at first." A high-knowledge subject is quicker and more accurate than a low-knowledge subject at verifying the inference "Chase threw the ball to the first baseman." In fact, high-knowledge subjects are as fast at verifying the truth of such an inference as at verifying the truth of an event described explicitly in the text (Post, Greene, & Bruder, 1982).

The schemata that are used in such text-inference processes may be activated without effort by the reader. The text itself triggers the appropriate schemata in most instances. Texts written to be vague, metaphorical, or misleading work because they do not achieve the appropriate activation. The knowledge a skilled reader applies to the well-written text is applied not through effortful retrieval but through more or less "automatic" activation.

4. Text Structures

Part of the reader's knowledge that serves the construction of the text model includes the structure of text types. Stories have a structure that can be described in terms of story grammars (Mandler & Johnson, 1977; Stein & Glenn, 1979; Thorndyke, 1977) and causal event structures (Omanson, 1982; Warren, Nicholas, & Trabasso, 1979). In general terms, story grammars describe the syntax of stories, and other models of event structures describe the semantics of stories.

The syntax can be described as a setting and a series of embedded events. The reader may be able to use his implicit knowledge of the narrative form to help guide his construction of a text model. Knowing, for example, that he is reading a story, the reader can anticipate a *setting* (although it might not come first in the story). Having encoded a *setting* and some *initiating event,* the reader can anticipate some psychological reaction *(internal reaction)* in the protagonist and some subsequent efforts to influence events *(attempt).* (The italicized words are categories of story grammar used by Stein & Glenn, 1979.) At a semantic level, stories relate series of events linked by causal connections (and other connections) (Omanson, 1982). Also, a character's plan for action may be a salient aspect of a story's structure (Lichtenstein & Brewer, 1980).

The importance of story structures for reading seems clear. Whether they should be thought of as structures analogous to sentence syntax or as problem-solving structures or as causal-event sequences is not a critical issue for some purposes. Certainly different structural descriptions are plausible, just as different theories of English syntax are plausible. The essential point for a Cognitive Model of Reading is that we must assume that some general knowledge aids the skilled reader in forming a model of the text. The possible forms of these texts have been well worked out in the case of narratives, but less so for other text types. The structure of texts for science, history, etc., is of obvious concern for reading in the classroom. The child's reading curriculum is dominated by stories for several years, but this changes with increasing demands of content subject matter.

5. Comprehension Strategies

Are there specific strategies of comprehension at the reader's disposal? In the discussion so far, it is possible to assume that most of the reading processes lie outside of conscious control. We spoke of even schema activation as "triggered" by the text. However, the reader is clearly able to take a more assertive role in reading. He does so when, for example, he decides whether he is studying a text for an exam or scanning it to find a name. It is this control over the reading activity that we refer to as *comprehension strategy.* There are two different but related issues of comprehension strategy for the the Cognitive Model of Reading. The first is the reader's allocation of processing resources. The second is the reader's monitoring of his comprehension.

A plausible expectation is that readers allocate more processing resources to important text. This expectation is confirmed, at least in part. In their eye-camera research, Just and Carpenter (1980) found that longer gaze durations occurred in sentences containing structurally important information in expository texts. Readers spent more time especially encoding definitional and causal information. Using stories, Cirilo and Foss (1980) found longer reading times for sentences with more important information. However, this result is not always found (Britton, Meyer,

Simpson, Holdredge, & Curry, 1979; Post, 1983). There may be other features of the text that determine whether more important information gets more processing time. One factor is the reader's opportunity to get the "more important" information from other information in the text. For example, a summary sentence has important information, but a reader has a chance to get the information from other parts of the text. Other important information can be partly inferred by the reader if he is knowledgeable and the text is coherent. Thus the principle that readers allocate processing resources in response to text importance may be too general to be very meaningful without heavy qualification. Of course, we are talking here about allocation of resources during reading. That readers, even children, are aware of relative importance of text material is well established (Smiley, Oakley, Worthen, Campione, & Brown, 1977).

The second issue of comprehension strategies is comprehension monitoring. A reader who can detect problems in the text, e.g., logical contradictions, is implicitly monitoring his comprehension. So is a reader who can predict his level of recall of a text. The first of these, detection of local inconsistencies in a text, is something that even some skilled adults do not always do well (Wilkinson, Epstein, Glenberg, & Morse, 1980). However, being able to notice that a text is difficult and assuming that it will be difficult to remember are a part of the normal monitoring ability of skilled readers.

D. Verbal Efficiency

Finally, we need to consider reading processes in the framework of cognitive processing structures. The processes we have discussed, including both lexical access and comprehension access, are carried out in part in a limited resource system. The limitations of cognitive resources affect reading very directly. The reader must allocate resources to many activities. To mention a few of those we have described, the reader must access words, retrieve meanings, encode propositions, make inferences, apply schemata, and build a text model. Resources can be allocated to other things as well—decoding an unfamiliar name, searching memory for an antecedent, searching the written page for a previously read fact, etc. The reader's ability to do enough of these things well is the key to successful reading.

Verbal efficiency theory assumes that construction of a quality text model depends critically on the assembly and integration of propositions in working memory. Therefore, any processing factor that affects encoding of propositions will affect overall reading comprehension. Proposition encoding takes place within a limited-capacity system of working memory.

The constraint on working memory is the number of elements that can be activated at one time. It is possible also to conceptualize working memory as part of a structurally separate short-term memory (Atkinson & Shiffrin, 1968). However, a model with a single permanent memory system (Anderson, 1976) may be more congenial to the activation processes which are so prevalent a part of our Cognitive Model of Reading. Thus, working memory refers to the limited number of permanent memory units that are activated at any one time. In the case of reading, working memory serves comprehension by storing the results of partly processed sentences. For example, the first phrase or clause of a sentence is held in memory, and words are grouped into tentative structures as they are encountered.

For reading, an important fact about working memory is that only a limited amount of information can be activated at any one time. Perhaps this limitation can be expressed as a few propositions or a certain number of words, but any such estimate may seem arbitrary (see Kintsch & van Dijk, 1978). However, there is some limit that affects comprehension.

Verbal efficiency theory (Perfetti & Lesgold, 1977; Perfetti, 1985) assumes that this processing limit can be handled to the extent that some components of reading can execute without high cost to processing resources. Potentially, the components that could have this low-cost property include all the reading processes already discussed—lexical access, proposition encoding, schema activation. However, two of these three process types, lexical access and schema activation, are much more likely to be low in resource cost. Proposition encoding is likely to be high in resource cost. This follows from the facts that proposition encoding requires relational links among words to be established and that integration of propositions requires retrieval of previously assembled propositions. The integration is relatively easy when the required antecedent proposition is still in working memory, but more difficult if the antecedent must be "reinstated" (Kintsch & van Dijk, 1978). In either case, the reader's "text work" must be carried out in working memory. (See Perfetti, 1985, for a discussion of text work.) The main text work is proposition encoding, and it must be expected to be resource costly.

By contrast, lexical access and schema activation could be executed at low resource cost. The concept of automaticity is relevant here. Word access can become very facile with practice. Words can be recognized, if not exactly automatically, at least with relatively low expenditure of resources. Relevant schemata are triggered by text elements, in part by lexical access. Their application does not require resources, in principle. Of course, if a misunderstanding of the text has resulted from the application of the wrong schema, then a conscious or effortful search for appropriate schemata may follow. But the general principle is that both lexical access and schema activation are potentially low-resource processes, relative to proposition encoding.

This means, in effect, that lexical access is the process most promising for becoming less resource costly. It begins, after all, as a very costly process for the beginning reader. With practice it can become a fluent process, automatic for practical purposes. The hallmark of skilled reading, indeed, is the rapid and effortless activation of a word concept from a letter string.

An implication of verbal efficiency theory for instruction is that students need to develop a high level of lexical processing skill. Identifying words and encoding their meanings in context are processes that can be refined with practice to skills well beyond the rudimentary process of accurate word recognition.

E. Summary

Skilled reading is described by a Cognitive Model of Reading that reflects lexical access and comprehension processes. Lexical access can be understood as an interactive process in which letters, phonemes, and words are represented as interacting levels of information. Comprehension can be understood as a complex of overlapping processes, beginning with semantic encoding of words and including assembly and integration of propositions, activation of schemata, and inference making. Construction of a text model is an ongoing process, the representational "product" of comprehension. These processes, both lexical and higher level, depend in part on limited processing resources. Verbal efficiency theory claims that lexical access has the highest potential for becoming low in resource cost, thus enabling more resources to go to other processes.

III. BEGINNING READING

The Cognitive Model of Reading has been a (more or less) consensual view of how reading skill is used. We turn now to acquisition of reading skill, perhaps the most important acquisition in the child's schooling. Beginning reading has probably received more attention in research than skilled reading, but less attention from cognitive psychology. Nevertheless, we shall try to describe a Cognitive Model of Reading Acquisition parallel to our Cognitive Model of Reading.

A. The Cognitive Model of Reading Acquisition

There are many ways to learn how to read. How a child begins and progresses in his or her acquisition depends on many factors. The child who begins to read at home at age 4 may have a different acquisition from the child who begins only in first grade at age 6. A child who is in a "phonics" curriculum may learn in a different way from a child in a "language-experience" or "meaning-emphasis" curriculum. And, more fundamentally, a child who learns to read in an alphabetic script and a child who learns to read in a nonalphabetic script do not necessarily learn by the same procedures. Nevertheless, it is possible and indeed necessary to extract general principles of learning from these many different possibilities. Although children can begin to learn in different ways, there is common ground in two respects: the principles of acquisition and what it is that is eventually acquired. Within a given script system, all children will acquire more or less the same reading knowledge.

1. What Is Acquired?

Learning to read English or German is different from learning to read Chinese. The essential difference among writing systems is how the script codes the units of language. It is possible for scripts to code units of meaning, and logographic scripts do this. Chinese remains the most widely used meaning-based writing system in a world in which most scripts are alphabetic.

The logographic system is instructive for the learning principles it entails. The reader must make associations between units of meaning—words and morphemes—and units of writing. In the case of Chinese, the writing units are characters that include simple ideographs, pictographs, and phonetic compounds. The last category combines a radical, which has semantic value, and a phonetic, which has pronunciation value. Since this category accounts for about 80% of Chinese characters (Leong, 1973), it is somewhat misleading to refer to Chinese script as an ideographic or meaning-based system. The contrast with an alphabetic script is fundamental, however. An alphabetic script associates meaningless script units, or letters, with meaningless language units, or phonemes. In written Chinese, there are no script units corresponding to phonemes.

In such a meaning-based script, what is acquired is *associations*. The child must learn links between a complex script symbol and a word in his spoken language. (The "word" includes features of both pronunciation and meaning.) In Chinese, the degree of literacy depends on the number of these associations that are acquired. In elementary schools, children learning Chinese are expected to acquire about 500 or 600 per year during the six years of reading instruction (Leong, 1973). Chinese children spend significant time at home working on characters. Presumably, this is necessary or at least very helpful for the formidable task of acquiring so many associations, largely arbitrary ones between script stimuli and language responses. A literate Chinese adult typically learns between 5,000 and 7,000 of these associations.

The case of logographic script makes clear the point that a large number of associations can be established in learning to read. Equally clear is the value of an alphabetic system for economy of learning. An alphabet, which associates script units with meaningless speech units, reduces the number of associations to be learned by a large magnitude. The 26 letters of the Roman alphabet, the 24 letters of the Greek alphabet, and the 32 letters of the Russian alphabet all represent very economical script systems. Each letter is associated with one or more phonemes, and as the learner masters these associations reading becomes *productive*. That is, a relatively small number of symbols produce an indefinitely large reading vocabulary. The child who acquires the *alphabetic principle,* the principle of association between meaningless script and meaningless speech, is able to read words not encountered previously. This is productive reading; by contrast, in logographic systems the reader often must learn a new association in order to read a new word.

Thus, the question of what is acquired depends on the script. On the other hand, associations are part of what is acquired, regardless of script. The associations acquired in an alphabetic system are productive. They allow decoding of novel word forms.

2. Obstacles to Acquisition

There are some problems facing the learner of an alphabetic script. One is that phonemes, especially consonants, are abstract perceptual categories. Thus the reader is forced to learn associations between letters and abstract perceptual units. A second obstacle is that existing alphabets do no uniquely code each vowel phoneme. Thus the reader faces probabilistic and context-dependent learning.

The first obstacle is intrinsic to speech perception. Phonemes are perceptual abstractions in all languages. The problem exists mainly for consonants, however, because vowels, while abstract, are relatively "concrete." Vowels have acoustic duration—they last long enough to be heard—and they are less dependent on context. Thus when a teacher points to the letter *a* in *man,* and says, "Aah," the child can hear a sound about the same as the *a* in *apple.* Vowel sounds, the phoneme /ae/ in this case, are relatively perceptible and invariant across contexts. By contrast, when the teacher refers to the letter *d* as having the sound of "duh" in *dime* and in *dome*, this is a bit misleading. The phoneme /d/ is an abstraction, a perceptual prototype of all the [d] sounds that actually occur. It is very dependent on context and is not the same, acoustically, in *dime* as in *dome*. This means that acquiring associations between consonant graphemes and phonemes, e.g., *d* and /d/, can be a problem for the child, in principle.

The second obstacle to acquiring an alphabetic script arises from the design of alphabets. The price of economy has been to have complex correspondences for vowels. Thus American English has about a dozen vowel phonemes but only five standard vowel letters. For example, *cat, car,* and *cake* each use the letter *a* for a different vowel phoneme. This potential problem is solved to an extent by the orthography, i.e., the system of letter-sequencing rules. For example, the pronunciation of *a* in *cake* is determined by the presence of final *e*. For the beginning reader, the vowel problem complicates the learning task. Some of the associations to be learned are context dependent.

However, this is not a fundamental obstacle to learning an alphabetic script, but merely a feature of alphabet design. Alphabets can be more explicit—that is, have a different letter for every different vowel sound. The German alphabet, for example, is more explicit than the version of the Roman alphabet used for English. It uses diacritical marks in combination with letters (*ä* versus *a*). Generally there is a trade-off between an alphabet's explicitness and its economy. Since English is relatively less explicit, there have been proposals to alter the alphabet for teaching reading. For example, the Initial Teaching Alphabet designed by Pitman has 44 written symbols, one for each English phoneme. Many of these symbols combine letters into digraph symbols, e.g., *oi* is the symbol for the vowel in *boy*. Whether a more explicit alphabet makes learning easier is not clear (Chall, 1967). However, any problems that might occur in using such alphabets to teach reading must be purely technical, for example, the potential difficulty of producing transfer to the normal alphabet. In principle, an alphabet which codes all phonemes in a consistent and explicit manner has to make acquisition of letter–phoneme associations easier.

On the other hand, learning a less explicit orthography has advantages. Not only is it more economical in terms of number of symbols, but it also allows *morphological transparency*. By morphological transparency we mean that the semantic and syntactic relations among words are reflected in spelling. The letter *a* has a different vowel correspondence in *nation* than in *national*. An explicit alphabet that would use two different graphemes for the two different sounds could mask the morphological relationship between *nation* and *national*. English orthography makes transparent that these two words are a noun–adjective pair of the same lexical morpheme.

Thus whether the learner's problem is made easier or more difficult by a more explicit alphabet is a tricky question. It is partly a matter of what is acquired in the long run. It is possible that a less explicit orthography allows the reader to acquire a representation system that more fully links orthography with syntax and semantics. There is, however, no clear evidence that this results. Moreover, it is likely that the learner's initial progress in acquisition is made easier by a more explicit alphabet, provided care is taken with design features that affect transfer.

Another solution to the obstacles of alphabetic acquisition has been the use of the syllabary, a script system based on syllables. Syllables have acoustic duration and are relatively invariant across different contexts. Syllabary scripts remain the basis for some writing systems (e.g., Japanese Hiragana). An adaptation of a syllabary to initial reading instruction was carried out by Gleitman & Rozin (1973). They reported success at teaching children with prognosis for low reading achievement by means of a rebus-based syllabary. A rebus is a picture used as a name. For example, in Gleitman and Rozin's procedure, a picture of a can was first used for the word *can* and then for the syllable *can* as in *candy*. The point of this demonstration is not that syllabaries are superior writing systems that should be substituted for alphabets. Rather, it shows the importance of helping the child discover that the print system he encounters in reading corresponds to speech and not to meaning. This discovery is the key acquisition in learning to read in an alphabet.

Thus there are obstacles to learning to read in any system. In a meaning-based system the number of associations to be learned is very large because decoding principles cannot be applied. In alphabetic systems the number of associations is small, but the associations are partly abstract and context dependent. However, obstacles to learning the alphabetic principle can be overcome for most children, and special procedures designed to make the speech–print connection easier may be helpful for some children.

3. Linguistic Knowledge in Acquisition

It is clear that the child learning to read has to have some knowledge of language and speech. He learns to associate print units either with word meanings or with speech segments. Thus the learner's representation system would have to know about units of language. What does the child know about such things as phonemes, syllables, and words when he begins to acquire reading?

Prior to beginning school, children are reasonably competent language users. They have implicit knowledge of the syntactic structure of their language, as well as knowledge of how to use language for communication. Furthermore, their vocabularies are sufficient to allow carefully designed curricular materials to provide meaningful texts. However, there are questions about the details of the child's linguistic knowledge.

The question is usually put in terms of explicit versus implicit knowledge. A preschool child's implicit knowledge of language is adequate for most purposes of communication, but his explicit knowledge may not be adequate for learning how to read. Keep in mind that the learning problem in reading is to associate printed symbols with language units. The question is whether it is necessary to have explicit knowledge of such units in order to acquire the associations. Another way of stating the problem is to say that learning to read depends on the child's "linguistic awareness" (Mattingly, 1972). It is possible that in addition to having an implicitly adequate representation of the structure of language, the learner must be aware of the structural elements.

There is evidence that learning to read depends on this kind of linguistic knowledge, especially at the level of the phoneme. If a child is to learn associations between graphemes and phonemes, then it follows that having phonemes as units to operate on is necessary, or at least helpful, in forming the associations. Liberman, Shankweiler, Fischer, and Carter (1974) found that demonstrating explicit knowledge of phonemes is very difficult for preschool and kindergarten children. In their task, children have to tap once with a stick for each "sound" (phoneme) in a word, for example, three taps for *dog* and two for *he* when these words are spoken by the experimenter. Even first-grade children were not very successful in learning this task. (Tapping for the number of syllables in a word was more readily learned.) Performance on the phoneme tapping task, however, is related to early reading achievement (Liberman & Shankweiler, 1977). In one study described by Liberman and Shankweiler, the ability to phonemically segment words in kindergarten was the best predictor of first-grade reading achievement, as measured by the Wide Range Achievement Test, a test of oral word reading. This relationship between phoneme-knowledge and early reading achievement is quite general over a number of different phoneme knowledge tasks (Fox & Routh, 1976; Goldstein, 1976). Furthermore, the relationship endures over several years (Bradley & Bryant, 1983).

The question of whether phonemic knowledge is causally related to reading achievement is a bit more complex. A training study by Bradley and Bryant (1983) demonstrates that an increase in phonemic awareness, measured through a rhyme-detection task, produces gains in reading. Thus there is evidence for a causal relationship.

On the other hand, the causal relationship may also run in the other direction. Ehri (1980) has argued that visual memories of printed letters that are part of word forms allow the child to develop phonological knowledge. Perfetti, Beck, and Hughes, 1981 (described in Perfetti, 1985) conclude that skill in reading also causes increases in phonemic knowledge. In their longitudinal study of first-grade children's performance on a task which required deletion of a phoneme—for example, "Say *cat* without the 'kuh' "—they found that performance on the phoneme task improved following gains in reading, rather than vice versa. There was also a simple nonanalytic phoneme task in which the subject had to "blend" phonemes spoken in isolation into words and syllables. Performance on this task showed gains prior to gains in reading. Thus a reciprocal relationship seems to hold between phonemic awareness and learning to read. Each is cause and effect of the other at a general level. At a more specific level, a low-level phoneme awareness is sufficient for beginning to learn reading. A more articulated knowledge, analyzing words into segments, is not necessary. Instead, this knowledge is acquired through experience in reading.

4. Letters, Letter Names, and Phonemes

An important part of what the child learns in an alphabetic script involves letters. There are at least two different components to the letter-learning experience: (1) the perceptual learning of letter forms and (2) the associative learning of letter names. The perceptual learning of letter forms means that the child learns to recognize letters as letters and as parts of words. This eventually allows the child's representation to include spellings as routes to lexical access. Letters become familiar, letter patterns become familiar, and printed words become familiar. In a sense this perceptual learning is the main learning mechanism for the acquisition of reading skill (Gibson & Levin, 1975); LaBerge, 1976).

The letter name is incidental to this perceptual learning process. As a strictly perceptual learning issue, only visual forms are needed. In fact, it is sometimes claimed that learning the names of letters is detrimental, rather than helpful, to reading acquisition. However Ehri (1983) has examined the evidence concerning the learning of letter names and concludes that learning letter names is not detrimental.

One reason for arguing against letter-name learning is logical. The names of the letters are not the phonemes associated with the letters; "bee" is not the phonemic value of /b/ and "double you" is not even close to the phonemic value of /w/. So, the argument goes, it is misleading for the child to learn the name of the letter when it is the phoneme he needs to associate with it. However, Ehri points out that the important thing may not be whether the letter name is the correct phonemic value of the letter, but that it is a speech-based association. This may help the child discover the meaningless print–speech association needed for reading. Furthermore, a letter name does typically include some of the phonemic value of the letter. There is a /b/ (as a perceptual abstraction) in "bee" and there is a /s/ in "ess." Also, as Read (1971) and Chomsky (1977) demonstrated, beginning readers spell by using the phonemic information in the letter names. Although it is very imperfect, there is useful reading information in the letter name. Thus, as Ehri suggests, the fact that the name is "misleading" may not be an obstacle.

5. Acquisition Stages

Although we have emphasized that the alphabetic principle is the key discovery in learning to read, the example of learning Chinese characters should be kept in mind. Clearly, a person can learn to read without the alphabetic principle. It is also possible, accordingly, that even a child who eventually acquires an alphabetic system such as English can begin as if he were learning Chinese. That is, the child can learn by associating a spoken word with a printed word.

Gough & Hillinger (1980) have suggested that learning to read does typically begin in this way. There is an initial phase of associative learning and a later stage of true alphabetic learning. In the associative-learning phase, the printed word has some critical perceptual feature which the child uses to associate it with an oral language word. What the critical feature is is variable and unprincipled. The word *Budweiser,* as Gough and Hillinger (1980) point out, could be an early word read by the child on the basis of its length or its distinctive typography in advertisements or on beer cans. Similarly, *stop* may be read through the distinctive features of a stop sign. This may not seem much like reading, and it is not if this is all the child can do. However, it is reading to the extent that the child can read words out of their original context. The critical stimulus feature can change, and the child can eventually learn an invariant association between the letter string *s t o p* and the word *stop*.

Thus the principle of Phase 1 learning is that associations are acquired between specific printed letter strings and specific words. It is nonproductive learning. The child cannot read an unfamiliar word on its first encounter. Eventually, the memory burden becomes rather large, as more and more specific associations are learned. At some point the second phase—true reading—must begin. The child learns that words have constituent letters and catches on to the alphabetic principle: The letters stand for sounds.

The transition to the true reading phase is the acquisition of a word-identification process that is under the control of intrinsic word features rather than extrinsic features. Extrinsic features include the contexts that allow meaning to guide "expectations" about word identities. Such expectations play an important role before the child begins to master intrinsic word features. Early in the first grade, errors made in oral reading tend to be appropriate for the context, even when they show little graphemic resemblance to the printed word. By the end of first grade, children's oral reading errors show much greater graphemic overlap with the printed word. Thus the child begins the reading-acquisition process with considerable knowledge concerning the target product of reading—i.e., what is read is supposed to make sense—and he uses this knowledge to guide his reading. However, the successful learner will quickly master some of the intrinsic word information that allows reading to be less dependent on context.

During this learning period, constituent letters are important features for the child. Evidence suggests that the first letter of a word is an especially important word feature to the child (Rayner & Hagelberg, 1975). Global word shape cues, which are often said to be important in reading, are actually not important as cues in learning to read once instruction has begun. (They may be important for the early *stop*-type reading mentioned above.) However, shape cues for words that include features of letters, rather global word shapes, may have some role in word identification (Rayner & Hagelberg, 1975). Letter identities also seem to play a larger role than phoneme identities in children's judgments of printed word similarity (Beverly & Perfetti, 1983). In general, acquisition is partly a matter of learning specific features of print, especially specific letter constituents.

This two-phase description need not be correct for all children for all learning environments. In fact, it is likely that children use specific letter constituents very early in learning to read. But it is useful in giving us a general framework for acquisition. True productive reading depends on decoding. But procedures of decoding and "holistic" association can exist side by side. It is important to realize that beginning to learn to read does not depend on the alphabetic principle. True progress in learning how to read does, however.

B. Summary

The acquisition of reading depends on learning environments and the script system to be learned. Alphabetic systems demand that the learner acquire the alphabetic principle that maps meaningless speech segments to meaningless script units. Knowledge of speech is important for this association to take place, and the child's knowledge of speech segments is not very explicit prior to learning to read. Learning how to read depends in part on simple knowledge of speech segments, but more analytic knowledge of phonemes may be the result of rather than the prerequisite for learning to read. This proposal makes sense especially in light of a two-phase learning model. The first phase is characterized by making associations between printed and spoken words, and the second phase is characterized by applying the alphabetic principle and learning to decode novel word forms. The transition between these stages is marked by increasing attention to constituent letters as the control features of word identification.

IV. INSTRUCTION IN READING

In this section we discuss the ways reading is and can be taught in light of the cognitive models of reading. We first consider beginning reading.

The first question is how we should view the relationship between cognitive models of reading and the teaching of reading. In fact, a cognitive model of a skill is not sufficient. Instructional design includes an analysis of competent performance and an analysis of how a learner moves from an initial state of relative incompetence to a later state of competence. Glaser (1976, 1982) has made this general point explicitly. He notes that a science of instructional design includes (a) a model of skilled performance, (b) a model of the learner's knowledge at particular points in learning, and (c) a model of the conditions that promote the acquisition of competence. Furthermore, in order to know about the learner's knowledge at intermediate levels of performance, we have to have assessment and monitoring techniques that are sensitive to the underlying knowledge states that comprise skilled performance (Glaser, 1982). So far, we have suggested a detailed model of skilled performance in reading, a very sketchy statement of the child's competence prior to instruction, and a minimal sketch of the state transformations in learning to read. A genuine model of these state transformations, i.e., a model of learning how to read with comprehension, remains a job for the future. It is, indeed, the single component of the cognitive psychology of reading most in need of attention.

However, this does not mean that there is little to say about instruction. Instruction goes on with good, bad, or nonexistent models of learning. Moreover, there are reasonably clear conclusions concerning some issues of instruction.

A. Instruction in Light of the Cognitive Model of Skilled Reading

Instruction even in beginning reading is informed by a model of skilled reading. The model we have used emphasizes certain important target competencies. For example, a target competency is skilled lexical access, the fluent recognition of words independent of context. A second target competency is appropriate schema activation (Spiro, 1980). A third is the application of appropriate comprehension strategies (Brown & Palincsar, 1982). There are many other skills that are part of these general competencies. For example, word knowledge (vocabulary) is a critical target skill that, in part, links lexical access and schema activation.

What application can be made of this knowledge of skilled reading? Again, we need guidance from models of learning, which are not available for some of these components. However, let us assume certain target competencies and speculate on the conditions of learning: The target competencies are fluent identification of printed words and comprehension of text. These are considered below in terms of their acquisition and instruction.

B. Lexical Access

The target goal for lexical access is fluent word recognition that is not costly to processing resources. However, it seems reasonable to suggest two target competencies along the way: (1) a stage of accurate word recognition and (2) a stage of fluent word recognition. Presumably these are not so much stages as they are overlapping levels of skill. Fluency in lexical processes enables the reader to achieve more text comprehension; however, it is preceded by lexical accuracy, which is necessary for any real progress in beginning reading. Accuracy becomes fluency with practice.

Of course, accuracy refers to a measurable performance rather than an underlying knowledge. So does fluency. Accuracy refers to some standard of single isolated word identification—e.g., how many words can a child read correctly from a standardized list? Fluency refers to a standard of speed or ease of recognition, perhaps also on a standardized list. However, what the child learns goes beyond these performances. Accuracy and speed both reflect the child's lexical knowledge: knowledge of specific words, implicit knowledge of orthographic patterns, and implicit knowledge of roles relating such patterns to word formations.

Thus the learning assumption is that a child will learn "specific forms." Many of these will be high-frequency forms for which decoding rules are not quite sufficient or, more generally, very context dependent. *The, of, you,* and many other short high-frequency words are learned as specific patterns. However, even longer words can be learned as specific units, including words that are quite "regular," i.e., words having relatively context-free decoding rules. We can think of the highly skilled reader as having acquired many word-specific forms. Given the right string of letters, the specific word form is activated. The child acquiring reading builds up a store of these specific word forms.

However, there is something else the child is learning. He is acquiring a vast "vocabulary" of printed letter sequences and a corresponding decoding system that maps these sequences onto syllables and words. These letter patterns occur in many different words encountered by the reader. Thus there is an inductive learning mechanism: Encountering words that recycle, for English, 26 grapheme forms through a few hundred two-, three-, and four-letter patterns allows these patterns to be extracted and to serve lexical access. It is also likely that the abstract principles that organize these patterns are induced. Thus the child induces a system that recognized *str* as a three-letter pattern at the beginning of a word, but not as a pattern for the end of a word. For *rts* he induces the reverse.

He also learns mappings, including some implicit abstractions. For example, he learns that $f \rightarrow$ /f/ and $d \rightarrow$ /d/ in nearly all contexts. And he learns that *a* and *i* have variable context-sensitive mappings. Thus one abstraction that he implicitly learns is that consonants are less context sensitive than vowels. But of course he also learns that certain digraph patterns have their own mappings, e.g., *th* and *sh*.

Both the orthographic patterns and the mappings are essential for the learner and the skilled reader. They enable unfamiliar words to be "recognized" or at least decoded into speech forms. Furthermore, they provide additional representations for lexical access. It is possible, although this has not yet been demonstrated, that fluency in lexical access comes because of redundant representation systems. That is, a word can be accessed from specific single letters, from specific orthographic patterns, and from speech-coded representations. The more representations the reader has, the more accurate and the more fluent word identification will be.

Induction or Direct Teaching?

So far, we have assumed that the representation system a reader needs can be acquired by induction. That is, some of the representation system is the result of extracting patterns and then inducing, implicitly, a new level of representation. Specifically, letter patterns and their phonological mappings are induced from reading words. There is no question that human beings are prolific pattern inducers. Moreover, there is clear evidence that people implicitly learn orthographic rules when they are built into a novel alphabet-learning task (Brooks, 1977). Young children also show an ability to make use of the regularity of English orthographic patterns (Pick, Unze, Brownell, Drozdal, & Hopmann, 1978). Thus, we can conclude that one powerful condition for learning this part of reading—the backup representation system—is the exposure to printed words.

But what kind of exposure? It is doubtful that significant pattern induction will occur through repeated passive exposure to words. At minimum, the child has to learn associations between printed words and something else. In the process of learning these associations, the child comes to be able to read *and* to induce the patterns and mappings that will promote further skill in reading.

Now there is another question: What is the "something else" with which the printed words become associated? In principle, the printed word form can become associated with any pre-existing or new representation that the child can establish. Clearly, however, it is the spoken word form and its associated semantic values that provide the representation. The spoken language form is the key representation for learning to read.

This brings us to the central pervasive issue in learning lexical access through print. How should the associations be taught? We have argued that pattern induction is a powerful procedure that will do the job in principle. However, the problem is that the learner must be able to read in order to induce the patterns. It would help if he had some of the system—the speech mappings. In an alphabetic system, it seems a terrible waste to keep the principle that would enable this reading hidden from the learner. However, this is a consequence of the approach to reading instruction favored by Goodman (1967) and Smith (1973). This approach insists that the print–speech mapping system not be directly taught.

Meaning versus Code. The issue here goes under different labels that are correlated. *Phonics versus whole word* and *meaning emphasis versus code emphasis* are two of these labels. Whether the child is taught mappings between print and speech at the subword level is really the issue. It is simply not possible to ignore these mappings at the word level. Some fear that teaching mapping directs attention away from meaning and interferes with learning to read. However, there is no evidence for this curious claim.

On the contrary, the evidence on beginning reading instruction points to the conclusion that code-emphasis programs are somewhat more effective than meaning-emphasis programs. This was the conclusion of Jeanne Chall (1967, 1983) based on an evaluation of the many studies that compared teaching methods, and it was also the conclusion of Williams (1979) based on still more studies. However, as both Chall and Williams emphasized, the advantage of phonics or code-emphasis programs seems relatively small and perhaps does not persist beyond the first two grades. The relatively slight advantage of direct code teaching on the one hand, and on the other hand the obvious importance of the code for lexical access, suggest that meaning-emphasis programs do not ignore the code altogether. The speech-mapping functions of subword units (the code) are part of what is learned in any program. Mappings can be partly induced and partly directly taught. Direct teaching of the code appears to be a bit more effective in establishing early learning than indirect teaching. It may also be especially effective for children who are poor risks to induce the code on their own. Certainly there is no reason to avoid code teaching. In fact, the fear that children who are taught by direct code methods will miss out on meaning has been clearly invalidated by a longitudinal comparison study (Lesgold & Curtis, 1981; Lesgold & Resnick, 1982). Lesgold & Curtis report that oral reading errors in first grade are usually appropriate for the meaning context even for children who have been taught only grapheme–phoneme correspondence and have had no explicit instruction in "reading for meaning."

Meaning-emphasis programs, as we have noted, do not necessarily ignore the code. Indeed these "basal" programs, in which children read stories from the very beginning of instruction, are supplemented by workbooks and teaching activities which help get the job done. The main difference is that the content of the basals is less well controlled. That is, whereas code programs introduce words that are orthographically regular and use few letter–phoneme correspondences, the basals introduce words without regard to regularity and mappings predictability (Beck, 1981; Willows, Borwick & Hayvren, 1981). In Beck's (1981) comparison of code programs with basal programs, she found that the basal stories read early in the first grade had hardly any words for which all the letter–phoneme correspondences were taught. Code programs used vocabulary that was 79%–100% decodable according to taught correspondences. Thus the basals place the burden on the learner to induce correspondences on his own, or on the teacher to teach them later.

Thus the instructional issue becomes a technical issue of when and how to teach rather than whether to teach. Indeed, that is a proper level for the issue, given that the cognitive requirements of reading in an alphabetic language assure that something of this sort must be learned eventually. However, we are probably at the limits of what we can say about these technical issues based just on the cognitive models of skilled reading and reading acquisition. Research that traces the states of learners through different instructional environments would shed some light on the remaining instructional issues. At present, we know very little about what exactly learners know about words—how they represent words, letter patterns, and speech mappings—at various stages of learning under different conditions of instruction.

C. Comprehension Instruction

We turn now to a consideration of comprehension. Comprehension, of course, is part of all reading right from the beginning, provided the child is reading text. Comprehension instruction, however, is an issue only to the extent that the components of comprehension are not acquired and used by the child outside of the reading curriculum.

1. Schemata and Schema Theory in Instruction

Schemata, or conceptual knowledge structures, have an important role in reading as they do in all cognition. Indeed, our consensual Cognitive Model of Reading included a major role for schemata in comprehension. However, this general model does not single out schemata for any special instructional emphasis. Schemata are critical for comprehension, but they comprise a too-diffuse set of learnings to allow any instructional emphasis. Everything a person knows can be represented as a schema, and without much more than this there are no implications for instruction, except that children should learn a lot.

However, there is another point of view on this matter which sometimes goes under the label of *schema theory*. The difference is perhaps one of emphasis. Schema theory, rather than viewing schemata as an integral part of complex cognitive activities, seems to assign privileged status to schemata. As an issue of comprehension theory, the status of schemata is a matter for research that attempts to distinguish how and when conceptual structures make their contribution to text comprehension. Thus, schemata will deserve privileged status in comprehension theory to the extent that they are shown to make early deterministic contributions to, for example, the encoding of propositions. However, it does not follow that because schemata have a privileged status in comprehension theory they should have a privileged status in instruction. It is not always clear specifically what people are doing when they are teaching reading "according to schema theory." However, it is a clear consequence of what we know about reading that teaching according to schema theory should not serve as a substitute for teaching about the code. Schema theory, if we give attention to this point, can be prevented from becoming for this generation of teachers of reading what the "psycholinguistic guessing game" was for the last generation.

With that caveat, there may be something to say about schema teaching. The first assumption is that there is no privileged status for schemata in instruction, but that schemata play a role in reading and reading comprehension. A second assumption is that schemata are learned without instruction. The everyday conceptual knowledge that a reader must have to understand ordinary texts is acquired through everyday experience. However, the specific knowledge needed to understand science texts is the result of both everyday experience and specific schooling. Now neither everyday knowledge nor specifically schooled knowledge is distributed equally among children. So there are opportunities to increase both kinds of knowledge within the classroom, but it makes no sense to make such opportunities the centerpiece of instruction in reading. The acquisition of schemata is what all learning is about, a claim as vacuous as it is true.

The useful implications of schemata may lie less with the existence of knowledge structures than with the conditions of their use. Spiro (1980) referred to the problem of *schema selection:* The reader must not merely have schemata, he must select the one required by the text. By the account of the Cognitive Model we have described, this is not so much a selection process as an activation process. For a well-written text and a skilled reader, features of the text should trigger or activate appropriate schemata. However, for a learning reader or an older reader of low skill, these activation processes may be less likely to occur. For example, if a reader has low-level word-identification skills, the schema-activation processes may occur either less often or less fortuitously. Alternatively, the schema may deactivte because of effortful word identification and proposition encoding.

An implication of this is that children should be provided with information that they need before or during their reading. This is in effect what teachers do when they provide oral discussion about certain things prior to the child's reading a story about these things. However, it is important to realize that this preactivation instruction does not have to be restricted to simple concepts, but can include more complex structures central to events in a story. It is often the case that children have the necessary knowledge, and the preactivation may remind them of this knowledge.

This seems to be the most generally useful implication of schemata for instruction in reading. It is impossible to ensure that every reader has all the relevant knowledge required by a text selection. Indeed, learning to read makes the reader less dependent on prior knowledge and more able to acquire new knowledge. Meanwhile, certain procedures can increase the chances that the child will use the knowledge that he or she has.

Story Structures. One particular example of schema instruction is in story schemata. It is possible that the cognitive role of story structures, or other text structures, is mirrored by an instructional role. The general principle that structures are learned is undoubtedly true. Since children have story-structure knowledge by school age (Stein & Glenn, 1979), explicit instruction in story structures is not likely to be especially needed. However, it is possible that some children are missing knowledge of story structures just as it is possible to lack knowledge about anything else. There have been attempts to teach story structures to low-achieving students, on the assumption that their reading comprehension might be low because of failure to use story structures. At least two studies have been successful in this (Fitzgerald & Spiegel, 1983; Short & Ryan, 1982), and there have been some without success (Dreher & Singer, 1980). It is not completely clear what determines a successful outcome from this kind of comprehension instruction. However, one possibility, consistent with the conditions of the successful studies, is that the instruction that has good results is rather minimal, serving perhaps to remind children of what they already know so that they can use it in a reading situation. This is in effect the teaching of a comprehension strategy in which a child begins to apply knowledge to a processing task. This does not imply that story-structure instruction should be a curriculum component. Rather, it demonstrates the one possibility, perhaps limited, for helping children who have not made much progress in reading comprehension.

2. Comprehension Strategies

Story-structure instruction can be an example of comprehension-strategy instruction or merely an example of specific schemata instruction, depending upon how it is done. The general distinction is that instruction in comprehension strategies focuses on the procedures a reader uses rather than on the knowledge these procedures work on. The question of whether there is a place for comprehension-strategy instruction in the curriculum is clear in general. Any time a teacher says, "Read something twice to understand it better," or the like, instruction in comprehension instruction has occurred. To make such instruction more systematic than this is to make comprehension-strategy instruction part of the curriculum. Some would resist this suggestion on the grounds that comprehension depends on specific knowledge domains and that generalized procedures for comprehension either do not exist or cannot be taught. However, there is nothing in what we know about reading comprehension (including our description of the Cognitive Model of Reading) that suggests that comprehension strategies, whether they are general or more specific, are automatically used without instruction. The generality of comprehension strategies seems to be something of a pseudoissue. The only question is how broadly they transfer.

A more serious problem is the identification of comprehension strategies which are beyond the obvious ones used by any teachers. All comprehension strategies can be directed toward increasing the chances that the reader will construct a mental text model that corresponds to the underlying model of the actual text. This is accomplished through explicit attempts to extract the higher level (important) text elements, either through the allocation of resources, the monitoring of comprehension, or various combinations of these strategies. It has long been known that questions strategically interspersed throughout a text can increase comprehension of the text as a whole under certain conditions (Rothkopf, 1971). Requesting a reader to answer questions following text selections seems to encourage a kind of regular updating of the text model. This in turn may foster what Rothkopf termed *mathemagemic* behaviors, the generalizable learning process that, in the case of reading texts, includes the kinds of monitoring skills usually taught—self-questioning and summarizing, especially.

There have been successful attempts more recently to teach such comprehension strategies in the classroom. Palincsar and Brown (1984) taught seventh-grade low-achieving readers certain monitoring procedures, including summarizing, questioning, clarifying, and predicting. Children successfully learned to perform the monitoring activities and showed gains in measures of text comprehension. It is impossible to say what specifically produced the gains but it is possible to speculate that any activity that increases the child's attention to the text and/or his understanding of it will help the child who has difficulties (even if these things are not the source of the difficulties). It also appears that children can be trained to form inferential elaborations that are needed for comprehension (Bransford et al. 1982). Thus it is becoming clear that comprehension strategies not only can be learned, they can also be taught. They probably work—when they do—by reminding the reader about procedures that he would use in other situations but fails to use in reading texts, or by providing some procedures that help compensate for a reading problem.

3. Instruction in Verbal Efficiency

Finally, we return to lexical access in the context of comprehension. We have pointed out the need to consider lexical access as a fluent process as well as an accurate one. It is especially in comprehension that this point becomes important. It is quite clear that lexical-access processes that are nonfluent can interfere with comprehension (see Perfetti, 1985). It is also clear that instruction in lexical access is not normally carried out with a fluency criterion in mind. One implication for instruction suggested by the Cognitive Model of Reading with its verbal efficiency component is that perhaps it should be.

How continued practice at word identification can best be achieved remains an open question. There is naturally a reluctance to have prolonged direct instruction on the code as part of reading. A fourth-grade teacher does not want to teach grapheme–phoneme correspondences. Furthermore, it is not clear that this is warranted except in a few cases.

However, it is clear that many children complete their primary grades' reading instruction without knowing enough about decoding. Their weakness shows up in speed of word identification, even if their accuracy is adequate to meet the demands of their texts. However, the speed itself is merely a symptom of inadequate knowledge about words and word formations. This means that practice at speeded responding itself will not necessarily help comprehension, although it might if carried out long enough. It is clear that short sessions at speeded word identification have no effect.

Nevertheless, there are many possibilities for increasing word-identification fluency. Beck (1981, 1983) has suggested that extended word-identification practice can be part of the regular text-reading curriculum. She proposed a two-strand reading program, one-strand including only conceptually easy material and the other more challenging material. The easier material would allow even slower students to practice word-identification skills (and to continue to build up lexical knowledge) in the context of comprehension.

A second method is computer-aided instruction. Computer instruction, of course, can be used in many curriculum areas. In word identification it may be especially useful in making practice more engaging, especially in the quantity that is needed to have an impact. Game environments have been developed to present many different word tasks to children, and research so far is encouraging for the value of such tasks (see Frederiksen et al., 1983).

The general point may be that decoding instruction does not have to be aversive. It can be part of regular text reading, provided texts are carefully controlled, or part of engaging computer games, provided tasks are carefully designed. Other possibilities exist. Instruction in extended word practice can be part of a reading comprehension curriculum as well as a beginning reading curriculum.

D. Summary

In light of cognitive models of reading and reading acquisition, certain instructional issues are raised. However, there remains a need to analyze the acquisition process more fully so that instructional procedures are informed by an understanding of how a learning reader makes progress. Still, there are ample theoretical and empirical grounds for links to instruction. For beginning reading, it is clear that direct teaching of decoding has much to recommend it and has no harmful side effects. It is also clear that progress in reading can take other routes because human beings are prolific pattern inducers. As for comprehension, most children have what they need minimally to comprehend some texts. However, a failure to have schemata activated by text features may characterize children with low reading skills, perhaps because of inefficient word-identification skills. Procedures that help children apply what they know to texts can be and often are part of reading lessons. Procedures that help the child monitor his or her comprehension appear to be especially valuable. Finally, extended word practice also can be made a painless part of the reading curriculum.

V. SUMMARY

Linkages between the theoretical analysis of a cognitive skill and the acquisition of the skill in instruction are important in establishing a strong scientific basis for instructional practice. The case of reading is especially important because of its centrality in curricula. We have described a cognitive model for reading comprehension and one for reading acquisition. These models represent significant progress in the cognitive analysis of reading skill and reading acquisition. The development of reading instruction perhaps has proceeded without sufficient contact with such analysis. There is more needed to make this contact meaningful, namely, more analysis of the conditions of learning than we have seen. However, there is plenty to say about the instructional implications of what we do know.

ACKNOWLEDGMENT

The authors wish to acknowledge the support of the Learning Research and Development Center which is funded in part by the National Institute of Education, which is not responsible for the views expressed.

REFERENCES

Anderson, J. R. (1976). *Language, memory, and thought*. Hillsdale, NJ: Erlbaum.
Anderson, R. C., Reynolds, R. E., Schallert, D. L., & Goetz, T. E. (1976). *Frameworks for comprehending discourse* (Technical Report No. 12). Urbana: University of Illinois, Laboratory for Cognitive Studies in Education.
Anderson, R. C., Spiro, R. J., & Anderson, M. C. (1978). Schemata as scaffolding for the representation of information in connected discourse. *American Educational Research Journal, 15*, 433–440.
Atkinson, R. C., & Shiffrin, R. M. (1968). Human memory: A proposed system and its control processes. In K. W. Spence & J. T. Spence (Eds.), *The psychology of learning and motivation*, (Vol. 2). New York: Academic Press.

Baron, J. (1979). Orthographic and word specific mechanisms in children's reading of words. *Child Development, 50,* 60–72.

Beck, I. L. (1981). Reading problems and instructional practices. In T. G. Waller & G. E. MacKennon (Eds.), *Reading research: Advances in theory and practice,* (Vol. 2, pp. 53–95). New York: Academic Press.

Beck, I. L. (1983). Developing comprehension: The impact of the directed reading lesson. In R. Anderson, R. Tierney, & J. Osborn (Eds.), *Learning to read in American schools* (pp. 3–20). Hillsdale, NJ: Erlbaum.

Beverly, S. E., & Perfetti, C. A. (1983). *Skill differences in phonological representation and development of orthographic knowledge.* Paper presented at the Biennial Meeting of the Society for Research in Child Development, Detroit, Michigan.

Bradley, L., & Bryant, P. E. (1983). Categorizing sounds and learning to read—a causal connection. *Nature, 301,* 419–421.

Bransford, J. D., & Johnson, M. K. (1973). Considerations of some problems of comprehension. In W. G. Chase (Ed.), *Visual information processing* (pp. 383–438). New York: Academic Press.

Bransford, J. D., Stein, B. S., Vye, N. J., Franks, J. J., Auble, P. M., Mexynski, K. J., & Perfetto, B. A. (1982). Differences in approaches to learning: An overview. *Journal of Experimental Psychology: General, 111,* 390–398.

Britton, B. K., Meyer, B. J. F., Simpson, R., Holdredge, T. S., & Curry, C. (1979). Effects of the organization of text on memory: Tests of two implications of a selective attention hypothesis. *Journal of Experimental Psychology: Human Learning and Memory, 5,* 496–506.

Brooks, L. R. (1977). Visual pattern in fluent word identification. In A. Reber & D. Scarborough (Eds.), *Toward a psychology of reading: The proceedings of the CUNY conferences.* Hillsdale, NJ: Erlbaum.

Brown, A. L., & Palincsar, A. S. (1982). Inducing strategic learning from text by means of informed, self-control training. *Topics in Learning and Learning Disabilities, 2*(1), 1–17.

Carpenter, P. A., & Just, M. A. (1981). Cognitive processes in reading: Models based on readers' eye fixations. In A. M. Lesgold & C. A. Perfetti (Eds.), *Interactive processes in reading,* (pp. 177–213). Hillsdale, NJ: Erlbaum.

Chall, J. (1967). *Learning to read: The great debate.* New York: McGraw-Hill.

Chall, J. (1983). *Learning to read: The great debate* (updated ed.). New York: McGraw-Hill.

Chiesi, H. L., Spilich, G. J., & Voss, J. F. (1979). Acquisition of domain-related information in relation to high and low domain knowledge. *Journal of Verbal Learning and Verbal Behavior, 18,* 257–274.

Chomsky, C. (1977). Approaching reading through invented spelling. In L. B. Resnick & P. A. Weaver (Eds.), *Theory and practice of early reading* (Vol. 2, pp. 43–66). Hillsdale, NJ: Erlbaum.

Cirilo, R. K., & Foss, D. J. (1980). Text structure and reading time for sentences. *Journal of Verbal Learning and Verbal Behavior, 19,* 96–109.

Collins, A., & Loftus, E. (1975). A spreading-activation theory of semantic processing. *Psychological Review, 82,* 407–428.

Coltheart, M. (1978). Lexical access in simple reading tasks. In G. Underwood (Ed.), *Strategies of information processing* (pp. 151–216). London: Academic Press.

Curtis, M. E. (1980). Development of components of reading skill. *Journal of Educational Psychology, 72,* 656–669.

Dooling, D. J., & Lachman, R. (1971). Effects of comprehension on retention of prose. *Journal of Educational Psychology, 88,* 216–222.

Dreher, M. J., & Singer, H. (1980). Story grammar instruction unnecessary for intermediate grade students. *The Reading Teacher, 34*, 261–268.

Ehri, L. C. (1980). The role of orthographic images in learning printed words. In J. F. Kavanagh & R. Venezsky (Eds.), *Orthography, reading and dyslexia*. Baltimore: University Park.

Ehri, L. C. (1983). A critique of five studies related to letter-name knowledge and learning to read. In L. M. Gentile, M. L. Kamil, & J. S. Blanchard (Eds.), *Reading Research Revisited*. Columbus, OH: Merrill.

Ehrlich, S. F., & Rayner, K. (1981). Contextual effects on word perception and eye movements during reading. *Journal of Verbal Learning and Verbal Behavior, 20*, 641–655.

Fitzgerald, J., & Spiegel, D. L. (1983). Enhancing children's reading comprehension through instruction in narrative structure. *Journal of Reading Behavior, 14*, 1–18.

Forster, K. I. (1979). Levels of processing and the structure of the language processor. In W. E. Cooper and E. C. T. Walker (Eds.), *Sentence processing: Psycholinguistic studies presented to Merrill Garrett*. Hillsdale, NJ: Erlbaum.

Fox, B., & Routh, D. K. (1976). Phonemic analysis and synthesis as word-attack skills. *Journal of Educational Psychology, 68*, 70–74.

Frederiksen, J. R., Weaver, P. A., Warren, B. M., Gillotte, H. P., Rosebery, A. S., Freeman, B., & Goodman, L. (1983). *A componential approach to training reading skills* (Report No. 5295). Cambridge, MA: Bolt Beranek and Newman.

Gibson, E. J., & Levin, H. (1975). *The psychology of reading*. Cambridge, MA: MIT Press.

Glaser, R. (1976). Components of a psychology of instruction: Toward a science of design. *Review of Educational Research, 46*, 1–24.

Glaser, R. (1982). Instructional psychology: Past, present, and future. *American Psychologist, 37*, 292–305.

Gleitman, D. M., & Rozin, P. (1973). Teaching reading by the use of syllabary. *Reading Research Quarterly, 8*, 447–483.

Goldstein, D. M. (1976). Cognitive-linguistic functioning and learning to read in preschoolers. *Journal of Educational Psychology, 68*, 680–688.

Goodman, K. S. (1967). Reading: A psycholinguistic guessing game. *Journal of the Reading Specialist, 6*, 126–135.

Gough, P. B. (1972). One second of reading. In J. F. Kavanaugh & I. G. Mattingly (Eds.), *Language by ear and eye: The relationship between speech and reading* (pp. 331-358). Cambridge, MA: MIT Press.

Gough, P. B., & Hillinger, M. L. (1980). Learning to read: An unnatural act. *Bulletin of the Orton Society, 20*, 179–196.

Just, M. A., & Carpenter, P. A. (1980). A theory of reading: From eye fixations to comprehension. *Psychological Review, 87*, 329–354.

Just, M. A., Carpenter, P. A., & Masson, M.C. J. (1982). What eye fixations tell us about speed reading and skimming (Eye-Lab Technical Report). Pittsburgh, PA: Carnegie-Mellon University.

Kintsch, W. (1974). *The representation of meaning in memory*. Hillsdale, NJ: Erlbaum.

Kintsch, W., & Keenan, J. W. (1973). Reading rate as a function of the number of propositions in the base structure of sentences. *Cognitive Psychology, 5*, 257–274.

Kintsch, W., & van Dijk, T. A. (1978). Toward a model of text comprehension and production. *Psychological Review, 85*, 363–394.

Kliegl, R., Olson, R. K., & Davidson, B. J. (1982). Regression analyses as a tool for studying reading processes: Comments on Just and Carpenter's Eye Fixation Theory. *Memory and Cognition, 10*, 287–296.

LaBerge, D. (1976). Perceptual learning and attention. In K. W. Estes (Ed.), *Handbook of learning and cognitive processes: Vol. 4. Attention and memory*. Hillsdale, NJ: Erlbaum.

LaBerge, D., & Samuels, S. J. (1974). Toward a theory of automatic information processing in reading. *Cognitive Psychology, 6,* 293–323.

Leong, C. K. (1973). Reading in Chinese with reference to reading practices in Hong Kong. In J. Downing (Ed.), *Comparative reading: Cross-national studies of behavior and processes in reading and writing.* New York: Macmillan.

Lesgold, A. M., & Curtis, M. E. (1981). Learning to read words efficiently. In A. M. Lesgold & C. A. Perfetti (Eds.), *Interactive processes in reading.* Hillsdale, NJ: Erlbaum.

Lesgold, A. M., & Resnick, L. B. (1982). How reading disabilities develop: Perspectives from a longitudinal study. In J. P. Das, R. Mulcahy, & A. E. Wall (Eds.), *Theory and research in learning disability.* New York: Plenum.

Liberman, I. Y., & Shankweiler, D. (1977). Speech, the alphabet and teaching to read. In L. B. Resnick & P. A. Weaver (Eds.), *Theory and practice of early reading.* Hillsdale, NJ: Erlbaum.

Liberman, I. Y., Shankweiler, D., Fischer, F. W., & Carter, B. (1974). Explicit syllable and phoneme segmentation in the young child. *Journal of Experimental Child Psychology, 18,* 201–212.

Lichtenstein, E. H., & Brewer, W. F. (1980). Memory for goal-directed events. *Cognitive Psychology, 12,* 412–445.

Lindsay, P. H., & Norman, D. A. (1977). *Human information processing: An introduction to psychology.* New York: Academic Press.

Mandler, J. M., & Johnson, N. S. (1977). Remembrance of things parsed: Story structure and recall. *Cognitive Psychology, 9,* 111–151.

Massaro, D. W. (1975). *Understanding language: An information-processing analysis of speech perception, reading and psychololinguistics.* New York: Academic Press.

Mattingly, I. (1972). Reading, the linguistic process, and linguistic awareness. In J. Kavanah & I. Mattingly (Eds.), *Language by ear and by eye.* Cambridge, MA: MIT Press.

McClelland, J. L., & Rumelhart, D. E. (1981). An interactive activation model of context effects in letter perception: Part 1. An account of basic findings. *Psychological Review, 88,* 357–407.

McConkie, G. W., & Rayner, K. (1973). *The span of the effective stimulus during fixations in reading.* Paper presented to the American Educational Research Association, New Orleans.

McConkie, G., & Zola, D. (1981). Language constraints and the functional stimulus in reading. In A. M. Lesgold & C. A. Perfetti (Eds.), *Interactive processes in reading* (pp. 155–175). Hillsdale, NJ: Erlbaum.

Omanson, R. C. (1982). An analysis of narratives: Identifying central, supportive, and distracting content. *Discourse Processes, 5,* 195–224.

Palincsar, A. S., & Brown, A. L. (1984). Reciprocal teaching of comprehension-fostering and comprehension-monitoring activities. *Cognition and Instruction, 1,* (2), 117–175.

Perfetti, C. A. (1985). *Reading Ability.* New York: Oxford University Press.

Perfetti, C. A., Beck, I. L., & Hughes, C. (1981, April). *Phonemic knowledge and learning to read.* Paper presented at the Society for Research in Child Development Symposium, Boston.

Perfetti, C. A. & Goldman, S. R., & Hogaboam, T. W. (1979). Reading skill and the identification of words in discourse context. *Memory & Cognition, 7,* 273–282.

Perfetti, C. A., & Lesgold, A. M. (1977). Discourse comprehension and sources of individual differences. In M. A. Just & P. A. Carpenter (Eds.), *Cognitive processes in comprehension* (pp. 141–183). Hillsdale, NJ: Erlbaum.

Perfetti, C. A., & McCutchen, D. (1982). Speech processes in reading. In N. Lass (Ed.), *Speech and language: Advances in basic research and practice* (Vol. 7, pp. 237–269). New York: Academic Press.

Perfetti, C. A., & Roth, S. F. (1981). Some of the interactive processes in reading and their role in reading skill. In A. M. Lesgold & C. A. Perfetti (Eds.), *Interactive processes in reading* (pp. 269–297). Hillsdale, NJ: Erlbaum.

Pick, A. D., Unze, M. G., Brownell, C. A., Drozdal, J. G., Hopmann, M. R. (1978). Young children's knowledge of word structure. *Journal of Child Development, 49,* 669–680.

Post, T. A. (1983). *Text processing and chronometric models of comprehension.* Unpublished master's thesis, University of Pittsburgh, Pittsburgh, PA.

Post, T. A., Greene, T., & Bruder, G. (1982). *"On-line" text processing in high- and low-knowledge individuals.* Paper presented at the twenty-third annual meeting of the Psychonomic Society, Minneapolis.

Rayner, K. (1975). The perceptual span and peripheral cues in reading. *Cognitive Psychology, 7,* 65–81.

Rayner, K., & Hagelberg, E. M. (1975). Word recognition cues for beginning and skilled readers. *Journal of Experimental Child Psychology, 20,* 444–455.

Rayner, K., McConkie, G. W., & Zola, D. (1980). Integrating information across eye movements. *Cognitive Psychology, 12,* 206–226.

Read, C. (1971). Pre-school children's knowledge of English phonology. *Harvard Educational Review, 41,* 1–34.

Rothkopf, E. Z. (1971). Experiments on mathemagenic behavior and the technology of written instruction. In E. Z. Rothkopf & P. E. Johnson (Eds.), *Verbal learning research and the technology of written instruction.* New York: Teachers College Press.

Rumelhart, D. E., & McClelland, J. L. (1981). Interactive processing through spreading activation. In A. M. Lesgold & C. A. Perfetti (Eds.), *Interactive processes in reading* (pp. 37–60). Hillsdale, NJ: Erlbaum.

Rumelhart, D. E., & McClelland, J. L. (1982). An interactive activation model of context effects in letter perception: Part 2. The contextual enhancement effect and some tests and extensions of the model. *Psychological Review, 89,* 60–94.

Schank, R. C., & Abelson, R. P. (1977). *Scripts, plans, goals, and understanding: An inquiry into human knowledge structures.* Hillsdale, NJ: Erlbaum.

Short, E. J., & Ryan, E. B. (1982). Remediating poor readers' comprehension failures with a story grammar strategy. Paper presented at the Annual Meeting of the American Educational Research Association, New York.

Smiley, S. S., Oakley, D. D., Worthen, D., Campione, J. C., & Brown, A. L. (1977). Recall of thematically relevant material by adolescent good and poor readers as a function of written and oral presentation. *Journal of Educational Psychology, 69,* 881–887.

Smith, E. E. (1978). Theories of semantic memory. In W. K. Estes (Ed.), *Handbook of learning and cognitive processes: Vol. 6. Linguistic functions in cognitive theory* (pp. 1–56). Hillsdale, NJ: Erlbaum.

Smith, F. (1973). *Psycholinguistics and reading.* New York: Holt.

Spilich, G. J., Vesonder, G. T., Chiesi, H. L. & Voss, J. F. (1979). Text-processing of domain-related information for individuals with high and low domain knowledge. *Journal of Verbal Learning and Verbal Behavior, 18,* 275–290.

Spiro, R. J. (1980). Constructive processes in prose comprehension and recall. In R. J. Spiro, B. C. Bruce & W. F. Brewer (Eds.), *Theoretical issues in reading comprehension* (pp. 245–278). Hillsdale, NJ: Erlbaum.

Stanovich, K. E., & West, R. F. (1981). The effect of sentence context on on-going word recognition: Tests of a two-story theory. *Journal of Experimental Psychology: Human Perception and Performance, 7,* 658–672.

Stein, N. L., & Glenn, C. G. (1979). An analysis of story comprehension in elementary school children. In R. Freedle (Ed.), *Advances in Discourse Processing: Vol. 2. New directions in discourse processing.* Norwood, NJ: Ablex.

Sticht, T. G., Beck, L. J., & Hauke, R. N. (1974). *Auding and reading: A developmental model*. Alexandria, VA: Human Research Organization.

Swinney, D. A. (1979). Lexical access during sentence comprehension: Reconsideration of context effects. *Journal of Learning and Verbal Behavior, 18,* 645–659.

Thorndyke, P. W. (1977). Cognitive structures in comprehension and memory of narrative discourse. *Cognition, 9,* 77–110.

Tulving, E., & Gold, C. (1963). Stimulus information and contextual information as determinants of tachistoscopic recognition of words. *Journal of Experimental Psychology, 66,* 319–327.

Vellutino, F. R. (1982). Theoretical issues in the study of word recognition: The unit of perception controversy reexamined. In S. Rosenberg (Ed.), *Handbook of applied psycholinguistics* (pp. 33–197). Hillsdale, NJ: Erlbaum.

Venezky, R. L. (1970). *The structure of English orthography*. The Hague, The Netherlands: Mouton.

Venezsky, R. L. (1975). The curious role of letter names in reading instruction. *Visible Language, 9,* 7–23.

Warren, W. H., Nicholas, D. W., & Trabasso, T. (1979). Event chains and inferences in understanding narratives. In R. Freedle (Ed.), *Advances in discourse processes* (Vol. 2). Norwood, NJ: Ablex.

West, R. F., & Stanovich, K. E. (1978). Automatic contextual facilitation in readers of three ages. *Child Development, 49,* 717–727.

Wide Range Achievement Test. (1978). Wilmington, DE: Jastak Associates.

Wilkinson, A. C., Epstein, W., Glenberg, A. M., & Morse, E. (1980). *The illusion of knowing in studying texts*. Paper presented at the annual meeting of the Psychonomic Society, St. Louis.

Williams, J. (1979). Reading instruction today. *American Psychologist, 34,* 917–922.

Willows, D. M., Borwick, D., & Hayvren, M. (1981). The content of school readers. In G. E. MacKinnon & T. G. Waller (Eds.), *Reading research: Advances in theory and practice* (Vol. 2). New York: Academic Press.

3

Writing

**MARLENE SCARDAMALIA and
CARL BEREITER**

*Centre for Applied Cognitive Science
Ontario Institute for Studies in Education
Toronto, Ontario, Canada M5S 1V6*

I. THE NATURE OF HIGHER ORDER ABILITIES

All language abilities are complex and impressive in their power. Unlike many other abilities dealt with in school, language tends to be highly automated and to enable considerable untutored competence in speaking, listening, and (after a certain amount of initial instruction) reading and writing. Naturally occurring aspects of language use in reading and writing have received a great deal of attention (Clay, 1975; Goodman, 1967; Graves, 1983; Harste & Burke, 1980; Rentel & King, 1983; Smith, 1971). The language arts community has stressed the inherent naturalness of abilities, and the call for educational reform has been a plea to provide contexts for writing that will enable students to exercise their natural talents. This emphasis has, however, tended to obscure the fact that there are effortful, higher order processes needed to manage more naturally occurring abilities. Within the past several years cognitive scientists have identified qualitatively distinct procedures that are part of the expert's but not of the novice's repertoire. Instructional experiments aimed at fostering expert strategies suggest that an additional order of educational objective may be required if adequate attention is to be given to these more effortful and specialized aspects of competence.

The case for distinctions between relatively automated abilities supported by ordinary social interchange and more purposefully constructed, effortful abilities has been made for a broad range of school abilities (Brown, Bransford, Ferrara, & Campione, 1983). Likewise, distinctions uncovered between expert and novice procedures in a variety of domains can in a sense be considered distinctions between routine execution of

59

learned rules and subordination of such procedures to more goal-directed or strategic processes (Evans, 1984; Resnick, 1983; Reif & Heller, 1982; White, 1984). Research in the area of written communication has identified distinctions between lower order and higher order processes and between novice and expert strategies similar to those found in other subjects across the school curriculum. As in other domains, it has been found that even relatively advantaged students with years of schooling tend to exhibit strategies that are more novice- than expertlike, but instruction designed on the basis of cognitive strategy models is demonstrating considerable promise. Further, as instructional efforts uncover inadequacies in typical student procedures, they also point to needed refinements in models and methods of presentation. The result is a spiraling agenda for scientific analysis and instructional advance, with advances in every domain contributing to advances in others.

Perhaps the main thing that research on writing has to offer for an understanding of higher order abilities in general is a case in which novice competence tends to be highly organized and effective for coping with school tasks and not simply a downscale version of expert competence. Thus the comparison of expert and novice strategies is unusually informative about the many-faceted nature of higher order abilities. The rest of this paper concentrates on such comparisons.

II. THE DISTINCTIVE NATURE OF HIGHER ORDER MENTAL ACTIVITY IN WRITTEN COMPOSITION

The typical novice strategy is a way of writing that is explainable within a "psychology of the natural"—a way of writing that makes maximum use of natural human endowments of language competence and of skills learned through ordinary social experience, but that is also limited by them. This way of writing has been termed knowledge telling (Bereiter & Scardamalia, 1983, 1985; Scardamalia & Bereiter, 1985). The higher order way of writing requires a "psychology of the problematic" for its explanation. It involves going beyond natural endowments and skills learned through ordinary social experience to incorporate, within the competence of the individual, capabilities for the reprocessing of knowledge that are normally achieved only in the social group. This model of writing is termed *knowledge transforming* (Bereiter & Scardamalia, 1984; Scardamalia & Bereiter, in press). This two-model view of composing makes it possible to account for bifurcations in the literature between treatments of writing as a natural consequence of language development, needing only a healthy environment in which to flourish, and treatments of writing as a difficult task, mastered only with great effort. Treatments of writing as a relatively natural language task follow from numerous reports of children taking readily to written expression and literary creation (Brandt, 1982; Clay, 1975; Graves, 1983; Rentel & King, 1983). Treatments of writing as a task requiring extraordinary intellectual and educational efforts follow from intuitive analyses of writing as one of our most advanced intellectual achievements, an achievement that burdens many of its most accomplished artists and defies the efforts of relatively favored university students (Lyons, 1976) and professionals (Odell, 1980).

Models representing what comes naturally and what comes with extraordinary effort both represent distinct human capabilities with distinctive values. But to understand human diversity and in particular to design educational experiences that will enable a full range of competence, it must be understood that these models are not alternative manifestations of the same competence.

III. THE ACQUISITION OF HIGHER ORDER COMPETENCE: FROM CONVERSATION TO KNOWLEDGE TELLING TO KNOWLEDGE TRANSFORMING

A. Conversation to Knowledge Telling

The child who comes to school already a proficient user of oral language has a number of hurdles to get over on the way to becoming a proficient writer. The most immediate, of course, is the attainment of literacy. Other, less obvious hurdles lie beyond. Generally, these hurdles have to do with problems of sustaining discourse without the numerous kinds of support provided by a conversational partner. There are problems in thinking of what to say, in staying on topic, in producing an intelligible whole, in making choices appropriate to an audience not immediately present. At a deeper level there are problems of searching memory without external cues and executive problems of holding the various subprocesses of discourse together for extended periods.

These are significant problems, but there are natural solutions to them. One solution is to stick to telling stories or relating personal experiences. But for expository writing, which students find themselves having to face sooner or later, the natural solution is the knowledge-telling strategy of composing. This strategy was expressed by a 12-year-old student as follows:

> I have a whole bunch of ideas and write down until my supply of ideas is exhausted. Then I might try to think of more ideas up to the point when you can't get any more ideas that are worth putting down on paper and then I would end it.

The current conception of how this strategy works is shown in the model diagramed in Figure 1. It is a strategy specifically geared to dealing with school writing tasks, and so it starts with the writer's constructing some mental representation of a writing assignment. The assignment is analyzed to locate identifiers of topic and genre. The assignment might, for instance, be to write an essay on whether animals should be kept in zoos. Topic identifiers would be *animals* and *zoos*. The specification of the essay form

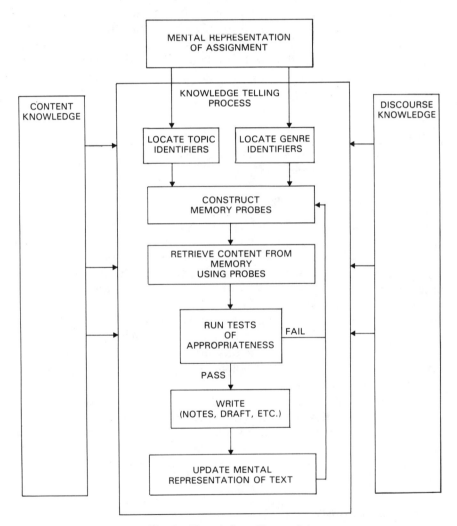

Fig. 1. Knowledge-telling model.

and of an issue would permit identifying the genre as that of the argument or opinion essay, which calls minimally for the statement of a position and one or more supporting reasons. The topic and genre identifiers function as memory probes, permitting the student to retrieve relevant content from memory in an appropriate order for presentation. Thus, the probes *animals, zoos,* and *statement of position* might bring forth the opinion that animals do not belong in zoos. This item of content, since it meets tests of topic and genre appropriateness, is then translated into notes or language suitable for the essay. It then becomes a source of further probes for memory search. New probes, *animals don't belong in zoos* and *reason,* may bring forth an idea such as "If they are in zoos, there won't be many animals left in the wild." This think–say process continues until the page is complete or the store of ideas that comes to mind is depleted. It is not assumed, of course, that the writer consciously formulates the memory probes, any more than the producer of a sentence consciously formulates the need for a certain part of speech. On the contrary, we assume that the process is most of the time rapid and virtually automatic.

Knowledge telling provides a natural and efficient solution to problems encountered by the young writer in school. The solution is efficient because, given any reasonable specification of topic and genre, the writer can get started in a matter of seconds and speedily produce an essay that will be on topic and that will conform to the type of text called for. The solution is natural because it preserves as much as possible of the discourse procedures (although not necessarily the language forms) already acquired through conversation. That is, knowledge telling makes maximum use of external cues and cues generated from language production itself. It preserves the straight-ahead form of oral language production and requires no significantly greater amount of planning, revision, or goal setting than does ordinary conversation. It is serviceable, even though it does not answer to the culture's highest needs. Hence there is little wonder if such an approach to writing is retained on into university and career, even if its shortcomings become increasingly significant.

The following is a brief review of evidence that supports the knowledge-telling model:

1. *Text characteristics.* Although the knowledge-telling model deals with how texts are generated and not with what those texts will be like, the model does suggest certain text characteristics that would result from knowledge telling.
   a. *Topical coherence.* Texts generated by knowledge telling should tend to stick to their simple topics. That is, a text on the topic of whether television is a good or bad influence on children would be expected to deal with television watching and children, although not neces-

sarily sticking to the issue of the influence of the former on the latter. This is precisely what McCutchen and Perfetti (1982) have found in their research on coherence in elementary school writing. They found that in fourth-grade texts the simple topic was usually the only reference for given (as opposed to new) information in text sentences, so that sentences were coherent with the topic but not with each other, as they would be in a more planful treatment of an issue.

b. *Well-formedness.* Because knowledge of discourse structures is hypothesized to prompt content generation, the model predicts that texts will tend to conform to the structural requirements of literary forms, although not necessarily achieving the goals of those literary types. In their longitudinal study of beginning writers, Rentel and King (1983) found that by the second year of school most children had begun to write stories that had the characteristic elements of narrative. But in a national assessment of stories produced by 17-year-olds, almost a third were judged to fall short of showing "evidence of the story-teller's obligation to structure a plot and elaborate it with appropriate details" (National Assessment of Education Progress, 1980a, p. 14). Similarly, in persuasive writing, knowledge telling ought at a minimum to produce a statement of belief accompanied by a list of reasons, but not a developed line of argument. Texts fitting this description proved to be the modal type for both 13-year-olds and 17-year-olds in the National Assessment of Educational Progress (1980a, 1980b) evaluations of persuasive writing.

c. *Writer-based prose.* As defined by Flower (1979), this pervasive kind of student writing (identified by studying novice, university-level writers) presents ideas in a form and in an order that are reasonable from the standpoint of the writer's thinking of them but that are not suited to the reader's uptake of the information. Such writing, Flower notes, is appropriate for a first draft, but with novice writers it tends to persist in the final draft. The knowledge-telling model hypothesizes a think–say composing process and limited means for operating on knowledge about reader reactions that could be expected to yield prose of this type.

2. *Self-reports.* Interview statements by elementary school students of the type presented above indicate that they see writing as primarily a matter of recalling what they know about a topic and writing down either all their ideas or the best of those they had retrieved. Such evidence is anecdotal. It permits no conclusion about how young people in general write, but it does serve as evidence that at least some young people consciously approach writing in the way indicated by the knowledge-telling model. This is an important point to establish, be-

cause it is quite possible for a theory to give an adequate account of the products of cognition (for instance, to account for text characteristics) without corresponding in any way to the process by which those products were generated (Chomsky, 1980).

3. *Absence of protocol evidence of goal setting, planning, and problem solving.* Absence of protocol evidence is not conclusive, since it could mean simply that immature writers carry on processes covertly that are more overt in mature writers. But it should also be pointed out that that argument would be at least equally convincing turned the other way around. That is, if novice writers were in fact deliberately setting goals and striving to achieve them one might expect them to be engaged in more conscious problem solving than experts, for whom greater portions of the writing task would have become automatic. Thus, although it is not conclusive, the protocol evidence should not by any means be dismissed.

4. *Start-up time.* If young writers were carrying on significant amounts of planning, this might not be revealed in their thinking-aloud protocols, but it would nevertheless take time. Consequently, the speed with which young writers began writing, once given an assignment, and the finding that start-up time was unrelated to time and length constraints (Zbrodoff, 1984) argue against any composing process that involves a great deal more deliberation than is hypothesized by the knowledge-telling model.

5. *Limitations on revision.* A consistent finding is that revision, even among university students, is largely limited to proofreading, cosmetic alterations, spelling, punctuation, grammer, and word choice (Bridwell, 1980; National Assessment of Educational Progress, 1977; Nold, 1981; Perl, 1979). One of the strongest points of the model is that it makes students' avoidance of revision something that is predictable from the way they write rather than some additional phenomenon in need of special explanation (and special treatment). Whereas expert writers can check what they have produced against goals and translate perceived deficiencies into problems to be solved, the knowledge-telling model supports a "try again" approach to revision of content. Consequently, revision other than through deletion or through cosmetic changes is likely to prove unrewarding.

6. *Evidence of a similar strategy in reading.* A comprehension strategy very similar to knowledge telling has been identified (Brown et al., 1983; Scardamalia & Bereiter, 1984). Both strategies involve discrete items of content linked to topics and both function without goal formulation, problem solving, or construction of high-level syntheses of content. This parallelism serves to buttress the validity of the knowledge-telling model, because, as van Dijk and Kintsch (1983, p. 262)

remark, "It seems highly implausible that language users would not have recourse to the same or similar levels, units, categories, rules, or strategies in both the productive and the receptive processing of discourse."

B. Knowledge Telling to Knowledge Transforming

Knowledge telling gains its efficiency by turning expository writing into a routine. This does not mean that writing is easy or unstressful for immature writers. Often it is quite the opposite (Daly & Miller, 1975). But knowledge telling does make one writing task much like another, thus allowing it to be handled in an orderly manner, minimizing the need for planning and problem solving. Such orderly procedures are not learned overnight, of course. Most of the young elementary school writers studied by the Toronto Writing Research Group have had trouble sustaining coherent text production, while older school-age writers have mastered knowledge telling in a variety of genres. Few have shown signs of going beyond it. The schools where we have worked are among the best we have seen, both in amount of school time devoted to writing and in concern and skills of teachers. It is unlikely that the results are atypical, at least not atypically low.

Clear indications of a model of writing distinct from knowledge telling may be obtained by looking at graduate students, however. Although they may not be expert writers by literary standards, these more advanced students give evidence of a distinctly more complex approach to writing than do younger students. This more complex approach is marked by an active reworking of knowledge as it is used in writing.

This reworking or transforming of knowledge has been described in a variety of ways by professional writers (Lowenthal, 1980; Murray, 1978; Odell, 1980). Aldous Huxley described the process as follows:

> Generally, I write everything many times over. All my thoughts are second thoughts. And I correct each page a great deal, or rewrite it several times as I go along. . . . Things come to me in driblets, and when the driblets come I have to work hard to make them into something coherent. (from interview in *Writers at Work*, 1963, p. 197)

Compare this to the orderly and painless process described by a sixth-grader:

> I have a whole bunch of good ideas and I start writing the major ones first because they are the ones that are in the front of my mind. Then the smaller ones start coming three-quarters of the way in the page and maybe a whole bunch of those . . . a swarm of those. So I might write as many of them as I can. . . . It doesn't take that long.

What is the more complex, knowledge-tranforming model like? Figure 2 shows the model as we currently conceive of it. It will be noted that

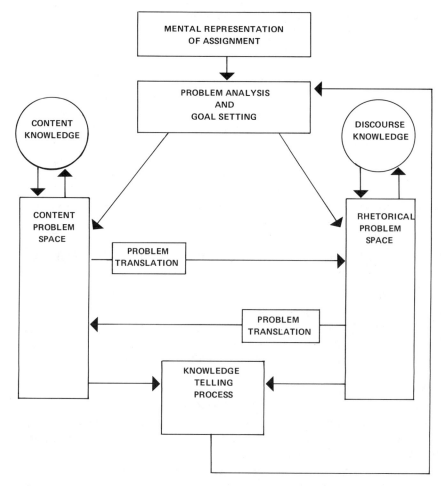

Fig. 2. Knowledge-transforming model.

the knowledge-telling process, as depicted in Figure 1, is still there, but it is now embedded in a more complex problem-solving process involving two different kinds of problem spaces. In the content space, problems of belief and knowledge are worked out. In the rhetorical space, problems of achieving goals of the composition are dealt with. Connections between the two problem spaces indicate output from one space serving as input to the other—for instance, a rhetorical problem of achieving clarity being translated into the need to reconsider the meaning of some concept represented in the content space. It is this interaction between problem spaces that, we argue (Scardamalia, Bereiter, & Steinbach, 1984), is the basis for reflective thought in writing. The knowledge-telling process is relegated to handling nonproblematic phases of composition—in producing routine or familiar stretches of prose, for instance, or in the uninhibited writing of first drafts, when the writer may intentionally suppress problem-solving operations.

The work of Flower and Hayes (1980a, 1980b, 1981) makes it clear that composition is a highly resource-demanding task for experts and that what makes it resource demanding is the complexity of problems the experts set for themselves. The fact that they establish the complexity of the task rather than having the level of complexity determined by the assignment is perhaps the single most significant fact about expert composing. Even though the impetus for the task may have come from some external source such as an assignment or a deadline, the task becomes self-defined. In turn, it gains meaning. From this perspective, making a task meaningful is part of the writer's expertise.

What follows is a brief overview of the kinds of mental activities identified in expert composing. It is through these mental activities that experts sustain self-definition of constraints and goals.

1. *Alternating, checking, and coordinating procedures.* Experts alternate between types of composing activities (e.g., generating content and detecting problems), check the adequacy of courses of action that they have embarked on, and manage to coordinate the various results of these efforts. Basically, they execute self-regulatory strategies—strategies for managing their cognitive behavior.

To be an expert writer you must obviously have a repertoire of powerful rhetorical strategies; by contrast, the best self-regulatory strategies in the world will not make you a good writer. But the learning of rhetorical strategies presupposes an executive structure within which those strategies may function. That implies a structure for setting goals to be achieved through the composition and for monitoring progress toward those goals, for identifying obstacles, solving problems, and so on. As we have seen, the executive structures that guide the composing processes of novice writers tend not to have these capabilities.

2. *Memory search.* Searches for content appropriate to a text appear as odysseys through hard-to-get-at memory stores for experts while they appear as nonproblematic—take what comes next—operations for novices.

Heuristic search is the name given to memory search procedures that employ strategies for increasing the likelihood of finding what one is looking for (Newell & Simon, 1972). The search strategy that has been examined most carefully is the strategy of elaborating constraints (Flower & Hayes, 1980a). The expert elaborates constraints and thus generates more conditions for solution than would otherwise be the case. The effect of elaborating constraints, however, is to produce an increasingly integrated analysis of the problem. When people are continually engaged in problem analysis, they develop representations of problem and solution types that render many situations no longer problematic (Chi, Feltovich, & Glaser, 1981). This frees mental capacity to pursue more advanced problems, which in turn generate representations that render problem solving unnecessary, thus permitting attention to shift to a still higher level of problem, and so on. Such a process seems to characterize expert writers. By comparison, the novice uses the givens of the assignment rather than personally elaborated constraints. Accordingly, the number of constraints to be dealt with is lower, and so is the potential for activating, integrating, and reformulating content.

3. *Mental representations of text.* Cognitive analyses of expert–novice differences in writing typically focus on differences in the mental operations that are performed. Closely associated with mental operations are the mental representation that they apply to and that enable different operations.

Text can be represented at many different levels. The lowest level would be near photographic representation of the physical text. At levels progressively further removed from the physical text are verbatim representations, representations of detailed content (*microproposition,* in Kintsch and van Dijk's terms, 1978), representations of the gist *(macropropositions),* structural representations, problem representations, and intentional or goal representations.

Mature writers give evidence of all these kinds of representations. Immature writers give evidence of representations at a lower level, closer to the surface text (Burtis, Bereiter, Scardamalia, & Tetroe, 1983). Mature writers also interconnect the representations they construct. For immature writers the interconnections are infrequent, and when they do appear the degree of integration tends to be minimal (Scardamalia & Paris, 1985). These findings are in keeping with distinctions between the knowledge-transforming and knowledge-telling models of written composition. The knowledge-transforming model describes how goals are generated and how problem-solving processes operate on goals, structural representations, and gist representations. The knowledge-telling model describes how text is generated without the need to operate on high-level representations of purpose or gist.

IV. INSTRUCTION: CURRENT EFFORTS AND ADVANCES TOWARD KNOWLEDGE-TRANSFORMING STRATEGIES

Many new things have started to happen in the teaching of writing. Children are being encouraged to start writing before they have learned to read, inventing their own spellings (Clay, 1975). Some schools are greatly increasing the amount of time devoted to writing. Children are writing in teams or sharing their productions with one another in workshops (Crowhurst, 1979). *Conferencing*—the term used to describe teacher–student and student–student dialogue and feedback regarding writing—is the mainstay of many progressive programs (Graves, 1983). Microcomputers are being used to ease revision, to produce presentable newspapers and other realistic applications of writing, and even for long-distance communication among student writers (Quinsaat, Levin, Boruta, & Newman, 1983). At the college level the "new rhetoric" (Young, 1976) is bringing a new emphasis on student's exploring and developing their ideas before writing. In general, there seems to be a growing emphasis on making writing a worthwhile and intrinsically satisfying activity for students.

Not enough children have grown up on a rich diet of meaningful writing experience for us to know whether they will emerge with a fundamentally different kind of writing competence or whether they will emerge with only an improved version of knowledge telling. The only point that can be insisted upon strongly at present is that educators ought to be wondering what the outcomes are and trying hard to find out.

In addition to the curriculum efforts mentioned above, there have been instructional experiments based on expert–novice models for composing. Each of these experiments has been of relatively short duration, and they have not been designed with classroom use as their primary objective. Their overriding aim has been to convey to students the activity underlying expert competence and to determine the extent to which the cognitive behavior and strategies of novices can be rendered more expertlike.

In the area of writing, refinements in instructional means have resulted in a technique termed *procedural facilitation* (Bereiter & Scardamalia, in press; Collins & Brown, in press; Scardamalia & Bereiter, 1983). Procedural facilitation consists of routines and external aids designed to reduce the processing burden involved in taking on the advanced self-regulatory strategies of the expert. The main steps in designing a procedural facilitation are:

1. Identify a self-regulatory function that appears to go on in expert performance but that does not go on or that goes on in an attenuated form in student performance.

2. Describe the self-regulatory function as explicitly as possible in terms of mental operations or functions.

3. Design a way of cueing or routinizing the onset and offset of the process to make minimal demands on mental resources.

4. Design external supports or teachable routines for reducing the information-processing burden of the mental operation.

It is important to distinguish such efforts from practices that involve the teacher as director of the procedure, insuring that the child carries out certain procedures or types of activities. These latter types of efforts have been termed *substantive facilitation* (Scardamalia & Bereiter, 1985) because a good deal of the executive control remains in the teacher's hands. By necessity, procedural facilitations represent simplified versions of the mature executive. If the novice were advanced enough to understand expert procedures straightaway, the need for intermediate measures would not arise. But intermediate measures are needed, and this is where techniques such as procedural facilitation and reciprocal teaching (Palincsar & Brown, 1984) come in.

Instructional interventions that have aimed to demonstrate cognitive strategy change in writing—those employing procedural facilitations—have ranged from single sessions to sessions of a few weeks to one of about half a year. Accordingly, at this point we must rely on currently available short-term indications of cognitive behavior changes that point to more fundamental structural changes. These short-term indications include:

1. *Evidence of problem-solving effort.* Central to expert competence is the ability to detect and address problems that emerge in the course of writing. The extent and variety of problem solving distinguishes the knowledge-transforming model from the knowledge-telling model. Results of studies using procedural facilitation show students dealing with more varied and complex types of problems than they do when using their normal writing procedures.

2. *Internalizing a new feedback loop.* Knowledge telling is essentially a straight-ahead process. Anything that gets students to reconsider a decision, to judge one output against another, to represent something in a different way–anything that gets students to do these things under their own direction—introduces the potential for self-modification into the system. Instructional studies (Bereiter & Scardamalia, in press; Scardamalia & Bereiter, 1983; Scardamalia et al., 1984) have demonstrated that, with the help of procedural facilitations, children can shift attention between content generation on the one hand and problem identification and analysis on the other. Further, their performance is aided, not deterred, by this shifting of attention. This is a finding of much importance. It suggests that the primary means available to adults for reducing the load of writing— breaking the task into more manageable subtasks—is available to immature writers under suitably facilitating conditions. What students appear to lack is the executive routine to manage such activity. As we clarify and refine our understanding of the underlying operations and manage to convey them to children, even more effective executive procedures should be teachable.

3. *Generalizability of transformational procedures.* The previously cited instructional studies have aimed to determine the extent to which performance demonstrated with procedural supports available was also demonstrated when they were withdrawn. These analyses suggest that students have begun to internalize new procedures and can conduct them, although in somewhat attenuated form, even when working on their own in a test situation. One follow-up study, conducted one year after the intervention, showed evidence of competence in knowledge-transforming operations that had not been taught directly (for example, note making, information assembly from library resources, and revision).

4. *Incorporating into individual competence abilities normally dependent on social interaction.* In studies using procedural facilitation, results were obtained under conditions where students were working independently, without the benefit of teacher evaluations or suggestions for improvement. It is thus particularly significant that in both studies of revision (Scardamalia & Bereiter, 1983) and studies of reflective processes (Scardamalia et al., 1984), changes in measures of text characteristics, surface behavior, *and* cognitive behavior have shown significant improvement. Frequently the most noticeable advances have been with students previously showing little talent. Also, with rare exceptions, it has been possible to trace improvement to each student in the class.

5. *Understanding the composing process.* Another form of data depends on the sometimes neglected fact that one is dealing with sentient beings, who can tell about the experience of attempting the new procedure. Their reports of cognitive change (to be distinguished from reports of enjoyment or improved performance) provide valuable information. Student responses to procedural facilitations have been virtually unanimous in declaring that evaluating and considering changes of their texts was a new experience for them, and they generally communicated a sense of having acquired a new intellectual power, not just a procedural trick. In general, students report much more profound changes in their thinking than are reflected in their performance. This is not surprising, but it often suggests where the points of strongest contrast are between the students' existing strategies and the procedures to which they have been exposed. It is a rare student who is able to explain his or her own composing strategy. But it is common for students to express the sense of a day-versus-night difference between the way some procedural facilitation has enabled them to function and the way they perceive their normal functioning in writing. If their reports are consistent with the kind of strategy change that was envisioned— which they have been—this too constitutes provisional evidence that the instruction has moved them in the direction of a more mature strategy.

V. ASSESSMENT OF WRITING

In order to assess the effects of writing instruction on cognitive processes it is essential to have a model that indicates what development of cognitive processes in writing would consist of. In the absence of appropriate theoretical models, two mistakes are frequently made:

1. *Overinterpretation of surface manifestations of change.* It is possible, often by very simple means, to double the amount children write, increase the amount and level of revision, and elicit dramatic testimonials about the value of what has been done. Demonstrating that cognitive changes have actually occurred requires more penetrating investigation and will often show that the superficial indicators were misleading.

2. *Error in attribution.* In virtually every classroom situation the teacher provides some measure of help to students in their writing. Consequently there is a problem in judging what aspects of the final product to attribute to the teacher and what to attribute to the student. The confounding becomes particularly serious when methods employing substantive facilitation are at issue. These procedures, by definition, involve more active help from the teacher and help at higher levels (in identifying goals and problems, in formulating gists, etc.).

It is popular at this time to distinguish between instruction that focuses on the "product" and that which focuses on the "process." But in fact the word *process* means different things to different investigators, and current efforts almost universally lay claim to a process orientation. The following four types of outcome variables address distinctions that are meant to clarify the level at which processes underlying performance are addressed:

1. *Text characteristics.* The traditional concern of writing instruction has been to produce better compositions. It remains that the great bulk of instructional research, although it may employ quite nontraditional teaching methods, still focuses on text quality as the outcome of principal interest.

2. *Surface behavior.* One meaning of *process* is observable behavior such as taking notes, outlining, and revising (especially revising). We would also include in this category such outcomes as spending more time at writing and writing more words or producing more changes or more drafts of a composition. According to this view of process, then, instruction is successful it if leads students to show more of the intended observable behaviors.

3. *Cognitive behavior.* Here the emphasis is on mental activities that lie behind the observable text and observable writing behavior: planning (which may or may not involve notes and outlines), rethinking or reprocessing (which may or may not involve physical changes to already written text), etc.

4. *Cognitive strategies.* Here the emphasis is not on particular cognitive behaviors but on the way cognitive behavior is organized in writing. The outcome of interest, therefore, is structural change in the student's executive system for composing. Procedural facilitations, which make use of content-free external supports that are managed by the child, permit fairly precise gauging of what is available and what is lacking in students' strategic repertoires.

Procedural facilitation aims to influence all four types of outcome. In contrast, traditional and newer procedures for improving writing have not been based on explicit models of cognitive behavior and their aim, accordingly, has not been to assess advances based on such models. It follows that only data on the first two types of outcome variables are available for traditional and for most current instructional efforts.

Although outcomes of all kinds have to be assessed from observation, it is worth noting that the assessment of each type of outcome involves risky inference beyond what is directly observable. This is obvious in the case of cognitive-behavior and cognitive-strategy outcomes, but the inferences are no less problematic in the case of supposedly more objective outcomes. If one is interested in text-quality outcomes, it is surely with some expectation of improving the quality of writing people do outside the writing class. And so there is a problem of empirical generalization to other situations and other kinds of writing. How well can one infer from the quality of students' personal essays or literary ventures how they will perform with real-life reports, memoranda, etc.? Another serious difficulty in interpreting results of holistic ratings of text quality is the fact that, for the writing of school age students, the more words students write, the higher the ratings of their text tend to be. Simply asking students to write more is sufficient intervention to produce significant gains in rated quality of texts (Scardamalia, Bereiter, & Goelman, 1982).

Surface-behavior outcomes likewise involve extremely risky inferences. For seldom is the observable behavior valuable in itself. It has to be assumed that note taking or outlining imply some worthwhile planning and organizing going on covertly, and that changing words and moving text around imply constructive rethinking. To cite a cautionary example, a colleague of ours, examining a computer "dribble" file, was so impressed by the amount of revision activity recorded for one student that he went to watch the student at work. He discovered that the student whiled away unproductive moments at the computer by deleting bits of text and then making them reappear. The example would be trivial were it not that data on word counts and frequency of text changes appear to provide the main empirical basis at present for claims about the pedagogical value of word processors. In general, it seems that researchers who focus on surface-behavior outcomes are assuming cognitive-behavior outcomes but are not providing a reasoned basis for their assumptions nor carrying out empirical checks to see whether the intended cognitive behavior is actually taking place.

There is a more profound reason, however, for being dubious about instruction that focuses on text- or surface-behavior outcomes. Novices are already too dominated by what is on the surface. Difficulties in both revision and planning appear to result from domination by tangible products. Abstract (i.e., remote from the physical text) planning carried out by expert writers is seldom seen, and when it is modeled for younger students it tends to get reduced to thinking of things to put into the text. Students' comprehension of text also tends to be dominated by what is superficial in the text—topic identifiers, the flow of language, specific statements considered in isolation—and to miss those meanings that would have to be constructed by themselves by abstraction from what is presented in the surface text (Brown & Day, 1983; Scardamalia & Bereiter, 1984).

Instruction that focuses on text characteristics and on the more tangible elements of writing practice need not be superficial, of course. See, for instance, White's appreciation of Strunk as a teacher in the introduction to Strunk and White (1959). But the one big inference we might draw from what is already known about writing and reading strategies is that novices need somehow to be put in touch with those great reaches of mental activity in text processing that do not show and that are not directly suggested by observable features of the task. That would seem to be the major educational justification for focusing on cognitive behavior and cognitive strategies.

VI. KNOWLEDGE-TRANSFORMING PROCEDURES WITHIN THE GENERAL CONTEXT OF HIGHER ORDER SKILLS

Students have frequently referred to instruction based on expert models of composing as having taught them "how to think" rather than how to write. It is interesting that after all the talk with these students about writing, they remember the efforts as being about thinking. Of course they are correct. At the most general level they learned to execute the same kinds of problem-solving efforts that distinguish experts in other domains— shifting attention between different problem possibilities, evaluating alternatives, redefining goals as the problem emerges rather than rigidly adhering to a predetermined course of action. What had not been anticipated was that this fact would be so transparent to young students. Several students throughout the course of instruction actually offered information about how they had used the procedures in contexts other than writing.

The point to be stressed is that the self-regulatory mechanisms that typify expert procedures can contribute not only to immediate performance but also to the further development of the system. When executive functions such as planning and evaluating are incorporated into the system of cognitive behavior, they generate information that may lead to strategic changes in behavior (Flavell, 1979). In other words, these self-regulatory mechanisms may constitute change-inducing agents that will have the effect of altering the rules by which the system operates. Instead of fostering self-regulation whereby the individual takes charge, contemporary school practices of all kinds seem to encourage a more passive kind of cognition. One set of school practices favors passivity by continually telling students what to do. Pearson and Gallagher (1983) report that it is common for elementary school teachers to restate the content of every text passage for students, on the assumption that many will have failed to grasp it. The opposing set of practices favors passivity by encouraging students to follow their spontaneous interests and impulses. The failure of many adolescents to perform at a formal level on Piagetian tasks (Lawson & Renner, 1974) may be taken as symptomatic, insofar as formal thought involves deliberate operations on one's knowledge. Recent evidence of the persistence of prescientific schemata in students who have studied physics (McCloskey, Caramazza, & Green, 1980) further bespeaks a failure of students to revise their existing cognitive structures in light of new information. Largely absent from current schooling efforts, scarcely even contemplated, are school practices that encourage students to assume responsibility for what becomes of their minds.

It is unlikely that improvement will come from having schools do better what they already do. Development of higher order abilities appears to require higher levels of educational objectives than are currently being pursued. These higher level objectives involve imparting to the students those kinds of competence that have previously been reserved to the teacher. It has been the teacher who is expected to know what is worth learning and how it relates to what was learned previously. It has been the teacher's job to establish links between current activities and the student's needs and interests. It has been the teacher's job to recognize the spark of originality in the student's work and fan it into a flame. It has been the teacher's job to ask the probing question, to reveal the unexamined premise. Expert performance clearly demonstrates that these executive procedures, handled in schools by the teacher, are, for expert problem solvers, under self-direction.

Writing would seem to offer an especially promising domain in which to help students develop skills of setting and pursuing cognitive objectives. It allows students to work with whatever knowledge they have and to concentrate on its implications and interrelationships. Goals to understand, to solve, to evaluate, to define, and many others of this kind are amenable to pursuit either as primary or as secondary objectives of a writing project. But being able to set and pursue such goals autonomously means functioning according to a knowledge-transforming rather than a knowledge-telling model.

Enabling students to develop a knowledge-tranforming model of composing—a model that permits them to set and pursue their own goals in writing—seems likely to require more than simply a rich diet of relatively unrestricted writing experience, with a teacher involved as collaborator, respondent, and guide. The following additional elements appear necessary:

1. Students (and teachers) need to be made aware of the full extent of the composing process—that it is not just what one does while putting words on paper but that it includes the setting of goals, the activation of nodes in memory, the formulation of problems, and so on. It needs to be constantly clear to students that the ultimate goal is that they should be able to take charge in a competent way of the whole process.

2. The problems of acquiring higher levels of competence need to be made the students' problems and not only the teacher's. Ideally, this should not mean burdening students with the teacher's cares and woes. Rather it should mean getting students involved in inquiries and problem-solving experiments that they will find fascinating and illuminating.

3. The teacher needs to model for the students and the students need to model for each other those major aspects of the composing process that do not normally show. What particularly needs to be modeled is the process of leading oneself to new insights through reflection. Of course, experts as well as novices run into many problems along the way. For experts these problems serve as important clues. Young students, by comparison, tend to feel threatened by problems and thus avoid them. Part of what students need to gain is an understanding of the "debugging" process that adults go through and encouragement to treat "bugs" and confusions as important sources of data.

4. The use of procedural facilitation—simplified routines and external supports—can help students get a start on more complex executive processes. As much as possible, however, the students need to share in an

understanding of the purpose, of where the facilitation is supposed to be helping them go. Without such purposefulness, students are likely to assimilate the new procedure to their existing one and thus obtain only superficial benefits.

Analogous ways of fostering higher order abilities have begun to show effect in reading comprehension (Bereiter & Bird, 1985; Palincsar & Brown, 1984). In domains such as mathematics and science, where there are extensive bodies of content to master, the problems of higher order abilities are somewhat different. But if students can develop powerful knowledge-transforming skills in writing and reading, this could go a long way toward enabling them to become active builders of their own knowledge in all domains.

ACKNOWLEDGMENTS

The work reported in this paper was supported by the Ontario Ministry of Education through a block grant to the Ontario Institute for Studies in Education and by grants from the Alfred P. Sloan Foundation and the Social Sciences and Humanities Research Council of Canada. An early version of this paper was prepared for an American Educational Research Association Task Force subgroup on "Higher Order Academic and Thinking Skills Needed for Future Education and Career Success."

REFERENCES

Bereiter, C., & Bird, M. (1985). Use of thinking aloud in identification and teaching of reading comprehension strategies. *Cognition and Instruction, 2,* 131–156.

Bereiter, C., & Scardamalia, M. (1983). Does learning to write have to be so difficult? In A. Freedman, I. Pringle, & J. Yalden (Eds.), *Learning to write: First language, second language* (pp. 20–33). New York: Longman.

Bereiter, C., & Scardamalia, M. (1984). *Reconstruction of cognitive skills.* Paper presented at the meeting of the American Educational Research Association, New Orleans.

Bereiter, C., & Scardamalia, M. (1985). Cognitive coping strategies and the problem of "inert knowledge." In S. F. Chipman, J. W. Segal, & R. Glaser (Eds.), *Thinking and learning skills: Research and open questions* (Vol. 2, pp. 65–80). Hillsdale, NJ: Erlbaum.

Bereiter, C., & Scardamalia, M. (in press). *The psychology of written composition.* Hillsdale, NJ: Erlbaum.

Brandt, A. (1982). Writing readiness. *Psychology Today, 16,* 55–59.

Bridwell, L. S. (1980). Revising strategies in twelfth grade students' transactional writing. *Research in the Teaching of English, 14,* 107–122.

Brown, A. L., Bransford, J. D., Ferrara, R. A., & Campione, J. C. (1983). Learning, remembering, and understanding. In J. H. Flavell & E. M. Markman (Eds.), *Handbook of child psychology: Vol. 3. Cognitive development* (4th ed.) (pp. 77–166). New York: Wiley.

Brown, A. L., & Day, J. D. (1983). Macrorules for summarizing texts: The development of expertise. *Journal of Verbal Learning and Verbal Behavior, 22,* 1–14.

Burtis, P. J., Bereiter, C., Scardamalia, M., & Tetroe, J. (1983). The development of planning in writing. In G. Wells & B. M. Kroll (Eds.), *Explorations in the development of writing* (pp. 153–174). Chichester, England: Wiley.

Chi, M. T. H., Feltovich, P. J., & Glaser, R. (1981). Categorization and representation of physics problems by experts and novices. *Cognitive Science, 5,* 121–152.

Chomsky, N. (1980). *Rules and representations.* New York: Columbia University Press.

Clay, M. M. (1975). *What did I write: Beginning writing behaviour.* Auckland, New Zealand: Heinemann Educational Books.

Collins, A., & Brown, J. S. (in press). The new apprenticeship: Teaching students the craft of reading, writing, and mathematics. In L. B. Resnick (Ed.), *Cognition and instruction: Issues and agendas.* Hillsdale, NJ: Erlbaum.

Crowhurst, M. (1979). The writing workshop: An experiment in peer response to writing. *Language Arts, 56,* 757–762.

Daly, J. A., & Miller, M. D. (1975). Further studies on writing apprehension: SAT scores, success expectations, willingness to take advanced courses, and sex differences. *Research in the Teaching of English, 9,* 242–249.

Evans, G. (1984). *How much in control? A view of adolescent and adult performance in four task areas.* Paper presented at the meeting of the Centre for Applied Cognitive Science, Toronto.

Flavell, J. H. (1979). Metacognition and cognitive monitoring: A new area of cognitive-developmental inquiry. *American Psychologist, 34,* 906–911.

Flower, L. S. (1979). Writer-based prose: A cognitive basis for problems in writing. *College English, 41,* 19–37.

Flower, L. S., & Hayes, J. R. (1980a). The cognition of discovery: Defining a rhetorical problem. *College Composition and Communication, 31,* 21–32.

Flower, L. S., & Hayes, J. R. (1980b). The dynamics of composing: Making plans and juggling constraints. In L. W. Gregg & E. R. Steinberg (Eds.), *Cognitive processes in writing* (pp. 31–50). Hillsdale, NJ: Erlbaum.

Flower, L. S., & Hayes, J. R. (1981). The pregnant pause: An inquiry into the nature of planning. *Research in the Teaching of English, 15,* 229–244.

Goodman, K. S. (1967). Reading: A psycholinguistic guessing game. *Journal of the Reading Specialist, 6,* 126–135.

Graves, D. H. (1983). *Writing: Teachers and children at work.* Exeter, NH: Heinemann Educational Books.

Harste, J. C., & Burke, C. L. (1980). Examining instructional assumptions: The child as informant. *Theory Into Practice, 19,* 170–178.

Kintsch, W., & van Dijk, T. A. (1978). Toward a model of text comprehension and production. *Psychological Review, 85,* 363–394.

Lawson, A. E., & Renner, J. W. (1974). A quantitative analysis of responses to Piagetian tasks and its implications for curriculum. *Science Education, 58,* 545–559.

Lowenthal, D. (1980). Mixing levels of revision. *Visible Language, 14,* 383–387.

Lyons, G. (1976, September). The higher illiteracy. *Harper's,* pp. 33–40.

McCloskey, M., Caramazza, A., & Green, B. (1980). Curvilinear motion in the absence of external forces: Naive beliefs about the motion of objects. *Science, 210,* 1139–1141.

McCutchen, D., & Perfetti, C. A. (1982). Coherence and connectedness in the development of discourse production. *Text, 2,* 113–139.

Murray, D. M. (1978). Internal revision: A process of discovery. In C. R. Cooper & L. Odell (Eds.), *Research on composing* (pp. 85–103). Urbana, IL: National Council of Teachers of English.

National Assessment of Educational Progress (1977). *Write/rewrite: An assessment of revision skills; selected results from the second national assessment of writing* (Tech. Rep. No. 05-W-04). Washington, DC: U.S. Government Printing Office. (ERIC Document Reproduction Service No. ED 141 826)

National Assessment of Educational Progress (1980a). *Writing achievement, 1969–79: Results from the third national writing assessment: Vol. 1. 17-year-olds* (Tech. Rep No. NAEP-R-10-W-01). Denver: National Assessment of Education Progress. (ERIC Document Reproduction Service No. ED 196 042)

National Assessment of Educational Progress (1980b). *Writing achievement, 1969–79: Results from the third national writing assessment: Vol. 2. 13-year-olds* (Tech Rep. No. NAEP-R-10-W-02). Denver: National Assessment of Educational Progress. (ERIC Document Reproduction Service No. ED 196 043)

Newell, A., & Simon, H. A. (1972). *Human problem solving*. Englewood Cliffs, NJ: Prentice-Hall.

Nold, E. W. (1981). Revising. In C. H. Frederiksen & J. F. Dominic (Eds.), *Writing: The nature, development and teaching of written communication* (pp. 67–79). Hillsdale, NJ: Erlbaum.

Odell, L. (1980). Business writing: Observations and implications for teaching composition. *Theory into Practice, 19,* 225–232.

Palincsar, A. S., & Brown, A. L. (1984). Reciprocal teaching of comprehension-fostering and monitoring activities. *Cognition and Instruction, 1,* 117–175.

Pearson, P. D., & Gallagher, M. C. (1983). The instruction of reading comprehension. *Contemporary Educational Psychology, 8,* 317–344.

Perl, S. (1979). The composing processes of unskilled college writers. *Research in the Teaching of English, 13,* 317–336.

Quinsaat, M. G., Levin, J. A., Boruta, M., & Newman, D. (1983). *The use of a word processor in classrooms*. Paper presented at the meeting of the American Educational Research Association, Montreal.

Reif, F., & Heller, J. I. (1982). Knowledge structure and problem solving in physics. *Educational Psychologist, 17,* 102–127.

Rentel, V., & King, M. (1983). Present at the beginning. In P. Mosenthal, L. Tamor, & S. Walmsley (Eds.), *Research on writing: Priniciples and methods* (pp. 139–176). New York: Longman.

Resnick, L. B. (1983). Mathematics and science learning: A new conception. *Science, 220,* 477–478.

Scardamalia, M., & Bereiter, C. (1983). The development of evaluative, diagnostic, and remedial capabilities in children's composing. In M. Martlew (Ed.), *The psychology of written language: Developmental and educational perspectives* (pp. 67–95). London: Wiley.

Scardamalia, M., & Bereiter, C. (1984). Development of strategies in text processing. In H. Mandl, N. Stein, & T. Trabasso (Eds.), *Learning and comprehension of text* (pp. 379–406). Hillsdale, NJ: Erlbaum.

Scardamalia, M., & Bereiter, C. (1985). Research on written composition. In M. Wittrock (Ed.), *Handbook of research on teaching* (3rd ed., pp. 778–803). New York: Macmillan.

Scardamalia, M., & Bereiter, C. (in press). Knowledge telling and knowledge tranforming in written composition. In S. Rosenberg (Ed.), *Advances in applied psycholinguistics* (Vol. 1). New York: Cambridge University Press.

Scardamalia, M., & Bereiter, C., & Goelman, H. (1982). The role of production factors in writing ability. In M. Nystrand (Ed.), *What writers know: The language, process, and structure of written discourse* (pp. 173–210). New York: Academic Press.

Scardamalia, M., & Bereiter, C., & Steinbach, R. (1984). Teachability of reflective processes in written composition. *Cognitive Science, 8,* 173–190.

Scardamalia, M., & Paris, P. (1985). The function of explicit discourse knowledge in the development of text representations and composing strategies. *Cognition and Instruction, 2,* 1–39.

Smith, F. (1971). *Understanding reading: A psycholinguistic analysis of reading and learning to read.* New York: Holt.

Strunk, W., Jr., & White, E. B. (1959). *The elements of style.* New York: Macmillan.

van Dijk, T. A., & Kintsch, W. (1983). *Strategies of discourse comprehension.* New York: Academic Press.

White, B. Y. (1984). Designing computer games to help physics students understand Newton's laws of motion. *Cognition and Instruction, 1,* 69–108.

Writers at work: The Paris Review interviews (2nd ser.). (1963). New York: Viking.

Young R. E. (1976). Invention: A topographical survey. In G. Tate (Ed.), *Teaching composition: Ten bibliographical essays* (pp. 1–43). Fort Worth, TX: Christian University Press.

Zbrodoff, N. J. (1984). *Writing stories under time and length constraints.* Unpublished doctoral dissertation, University of Toronto, Toronto.

4

Second Language

JOHN B. CARROLL
Department of Psychology
University of North Carolina
Chapel Hill, North Carolina 27514

I. INTRODUCTION

Partly from research in psycholinguistics and partly from more general work on information processing, memory, and similar topics, cognitive psychology ought to have much to say about language learning in all its forms. But there are special difficulties in applying cognitive psychology to foreign language learning. One is that most of the available theory about knowledge representation and skill acquisition has seen very little application to foreign language learning. A more fundamental difficulty stems from the possibility that "knowing" a foreign language may be a very different kind of knowledge from "knowing" a subject like arithmetic, geometry, physics, or American history.

As one who has lived through a number of phases of theory development in psycholinguistics and cognitive psychology, my only recourse is to serve as a kind of filter in conveying from these developments what seems now to be most relevant, meaningful, useful, and important in considering foreign language learning. In so doing I find it desirable to examine issues from the perspective of foreign language teachers, because I believe these people are much closer to the real problems of foreign language learning and teaching than cognitive psychologists—or even psycholinguists—usually are. I therefore draw extensively on the thinking and writings of authorities on foreign language teaching, many of whom have given attention to possible applications, in their field, of cognitive psychology and psycholinguistics.

The emphasis will be on cognitive processes and demands related to what has to be learned, and how that is learned, in acquiring a second language. I can make only occasional mention of many other factors—

COGNITION AND INSTRUCTION

factors of a social, sociolinguistic, motivational, or affective nature. These factors are so important that many second language teaching authorities give them a large share of their attention. For discussions, see writings of Brown (1980, chap. 7), McDonough (1981, chap. 6), Stevick (1976, 1980), and Stern (1983, Part IV).

I begin with an overview of the history of language teaching in relation to different goals of instruction, different views of what a language is, and different theories of language learning. Next I turn to a discussion of some current proposals about language learning and teaching in relation to possible contributions of cognitive psychology. Against this background, I then discuss what I see as critical issues in designing second language instruction. Finally, I suggest next steps and possibilities for innovation, research, and application.

II. CHANGING CONCEPTS OF LANGUAGE AND LANGUAGE TEACHING

For at least 25 centuries (Kelly, 1969) there has been a profession of second language teaching. For students, learning a second language has meant different things. For some, it has meant primarily learning to read the language—for example, to read literary classics, foreign newspapers, or whatever. For others, it has meant learning to use the language in practical spoken communication with people who have that language as their first and perhaps only language. The different goals of students have had an important influence on purposes and methods of teaching and even on conceptions of what a language is or consists of.

When the teaching is focused primarily on reading, the student's problem has been considered to be that of acquiring a knowledge of the vocabulary and grammar of the language so that printed texts can be deciphered or decoded, as it were, and converted into something more readily comprehensible, like a translation in the student's native language. This is the setting in which the *grammar–translation teaching method* has been developed and used for centuries. The student is presented with texts in the second language—at first simple, then more advanced, and expected to learn to translate and understand those texts by applying rules of grammar and consulting dictionaries and word lists. The second language is viewed as another system for conveying meanings, different in strange and not readily understandable ways from the first language, but a system embodied most immediately in its written form—its printed symbols. The language is presented to students most directly in its written form, often with little if any concern for how the written language is to be pronounced.

The language system is regarded as a vast collection of facts to be learned about vocabulary, word formation, and grammar.

When the teaching is focused primarily on the spoken language, the language is viewed first of all as a system of sounds, not as a system of printed symbols. Teachers may recognize that the system can be described in terms of a grammar, and that its words can be listed in dictionaries, but they may consider it debatable whether the learner's attention has to be drawn to rules of grammar. One strategy of teaching a spoken language has always been a "natural" or "direct" method whereby the teacher simply tries to establish communication with students in the second language by speaking the language in situations that suggest the meanings of utterances and by gradually encouraging students to imitate speech and use it for communication. This is often done with no attempt to explain the grammar of the second language. Students are expected to acquire competence in the second language in somewhat the same manner that they acquired competence in their native language.

Over a large part of the history of second language teaching, the grammar–translation method has been predominant, especially in formal schooling. It has been thought that students who wished to acquire competence in the spoken language could do that in advanced phases of instruction, after competence in reading has been reasonably well established.

In modern times scholars have increasingly tended to devote themselves to the systematic study of language in general as a human social institution. A science of language, called *linguistics,* has emerged, concerned with describing and comparing languages and addressing general questions about the nature and universal properties of languages. In linguistics, particular languages are studied only as exemplars of the general phenomenon, and the systematic examination of such languages has been conducted largely independently of pedagogical concerns.

Linguistic scientists have had thoughts and opinions about language teaching, however, and their views on the nature of language have attracted the attention of language teachers. The views of two linguistic scientists— Leonard Bloomfield and Noam Chomsky—have had important influences on developments in language teaching in the present century.

Leonard Bloomfield, the founder of what is now often called *structural linguistics,* stressed the fact that a language is a system primarily of sounds, not of printed symbols. He considered the written form of a language to be a secondary, auxiliary system that evolved only in the more advanced civilizations. As expressed in various writings (Bloomfield, 1914, 1933, 1942), Bloomfield's views were influential in moving language teaching in American schools away from the grammar–translation method and toward an emphasis on the spoken language. First in the 1940s (in the armed services) and later in the early 1950s (in schools and colleges) teachers emphasized the goal of having students learn to speak and understand the second language being taught. Students could also learn to read and write the language, either simultaneously with acquiring the spoken form or after speaking competence was gained, but this was secondary.

Bloomfield's views on the nature of language learning were also influential. He stated that language use involves a system of habits—habits pertaining to the perception and production of spoken forms. Even in his earliest writings on the matter, Bloomfield warned against regarding language teaching as "the imparting of a set of facts." He pointed out that the "facts" of language are exceedingly complex; he felt that an intellectual knowledge of such facts would be of little use in real-life communication situations. As he said, "Language is not a process of logical reference to a conscious set of rules: the process of understanding, speaking, and writing is everywhere an associative one. Real language-teaching consists, therefore, of building up in the pupil those associative habits which constitute the language to be learned" (Bloomfield, 1914, p. 294). This theme was implicit also in remarks to be found in his later writings: "The matter that is to be presented, the thousands of morphemes and tagmemes of the foreign language, can be mastered only by constant repetition" (Bloomfield, 1933, p. 505); "practice everything until it becomes second nature" (Bloomfield, 1942, p. 16). At the same time, Bloomfield (1933) recommended that language be acquired in meaningful situations: "The nucleus of the foreign language should be presented in connection with practical objects and situations—say, of the classroom or of pictures" p.505).

Bloomfield's views became the inspiration for what came to be known as the *audio-lingual method* (Brooks, 1964). In this method, it was recognized that language learning is in many respects learning of perceptual–motor skills, particularly in connection with the second language sound system. Stress was placed on the accurate perception and pronunciation of foreign sounds; students were encouraged to mimic sounds spoken by native speakers, but help was also given in the form of lectures and hints about phonetics and articulation. In effect, this was attempted cognitive guidance of a perceptual–motor skill.

An important feature of the audio-lingual method was the memorization of dialogues in the second language, in the hope that students would acquire a feel for the grammatical patterns exemplified in these dialogues. Another feature of the audiolingual method was the use of the language laboratory (Stack, 1960), where students could listen to tape recordings and perform extensive practice and drill in varying grammatical patterns.

A further consequence of Bloomfield's views was the development of what became known as *contrastive linguistics* (Lado, 1957), that is, the systematic comparison of the second language with the first language, in order to identify features of the learner's first language that were likely to cause interference in learning the second language. This was based on Bloomfield's notion of language learning as the formation of new habits. It was thought that through contrastive studies of first and second languages with respect to their sound structures, grammatical rules, and systems of word meanings, learners could be helped to avoid the errors that could arise on account of interference between first and second language habits.

Ultimately, some of the assumptions and procedures of the audio-lingual method were challenged by the development of a new school of thought in linguistics called *transformational generative grammar*. The publication of Chomsky's (1957) *Syntactic Structures* heralded what many regarded as a revolution in linguistic theory and method. Briefly, Chomsky thought of a language as essentially a property of the native speaker's mind, inhering in a capability (1) to generate—"create"—or understand an infinity of grammatical utterances based on a finite system of rules and (2) to evaluate whether a given possible utterance would be grammatical in the speaker's native language. Chomsky drew a distinction between *surface* and *deep structures* and pointed out that at least in English, many sentences may be ambiguous in form or meaning in the sense that they can be derived from different deep structures. (A famous example was the sentence "Flying planes can be dangerous.") According to Chomsky, the rules of a language pertain largely to the manner in which *phrase structures* are formed and used in *transformations* of deep structures whereby different kinds of grammatical utterances (sentences) may be shown to be related— for example, active, passive, negative, and interrogative forms of sentences. Structural and transformational rules could be codified in quasi-mathematical terms.

The school of transformational generative grammar placed much less emphasis than Bloomfield and the structuralists on the primacy of speech over writing. The basic structures of a language were thought to apply with at least as much force to written language as to spoken language. To the extent that written language is "edited" by language users, it would exhibit the standard form of the language even more clearly than spoken language. It was thought that the fundamental unit of language is the complete, grammatical sentence; complete sentences are the kinds of structures that are more prevalent in written language than in spontaneous speech, with its frequent false starts, hesitations, and sentence fragments.

What this seemed to mean for language learning was that the important rules to learn would be those pertaining to the deep structures and their transformations to surface structure. This idea was applied not only to rules pertaining to the order of words in sentences, but also to the way in which different morphological variants of words are formed (plurals, tense forms, compounds, etc.), with variations in sound values. The status of the phoneme, so much labored over by structural linguists, became fundamentally altered in Chomsky's system (Chomsky & Halle, 1968).

The views of transformational grammarians on the role of written language may have encouraged some language teachers to return to placing emphasis on the written language, but there has been a carryover from the days when structural linguists were preaching the primacy of spoken language. In recent years, the "speaking objective' has continued to dominate language-teaching programs.

Although Chomsky opined that linguistics is essentially a branch of psychology, he vehemently rejected (Chomsky, 1959) the behaviorist interpretations of language behavior and learning advanced by Skinner (1957). He asserted that language use and learning cannot be described in terms of the formation and reinforcement of habits. He also came to support a form of nativism, claiming that specific capacities for language learning—that is, capacities for learning particular forms of possible grammars—are innate and, as it were, "wired in" to the human brain. To the extent that capacity for language learning is innate, it would be useless or unnecessary to examine or try to guide its processes; therefore, all the learner needs is appropriate language input.

In the period since Chomsky's introduction of transformational generative grammar, linguistic theories have multiplied. Chomsky's own theories have exhibited considerable development and refinement, not only by Chomsky himself (1965) but at the hands of others (e.g., Chafe, 1970; Lyons, 1968; McCawley, 1968). One trend has been toward greater emphasis on the analysis of meaning in language and of the contexts in which different forms of language are relevant or appropriate.

All varieties of linguistic theory have been essentially concerned with the *formal analysis* of language systems as abstract objects. Although such analysis may be helpful in selecting materials for language teaching and providing explanations of grammatical phenomena, it gives little guidance regarding the conceptual design and sequencing of a language learning curriculum. On the whole, language teachers have remained neutral or eclectic as to the type of grammatical theory needed as a basis for language teaching. Attempts to base language teaching explicitly on phrase structures and their transformations have apparently not produced the large improvements in language proficiency that were hoped for (see, for example, contrasting viewpoints of James, 1969, and Lamendella, 1969, and comments of Carroll, 1971). Actually, the transformational grammarians offered no new, positive theory of language learning and performance. Their main contribution was the suggestion that, as Stern (1983) puts it, "teaching techniques which make learners respond automatically or repeat mechanically are less appropriate than techniques which lead to creative language use" (p. 174).

Language teaching today exists in many varieties, as it always has. Examples of grammar–translation and audio-lingual methods can still be found. As a result of the Chomskyan revolution, however, teachers have tended to shift towards methods that seek to endow the learner of a second language with the kind of creative competence described by Chomsky. The theory of language teaching has also been considerably influenced by developments in psycholinguistics, particularly research on first language acquisition. Many language teachers see first language acquisition as an important model for looking at how a second language can best be taught.

III. SOME CURRENT VIEWS OF SECOND LANGUAGE LEARNING

A. A Framework for Examining Second Language Learning

Seeking a basis for analyzing the models offered by various authorities, Stern (1983, p. 338) offers the chart shown (with slight modifications) in Figure 1. It groups the variables to be considered under five headings: (1) social context, (2) learner characteristics, (3) learning conditions, (4) learning process, and (5) learning outcomes. There are implications for cognitive psychology in each of these categories; for example, the social context may influence the type of input the learner has, and this input may constitute one of the factors under the category of learning conditions. For present purposes, however, let us concentrate on the learning process, which Stern (1983) discusses as follows:

> The learning process can be looked upon as consisting overtly of strategies and techniques employed by the learner and, covertly, of conscious and unconscious mental operations. The problem is and has been how best to study them. A first approach would be one which openly examines the actual language learning behaviour: what do learners do to learn a language in the classroom or in a free learning situation? Another approach might be to tap the insights of the learners themselves and to inquire into their objectives, strategies, and techniques, their thoughts and feelings about language learning as well as steps and stages perceived by them as necessary to master the language. Another approach might be to make experimental, observational, or introspective studies of cognitive processes involved in language learning, such as: attending, discriminating, imitating, memorizing, rehearsing, probing, matching,

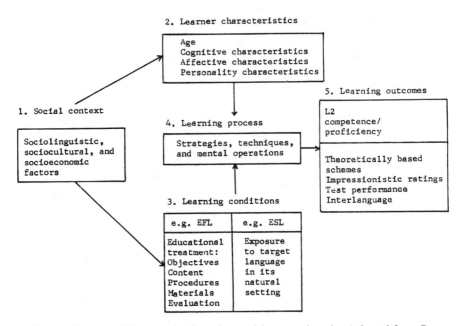

Fig. 1. Framework for examination of second language learning (adapted from Stern, 1983, p. 338).

guessing, comparing, inferring, forming hypotheses, generalizing, verifying, and planning. It would also be valuable to explore by observation, experiment, or introspection the motivational and affective concomitants of the learning process, for example, persistence, elation, frustration, resistance, humour, and so on. Any of these suggested approaches can be repeated over a period of time in order to obtain a longitudinal account of language learning development. It should further be possible to compare different learners in the same situations or groups of learners in different situations in order to discover individual or group differences among learners in response to variations in the learning conditions. At present, we are still at the beginning of the direct study of second language learning behaviour. (p. 339)

If nothing else, this passage suggests the immensity of the task of studying second language learning processes and strategies. Each of the cognitive processes mentioned (attending, discriminating, etc.) constitutes a major category of psychological theorizing and experimentation. It is impossible to consider them all here in detail. It seems useful, however, to approach them from the perspective of a series of interrelated "hypotheses" advanced by Stephen Krashen, a second language teacher and writer on second language teaching methods, in presenting what he calls the Monitor Model. For convenience, I list these hypotheses, quote from his remarks about them, and discuss them in the order in which he gives them in a published lecture (Krashen, 1982b), but he has written about them extensively in other publications (Krashen, 1981a, 1981b, 1982a).

B. Krashen's Monitor Model: Some Hypotheses

1. The Acquisition–Learning Distinction Hypothesis

Basic to Krashen's model is a proposed distinction between two types of language learning: first, *acquisition,* the "natural" kind of language learning exemplified in the way children acquire language, "subconsciously, through informal, implicit learning"; and second, *conscious language learning.* Krashen always means conscious learning when he uses the word *learning.* "This is knowing about language, explicit, formal linguistic knowledge of the language. We generally see this in language classrooms."

Acquisition, i.e., "natural" learning, is presumed to occur in situations in which people use a language in exchanging information, asking questions, and giving directions, often with respect to the immediate environment, persons, concrete objects, emotions, felt sensations and desires, etc. Children acquire most of their first language competence in such environments, but Krashen believes it is possible to create environments at least approximately like this for adults learning a second language.

While this distinction between acquisition and learning may well be drawn, one wonders whether it is really a distinction between subconscious, tacit learning and conscious learning. A perennial problem in psychology has been whether learning can occur without some kind of conscious attention. In contemporary cognitive psychology, it has been asserted (Schneider & Shiffrin, 1977) that initial learning is accompanied by conscious attention, but at later stages, after practice, the role of conscious attention is reduced as the learner progresses towards "automatized" behavior. Even in the "natural " learning behavior postulated by Krashen, the learner (whether a child or an adult) has to *attend* to something—*notice* something, at least in the first phases of the learning of some particular response. The distinction may not, therefore, be between subconscious and conscious learning, but between learning of communicative responses in situations naturally evoking them and a kind of metalinguistic knowledge *about* such responses, as is ordinarily imparted in textbooks and classroom presentations. Alternatively or in addition, as we may see in the description of the Monitor hypothesis explained later, the distinction may be between learning that takes place without attention to the learning itself, and learning that takes place when one is attending (with the Monitor) to the learning and to one's performance. Krashen is not saying that conscious learning should be discouraged in second language teaching, but he does seem to claim that the subconscious acquisition process is somehow more fundamental, and that it produces more enduring learning. If so, it behooves cognitive psychologists to examine carefully the circumstances in which this type of learning takes place. In classical learning theory, Krashen's acquisition might be regarded as a form of incidental (as opposed to intentional) learning. Since psychologists find intentional learning to be generally better and more productive than incidental learning, it is somewhat surprising that a form of incidental learning could be claimed to be in some way superior to intentional learning.

2. The Natural Order of Acquisition Hypothesis

This hypothesis says that "in acquisition [in Krashen's sense] people acquire items in a predictable order." It stems first from the work of Roger Brown (1973) in studying first language acquisition. Brown found that among different children the order in which certain features of English were acquired was virtually invariant. There is now a considerable body of evidence (e.g., Anderson, 1978; Dulay & Burt, 1974) showing that not only do these orders occur in child and adult learners of English as a second language, but that comparable orders occur in learners of other languages—more or less independently of the input as characterized by the frequency of the features in spontaneous speech of interlocutors or the order and frequency of their presentation in instructional materials (textbooks and the like).

Explanations for these findings have tended to appeal to the linguistic analysis of the features. For example, early-acquired possessive markers depend on a more complex structure: *John's hat* being presumably derived from *the hat of John* or *John has a hat*. The hypothesis of *derivational complexity* has run into serious difficulties in explaining first language (L1) sentence comprehension in adults (see Clark & Clark, 1977), but it may well hold in early language comprehension. More generally, however, one may postulate that order of acquisition depends upon successive learning stages. In early stages, the learner can deal only with simple features; in later stages, having mastered the simple structures, the learner can assimilate more involved structures. It is to be understood, in all this, that mastery is measured and observed in natural, spontaneous speech situations—not necessarily in contrived testing situations. For example, errors in written tests do not necessarily show the same order of difficulty as errors in spontaneous speech.

What is cognitive psychology to make of this? The hypothesis implies that there are inherent characteristics of the content to be learned that determine the relative ease of acquisition when matched with learners' states of mastery. If so, what are these inherent characteristics and how are they internalized by the learner? As yet, there do not appear to be relevant models for this in cognitive psychology.

3. The Monitor Hypothesis

In essence, this central hypothesis of Krashen's model proposes a contrast between two possible states of a speaker in making an utterance: (1) fluent responding based on acquisition (see Hypothesis 1 above), and (2) the speaker's monitoring of his/her own speech output, based on what Krashen thinks of as conscious learning of particular linguistic forms and rules. That is, in monitoring, the speaker will try to recall and apply appropriate rules about what is grammatically acceptable, planning and guiding speech accordingly, or correcting errors as they occur. In speech performance (that is, the emitting of utterances), a speaker may alternate between these two states. In the nonmonitoring state, the speaker is fluent and nonhesitant. Monitoring behavior is reflected in nonfluency and hesitancy, although some speakers may be able to monitor their speech with enough facility to exhibit reasonable fluency.

Here again we see a distinction drawn between conscious and subconscious learning and between the consequences of each. However, the same remarks and strictures I have mentioned above would seem to apply here as well. The distinction may be more between the circumstances of learning in each case, the nature of what is learned, and the degree of automatization that is or can be attained. The individual in a monitoring state is one who may not have attained an adequate degree of automatization with respect to the linguistic features involved.

One might mistakenly understand the monitor hypothesis to imply that acquisition always yields linguistically correct behavior. This is by no means the case, and Krashen would be the first to deny such a conclusion. Even in acquisition situations, learners can draw false analogies from the input, forget or misremember what has been temporarily acquired (placed in an intermediate-term memory?), or simply become confused. They can make mistakes even when seeming to perform fluently. A learner may say "I goes to school every day" with perfect abandon, only to be corrected by a teacher. According to Krashen, teacher correction of student errors is aimed at learning, not acquisition, in the sense that it is intended to cause the learner to have a kind of metalinguistic awareness of a rule and its application.

4. The Input Hypothesis

This states simply "that the way we acquire language (not learn it) is through comprehensible input: focus on the message, not the form. . . . It claims that listening comprehension is of primary importance in language acquisition, and that speaking will emerge with time.'' Input becomes comprehensible when it consists of at least some material that the learner (or should one say *acquirer?*) has already absorbed, and when it becomes understandable through the linguistic or extralinguistic context. For the beginner it consists of *simple codes*—short utterances with simple structures. For the more advanced student it consists of much material already mastered, plus items or structures that are just beyond the learner's mastery or comprehension, but which the learner is "ready" to acquire. The context provides clues for understanding these new items or structures, and if they are understood they are likely to be acquired in the natural manner that Krashen contrasts with formal learning.

Evidence for this hypothesis is found in both first language and second language acquisition studies. Children acquiring their first language, as well as children and older people acquiring a second language, learn new structures when the input is roughly tuned to the individual's stage of learning. One sees here a relationship to the natural order of acquisition hypothesis, in that it is assumed that inputs can be characterized in terms of how their elements can be sorted into those appropriate to different learning stages.

Krashen believes that, optimally, the input is spoken. Could not the same principles regarding the readiness of learners to acquire items or structures just beyond their current stage of learning apply to written input? To a degree, yes, if reading comprehension is the objective. Consider this remark from the diary of an adult language learner about the input in a French class: "The written words were so *tangible,* unlike the elusive spoken words that went in one side of my short-term memory and out the other" (Bailey, 1980, p. 59). Krashen would probably comment on this that the concreteness of the written word is illusory, in that a written word does not constitute a really adequate surrogate for the spoken form. He implies that true language acquisition comes about only if the input is in spoken form. (Recall the structural linguists' insistence on the primacy of speech over writing.) It may take more time—more repetitions on different occasions—for the spoken form to be internalized, but this is a more genuine form of learning than learning a written form. Obviously, it leads to better transfer to proficiency in spoken communication.

This hypothesis is also relatable to the interesting finding of Postovsky (1974) about adult learners in an intensive course in Russian who were encouraged not to try to speak or imitate foreign sounds and words, but simply to listen and try to understand Russian language input for a few weeks. When they were finally allowed to speak and were tested, their fluency and pronunciation were better than that of learners in other classes who had been allowed, encouraged, or even required to imitate and speak from the outset.

There are several interesting points here for cognitive psychology. One is that the internal representation of foreign sounds, words, and structures may be qualitatively different when those representations are of speech as opposed to writing. There may, of course, be correspondences between representations of spoken and of written elements, but they are at least *separate* representations. A second is that representations of forms and grammatical structures, when those representations are meaningful and acquired with transferability, appear to include representations of extralinguistic context. This extralinguistic context, indeed, constitutes the meaning of the forms and structures. This point is easy to accept in the case of linguistic forms referring to concrete objects. The internal representation of /pom/ (French *pomme*, "apple") must be somehow similar to the internal representation of English /aepəl/ as it applies to a class of fruits, but how is one to characterize the representation of the French structure /eskə/ (*est ce que*, roughly translated as "is it that . . .?")? The representation apparently must include that of a situation in which a certain kind of question is being asked. Linguistic analysis has rarely been concerned with the specification of such extralinguistic contexts of higher order structures.

An even more difficult question has to do with the internal representation of word orders, if indeed it is meaningful to speak of such representation. For example, assume that in time a learner of German will acquire by natural learning the structures exemplified in the following German sentence (with literal and free translations):

> *Ich bin gestern in die Stadt gegangen.*
> I am yesterday into the city gone.
> (I went to town yesterday.)

At least two important word order structures are to be seen here: the postposition of the past participle *gegangen),* and the order of time words before place words. These orders are quite strict in German, and they are different from the English orders. In what sense does the speaker of German have psychological representations of these structures? How does a learner acquire them, in view of the fact that sentence inputs will vary widely (e.g., with different time and place words)? Can pattern acquisition be explained in terms of habits or expectancies? To what extent can conscious attention (through monitoring) guide the construction of utterances that conform to rules? I have no firm answers to any of these questions, nor has cognitive psychology or psycholinguistics, as far as I am aware. There is beginning to be some limited evidence on learning strategies from experiments on the learning of artificial languages (e.g., Mori & Moeser, 1983), tending to confirm Krashen's supposition that semantic aspects of messages are more critical than formal aspects, but such experiments are far from providing data on mechanisms of word order learning. The generalizability of findings from such experiments seems limited not so much by the use of artificial language materials (to a learner, even real second language materials are in a sense artificial) as by the rather artificial conditions under which they are conducted. That is to say, these experiments are conducted in a laboratory learning situation where there is nothing like verbal interaction between interlocutors; there is only learner interaction with printed language stimuli associated with static visual displays.

Let us, however, speculate about acquisition of word order structures. Suppose the problem is that of a German speaker learning the English word orders for time and place words. First, turn to Krashen's notion of simple codes. In a naturalistic situation one can suppose that the person might hear a variety of simple sentences with place words like

1. He went to school.
2. I'm going upstairs.
3. I made it in the kitchen.
4. They were playing in the yard.
5. Put it on the table.
   . . . etc.

as well as simple sentences with time words like

6. I'm going tomorrow.
7. He left yesterday.
8. You do it right now.
9. He's coming this afternoon.
10. I haven't seen him yet.
    . . . etc.

from which the learner might come to expect place and time words to come after the verb phrase. At this stage the learner might be expected to hear and just barely understand more complex sentences with both place and time words like

11. He didn't go to school yesterday.
12. They left for America last month.
13. I went to town this morning.
    . . . etc.

Of course, the order of time and place words is somewhat freer in English than it is in German, but sentences 11–13 exemplify the usual order for these contexts; they "sound right" to a native English speaker—better than sentences like

14. He didn't go yesterday to school.
15. I went this morning to town.

After hearing a sufficient variety of acceptable simple sentences like 11–13, the learner might well learn to expect place words before time words, and to use this order in his own attempted utterances. It is also possible that the learner would come to perceive the verb phrase with a place phrase as a unified component (a "constituent") to which a time phrase is appended:

[(I went) + to town] + this morning.

The problem harks back to the debates between stimulus–response theorists and psycholinguists who followed Chomsky in inveighing against habit-formation theories. In my view, Chomsky and his followers went too far in criticizing habit-formation theories. They may have been jusitified in asserting that one could hardly acquire grammatical structures simply by memorizing sentences. But language teachers who used sentence memorizing techniques probably did not expect students to acquire grammatical structures *directly* from memorized sentences. They assumed only that memorized sentences would serve as *examples* of grammatical structures and that the structures would be acquired by a process of subconscious analysis and interiorization on the part of the learner—a process not unlike what a learner might use in receiving, understanding, and analyzing language heard in naturalistic situations. The output of such processing might well be the formation of perceptual and motor habits relating to the phonemic and morphemic composition of linguistic forms and constituents, the orders in which they occur, and the points in a sequence where optional fill-ins are acceptable. Clearly, the ready pronunciation of a long second language word would require a degree of automatization of the articulatory programming involved in such pronunciation, and automatization may be equated with habit formation. Probably Bloomfield's advice (quoted above) to practice memorized sentences "until you can rattle them off without an instant's hesitation" was intended mainly to support the automatization of articulatory habits, with an incidental transfer, on occasion, to transformation of habits involving the ordering of higher order constituents. The issue really has to do with what units, constituents, and regularities become involved in linguistic habit formation. The mistake that was made in some early psycholinguistic investigations was that the complexity of linguistic structure was not fully appreciated. For example, the ordering of transitional probabilities found in Johnson's (1965) studies of sentence memorization was a consequence of the stimuli used; different probabilities might have been found with a greater variety of stimuli.

Furthermore, let us return to a point only hinted at above, namely, that any linguistic habit that is formed necessarily must be associated with some kind of stimulus element. Here I am thinking of the habits that must be formed to support language *production*. The speaker learns to use particular linguistic structures in response to particular stimulus situations. These stimulus situations may be hard to describe or analyze—a circumstance that explains in part the lack of linguists' attention to such matters—but they are surely present, whether in external communication contexts, in the speaker's thinking processes, or in observable linguistic contexts. Examples of the latter are easiest to give: If a speaker is asked a question, the form of the question constitutes a stimulus that may determine, at least in part, the linguistic form of the answer. Language performance has its creative aspects, to be sure, but to a major extent it can be stimulus bound. A large part of the learning or acquisition that occurs in naturalistic contexts must certainly include apprehension of the stimulus conditions associated with language forms and structures. (In several publications concerned with a possible "performance grammar" of English, I have suggested stimulus conditions associated with a number of English structures [Carroll, 1973, 1974, 1980]).

5. The Attitude Hypothesis

According to Krashen, this says that "people with certain personalities and certain motivations perform better in second language acquisition, and also that certain situations are more conducive to second language acquisition." Krashen has little to say about this hypothesis (at least in the source quoted) beyond remarking that low-anxiety situations are more conducive to language acquisition and that people with high self-confidence are usually faster learners. I see little immediate interest in this hypothesis for cognitive psychology and will therefore leave it without discussion, except to suggest that acquisition is more likely to occur in low-anxiety situations, while conscious learning is likely to be associated with situations involving at least a moderate degree of arousal.

6. The Aptitude Hypothesis

This hypothesis happens to have high interest for me, because it relates to work I have done on foreign language aptitude. Krashen's speculation is that *attitude* (Hypothesis 5) relates to acquisition (in his sense), while *aptitude* (defined as "how well you do on the Modern Language Aptitude Test") relates "directly to conscious learning." That is, he believes aptitude relates to success in formal language courses in which there is much emphasis on conscious learning, but shows little if any relation to success in acquiring language in informal, naturalistic contexts in which the learner has an appropriate low-anxiety attitude.

There is surely some basis for this hypothesis. I have written extensively on factors in learning situations that seem to determine the extent to which aptitude measures are correlated with success (Carroll, 1962, 1981). Quality of instruction, opportunity to learn (amount of time allowed, and indirectly, the pace of instruction), and student perseverance (willingness to spend time necessary to achieve mastery) are among such factors. I have noted that aptitude tests tend to have particularly high validity in courses that emphasize formal grammar (and thus, Krashen would say, conscious learning). But I am inclined not to agree that aptitude is associated exclusively with conscious learning. Aptitude is associated with *rate of learning,* whether in formal or informal learning situations. Experience with the test in a wide variety of learning situations, including many intensive, "immersion" courses in which I am reasonably sure instructors tried to establish natural acquisition contexts of the sort that Krashen recommends, suggests that aptitude is associated not only with conscious learning but also with rate of acquisition in contexts that could be regarded as relying on what Krashen thinks of as subconscious learning or acquisition.

This may be particularly true of certain components of second language aptitude, one of which is what I have termed *phonetic coding ability.* Essentially, this seems to be the ability to "code sounds," that is, to form internal representations of heard sounds—either specific phonemes or constellations of phonemes as represented by words or even phrases and sentences. Phonetic coding ability correlates with the ability to imitate heard words and phrases accurately and with an approximation to the foreign pronunciation, at least within the span of immediate memory. It also appears to correlate with the ability to remember novel phonemic materials despite interfering stimuli. There are wide individual variations among both children and adults in this ability, and since imitation and remembrance of novel phonemic materials must be required even in naturalistic learning situations, it seems to follow that aptitude would be related to rate of learning in such situations.

Another component of aptitude is what I have called *grammatical sensitivity,* the ability to become aware of the grammatical functions of linguistic forms—whether through conscious instruction or through less conscious inductive processes. For whatever reason, there are striking individual variations in this ability, regardless of whether individuals have had instruction in the grammar of their own or other languages. It tends to be most highly correlated with success in courses emphasizing grammar instruction, but it shows at least some relation to success in courses not emphasizing grammar instruction and formal analysis of language—even in those contexts in which Krashen claims more acquisition than learning occurs. This could be because some kind of awareness of grammatical function, even at a subconscious level, may be required in acquisition contexts. People acquiring language in those contexts have to notice things about the speech they hear and about the utterances they attempt. Their ability to induce the structural features and functions of speech constituents must have at least some influence on their rate of learning. Even as first language learners, children notice things about the language they are learning and can be quite explicit about their observations (Gleitman, Gleitman, & Shipley, 1972); it is reasonable to suppose that similar phenomena occur in second language acquisition.

Of course, the fact of individual differences, in itself, is of little interest in cognitive psychology; the fact that the dimensions of individual differences relate to specific cognitive processes is, however, of potentially great importance. Although I cannot agree completely with Krashen's formulation of an aptitude hypothesis, I agree with its spirit, to the extent that it suggests the operation of different cognitive processes in different learning contexts.

7. *The Filter Hypothesis*

Here Krashen takes up the suggestion of Dulay and Burt (1977) that "an affective filter," associated with high anxiety, can keep input from getting in. "What the filter hypothesis says about pedagogy is that the more we do to lower the filter, i.e., the more our classes are low-anxiety, the better off our students will be." "The new methods . . . provide a relaxed classroom where the student is not on the defensive."

The filter hypothesis appears to be an extension of Hypothesis 5, the attitude hypothesis, and thus requires no further discussion here.

8. *The L1 Hypothesis*

Here Krashen extends his Monitor Model to point out that learners—particularly adults—often use forms and structures directly or indirectly from their first language (L1) when they don't have sufficient competence in the second language (L2). Further, he believes, L2 teachers and instructional materials frequently encourage such behavior inadvertently through the formal way in which languages are taught.

The L1 hypothesis speaks to the problem of interference between L1 and L2. There is ample evidence that such interference occurs, not only from common observation of second language speakers but from research using error analysis (Corder, 1981). What Krashen seems to be suggesting here is that the kind of interference that occurs in acquisition contexts differs from what occurs in formal, conscious learning contexts. For example, Burmeister and Ufert (1980) found that the kinds of errors that a six-year-old native speaker of German made in English differed depending on whether they occurred in "spontaneous" as opposed to "elicited" contexts. One may suppose that the spontaneous speech errors came from acquisition whereas the elicited speech errors arose from more formal learning contexts. Burmeister and Ufert argue that the child used different strategies in the two situations.

There has been continued interest in how features of the L1 system influence the acquisition of the L2 system. Stern's (1983) characterization of the learner's problem is interesting:

> *Cognitively,* the learner at the start faces disorientation with regard to all linguistic, semantic, and sociolinguistic aspects of the second language. While first language competence is experienced as compelling and completely self-evident—a secure and familiar frame of reference—the second language system appears, to begin with, as indistinct, arbitrary, puzzling, almost entirely meaningless, and often as artificial, even "wrong," sometimes absurd, and, on many occasions, disconcertingly confusing.
>
> The task for the learner is, first of all, to overcome the disorientation and constraints that characterize the early stage of contact with the new language, and to build up, cognitively and affectively, a new reference system and a system of meanings, to develop a feeling for right and wrong in language use, a sense of familiarity and order, and eventually to acquire the capacity to use the language "creatively," that is, to be able to respond to communicative situations appropriately and spontaneously and to be able to think in the second language. This process has often been described—as in first language acquisition—as "internalization," "interiorization," or "incorporation." (p. 398)

Selinker (1972) introduced the concept of *interlanguage* to describe the mixed L1–L2 system that a learner constructs for him/herself in the course of learning L2. According to Hatch (1978) there is considerable regularity in the interlanguages that different learners construct—a regularity partly evidenced by the order in which features are learned (see Krashen's Hypothesis 2). The point is that a learner's interlanguage is a *cognitive construction* derived from the inputs—in both acquisition and learning contexts—to which the learner has been exposed. Errors in these interlanguages arise both from confusions in interpreting L2 input (partly on the basis of L1 competence) and from confusions in understanding formal instruction. Because such confusions are undoubtedly highly specific to the exact nature of the input in each case, it would probably be difficult to arrive at generalizations about their nature and origins. Nevertheless, experimental work along the lines of Slobin and Bever's (1982) crosslinguistic study of children's use of *canonical sentence schemas* might be suggestive. A rather detailed analysis of how second language learners use first language patterns in constructing L2 systems is offered by Hatch (1983).

9. Individual Variation in Monitor Use

Krashen speculates that some people, particularly adults taught in a formalistic way and those with overconscientious attitudes, *overuse* the

Monitor. They "don't trust acquisition" and exhibit a tendency to plan their utterances by conscious application of grammar rules. They are hesitant, and are able to get out a sentence only with great difficulty. At an opposite extreme are "underusers," people who "just talk"; they have "no conscious grammar to speak of." ("These are people who don't know a prepositional phrase from their elbow," Krashen remarks.) They rely almost totally on their acquired competence. "What is very interesting about these people is that they often do quite well with the language." They make errors, but they can understand and communicate. Krashen recommends, however, that "our pedagogical goal should be to produce optimal users" of the Monitor. Monitoring is useful, but it should not get in the way of communication. Optimal Monitor users are "people who refer to conscious rules when they can, but do not get hung up on them. They use them in written language and in prepared speech. But in normal day-to-day conversation they may use them very little."

It seems that optimal Monitor use demands that the second language speaker maintain a fine balance between risk taking (using whatever L2 patterns seem appropriate for communication, regardless of whether they are "correct") and caution (making sure that the patterns selected will serve well in communication and will not confuse hearers/readers or make them overly critical of the speaker's competence). Risk taking is possibly related to learner personality (Beebe, 1983) and the cognitive style associated with *field independence* (Brown, 1980, pp. 90–93).

IV. COGNITIVE PROCESSES IN SECOND LANGUAGE LEARNING

In a brief discussion it is possible only to suggest the kinds of contributions that cognitive psychology has made and could make to second language teaching. Research in cognitive psychology is already large in both scope and volume, and the kinds of cognitive phenomena that occur in L2 acquisition are too varied to permit simple generalizations. Hatch (1983) provides good coverage of research in psycholinguistics that pertains to second language learning.

A. Information Processing

Research and discussion in cognitive psychology address how "information" is "processed." Much experimental work in the field concerns phenomena of memory and problem solving. According to most models of memory, information is initially received in a sensory buffer, referred to long-term memory for its interpretation, and put into short-term or working memory where it may be either further processed and transferred to a long-term store (with consequent changes in the contents of the long-term store), or lost from the working memory—perhaps never to return. Models of problem solving consider how the working memory is used to perceive a problem and its elements and how it draws on the long-term memory store to combine, transform, and supplement problem elements to arrive at a solution that may be either acceptable or unacceptable according to a given criterion. Discussions of memory often appeal to Tulving's (1972) distinction between *episodic* and *semantic memory*. Episodic memory pertains to memories for particular experiences (episodes) while semantic memory pertains to long-term memories for information, often of a linguistic nature, that are not associated with particular episodes of learning—at least so the theory goes. In any event, L2 learning involves both memory and problem solving (either conscious or subconscious).

In applying cognitive psychology to L2 learning (for the time being, let us lay aside any distinction between acquisition and learning), we need first to inquire into what kinds of information have to be dealt with by the L2 learner. This information is of many kinds, and it is normally quite complex, having to do simultaneously with many different levels of language structure—phonological (and/or graphemic), morphological, syntactical, semantic, and discursive. Units of information can exist at all of these levels, and utterances that occur in communicative contexts contain at least some of them—sometimes nearly all of them. For example, a single word *never!* uttered to indicate negation has phonological, morphological, syntactic, and semantic information, as well as affective information. Even in the simplest kind of learning situation—whether in what Krashen would call a natural acquisition context or in the first stages of formal instruction, a learner might be called on to deal with any or all of these kinds of information.

The learner's continual problem is to process linguistic information in such a way as to *notice regularities* in the structure of L2. I am using the terms *regularity* and *notice* as the most general, neutral terms I can think of to refer to what is noticed and how it is processed, respectively. The process may be subconscious in the sense that the learner may not notice that he is noticing something, or not notice that what he is noticing is a regularity. The noticing of regularities seems, in any event, to be a minimal cognitive process necessary in acquiring L2. It is apparently the kind of cognitive process that Krashen thinks can occur in natural acquisition contexts. What is added in formal instruction is that someone (usually a teacher) points out the regularity, with the goal of having the learner notice it.

The regularity that is noticed on a particular occasion may be only a particular sequence of sounds, or it may be what may turn out to be a syllable, word, or phrase. At later stages of acquisition, it may be a regularity that occurs in the context of other regularities that have already been noticed and understood, e.g., it may be a new vocabulary item or a new grammatical construction embedded in an utterance most of which is well understood. What are the minimal conditions for noticing a regularity? I propose the following:

1. The regularity must in some sense be approximately within the learner's current span of apprehension. (The span of apprehension may be dependent on what other regularities the learner has noticed and understood; thus, a new word or grammatical construction can be within the span of apprehension because the remainder of the utterance in which it is embedded is understood.)

2. The regularity occurs in some particular context. (A speech event always occurs in at least *some* context.)

3. On different occasions, the regularity occurs in the same or highly similar contexts.

4. The regularity is noticed in contrast with other regularities, and this contrast is perceived to correlate with a contrast in contexts. (For example, on hearing "This is a hat," and "This is a bat," and observing appropriate pointings to a hat and a bat, the learner can notice the associations between sound and referent.)

A majority of linguistic regularities—perhaps all of them—have to do with meaning in some way. In many cases, contrasts in contexts provide direct clues to specific meanings (e.g., *hat* and *bat*—the baseball kind, let us say); in other cases, contrasts provide distinctions but no specific meanings, as in the case of distinctions between the phonemes /h/ and /b/. Some contrasts are associated with grammatical categories like noun, verb, and adjective; initially the learner may notice, for example, that certain regularities (nouns) are associated with classes of concrete objects, persons, etc., while other regularites (verbs) are associated with actions and motions. Later on, such categories become broadened. The particular contrasts that the L2 learner has to notice may or may not correspond to contrasts already acquired in L1. One is in the realm of concept-formation processes in considering what kind of information will enable the L2 learner to acquire the conceptual scheme characteristic of L2 to the extent that it may depart from that of L1. (For example, at some point in the learning of English, the individual will have to discover that the word *bat* has several meanings, and that in one of its semantic fields it can be both a noun and a verb. It would take us too long to detail the kinds of input needed for the learner to acquire such information.)

B. The Role of Context in Input

What makes L2 learning rather different from the learning of most other subject matters is that a special type of correspondence between language input and meaning must be acquired. If it is considered that speech has primacy over writing, and if the goal of learning is competence in talking and listening in L2, the special correspondence is one between spoken sounds and meaning. If the goal of instruction is restricted to competence in reading and writing a second language, the correspondence is between graphic forms and meaning. Meaning is essentially a cognitive process that operates on the individual's intentions, internal representations, and cognitive responses with respect to the nonlinguistic environment. A language system provides codifications of this cognitive process, and learning such a system therefore entails learning the particular codifications inherent in that system. It follows that the input to the learner must include the kind of context that will most directly and appropriately evoke the nonlinguistic-environment-related cognitive processes which are implied in linguistic codifications (that is, meanings).

We may classify such contexts under two headings: *extralinguistic context* and *linguistic context*. The first refers to anything in the environment that is not linguistic—objects, substances, persons, motions, changes, relations, attributes: in short, anything nonlinguistic about which a cognitive process can occur. Linguistic context, on the other hand, refers to language input that indirectly supplies meaning to a particular linguistic regularity. For example, in the sentence "'The gretch sighed," context "The . . . sighed" supplies certain kinds of information about what a *gretch* might be (assuming *gretch* constitutes a new or possible linguistic regularity). Both kinds of information constantly interact and it may be difficult to disentangle their separate effects.

It could be argued that L2 learning may not be different from learning many other subject matters, in that extralinguistic context occurs in those subject matters also. For example, laboratory work in physics or chemistry is included in instructional programs to give students experience with the "real-life" application of concepts imparted in those fields. On the other hand, insofar as those concepts are named (*gravity, force, ion,* etc.) it can also be argued that some of what happens in teaching physics or chemistry is teaching of language meanings. The relationship between a linguistic regularity and its meaning is a special type of relationship; the cognitive process whereby it is learned is of a special character.

In particular, it appears that learning the meaning of a regularity in a second language from an extralinguistic context is not the same, cognitively, as learning the meaning from a linguistic context when that context is the corresponding regularity in L1. To learn that French /pom/ means

English "apple" is not the same as learning to understand and use /pom/ in an extralinguistic context involving a real apple (or for that matter, a potato, since the French for potato is *pomme de terre,* "apple of the soil"). This difference is the basis of the distinction often drawn between *co- ordinate* and *compound bilingualism* (Ervin & Osgood, 1954). The co- ordinate bilingual is supposed to have two coordinate systems, both L1 and L2 having direct connections with their own systems of extralinguistic meanings, while the compound bilingual's L2 system of meaning is, at least partly, connected with the L1 system of meaning. While questions have been raised about the validity of a distinction between these forms of bilingualism, there is enough experimental evidence to support the no tion of the distinction at the level of cognitive learning and processing of meaning (Hatch, 1983, pp. 64–69; Hörmann, 1979, pp. 177–178). The dis- tinction is in any case useful in recommending, as does Krashen, that L2 learning be conducted in natural situations where L2 regularities can be directly associated with appropriate extralinguistic context. Obviously, such learning is much easier to make happen in teaching spoken forms; it is difficult to imagine a situation in which written forms could be directly associated with extralinguistic context without an associated speech con- text (one exception comes to mind, however: Söderbergh's [1971] pro- cedure, in teaching her child to read L1, of attaching printed labels to objects).

Extralinguistic and linguistic contexts (as long as they are in L2) may have different types of potentialities in L2 learning. The former are more valuable for learning direct referential meanings of major form classes such as nouns, verbs, and adjectives; they would also convey the meanings of certain morphological variants such as plurals, person endings, and possessives. They would also convey certain types of grammatical mean- ings, e.g., the contexts for sentence modes such as declarative, interro- gative, imperative, and exclamatory and the contexts for topic–comment contrasts and the role of "given" and "new" information (Halliday, 1967) in sentence formation. Linguistic contexts could contribute to the learning of all these types of meanings, but they would probably be more valuable in conveying regularities in the formation of higher order constituents like verb and prepositional phrases, relative clauses, etc., and in the ordering of such constituents.

C. The Internalization of Processed Input

A cognitive interpretation of the internalization of input follows: The noticing of a regularity may be regarded as a cognitive event that occurs on a single occasion, presumably in a short period of time, in working memory. It consists of a momentary representation of the regularity noticed, with any accompanying representations of features of the context, some of which may have been referred to, or matched with, representations in long-term memory. For example, the processing of a single syllable or word that has been noticed in input (e.g., *never*) may involve an observation that the word is in some way similar to a previously learned word (e.g., *ever*), or that its extralinguistic context is similar to one experienced previously.

Noticing of a regularity in working memory may or may not be accompanied by transfer of the working memory representation to longer term memory. Whether it is so transferred depends on several factors: (1) the strength of motivational aspects of the event—for example, the extent to which the regularity serves current needs of the learner; (2) whether the representation is covertly or overtly "rehearsed"; and (3) whether the representation corresponds to a memory trace of a similar representation noticed on a previous occasion. Thus, more frequently noticed regularities are more likely to be transferred to long-term memory.

The process is essentially one of converting something in episodic memory to a representation in semantic memory.

The phraseology used here contains no mention of *habit*. It uses only terms like *noticing* and *representation* to indicate putative cognitive events. We now have no reliable means by which such cognitive events can be publicly observed (through perhaps evoked potential techniques would be useful); we can only infer their existence by phenomenological introspection or by judging from certain kinds or performances—for example, memory recognition and recall performances. Recognition performances can depend solely on internal representations that have not become overt in any way. Recall performances can similarly depend on internal representations, but they are occasions on which internal representations control overt speech performances. We must assume that an overt speech performance comes about because, through working memory action, an internal representation programs a motor action.

Over time, and as the number of occasions on which a given regularity is noticed and referred to long-term memory increases, it appears that the speed and the accuracy of any responses that depend on this regularity also increase. Such increases are referred to by the term *habit formation;* they may also be described in terms of *automatization* (Schneider & Shiffrin, 1977). In fact, Schneider and Shiffrin's description of an *automatic process* seems particularly apt as a description of the formation of linguistic habits:

> An *automatic process* can be defined . . . as the activation of a sequence of nodes with the following properties: (a) The sequence of nodes (nearly) always becomes active in response to a particular input configuration, where the inputs may be externally or internally generated and include the general situational context. (b) The sequence is activated automatically without the necessity of active control or attention by the subject. . . . The same nodes may appear in different automatic sequences, depending on the context. . . . any new automatic process requires an appreciable amount of consistent training. . . . Furthermore, once learned, an automatic process is difficult to suppress, to modify, or to ignore. (p. 2)

An automatic process is to be contrasted with a *controlled process,* which Schneider and Shiffrin describe as "a temporary sequence of nodes activated under control of, and through attention by, the subject." The controlled process is what I believe occurs at the time of the *initial* noticing of a linguistic regularity. The "nodes" correspond to the particular features of the input and its context that are noticed by the learner. However, with repetition, the process gradually assumes the properties of an automatic one.

Schneider and Shiffrin speak of input configurations that may be either externally or internally generated. Externally generated configurations occur in what is often called *passive* control of language, i.e., *receptive* skill. A regularity perceived in language input evokes an internal representation of its meaning or function, and the more often this occurs, the more it is automatized to the point where "it is difficult to suppress, to modify, or to ignore." Internally generated configurations occur in *active* or *productive* use of language: they are what evoke the programming of corresponding motoric speech responses. These evocations, too, can become automatized, depending on such factors as the frequency with which they occur and the degree to which conscious attention is given to their programming. But it does not seem inappropriate to suggest that these responses are subject to what Skinner (1957) would call *shaping,* that is, the gradual modification or selection of responses that more accurately reflect the features of the input.

This account is an attempt to describe learning (acquisition, or internalization) of linguistic input regularities in cognitive terms. There exists a fairly large research literature (e.g., Underwood & Schulz, 1960) on the learning of certain kinds of linguistic regularities—a literature that is founded on a more functionalist, behaviorist type of theory than the one that has been adopted here. The findings about factors in learning reported in that literature deserve serious consideration as valid and useful, but I believe that (a) they are not inconsistent with cognitive theory, and (b) it is possible to give them deeper meaning and a more generalized interpretation if they are approached from the standpoint of cognitive theory as outlined here.

D. Cognitive Influences of Written Language

In L2 instruction, there has been a continual temptation on the part of both teachers and learners to utilize written, printed language as an aid in presenting language, language forms, and language regularities, even when the object of learning is control of the spoken language. Usually, L2 learners already have control of L1 in its written form, and it is natural for them to seek to attain control of L2 at least partly through a system of writing. For example, placed in an environment where most of her playmates had an American Indian language as their L1, my 11-year-old daughter was observed to make homemade phonetic transcriptions of the words and phrases she was learning in that language. Phonetic transcriptions are frequently used in L2 instruction, often to overcome the interference of L1 orthography and to provide an accurate representation of L2 phonological structure, especially where the L2 writing system departs significantly from that of L1 (French and Russian—the latter with a different alphabet—are examples that come to mind). Even if a phonetic transcription plays no part in the instruction, most L2 programs involve L2 in its written form, sometimes at the very outset.

Cognitively, L2 in its written form represents input from which the learner can observe significant regularities. The task for the learner is not unlike that of the learner of L2 in its spoken form; accepting Krashen's distinction between acquisition and conscious learning, we can say that there is an acquisition problem as well as a learning problem in learning to read L2. That is to say, the features of the L2 writing system need to be acquired by subconscious processes—they need to be *interiorized* and automatized quite as much as the features of the spoken language. Conscious learning comes about through instruction and the learner's conscious observation of correspondences between sounds and graphemic symbols, but these correspondences—as linguistic regularities—need to be automatized if fluency in reading is to be attained.

The processes involved in acquiring appropriate internal representations of the regularities in a second language writing system are similar to those described above for the acquisition of internal representations of the regularities in the spoken form of L2. That is to say, the learner has to notice regularities consisting of correspondences between graphemic symbols and sounds. But it would seem obvious that such regularities are best acquired *when the regularities in sound have already been acquired*. We can argue from analogy with the learning of reading in L1: Children nearly always learn to read L1 *after* they have acquired it in spoken form. To be sure, some children have certain difficulties in learning to read, but most L2 learners have already overcome most of these difficulties. There is some evidence that individuals suffering from dyslexia have particular difficulties in learning second languages, but it is not clear whether this is due to the inclusion of reading components in L2 instruction. Perhaps dyslexics would have less trouble in learning L2s in solely spoken form. In any event, the recommendation to delay L2 reading until after some mastery of the spoken language has been acquired would seem to have a sound practical and theoretical justification. The theoretical justification would come from the fact that the appropriate context of a graphemic regularity in L2 pertains to the sound system of L2 as already acquired by the learner; if that sound system has not been acquired, the learner is likely to develop incorrect generalizations based in part on his habits in L1.

E. The Problem of Irregularities

In both their spoken and written forms, all language systems (except possibly purely artificial languages like Esperanto) contain what may be regarded as *irregularities*. One way of describing an irregularity is to say that it is an exception to, or is not covered by, a general rule. English spelling is an example: it has been impossible to formulate rules to predict, from a knowledge of how it is sounded, the way every English word is spelled. Similarly, while it is possible to formulate a rule about how plural nouns in English are formed from the singular noun forms, this rule does not cover all cases. In the process of language acquisition (whether L1 or L2), learners are observed to behave as if they are constructing rules or generalizations about language input. Learners of English as L1 or L2 who say "mans" or "sheeps" appear to have formed a general rule—a provisional *regularity*—about plural formation; it so happens that this rule doesn't work for *man* and *sheep*.

Note, incidentally, that there is an ambiguity in the term *regularity*. In one sense there are only regularities and no irregularities in a particular language system: in standard English the plural forms of *man* and *sheep* are always *men* and *sheep*, and, in the sense we have been using the term, these are among the regularities of English that learners must acquire, even if they are irregular from the standpoint of a general rule about plural formation.

Ultimately, therefore, the learner of a language system acquires what is regular for the specific language form or context, at least when it is an exception to a general rule. A speaker of English can be expected to form the plural of a new word like *gretch* (assuming it is a noun) according to an implicit rule, but that speaker has had to learn a fair number of specific exceptions to such a rule (*men, sheep,* etc.). It does not appear, however, that the learner necessarily attains or maintains awareness of the exceptionality of such forms; they are eventually acquired naturally by L1 learners, and through a combination of conscious and subconscious processes by L2 learners.

F. Memory Processes: Echoic Memory

It seems certain that a process of *echoic memory* is involved in both L1 and L2 acquisition. This is the process of forming, from language input, an internal representation of a particular sound or sequence of sounds. It is on the basis of such an internal representation that the learner may recognize that sound or sound sequence when heard on a further occasion, and it is also on that basis that the learner programs a motoric speech act that he/she intends to make sound similar to what has been heard.

As noted in the discussion of Krashen's aptitude hypothesis, learners vary in their ability to form accurate internal representations of heard language input or to imitate it accurately. Some of the parameters of this process are undoubtedly like those of memory span: The length and complexity of input will control accuracy of immediate recognition and recall. As the number of occasions on which the input is heard increases, inputs can be recognized and reproduced with increasing accuracy and fluency. Likewise, as inputs become more meaningful, they are better handled.

These facts can be used to explain Postovsky's (1974) finding that learners' pronunciation of Russian was better if during early stages of instruction they were encouraged only to listen and not to speak. The early period of listening enabled the learners to perfect their internal representations of sound and thus have a better basis for programming and evaluating their speech productions when at last asked to speak.

G. Memory Processes: Long-Term Memory Storage

A language is a vast system of regularities. It is obvious and well accepted that this system can be acquired only gradually; the system is never acquired in its entirety, even by native speakers. Nevertheless, it appears that the capacity of long-term memory is virtually unlimited, in view of the fact that many individuals acquire a number of languages, each to a point approaching native fluency. On the other hand, considerable time—measured often in years—is required for such multilingual individuals to acquire each of their languages. The acquisition of a mass of language regularities requires time, much time—a fact that needs to be contemplated by anyone who wishes to acquire high competence in a second language. (According to evidence from studies of L2 aptitude, the time required will depend at least in part on individual aptitudes.)

Under suitable learning conditions, the elements of the phonological system, basic grammatical structures, and a functional vocabulary can be acquired in something like 500 hours of instruction (depending on the language, the individuals' learning aptitude, and the degree of mastery sought). After the acquisition of the basic sound and grammatical systems, the principal problem the learner faces is the acquisition of further vocabulary, both a larger recognition vocabulary and a larger vocabulary for active use and retrieval. The sheer quantity of lexical items to be acquired has caused researchers (e.g., Crothers & Suppes, 1967) to investigate ways of scheduling efficient ways of acquiring vocabulary, but my impression from such investigations is that no variables other than simple time of exposure and practice have ever been found to have any significant effects. There have been some experiments (e.g., McDaniel & Pressley, 1984) on the use of "keyword" and other mnemonic techniques to aid in vocabulary learning, but such techniques appear to have only very temporary effects and cannot be employed for the total task—they become unwieldy as applied to hundreds or thousands of vocabulary items. Traditional methods of making lists of new words encountered in texts or spoken discourse and frequently reviewing them until they are mastered seem not to be outdone by any novel method of vocabulary acquisition that has been proposed. Language teachers continually insist that vocabulary items are best learned in the contexts (linguistic and extralinguistic) in which they appear, and there is truth in this to the extent that such contexts furnish meaning in a way that mere translation equivalents may not.

H. Inductive Processes: Inferencing

The linguistic regularities that have to be noticed in order to be acquired are themselves frequently quite complex—complex, that is, beyond the simple association of words with meanings. This is true of many linguistic regularities concerned with the grammatical functions of particular forms, the composition of higher order structures, the ordering of constituents, and so on. Examples of such linguistic regularities governing the ordering of time and place words in English and in German have already been given. If language performance truly involves transformation rules (and there is controversy over this), acquisition of such rules would undoubtedly require a complex process of inference from a variety of examples in linguistic input. Although formal instruction may help the learner notice such regularities, ultimately the learner must acquire them on his own.

Carton's (1971) concept of *inferencing* may be useful in considering the inductive processes required or possible in L2 learning. He describes inferencing as occurring when "attributes and contexts that are familiar are utilized in recognizing what is not familiar.'' He suggests three types of inferencing: intralingual (based on the learner's intuitive knowledge of aspects of L2), interlingual (based on knowledge of other languages, including L1, as when one infers the meaning of a word from a cognate in L1 or some other language), and extralingual (based on the content and context of the message).

Certain refinements and revisions of these categories have been suggested by Bialystok (1983); her categories are *implicit knowledge, other knowledge,* and *context.* Bialystok conducted two experiments in an attempt to show how picture cues, a lesson in inferencing techniques, and provision of glossaries might help students of French gain better reading comprehension of French texts. The results were unimpressive, partly, I think, because the major concern was with lexical learning, and partly because her procedures did not come to grips with what I believe is the major problem: what kinds of information or, more specifically, what kind of language input is required to permit learners optimally and most efficiently to infer higher order grammatical regularities, either on an intuitive (subconscious) basis or on a conscious level. For example, what kind of linguistic and extra linguistic input would be required to allow a learner to infer that a language has a dual as well as a singular and a plural number category? What kind of language input would be required to permit a learner to infer that L2 is an OSV language—i.e., one in which the standard phrase structure has the order object–subject–verb? Cognitive psychologists could, I believe, make useful and interesting contributions to L2 teaching and learning by studying such questions. As of now there is little information of this sort to rely on. Yet L2 curriculum designers are continually pressed to prepare instructional materials that will permit learners to inference higher order grammatical regularities of these types.

V. INSTRUCTIONAL DESIGN

A. Methods versus Approaches

If there is any curriculum field in education which has been concerned above all others with teaching method, it is probably second language instruction. The reader can gain useful perspectives by referring to Kelly's (1969) review of 25 centuries of language teaching and Stern's (1983, Part VI) thoughtful analysis of recent trends. As one may see from these sources, there have been literally dozens of named methods: The *grammar–translation method,* the *direct method,* the *simplification method,* the *oral method,* the *audio-lingual method,* the *cognitive code-learning method,* the *natural method,* and so on. (I must confess to having inadvertently given one of these methods its name—the cognitive code-learning method; see Carroll, 1965; Chastain, 1976.)

Stern points out that second language teaching methodology has been promulgated to language teachers largely through "teachers' guides"—more accurately, textbooks on the subject that have had wide dissemination and acceptance. These teachers' guides are based largely on their authors' personal experiences in language teaching and their adoption of one or another theoretical position; they have in most cases not been based on any substantial amount of research in either psycholinguistics or second language teaching. Some writers (e.g., Mackey, 1965; Bosco & Di Pietro, 1970; Krashen & Seliger, 1975) have attempted to analyze teaching methods systematically, evolving a discipline that Stern calls *methodics*. In the end, however, Stern feels that "the method concept" has broken down. One of the most recent "teachers' guides" (Rivers, 1981) adopts an eclectic approach that affirms that there is some good in all of the methods. As Stern points out, however, even an eclectic approach assumes the conceptual distinctiveness of the different methods, and such an assumption can be called into question.

In the most general terms, a teaching method implies choices as to the objectives of teaching, what materials are to be taught, how they are gradated and sequenced, and how they are presented. Development of a language-teaching curriculum demands literally thousands of choices in these respects. Some major choices, however, are embodied in what may be called approaches, which become quite distinctive if they rigorously carry out the implications of those choices. As I see them, the major choices have to do with

1. the relative importance and the sequencing of skills with the spoken language (listening comprehension and speaking) versus skills with the written language (reading and writing);

2. the relative importance and the sequencing of receptive skills (listening and reading) versus productive skills (speaking and writing);

3. the relative importance of having the student acquire direct, intuitive competence with the language code versus having the student acquire conscious control of the language codes, that is, knowledge *about* the language as opposed to skill *in* the language;

4. the relative usefulness of presentation of material in a strict graded sequence versus presentation of material with relatively little concern for the gradation of input according to difficulty, transfer effects, and other considerations; and

5. the relative extent to which L2 and L1 are used or given emphasis in the instruction.

In what follows, I discuss considerations in making these choices according to cognitive psychology and relevant research. My recommendations may be thought of as leading to an approach rather than to a distinct method.

B. Spoken versus Written Language

The choice of relative emphasis on the spoken language versus the written language depends first of all on anticipated goals and desires of students. Some students (e.g., scholars or scientists wishing to acquire a reading knowledge of a foreign language of use to them) have a legitimate claim to seek only the reading objective. There are other students who have need of attaining only competence in the spoken language (e.g., persons being trained to listen to and monitor broadcasts in a foreign language). Surveys have shown that most American college students electing foreign language courses express a desire to acquire competence in both the spoken and the written language, with a preference for the spoken language; there are, however, notable individual variations in student preferences for spoken or written competence. In any event, it seems desirable to differentiate instruction according to student goals and preferences, when feasible. Research and experience have shown that it is possible to attain either type of competence independently of the other. Some L2 methodologists (e.g., Brooks, 1964) have fervently believed that the level of reading competence attained without competence in speech can never be as high as that attained when reading is learned only after training in the spoken language, but I know of no research that satisfactorily supports this belief (see, for example, the study by Scherer and Wertheimer, 1964, which compared traditional grammar–translation methods with the audio-lingual method, and the study of audio-lingual versus cognitive methods by Smith, 1970).

It can be argued, however, that the methods comparison studies done to date have not adequately tested the hypothesis that reading competence is superior when based on prior training in the spoken language. The studies just cited compared methods that included both speaking and reading instruction, but in different sequences and with different methods and emphases. They may not have adequately measured the degree and type of reading competence attained with methods having different emphases (see Carroll, 1969, for comment on Smith's study). From the analysis of reading competence presented here (Section IV, D), it is still a reasonable hypothesis that performance in reading in L2 is measurably superior in both speed and comprehension, and perhaps qualitatively different, when it is based on competence in the spoken language. Appropriate studies of this hypothesis still remain to be done. Pending such studies, it is reasonable to recommend that if superior reading competence is desired, it be based on attainment of considerable mastery of listening comprehension.

C. Receptive versus Productive Skills

Our cognitive analysis of the process of acquiring phonological, graphemic, and grammatical skills, and also the research findings of Postovsky (1974) and others reviewed by Postovsky (1977) give a strong signal that training in productive skills (speaking, and writing and spelling as well) should be delayed until the learner has had an opportunity to observe L2 input (spoken or written, as the case may be) and to internalize its system and features to the point where he/she can base productive performance on such internalizations.

This recommendation may come as a surprise to those who would follow the traditional principle that teaching procedures should elicit and emphasize from the outset the kinds of performances that are embodied in the ultimate objectives of the teaching. This principle would seem to dictate that if one wants a student to be able to speak a second language, one should require the student to try to speak even in the first lesson; if that speaking performance is not completely satisfactory, it might be claimed, it could be gradually improved through shaping, reinforcement, cognitive guidance, and other procedures. There is some evidence (Lane & Schneider, 1963) that such shaping of pronunciation can occur. Our cognitive analysis indicates, however, that what gets shaped and reinforced is the internal representation of regularities in the speech (or printed text) input. Shaping and reinforcement appear to occur optimally through cognitive processes resulting from continued exposure to input that is comprehended and analyzed internally, rather than through effects of rewards and corrections operating on attempted output. The process is in all likelihood more or less automatic as long as the learner gives careful attention to input. As internal representations of input become more accurate and in conformity to the actual characteristics of the L2 system, they become more satisfactory bases for programming speech or written productions. Learners can better evaluate their own productions because they have more accurate internal representations of L2 regularities.

The recommendation to delay the elicitation of language productions is not really in conflict with the principle of emphasizing training in the performances which are the behavioral objectives of teaching; it is simply a sound implementation of that principle.

D. Intuitive Competence versus Conscious Knowledge

Undoubtedly the most difficult and sensitive issue in language teaching methodology has to do with the extent to which the learner is led or encouraged to attain a metalinguistic awareness of the regularities in a second language and to employ them in receptive and productive use of the L2, as opposed to attaining a direct, intuitive competence in L2 similar to that of the native speaker, who presumably gets along quite well with little metalinguistic awareness of language regularities. This is also a sensitive issue in cognitive psychology because it may be difficult to define, describe, or measure metalinguistic awareness. That is, how are we to know the extent to which a learner attains such awareness, and how are we to know the extent to which it is involved in language use?

It may be helpful, first, to consider contrasts in language learning contexts and teaching methods insofar as they possibly relate to this problem.

Some varieties of what has been called the direct method attempt to establish a learning context that simulates, in many respects, the environment in which a learner acquires a language directly from language input and without a teacher who points out errors and gives explanations. In the direct method the classroom teacher seeks simply to model a native speaker of L2 who attempts to establish communication with students in that language. Use of L1 is minimal or avoided altogether, and few if any explanations about L2 are offered. Meaning is communicated by use of gestures, pictures and drawings, and other features of the immediate environment. Association between linguistic regularities and meanings is therefore said to be direct.

Such a learning context may be contrasted with one in which the teaching method involves much use of information about meanings and grammatical structures in L2. In the main, the students' L1 is used in giving such explanations. Meanings are conveyed largely by use of L1 equivalents (translations or glosses), and systematic explanations of grammar are given by listing conjugations, declensions, and the like. Students may be required to practice L2 grammatical regularities by means of "pattern drills," through which conscious control of grammatical patterns is to be achieved by the application of rules and other kinds of conscious knowledge. What I am describing here is a variety of the audio-lingual method. (It is slightly different from the strict audio-lingual method described by Brooks, 1964, in that Brooks recommended that grammatical pattern drills be conducted with more attention to meaning and content than to grammatical form. Brooks theorized that such pattern drilling is possible, but I have never been able to understand how students could perform such drills without at least some metalinguistic attention to grammatical form, because most pattern drills depend crucially on variation in grammatical forms.)

The fundamental issue at stake here is the extent to which provision of metalinguistic information about language regularities promotes the acquisition of competence. Consideration of how children acquire their first language would suggest that metalinguistic information is not needed in

L2 acquisition. But this does not answer the question of whether provision of metalinguistic information can facilitate L2 acquisition—and it does not exclude the possibility that such information can retard or otherwise interfere with L2 acquisition. Learning systematic metalinguistic information (e.g., conjugations and declensions) takes time and could conceivably interfere with L2 acquisition. Further, such metalinguistic information can divert attention from meaning.

On the other hand, if they are exposed to suitable inputs, learners will probably derive their own metalinguistic information—some of it accurate, some of it inaccurate. Provision of accurate information may prevent learners' induction of inaccurate information. Further, it is likely that learners will depend at least to some extent on metalinguistic information in actual language use. That is, they will on occasion make conscious choices guided by their information about the language.

It is apparently impossible to give any simple recommendation on this issue. No research comparing L2 teaching methods, to my knowledge, has studied in isolation the effect of providing metalinguistic information about language regularities. Nor does basic research on cognitive processes in L2 acquisition yield answers. Theory suggests, however, that the ultimate goal is internalization of language regularities without accompanying metalinguistic awareness or attention to such regularities. It also suggests that the ultimate goal is internalization of meanings associated with regularities. If the regime of language learning is so well organized that these meanings and regularities can be readily internalized without metalinguistic information, possibly by delaying requirements for language production, fine, but if metalinguistic information can be proved to facilitate such internalization, then it should be given. It may be difficult to convey some kinds of language meanings solely from extralinguistic or intralinguistic context; in such cases cognitive guidance may be needed—through the giving of translation equivalents, explanations of meaning contrasts, rules concerning grammatical structures and processes, and the like. It would seem preferable to present systematic phenomena like conjugations and declensions in meaningful contexts rather than in isolation, as has frequently been done in grammar–translation methods.

A useful kind of metalinguistic information to give would be direction about the situational contexts in which various sentence structures would be used. For example, the situations in which different forms of questions, polite requests, and direct commands are used can be arrayed, contrasted, and exemplified. Such arraying and contrasting of contexts would tend to give implicit metalinguistic information; it would focus attention on meaning, while differences in forms would be conveyed incidentally. In this way, instructional procedures would be designed to encourage the learner's noticing of regularities and contrasts while not emphasizing them explicitly. Language input must be designed to provide a delicate balance between ready comprehensibility and the challenge of learning regularities not previously understood.

E. Gradation versus Nongradation

A traditional principle in instruction, set forth long ago by Descartes and Comenius, is to divide content into small pieces, start with simple items, and gradually add items until the most complex materials can be presented and mastered. This principle is difficult to apply in language learning for at least two reasons: first, even the simplest piece of language input is complex, containing a number of features simultaneously, and second, the simpler aspects of language structure are not necessarily the most useful in meaningful language interactions. In fact, many of the structures that most frequently occur in day-to-day communication are among the more complex. Consider the fact that in English, for example, the most commonly occurring verbs tend to be the most irregular in their conjugations.

The gradation of linguistic content, therefore, requires the making of many compromises. Some writers (e.g., Noblitt, 1972) advocate the writing of "pedagogical grammars" to specify linguistic regularities in appropriate graded orders, but there is as yet no systematic agreement on principles of grading and ordering. Writers of instructional materials base their gradations of content on intuition and experience. Functionality and occurrence frequency of vocabulary and syntactic structures appear to be more important criteria for grading than sheer simplicity.

Some of the recommendations made above have implications for how material is graded. If learners are to acquire direct intuitive competence in the sense of interiorization of linguistic regularities with their meanings, materials presented in early stages of instruction must be those for which extralinguistic meaning contexts can be most easily provided. Such materials would include terms for concrete objects, observable movements, easily perceived temporal and spatial relations, and the like. Asher (1969) has conducted research confirming the effectiveness of his "total physical response" method, in which students listen to commands in L2 and learn to obey those commands (e.g., "stand up," "sit down," "put the ball under the table") by watching the instructor perform the actions. Such instruction illustrates the use of what Krashen (1980) calls simple codes. It can also illustrate the gradual introduction of new elements in frames that are already well understood and the use of contrasting contexts to convey new meanings ("put the ball on/under/in back of/in front of/to the right of the table"). At later stages, it would be possible to introduce more complex materials whose meaning could be inferred more from linguistic contexts than from extralinguistic contexts. Possible positive and negative transfers of items to items later in the instruction may also need to be taken into account.

Gradation also implies the sequencing of multiple opportunities for the learner to perceive linguistic regularities and to grasp their ranges of meaning and application. L2 reading materials are usually designed with deliberate control of repetitions of new items and with attention to the varying applications of meanings (for example, the word *toy* is used for various kinds of toys, physically all quite different, to convey the class meaning of the word). L2 learning can be organized to resemble a series of concept formation experiments.

The discussion thus far seems to imply that materials must always be well ordered and controlled for frequency and utility. Some grading and ordering is certainly desirable, but it can lead to monotonous, uninteresting instruction if carried too far. The problem is analogous to that in beginning reading instruction in English. Some reading programs begin only with words with a small number of "regular" spellings, but research and experience suggest that they are not as successful, ultimately, as programs that introduce a wider variety of words, such as "sight words" with irregular spellings.

One can recommend that in L2 instruction, teaching materials be of two types, one more or less carefully graded, and the other much less carefully graded and more representative of functional communication in the language. Learners can be expected to get at least some benefit from the latter type of input as they apply what linguistic knowledge they have to extract meaning from it. The informal speech of a teacher in the L2 classroom could be classified with this less carefully graded input, as could also selected reading materials from the daily press, magazines, and the like. Progress in learning from the carefully graded material would support increased learner success in dealing with less graded material.

F. Relative Use of L2 versus L1

A number of studies (e.g., Carroll, 1967, 1975) confirm that if spoken competence is the objective, the amount of classroom use of L2 by teachers and students is one of the most important instructional variables affecting student achievement. That is, to a degree, the more teachers use the spoken language in the classroom, and encourage students to use it, the greater the attainment of students in listening and speaking L2. This does not necessarily suggest that use of L1 should be completely excluded from the classroom; research studies have not compared teaching with limited use of L1 with teaching that avoids L1 use altogether.

In point of fact, it would be unusual to find a classroom in which use of L1 is completely excluded. The variation that occurs is between very little informal, spontaneous use of L2 and use of L2 for a major part of class time. What research studies suggest is that there is much benefit in exposing students to frequent and prolonged use of L2. In this way students are exposed to massive amounts of L2 input from which they can derive information about the language and can practice understanding and speaking it. The more meaningful this input is, the more students can benefit from it.

The residual issue is how L1 is employed. If it is used to give cognitive guidance about pronunciation, grammatical structure, and meanings in L2, it is beneficial to the extent that it does not interfere with, or substitute for, similar information that could be derived from exposure to L2. Some teachers are able to impart useful information of this sort (cognitive guidance about L2) directly in L2, resorting to L1 only when they perceive lack of comprehension on the part of students. In general, my recommendation is that L1 be used when necessary, but used to the least possible extent, not only because L1 use detracts from possible L2 use, but also because meanings (translations and the like) acquired solely through L1 are less likely to be properly incorporated into L2 competence.

VI. NEXT STEPS

Underlying much of the discussion in this chapter, either explicitly or implicitly, there has been a persistent problem: What does it mean to know a second language? What does this knowledge consist of? To what extent does it consist of information that the language user can bring to conscious awareness? Obviously some information is of this character: Language users are usually aware of lexical units and their meanings and are able to discuss and even explain them. But much information implicit in knowing a language is out of awareness and difficult to bring to awareness—certain information about language sounds, about grammatical functions and regularities, about "rules" of language use in interpersonal communication. How can that kind of information be acquired in the case of learning a second language? It would appear that traditional language-teaching methods that attempt to impart this kind of information solely on a conscious level are fundamentally erroneous. Similarly, it would be argued that language-testing methods that attempt to detect the presence of this information solely on a conscious level are misguided.

Krashen's hypothesis of a distinction between acquisition and learning represents the attempt of a second language teacher to understand second language learning. There is good reason to accept this hypothesis in view of many facts about both first language acquisition and second language acquisition in natural contexts. The proposal of Krashen and Terrell (1982) for a "natural approach" in language teaching has high appeal because it attempts to embody and utilize what psycholinguistic and cognitive research suggests about the language acquisition process. Educational research studies are needed to evaluate the practical effectiveness of such an approach with different kinds of students and under different social and motivational conditions.

At the same time, experimental cognitive studies are needed, in conjunction with such a teaching strategy, to determine whether there is a true cognitive difference between acquisition and learning. That is, we need to investigate in what way the cognitive processes involved in acquisition and in learning differ, if at all. We need to find out whether changes in behavior observed in an acquisition context are merely more automatized versions of behavior changes observed when learners gain conscious control of linguistic regularities, either through their own inductive processes or through having these regularities pointed out by others, as in formal instruction. As a final cheerful thought, I may add that the methodology that would have to be developed to answer these questions might lead to improved ways of testing second language competence in the deeper sense implied by current theories of language.

REFERENCES

Anderson, J. I. (1978). Order of difficulty in adult second language acquisition. In W. C. Ritchie (Ed.), *Second language acquisition research: Issues and implications* (pp. 91–108). New York: Academic Press.
Asher, J. J. (1969). The total physical response approach to second language learning. *Modern Language Journal, 53,* 3–7.
Bailey, K. M. (1980). An introspective analysis of an individual's language learning experience. In R. C. Scarcella & S. D. Krashen (Eds.), *Research in second language acquisition* (pp. 58–65). Rowley, MA: Newbury House.
Beebe, L. M. (1983). Risk-taking and the language learner. In H. W. Seliger & M. H. Long (Eds.), *Classroom oriented research in second language acquisition* (pp. 39–65). Rowley, MA: Newbury House.
Bialystok, E. (1983). Inferencing: Testing the "hypothesis-testing" hypothesis. In H. W. Seliger & M. H. Long (Eds.), *Classroom oriented research in second language acquisition* (pp. 104–123). Rowley, MA: Newbury House.
Bloomfield, L. (1914). *An introduction to the study of language.* New York: Holt. (Reprint, with introduction by J. F. Kess. Amsterdam: Benjamins, 1983.)
Bloomfield, L. (1933). *Language.* New York: Holt.
Bloomfield, L. (1942). *Outline guide for the practical study of foreign languages.* Baltimore: Linguistic Society of America & Waverly.

Bosco, F. J., & Di Pietro, R. J. (1970). Instructional strategies: Their psychological and linguistic bases. *International Review of Applied Linguistics, 8*, 1–19.

Brooks, N. (1964). *Language and language learning: Theory and practice.* New York: Harcourt Brace Jovanovich.

Brown, H. D. (1980). *Principles of language learning and teaching.* Englewood Cliffs, NJ: Prentice-Hall.

Brown, R. (1973). *A first language: The early stages.* Cambridge, MA: Harvard University Press.

Burmeister, H., & Ufert, D. (1980). Strategy switching? In S. W. Felix (Ed.), *Second language development: Trends and issues* (pp. 109–122). Tübingen: Gunter Narr.

Carroll, J. B. (1962). The prediction of success in intensive foreign language training. In R. Glaser (Ed.), *Training research and education* (pp. 87–136). Pittsburgh: University of Pittsburgh Press.

Carroll, J. B. (1965). The contributions of psychological theory and educational research to the teaching of foreign languages. *Modern Language Journal, 49*, 273–281.

Carroll, J. B. (1967). Foreign language proficiency levels attained by language majors near graduation from college. *Foreign Language Annals, 1*, 131–151.

Carroll, J. B. (1969). What does the Pennsylvania foreign language study tell us? *Foreign Language Annals, 3*, 214–236.

Carroll, J. B. (1971). Current issues in psycholinguistics and second language teaching. *TESOL Quarterly, 5*, 101–114.

Carroll, J. B. (1973). Some suggestions from a psycholinguist. *TESOL Quarterly, 7*, 355–367.

Carroll, J. B. (1974). Towards a performance grammar for core sentences in spoken and written English. *International Review of Applied Linguistics, 12*, Special Festschrift Issue for B. Malmberg, 29–49.

Carroll, J. B. (1975). *The teaching of French as a foreign language in eight countries.* Stockholm: Almqvist & Wiksell; New York: Wiley.

Carroll, J. B. (1980). A performance grammar approach to language teaching. In R. L. Schiefelbusch (Ed.), *Nonspeech language and communication: Analysis and intervention* (pp. 469–501). Baltimore: University Park.

Carroll, J. B. (1981). Twenty-five years of research on foreign language aptitude. In K. C. Diller (Ed.), *Individual differences and universals in language learning aptitude* (pp. 83–118). Rowley, MA: Newbury House.

Carroll, J. B., & White, M. N. (1973). Word frequency and age of acquisition as determiners of picture-naming latency. *Quarterly Journal of Experimental Psychology, 25*, 85–95.

Carton, A. S. (1971). Inferencing: A process in using and learning language. In P. Pimsleur & T. Quinn (Eds.), *The psychology of second language learning* (pp. 45–58). Cambridge, England: Cambridge University Press.

Chafe, W. L. (1970). *Meaning and the structure of language.* Chicago: University of Chicago Press.

Chastain, K. (1976). *The development of modern-language skills: Theory to practice* (2nd ed.). Chicago: Rand McNally.

Chomsky, N. (1957). *Syntactic structures.* The Hague: Mouton.

Chomsky, N. (1959). Review of B. F. Skinner's *Verbal behavior. Language, 35*, 26–58.

Chomsky, N. (1965). *Aspects of the theory of syntax.* Cambridge, MA: M.I.T. Press.

Chomsky, N., & Halle, M. (1968). *The sound pattern of English.* New York: Harper.

Clark, H. H., & Clark, E. V. (1977). *Psychology and language: An introduction to psycholinguistics.* New York: Harcourt Brace Jovanovich.

Corder, S. P. (1981). *Error analysis and interlanguage.* Oxford: Oxford University Press.

Crothers, E., & Suppes, P. (1967). *Experiments in second-language learning.* New York: Academic Press.

Dulay, H. C., & Burt, M. K. (1974). Natural sequences in child second language acquisition. *Language Learning, 24,* 37–53.

Dulay, H. C., & Burt, M. K. (1977). Remarks on creativity in language acquisition. In M. Burt, H. Dulay, & M. Finocchiaro (Eds.), *Viewpoints on English as a second language* (pp. 95–126). New York: Regents.

Ervin, S. M., & Osgood, C. E. (1954). Second language learning and bilingualism. In C. E. Osgood & T. A. Sebeok (Eds.), Psycholinguistics. *Journal of Abnormal and Social Psychology, 49* (Suppl.), 139–146.

Gleitman, L. R., Gleitman, H., & Shipley, E. (1972). The emergence of the child as grammarian. *Cognition, 1,* 137–164.

Halliday, M. A. K. (1967). Notes on transitivity and theme in English: II. *Journal of Linguistics, 3,* 199–244.

Hatch, E. M. (1978). Acquisition of syntax in a second language. In J. C. Richards (Ed.), *Understanding second and foreign language learning: Issues and approaches* (pp. 34–70). Rowley, MA: Newbury House.

Hatch, E. M. (1983). *Psycholinguistics: A second language perspective.* Rowley, MA: Newbury House.

Hörmann, H. (1979). *Psycholinguistics: An introduction to research and theory* (2nd rev. ed.). New York: Springer.

James, C. (1969). Deeper contrastive study. *International Review of Applied Linguistics, 7,* 83–95.

Johnson, N. F. (1965). The psychological reality of phrase structure rules. *Journal of Verbal Learning and Verbal Behavior, 4,* 469–475.

Kelly, L. G. (1969). *25 centuries of language teaching.* Rowley, MA: Newbury House.

Krashen, S. D. (1980). The theoretical and practical relevance of simple codes in second language acquisition. In R. C. Scarcella & S. D. Krashen (Eds.), *Research in second language acquisition* (pp. 7–18). Rowley, MA: Newbury House.

Krashen, S. D. (1981a). Aptitude and attitude in relation to second language acquisition and learning. In K. C. Diller (Ed.), *Individual differences and universals in language learning aptitude* (pp. 155–175). Rowley, MA: Newbury House.

Krashen, S. D. (1981b). *Second language acquisition and second language learning.* Oxford: Pergamon.

Krashen, S. D. (1982a). *Principles and practice in second language acquisition.* Oxford: Pergamon.

Krashen, S. D. (1982b). Theory versus practice in language training. In R. W. Blair (Ed.), *Innovative approaches to language teaching* (pp. 15–30). Rowley, MA: Newbury House.

Krashen, S. D., & Seliger, H. W. (1975). The essential contribution of formal instruction in adult second language learning. *TESOL Quarterly, 9,* 173–183.

Krashen, S. D., & Terrell, T. (1982). *The natural approach: Language acquisition in the classroom.* Oxford: Pergamon.

Lado, R. (1957). *Linguistics across cultures: Applied linguistics for language teachers.* Ann Arbor: University of Michigan Press.

Lamendella, J. T. (1969). On the irrelevance of transformational grammar to second language pedagogy. *Language Learning, 19,* 255–270.

Lane, H., & Schneider, B. (1963). Methods for self-shaping echoic behavior. *Modern Language Journal, 47,* 154–160.

Lyons, J. (1968). *Introduction to theoretical linguistics.* Cambridge, England: Cambridge University Press.

Mackey, W. F. (1965). *Language teaching analysis.* Bloomington: Indiana University Press.

McCawley, J. D. (1968). The role of semantics in grammar. In E. Bach & R. T. Harms (Eds.), *Universals in linguistic theory* (pp. 125–169). New York: Holt.

McDaniel, M. A., & Pressley, M. (1984). Putting the keyword method in context. *Journal of Educational Psychology, 76,* 598–609.

McDonough, S. H. (1981). *Psychology in foreign language teaching.* London: Allen & Unwin.

Mori, K., & Moeser, S. D. (1983). The role of syntax and semantic referents in learning an artificial language. *Journal of Verbal Learning and Verbal Behavior, 22,* 701–718.

Noblitt, J. S. (1972). Pedagogical grammar: Towards a theory of foreign language materials preparation. *International Review of Applied Linguistics, 10,* 313–331.

Oller, J. W. (1976). A program for language testing research. *Language Learning,* Special Issue No. 4, 141–165.

Posner, M. I. (1978). *Chronometric explorations of mind.* Hillsdale, NJ: Erlbaum.

Postovsky, V. A. (1974). Effects of delay in oral practice at the beginning of second language learning. *Modern Language Journal, 58,* 229–239.

Postovsky, V. A. (1977). Why not start speaking later? In M. Burt, H. Dulay, & M. Finocchiaro (Eds.), *Viewpoints on English as a second language* (pp. 17–26). New York: Regents.

Rivers, W. M. (1981). *Teaching foreign-language skills* (2nd ed.). Chicago: University of Chicago Press.

Scherer, G. A. C., & Wertheimer, M. (1964). *A psycholinguistic experiment in foreign-language teaching.* New York: McGraw-Hill.

Schneider, W., & Shiffrin, R. M. (1977). Controlled and automatic human information processing: I. Detection, search, and attention. *Psychological Review, 84,* 1–66.

Selinker, L. (1972). Interlanguage. *International Review of Applied Linguistics, 10,* 209–231.

Skinner, B. F. (1957). *Verbal behavior.* New York: Appleton.

Slobin, D. I., & Bever, T. G. (1982). Children use canonical sentence schemas: A cross-linguistic study of word order and inflections. *Cognition, 12,* 229–265.

Smith, P. D. Jr. (1970). *A comparison of the cognitive and audiolingual approaches to foreign language instruction: The Pennsylvania Foreign Language Project.* Philadelphia: Center for Curriculum Development.

Söderbergh, R. (1971). *Reading in early childhood: A linguistic study of a Swedish preschool child's gradual acquisition of reading ability.* Stockholm: Almqvist & Wiksell.

Stack, E. M. (1960). *The language laboratory and modern language teaching.* New York: Oxford University Press.

Stern, H. H. (1983). *Fundamental concepts of language learning.* Oxford: Oxford University Press.

Sternberg, S. (1969). The discovery of processing stages: Extensions of Donders' method. *Acta Psychologica, 30,* 276–315.

Stevenson, D. K. (1983). Foreign language testing: All of the above. In C. J. James (Ed.), *Practical applications of research in foreign language teaching* (pp. 153–203). Lincolnwood, IL: National Textbook.

Stevick, E. W. (1976). *Memory, meaning and method: Some psychological perspectives on language learning.* Rowley, MA: Newbury House.

Stevick, E. W. (1980). *Teaching languages: A way and ways.* Rowley, MA: Newbury House.

Tulving, E. (1972). Episodic and semantic memory. In E. Tulving & W. Donaldson (Eds.), *Organization of memory* (pp. 381–403). New York: Academic Press.

Underwood, B. J., & Schulz, R. W. (1960). *Meaningfulness and verbal learning.* Philadelphia: Lippincott.

5

Mathematics

RICHARD E. MAYER
Department of Psychology
University of California
Santa Barbara, California 93106

I. INTRODUCTION

The purpose of this chapter is to explore the relationship between the mathematics curriculum and the psychology of human learning and cognition. For purposes of the present chapter, we define the mathematics curriculum as the body of knowledge that is taught in mathematics lessons in grades K through 12, and we restrict our survey of the psychology of learning and cognition to the body of research that specifically focuses on the cognitive mechanisms underlying mathematical competence. We first attempt to provide an overview of the mathematics curriculum and the psychology of mathematics learning and then provide examples of how psychology can be related to the mathematics curriculum in areas such as counting, arithmetic computation, arithmetic application, algebraic computation, and algebraic application. This chapter is based on the premise that psychology has implications for organizing and teaching the mathematics curriculum, and that correspondingly the mathematics curriculum has implications for testing psychological theories that stand up to the demands of the real world.

II. THE MATHEMATICS CURRICULUM

Let us begin with a straightforward question: "What is the mathematics curriculum?" Although this may seem like a simple question, there is not a simple answer for it. Most federal and state agencies and associations refrain from answering the question because curriculum is viewed as a

COGNITION AND INSTRUCTION

domain that should be left to local school districts.[1] However, with thousands of school districts across the nation (e.g., California alone has over 1000 public school districts), there are many different answers to the curriculum question. In our search for a consensus concerning the curriculum question, this section explores four major sources of information: state and county departments of education, local school districts, standardized tests, and textbooks.

A. State and County Departments of Education

State and county departments of education may issue model curricula or proposed guidelines for curricula. Usually such pronouncements are developed by special panels or commissions. For example, Table 1 pre-

---

[1]Some states provide control over curriculum by mandating the use of certain textbooks.

TABLE 1

Some Suggested Program Objectives Involving Arithmetic Operations for Grades K through 6

Operations

Operations: Readiness
Using concrete objects, explore the process of joining and separating sets.
Using sets of concrete objects, explore addition and subtraction.

Operations: Kindergarten–Grade Three
Explore the skill of adding and subtracting whole numbers.
Develop the appropriate use of the operational symbols ($+$, $-$, $\times$, $\div$) between numbers.
Develop addition and subtraction facts.
Acquire addition and subtraction facts.
Acquire the skill of adding or subtracting with and without renaming.
Acquire the skill of adding and subtracting amounts of money.
Acquire the skill of using the terms *addend, sum, factor,* and *product.*
Maintain addition and subtraction skills for whole numbers through review and practice.
Explore the concept of multiplication.
Develop basic multiplication facts.
Acquire the basic multiplication facts.
Acquire an understanding of, and use of, the multiplication algorithm.
Develop the skill of adding and subtracting of decimal fractions (with and without renaming).
Acquire the skill of using number sentences.
Explore the meaning of division.
Develop basic division facts.
Acquire basic division facts.
Maintain multiplication and division skills for whole numbers through review and practice.

TABLE 1

Some Suggested Program Objectives Involving Arithmetic Operations for Grades K through 6 (*continued*)

Operations: Grades Four–Six

Maintain the addition and subtraction facts.

Acquire an understanding of, and skill in using, the operational symbols ($+$, $-$, $\times$, $\div$).

Develop mastery and accuracy in using addition and subtraction algorithms.

Maintain addition and subtraction skill for whole numbers through review and practice.

Maintain the basic multiplication and division facts.

Develop the division algorithm.

Acquire skill in using the division algorithm.

Develop skill in estimating sum, difference, product, and quotient of whole numbers.

Explore the use of positive and negative integers in everyday situations.

Develop the skill of adding and subtracting positive and negative integers.

Maintain skill in working with number sentences.

Maintain multiplication and division skill for whole numbers through review and practice.

Acquire computational skill for addition and subtraction of decimal fractions.

Acquire computational skill for multiplication and division of decimal fractions.

Develop the skill of converting a rational number into its equivalent fraction, decimal fraction, or percent forms.

Explore computational skill for the addition and subtraction of common fractions.

Explore computational skill for multiplying and dividing common fractions.

Explore percents through related work with fractions.

Develop the use of whole numbers as exponents.

Explore the skill of multiplying and dividing positive and negative integers.

Operations: Grades Seven–Eight

Develop the skill of using the standard order of operations in computations.

Explore shortcuts in the basic algorithm operations.

Develop the skill of multiplying and dividing positive and negative integers.

Acquire the skill of adding and subtracting rational numbers in fraction and mixed number forms.

Acquire multiplication and division skill for fractions.

Maintain computational skill for addition and subtraction of whole numbers and decimal fractions.

Maintain computational skill for the multiplication and division of whole numbers and decimal fractions.

Develop skill in estimating the sum, difference, product, and quotient of rational numbers.

Develop skill in rounding off.

Acquire the skill of using integers as exponents.

Acquire the skill of using numbers written in percent form.

Develop the skill of simplifying complex fractions.

Acquire the skill of solving simple equations by using the operations of addition, subtraction, multiplication, or division.

Acquire the skill of squaring a rational number.

Develop the skill of estimating square root.

Note. From *Mathematics Framework,* Sacramento: California State Department of Education, 1982.

sents a summarized portion of *Mathematics Framework* issued by the California State Department of Education (1982b). The typical level of curriculum description is very general, presumably because the state does not want to appear to usurp the local school districts' responsibility for establishing a specific curriculum.

B. Local School Districts

Most local school districts have documents which describe their curriculum in detail. Some districts list each of the "behavioral objectives" for each level of learning; others provide a "scope and sequence" which defines the major skills and the order in which they should be taught. Table 2 provides a summarized portion of the *Mathematics Continuum*

TABLE 2

Portion of Mathematics Continuum for a Local School District

3. WHOLE NUMBERS - ADDITION

	K	1	2	3	4	5	6
Concept of addition	░	▨	░	░	░	░	░
Notation of addition	░	▨	░	░	░	░	░
Facts through 10	░			░	░	░	░
Facts through 18	░	▨			░	░	░
Two digits - without renaming	░	░			░	░	░
Two digits with renaming	░	░			░	░	░
Three digits - without renaming	░	░			░	░	░
Three digits - renaming	░	░	░		░	░	░
Three addends	░	▨			░	░	░
Advanced addition	░	░	░	░			

4. WHOLE NUMBERS - SUBTRACTION

	K	1	2	3	4	5	6
Concept and notation	░	▨	░	░	░	░	░
Facts through 10	░			░	░	░	░
Facts through 18	░	▨			░	░	░
Two digits - without regrouping	░	░			░	░	░
Three digits - without regrouping	░	░			░	░	░
Two digits - with regrouping	░	░		░	░	░	░
Three or more digits - with regrouping	░	░	░				
Regrouping with zeros	░	░	░	░			

▨ Skills to be introduced and/or maintained - no test.

░ No emphasis at this level.

Note. From *Mathematics Continuum,* Goleta, CA: Goleta Union School District, 1978.

in effect at my local elementary school district (Goleta Union School District, 1978). The continuum was determined by a group consisting of the administrative and teaching staff of the district. While the continuum is fairly detailed, it is not necessarily used or even referred to by the teachers of the district; furthermore, it must be noted that each district may have a different continuum.

C. Standardized Tests

Another way of determining the mathematics curriculum is to examine the questions that appear on standardized tests. The questions are selected to be representative of the mathematics curriculum across a wide spectrum of school districts; in addition, standardized tests may be responsible for shaping the curriculum since teachers may attempt to "teach to the test." Table 3 lists the major categories for the fourth-grade mathematics sections of the Comprehensive Test of Basic Skills (1982), a standardized test of achievement used in many districts across the nation. Since standardized tests represent a "national test," they can be used to gauge what a national mathematics curriculum might look like.

D. Textbooks

Finally, the strongest determinant of the classroom curriculum in mathematics is the mathematics textbook (and related instructional materials).

TABLE 3

Types of Items on a Standardized Mathematics Achievement Test for Grade 4

Types of items	Number of items
Mathematics computation	
Add whole numbers	6
Add decimals or fractions	4
Subtract whole numbers	6
Subtract decimals or fractions	4
Multiply whole numbers or fractions	8
Divide whole numbers	9
Mathematics concepts and applications	
Numeration	10
Number sentences	7
Number theory	6
Problem solving	9
Measurement	9
Geometry	4

Note. From *Comprehensive Tests of Basic Skills, Preliminary Technical Report,* Monterey, CA: McGraw-Hill, 1982.

Many states restrict textbooks that may be used to those on statewide approved lists. This is a powerful way for states to exercise some influence over curriculum. Table 4 lists a portion of the table of contents of several fourth-grade math textbooks that are approved for use in California public schools. The state of California has approved approximately 12 series of books (California State Department of Education, 1981). In a typical school or district, a "textbook committee" selects books that best fit their needs. Thus, one way of gauging the mathematics curriculum is to examine the contents of a fairly small sample of textbooks, as well as the tests that accompany them.

In summary, determinants of what is taught in the mathematics classroom are, in order of decreasing importance: textbooks, standardized tests, local school district policy, and state/county department of education guidelines. Thus, in the United States, curriculum is determined to a large extent by several large commercial book publishing and testing companies, each trying to meet the needs and requirements of individual districts and states. Our answer to the curriculum question is "If you want to know what is taught in mathematics classrooms, take a careful look at standardized tests and popular textbooks."

III. THE PSYCHOLOGY OF HUMAN LEARNING AND COGNITION

The relationship between psychology and education has not always been a productive one. Thorndike (1922), working in the beginning of this century, attempted to use the scientific and theoretical tools of psychology to study school-related issues such as how children learn arithmetic. Unfortunately, Thorndike's tradition of merging education and psychology was not well accepted. During the middle of this century, psychologists tended to study theoretical issues using paradigms that seemed unrelated to school learning; correspondingly, many educational researchers focused on nontheoretical issues having to do with very specific classroom routines. However, as Ginsburg (1983) points out, during the past 20 years there has been a distinct change: Psychologists have finally begun to aim the powerful tools of psychology at complex problems including school learning, and educators have begun to bring new challenges to psychology. For the first time since Thorndike, there has been a consensual effort to develop a psychology of mathematics. For example, Resnick and Ford (1981) describe the role of subject matter researchers as follows:

> As psychologists concerned specifically with mathematics our goal is to ask the same questions that experimental and developmental psychologists ask about learning,

TABLE 4

Chapter Titles from Four Fourth-Grade Mathematics Textbooks

HBJ Mathematics	Holt Mathematics	Macmillan Mathematics	Scott Foresman Mathematics
Warm Up	Addition and Subtraction Facts	Reviewing Addition and Subtraction Facts	Numeration
Addition and Subtraction	Numeration	Place Value	Addition
Multiplication (One-Digit Multipliers)	Addition	Addition and Subtraction	Subtraction
Measurement	Subtraction	Multiplication and Division	Addition and Subtraction
Division (One-Digit Divisors)	Multiplication and Division Facts	Money, Time, Measurement	Decimals
Problem Solving	Measurement	Multiplying by Ones	Graphing
Geometry	Multiplication	Dividing by Ones	Multiplication Basic Facts
Fractions and Decimals	Division	Fractions	Multiplication: One-Digit Multipliers
Numbers	Fractions	Multiplying by Tens and Ones	Multiplication: One-Digit Multipliers
Multiplication (Two-Digit Multipliers)	Adding and Subtracting Fractions		Measurement
Division (Two-Digit Divisors)	Geometry		Division Basic Facts
Measurement and Graphing	Graphs and Probability		Division: One-Digit Divisors
			Ratio
			Geometry
			Meaning of Fractions
			Addition and Subtraction of Fractions
			Division: Two-Digit Divisors
			Perimeter, Area, and Volume

Note. From *HBJ Mathematics*, New York: Harcourt Brace Jovanovich, 1981; *Holt Mathematics*, New York: Holt, Rinehart and Winston, 1981; *Macmillan Mathematics*. New York: Macmillan Publishing Co., 1982; *Scott Foresman Mathematics*. Glenview, IL: Scott, Foresman and Company, 1980.

thinking, and intelligence, but to focus these questions with respect to a particular subject matter. What this means is that instead of asking ourselves the general question, "How is it that people think?" we ask ourselves, "How is it that people think about mathematics?" Instead of asking "How do people's thought processes develop?" we ask, "How does understanding of mathematical concepts develop?"

After a long period of mutual neglect, there is encouraging evidence that the content of the mathematics subject matter and findings in the nature of human cognition will be joined together by an emerging psychology of mathematics.

The traditional approach to analyzing the mathematics curriculum has been task analysis. For example, Gagne and his colleagues (Gagne, 1968; Gagne & Briggs, 1974) have used a *learning hierarchy* to describe various mathematical tasks. A learning hierarchy is generated by asking the following question: "What would you have to know how to do in order to perform this task, after being given only instructions?" For each subskill, the same question is applied. For example, Table 5 shows a partial hierarchy for several tasks selected from the K–12 math curriculum. The task analysis approach provides a hierarchy of tasks, suggesting which skills should be learned before which other skills. For example, children use counting as a way of computing simple additions and subtractions; in turn, knowledge of basic addition and subtraction facts is required for successful multidigit computation, and so on.

TABLE 5

Partial Learning Hierarchy for Six Tasks

Tasks	Examples
SOLVE ALGEBRA STORY PROBLEMS	John travels 100 miles in 2 days. At this rate, how far will he travel in 4 days?
SOLVE ALGEBRA EQUATIONS	$\frac{100}{2} = \frac{x}{4}$
SOLVE WORD PROBLEMS	John has 22¢. Sue gives him 33¢. How much does John have now?
COMPUTE MULTIDIGIT ARITHMETIC	22 + 33 + ___
RECITE ARITHMETIC FACTS	2 + 3 = ___
COUNT TO 10	How many dots? ⋯⋯

The cognitive approach to analyzing the mathematics curriculum provides an extension of the task-analysis approach. Rather than analyzing the task, the cognitive approach analyzes the cognitive processes and knowledge of the student—i.e., what must go on in the student's mind. Two key components in mathematical problem solving are: representation of the problem and implementation of a solution plan.

Which aspects of cognitive psychology are most relevant to the psychology of mathematics? The major contributions of cognitive psychology involve techniques for representing people's knowledge and people's cognitive processing (Mayer, 1981b). In particular, the following four tools of cognitive psychology are particularly relevant to the psychology of mathematics:

Comprehension models—Descriptions of how people translate words of a problem into an internal representation. For example, how is the sentence, "Tom has five more marbles than Pete," represented in memory?

Schema models—Descriptions of how people select and integrate information into a coherent representation. For example, given a collection of word problems, how can a person classify them into problem types?

Process models—Descriptions of the steps that a person goes through while carrying out some well-defined cognitive operation, such as the procedure for long division.

Strategy models—Descriptions of how people set, achieve, and monitor goals while carrying out some complex cognitive activity, such as generating a proof for a geometry problem.

Table 6 show how these techniques may be applied to each of six representative tasks from the mathematics curriculum. For each task listed on the left, the corresponding entry on the right shows a type of cognitive analysis that may be relevant. In the remainder of this chapter we explore

TABLE 6

Cognitive Analysis of Six Tasks

Tasks	Typical cognitive analyses
Solve algebra story problems	Representation, e.g., schema models
Solve algebra equations	Solution, e.g., strategy models
Solve word problems	Representation, e.g., comprehension and schema models
Compute multidigit arithmetic	Solution, e.g., process models
Recite arithmetic facts	Solution, e.g., process and strategy models
Count to 10	Solution, e.g., process models

how the tools of cognitive psychology can be related to the mathematics curriculum. In particular, we focus on five areas: counting, arithmetic computation (number facts and multidigit computation), arithmetic application, algebraic computation, and algebraic application.

IV. COUNTING

Counting problems involve telling how many items are in a given display. For example, a teacher puts three dolls on a table and asks, "How many dolls?" The child's job is to answer, "Three."

Klahr and Wallace (1976) investigated children's and adults' ability to tell how many dots are in a display, with the number varying from 1 to 10. Klahr and Wallace noticed that when only a few items were presented (such as 1, 2, or 3) responses were very fast and did not involve overt counting; they referred to this process of recognizing displays of 1–3 items as *subitizing*. However, for arrays of 4 items or more, most subjects had to count. The time to count each item beyond the subitizing range was about 1 for 5-year-olds and 3/10 s for adults. Thus, both 5-year-olds and adults tended to display the same counting patterns, but the time spent counting was longer for children. In addition, Klahr and Wallace noted that subitizing not only is faster than counting but also seems to develop earlier in children. In fact, Klahr and Wallace argue that subitizing is prerequisite for counting.

Figure 1 shows a process model which accounts for the performance. First, the subject points to the first item and sets a counter to 1, the counter is incremented rapidly for subitized sets and more slowly for large sets; the subject increments the counter by ones until reaching the end of the set, and then recites the number. Figure 2 shows a representation of children's counting based on Greeno, Riley, and Gelman's (1978) work. According to this model, children acquire a mental number line. The first few items (subitized range) can be counted quickly because they are perceptually groupable.

Gelman and Gallistel (Gelman, 1980; Gelman & Gallistel, 1978) have provided evidence that children as young as 3 years old seem to recognize that counting is related to addition and subtraction. In a typical experiment, children were shown a display containing three green mice as part of a "game." Then the same displays were shown later, but either with one item missing (subtraction) or with the line of mice shortened or lengthened (displacement). The children (aged 3, 4, and 5) expressed strong surprise

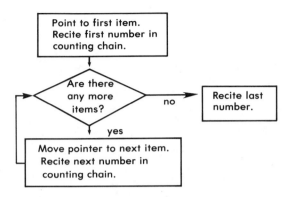

Fig. 1. A process model for counting.

at the subtraction treatment, but not at the displacement treatment. For example, one 3-year-old said of the subtraction treatment: "There was three animals in the can. Took one cuz there's two now." In contrast, the displacement treatment did not bother the children, because as one child said, "Even if it's mixed up, it's still three. Cuz, one, two, three." This research is consistent with the idea that even before formal instruction, children know that addition and subtraction can cancel each other out and are related to number, and that displacement does not alter number.

In another study (Gelman & Gallistel, 1978) children were asked to count displays consisting of 2–19 items. For small set sizes, 3-, 4-, and 5-year-olds all showed high levels of using one-to-one correspondence, i.e., pointing to each item as it is counted. For larger sets, the performance of the 3-year-olds fell off, suggesting that they have mechanical problems in dealing with large number sets, whereas the 4- and 5-year-olds maintained high levels of accuracy. More than 90% of the 4- and 5-year-olds

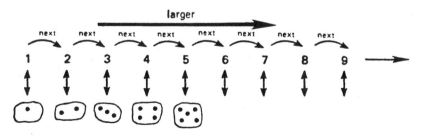

Fig. 2. The mental number line (from Resnick, 1982).

and 80% of the 3-year-olds used a *stable ordering,* i.e., recited the counting string in the same way each time. Use of the *cardinality* principle—recognition that the last number in the counting string corresponds to the value of array—was not clearly evident for the younger subjects and larger number sets. Finally, preschoolers seem able to count regardless of the specific items to be counted. Gelman (1980) concludes: "I am struck by the general willingness of preschoolers to count almost anything" (p. 62).

Gelman and Gallistel (1978) identified five principles that are required for counting: the *one-to-one principle* (each item receives one counting name), the *stable-order principle* (the counting words must be recited in the correct order), the *abstraction principle* (any display of objects can be counted), the *order-irrelevance principle* (the objects can be counted in any order), and the *cardinality principle* (the last item gives the numerical value of the set). The stable-order principle has been studied by Fuson, Richards, and Briars (1982) and Fuson & Hall (1983). They report that the stable order principle seems to be limited to a few numbers (e.g., up to 4 or 5) for young children, and this span increases with age. However, young children have trouble counting when they begin from a number other than 1 (Fuson, Richards, & Briars, 1982). Siegler and Robinson (1982) have provided some evidence that young children do not view the number line as an interval scale, but rather tend to represent the numbers in categories, such as small numbers, middle numbers, and large numbers. The cardinality principle has been studied by Markman (1979). She found that children's ability to exercise the cardinality principle correctly depended on the form of the counting question. When class names were used (such as *pigs* or *nursery school children),* performance on "How many?" questions was poor, but when collection names were used (such as *animal family* or *nursery school class),* performance was greatly enhanced. Apparently, young children are able to apply the cardinality principle but have some trouble seeing that counting and cardinality are related.

Implications

Apparently, children entering kindergarten already are proficient in counting: They can recognize small sets (up to about 4) without counting, they can count independently of the objects being counted, and they recognize that counting is related to the operations of addition and subtraction. Skills in reciting the number string, in one-to-one correspondence, and in the cardinality principle for small numbers are already emerging in children before formal instruction begins. However, counting skills need to be practiced so that they become automatic. Thus, it is reasonable to assume that children make use of these skills, with varying degrees of automaticity, in trying to understand number facts, as described in the next section.

V. ARITHMETIC COMPUTATION

Arithmetic computation refers to addition, subtraction, multiplication, and division of numbers. The California Assessment Program (California State Department of Education, 1982), a standardized achievement test, allocates 32% of its mathematics items to arithmetic computation (involving only whole numbers) in Grade 3, and approximately 21% of the Grade 6 test and the Grade 12 test covers arithmetic computation (including fractions and decimals). These figures suggest that arithmetic computation represents a fairly large component of the mathematics curriculum throughout Grades K–12. In this section, we explore two major subcategories of arithmetic computation: number facts and subtraction of whole numbers.

A. Number Facts

Addition number facts refer to simple addition problems of the form, $m + n =$ _____, where m and n are non-negative integers that sum to less than 10. Four major kinds of stages have been identified in children's learning of simple addition facts: *counting-all, counting-on, derived facts, known facts.*

Counting-all is an early strategy that makes use of the child's expertise in counting. For a problem such as $m + n =$ _____, the child's strategy is to set a counter to 0, increment it m times, then increment n times. For example, for the problem $3 + 4 =$ _____, the child might recite, "1, 2, 3 [*pause*], 4, 5, 6, 7, the answer is 7." In addition, the child might simultaneously extend a finger for each increment. In a recent study, Fuson (1982) found the approximately 20% of the 6- to 8-year-olds she tested used a counting-all strategy at least part of the time. Figure 3 provides a process model of the counting-all procedure. As you can see, the rectangles represent operations, the diamonds represent decisions, and the arrows show the flow of control.

Counting-on is a more sophisticated strategy that makes use of the child's expertise in counting. For a problem such as $m + n =$ _____ , the child's strategy is to set a counter to m and then increment it n times. For example, for the problem $3 + 4 =$ _____, the child might recite "3 [*pause*], 4, 5, 6, 7, the answer is 7." In addition, the child might put out 3 fingers when he/she says "3," adding one more for 4, one more for 5, one more for 6, and one more for 7. A modified version of counting-on is what Groen and Parkman (1972) call the *min model*. In this strategy, the child sets a counter to the larger of the two addends and then increments by the smaller of the two addends. For example, for the problem

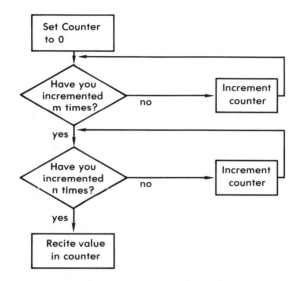

Fig. 3.   Counting-all procedure for addition.

$3 + 4 =$ _____, the child might recite "4, [*pause*], 5, 6, 7"; simultaneously, the child might extend four fingers, and then add one more,
one more, and one more. Figure 4 presents process models for two versions
of the counting-on procedure: counting-on from m and counting-on from
the larger of m or n.

The known-facts stage refers to students' memorizing a response for
each simple problem, such as the response "4" to the stimulus "2 + 2
= _____." The derived-facts stage refers to students' using their
knowledge of some addition facts to discover answers for related problems.
For example, Carpenter (1980) observed the following procedure for solving the problem $6 + 8 =$ _____: "6 + 6 is 12 and 2 more is 14."
Another student reasoned as follows: "I took 1 from 8 and gave it to 6.
7 + 7 = 14." These examples of derived facts show that students can
use a few known facts, coupled with knowledge of how to add and subtract
when an addend is 1 or 2, in order to solve many problems.

In a landmark study, Groen and Parkman (1972) asked first graders to
solve 55 addition fact problems with sums less than 10. If students tend
to use a counting-all procedure, then response time will be a function of
the sum of the problem—i.e., the total number of times the counter is
incremented corresponds to $m + n$. If students use a counting-on from
m procedure, then response time should be a function of the value of n—
i.e., the total number of times that the counter is incremented corresponds
to n. If students use counting-on from the larger of m and n, then response
time should be a function of the smaller of m and n—i.e., the total number

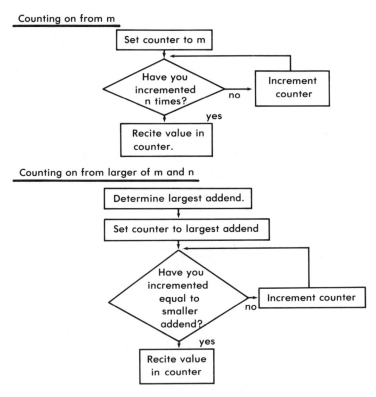

Fig. 4. Counting-on procedures for addition facts.

of times the counter is incremented corresponds to the value of the smaller addend. If students use a known-facts approach, then all problems should require about the same amount of time.

Figure 5 summarizes the mean response times for each problem. As can be seen, there is a pattern in which response time increases as a function of the smaller addend. This is the pattern that would be produced by counting on from the larger of m and n. Groen and Parkman found that this variety of the counting-on model best explained the results they obtained from first graders, thus suggesting that these children had developed fairly sophisticated counting algorithms. However, Figure 5 also shows that some problems were solved extremely quickly, such as the doubles $0 + 0, 1 + 1, 2 + 2, 3 + 3, 4 + 4$. Apparently, students have rapid memorized answers to these problems; this indicates that on some problems a known-facts approach is used.

Although counting models, such as Groen and Parkman's min model, seem to describe the performance of young children (e.g., first graders), performance of adults may not be best described by counting models. For

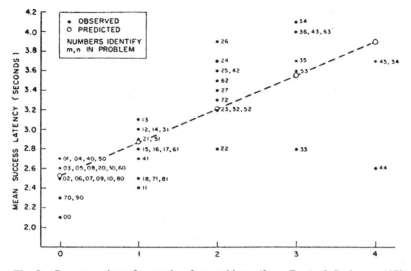

Fig. 5. Response times for number fact problems (from Groen & Parkman, 1972).

example, Groen and Parkman (1972) found that estimated time to increment a counter was 400 ms for first graders but 20 ms for adults. Ashcraft
and Battaglia (1978) have suggested that adults use "direct access" to
number fact problems—i.e., the answer is stored in memory and can be
directly retrieved without counting. Why is there a small (i.e., 20 ms)
slope in the response times? According to Ashcraft and Battaglia, on about
5% of the problems adults may revert to counting procedure because direct
access fails. In a series of experiments, Ashcraft and Battaglia were able
to show that counting models cannot account for adult performance; in
fact, the counting models tended to break down for children as young as
the fourth grade (Ashcraft & Fierman, 1982). Apparently, children move
from counting models to known facts as they move through the elementary
grades.

B. Subtraction of Whole Numbers

This category refers to subtraction of whole numbers involving two or
more columns. For example, the following problem is an example of subtraction of whole numbers:

$$\begin{array}{r} 210 \\ -\,162 \\ \hline \end{array}$$

The California Assessment Program found that 51% of the third graders
and 89% of the sixth graders were able to select the correct answer (48).

The most common error was to select 152 as the answer; this answer would be generated if the student subtracted the smaller number from the larger number in each column.

Large-scale assessments such as the California Assessment Program suggest that many students have trouble with computations involving carrying and borrowing. Recent cognitive research has provided a way of describing what the student knows in terms of a process model. Figure 6 shows a process model of the procedure for solving three-column sub-

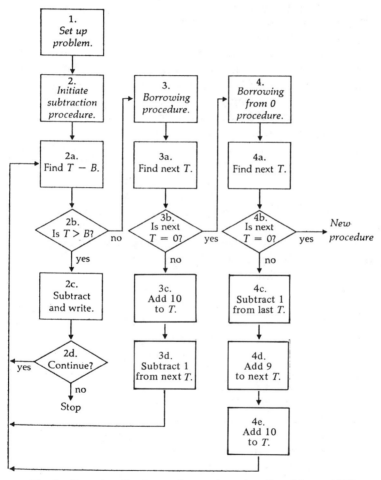

Fig. 6. Procedure for three-column subtraction (from Mayer, 1981).

$$
\begin{array}{r}
\text{Problem setup:} \quad T\,T\,T \\
-\ \underline{B\,B\,B}
\end{array}
$$

traction problems, such as is required to solve the above problem correctly (Mayer, 1981b). However, students who make errors such as selecting 152 as the answer may be using a procedure that has some bugs in it— for example, the student seems to ignore Step 2B. Brown and Burton (1978) argue that many errors can be attributed to systematic bugs in procedures rather than to random guessing.

In order to test this idea, Brown and Burton (1978) gave a set of 15 subtraction problems to 1,325 primary school children. Using a computer program called BUGGY, Brown and Burton attempted to locate the algorithm that each child was using. If the child was 100% correct, the BUGGY program would categorize the child as using the correct algorithm. If there were some errors, BUGGY tried to change the algorithm by adding one bug that would account for the errors. If no single bug could account for all the errors, then combinations of bugs were tried. Although BUGGY was based on hundreds of bugs or bug combinations, it was able to find algorithms for only about half the students. The other students may have been making random responses, may have been inconsistent, or may have been using bugs unfamiliar to BUGGY. A very common bug was "smaller from larger," in which the student always subtracted the smaller number from the larger number at each place value position. This bug, as we have explained, accounts for the students' answer 152 to the problem 210 − 162 = _____. Another common bug was "borrow from zero." When borrowing from a column whose top digit was 0, the student changed 0 to 9, but did not continue borrowing from the column to the left of the zero, for example, 103 − 45 = 158, or 803 − 508 = 395. Learning to comute means being able to use algorithms such as that shown in Figure 6 automatically and without bugs.

C. Implications

This section has shown how arithmetic computation can be represented in process models, and how individual differences in performance can be precisely described. For example, the process of subtraction can be represented as a flow chart with each box corresponding to a given decision or operation. One implication of this work is that learning of computational skills can be viewed as the development of more powerful "flow charts" in a child's memory. The development of more sophisticated procedures depends on the automaticity of the existing procedures; thus, children need practice and drill so that simple procedures may become automatic. Another implication is that students' misunderstandings of computational procedures can be diagnosed in more detail than has traditionally been used. For example, if we know that a child's solution procedure for subtraction includes the "borrow-from-zero" bug, we can design direct instruction aimed specifically at that bug.

VI. ARITHMETIC APPLICATION

Arithmetic application problems are word problems which require one or more arithmetic operations. For example, the California Assessment Program (California State Department of Education, 1982) included the following arithmetic application on tests given to third graders:

Ron had 7 peanuts.
Sue had 2 times as many peanuts as did Ron.
How many peanuts did Sue have?

Results indicated that 51% of the third graders selected the correct answer (14) and that the most common incorrect choice was 9. Apparently, some children decided to add 2 and 7 regardless of the words in the second sentence. The poor performance cannot be attributed to students' lack of knowledge of multiplication facts because 90% of the third graders successfully answered computational problems such as $2 \times 7 =$ _____.

Problem solving involves building a representation of the words of the problem and finding the solution of the problem using the rules of arithmetic and algebra. A major difficulty in students' performance on word problems seems to involve representation of the problem, i.e., moving from the words in the problem to a coherent mental representation of the problem. One major subcomponent in the representation process for word problems is the translation of each sentence.

As an example of the translation process, let us consider students' comprehension of relational propositions such as "Mary is twice as old as Betty." Recent work by Greeno and his colleagues (Greeno, 1980; Riley, Greeno, & Heller, 1982) involved asking children in primary grades to listen to and then repeat word problems. When the problem involved a relational sentence—e.g., "Joe has three marbles. Tom has five more marbles than Joe. How many marbles does Tom have?"—a common error was to forget the relational information and state, e.g., "Joe has three marbles. Tom has five marbles. How many marbles does Tom have?"

Confusion over how to translate relational sentences is not restricted to primary-school children. Soloway, Lochhead, and Clement (1982) asked college students to write equations to represent relational propositions such as "There are six times as many students as professors at this university." Approximately one third of the students produced a wrong equation, such as $6S = P$. Subsequent studies revealed that when students were asked to use BASIC programs to represent relational sentences, error rates fell dramatically.

In another series of experiments, Mayer (1982b) asked college students to read eight story problems and then recall them. The problems contained both relational propositions, such as "The rate in still water is 12 mph more than the rate of the current," and assignment statements, such as "The cost of the candy is $1.70 per pound." The recall results indicated a much higher error rate for recall of relational propositions (29%) than for recall of assignment propositions (9%). Subsequent analyses found that subjects tended to change relational propositions into assignments. For example, some subjects recalled "The rate in still water is 12 mph more than the rate of the current" as "The speed of the boat in still water is 12 mph."

There is some evidence that the ability to translate relational propositions increases with age. Riley et al. (1982) asked children to use wooden blocks to represent propositions such as "Joe has five more marbles than Pete." The frequency of correct answers increased steadily from Grades K to 3. Similarly, Trabasso (1977) found that correct encoding of relational facts, such as "The red stick is longer than the blue stick" increased from age 6 to adult.

A second aspect of representing word problems is to recognize problem types. There is growing evidence that children learn to categorize problems into types, that is, they acquire what could be called schemata for various problem types. Greeno and his colleagues (Greeno, 1980; Riley et al., 1983) have identified three general types of word problems:

Cause–change problems such as "Joe has 3 marbles. Tom gives him 5 more marbles. How many marbles does Joe have now?"

Combination problems such as "Joe has 3 marbles. Tom has 5 marbles. How many marbles do they have altogether?"

Comparison problems such as "Joe has 3 marbles. Tom has 5 more marbles than Joe. How many marbles does Tom have?"

As you can see, each of these problems requires the same arithmetical operation: $3 + 5 = 8$. However, childrens' performance seems to depend on problem type. For example, Greeno and his colleagues found that children in Grades K and 1 performed well on certain cause–change problems but poorly on comparison problems; in contrast, children in Grades 2 and 3 performed well on all types. This pattern suggests a developmental trend: Children begin with the idea that all problems are cause–change problems, and later learn to differentiate different types of schemata. Riley et al. (1982) have specified models that children acquire for representing word problems; as children develop, their models become progressively more sophisticated. Thus, errors may be due to students' using inappropriate schemata rather than to computational difficulties.

Weaver (1982) has distinguished between a unary-operation and binary-operation view of computation. The unary-operation approach is based on the idea that a problem like 5 + 3 means "add 3 to 5," whereas the binary-operation approach translates 5 + 3 into "combine 3 and 5." The unary-operation view is like Greeno's cause–change schema, and the binary-operation view is like Greeno's combination schema. Fuson (1982) has observed that the unary-operation view tends to be the first to develop in children, even before formal instruction.

Implications

Learning to solve word problems involves more than being able to carry out arithmetical operations. Unfortunately, some curricular materials provide no instruction in how to solve word problems; instead, word problems are included in problem sets as ways of teaching computation. The research cited in this section seems to show that learning to solve word problems also involves learning how to translate the sentences and combine them into a meaningful representation. For example, students have difficulty in translating relational propositions. Thus, instruction could provide practice in phrasing sentences in one's own words, or in writing equations to represent sentences. As another example, students may lack a particular schema such as the comparison schema for word problems. In this case, direct instruction could be provided along with practice in stating problems in one's own words. Examples of worked out problems provide another instructional technique.

VII. ALGEBRAIC COMPUTATION

Algebraic computation problems involve solving algebraic equations, including single equations and simultaneous equations. For example, the following problem is taken from the California Assessment Program's mathematics test for 12th graders (California State Department of Education, 1982a):

If $9X - 63 = 18$, then $X =$ _____.

Sixty-seven percent of the students selected the correct answer (9). The problem involved simple operations that the student could perform well— adding 18 and 63, dividing 81 by 9. However, one third of the students seemed to be unable to put these steps together to solve the problem.

The previous section on arithmetic computation demonstrated that solutions require both procedures (such as the model for how to add multidigit numbers) and strategies (such as how to organize the procedures into a solution plan). Cognitive psychologists have provided a technique for representing students' strategies: analysis of a problem as a problem space and analysis of the search through the problem space as a production system.

A problem space refers to the given state of the problem, the goal state of the problem, and all possible intervening states that could be generated by applying legal operations to each state. For example, Figure 7 shows a partial problem space for $6X - 8 = 3X + 22$. Note that only four kinds of operators are involved in the problem space: performing the same arithmetic operation to both sides of the equation involving numbers (MOVE NUMBER) or variables (MOVE VARIABLE), and carrying out an arithmetic operation on one side of the equation (COMPUTE NUMBER) or variables (COMPUTE VARIABLE). There are, of course, many other possible moves that are not shown in Figure 7, such as multiplying both sides by 2 or adding X to both sides.

A production system consists of a list of productions, with each consisting of a condition and an action. Table 7 lists a possible production system for searching the problem space for a problem such as $6X - 8 = 3X + 22$. The problem solver begins at the top of the production system and moves down until one of the conditions is met; if a condition is met, the problem solver sets carrying out the action as a goal. If the action can

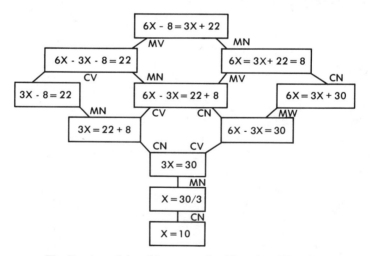

Fig. 7. A partial problem space for $6X - 8 = 3X + 22$.

TABLE 7

A Possible Production System for Solving Simple Equations

P1	If there are two numbers on one side of the equation, combine them using the rules of arithmetic (COMPUTE NUMBER)
	Example: $3X = 2 + 7 \rightarrow 3X = 9$
P2	If there are two Xs on one side of the equation, combine them using the rules of arithmetic (COMPUTE VARIABLE)
	Example: $2X + X - 7 = 2 \rightarrow 3X - 7 = 2$
P3	If there is a number on the left side, move it to the right side using the rules of algebra (MOVE NUMBER)
	Example: $3X - 7 = 2 \rightarrow 3X = 2 + 7$
P4	If there is an X on the right side, move it to the left side (MOVE VARIABLE)
	Example: $2X - 7 = 2 - X \rightarrow 2X + X - 7 = 2$
P5	If there are parentheses, clear the parentheses using the rules of arithmetic (CLEAR PARENS)
	Example: $2(X - 7) = 10 \rightarrow 2X - 14 = 10$

be directly carried out, it is carried out; however, if there is some obstacle in the way, then removing that obstacle is added as another goal. Then the problem solver returns to the top of the production list and moves down again.

Let us examine how the problem space and production system models would predict a person's performance. Given the problem $6X - 8 = 3X + 22$, the first production to fire is P3—there is a number on the left side. The action can be carried, resulting in the equation $6X = 3X + 22 + 8$. We return to the top of the list, and the first production to fire is P1; when the action is carried out, the resulting equation is $6X = 3X + 30$. We return to the top of the list, and the production to fire now is P4; when the action is carried out, the resulting equation is $6X - 3X = 30$. Next P2 fires, yielding $3X = 30$. Then, P3 fires, yielding $X = 30/3$. Then P1 fires, yielding $X = 10$. As you can see, if the productions had been in a different order in the list, the search through the problem space would have been different.

Recent experiments by Mayer (1982a) and Mayer, Larkin, and Kadane (1984) have suggested that the solution strategy that a person uses may depend on the format of the problem. For example, when a problem was presented as an equation, such as $(8 + 3X)/2 = 3X - 11$, people tended to use an *isolate strategy*. This strategy involves first trying to get all the

*X*s on one side and all the numbers on the other; for example, productions P3 and P4 would be placed on the top of the list. In contrast, people tended to use a *reduce strategy* when the problem was presented in words, for example, "Find a number such that if 8 more than 3 times the number is divided by 2, the result is the same as 11 less than 3 times the number." This strategy involves carrying out any indicated operations and clearing parentheses as soon as possible. Presumably, the word format was so crowded that subjects needed to reduce the amount of information. For example, productions P1, P2, and P5 would be placed at the top of the list.

In addition, Mayer, Larkin, and Kadane (1984) found individual differences among some subjects who solved very complex equations. Some tended to use a reduce strategy while others tended to use an isolate strategy. Thus, the problem space and production system analyses allow us to describe the strategies used by individual problem solvers.

Implications

The ability to solve algebraic equations involves, among other things, the achievement of some level of automaticity in carrying out basic operations and the development of planning skills. Although instruction tends to emphasize isolated operations such as how to add the same number to both sides, many students experience difficulty in determining when to apply the operations. One implication of this section is that students need drill and practice in carrying out algebraic operations. However, an examination of most textbooks suggests that this need is being met. Another implication is that students need practice in how to plan and how to monitor their plans. This need is not served by organizing problem sets so that all problems are solved in the same way. Instead, examples of instructional techniques aimed at teaching problem-solving planning are (1) asking students to describe their solution process and to compare their process to that of an "expert" and (2) asking students to select the sequence of necessary operations rather than actually to carry out the solution.

VIII. ALGEBRAIC APPLICATION PROBLEMS

Algebraic application problems are story problems that require the use of a basic algebraic formula such as rate = distance/time. For example, the sixth-grade mathematics test of the California Assessment Program (California State Department of Education, 1980) included the following problem:

If a distance of 350 miles is represented by a segment of 14 inches on a map, then on the map 1 inch represents: _____.

Sixty-one percent of the students selected the correct answer (25 miles). This is an example of a "direct variation problem," which can be represented as: $A/B = C/D$ where $A = 350$, $B = 14$, $C =$ the unknown, and $D = 1$.

As described in the section on arithmetic application, representation of story problems requires translation of each sentence as well as fitting the story information together into a coherent organization. In an interesting study, Paige and Simon (1966) gave students impossible problems such as

The number of quarters a man has is seven times the number of dimes he has. The value of the dimes exceeds the value of the quarters by two dollars and fifty cents. How many has he of each coin? (p. 79)

Some students translated the sentences into equatons without recognizing any inconsistencies. In contrast, other students read the problem and said, "This is impossible," while others misread the problem so that it was consistent, e.g., changing the second sentence to "The value of quarters exceeds the value of the dimes by two dollars and fifty cents." Apparently some students approach a problem mechanically while others try to make sense out of the problem.

How do students understand a problem? Hinsley, Hayes, and Simon (1977) have found that as students read the first few words of a story problem, they tend to make a decision concerning what type of problem it is. In one study (Hinsley et al., 1977) college students were given a collection of story problems and asked to sort them into categories. The results yielded 18 categories, such as *work, motion, interest, triangle,* etc. Subjects were able to perform the task and showed reasonable levels of agreement. Thus, there is some evidence that students have schemata for story problems.

In a follow-up study, Mayer (1981a) analyzed the story problems from a collection of algebra textbooks. In all, there were over 100 basic problem types. Categories such as *motion problems* could be broken down further into subtypes such as *overtake, closure, round trip, speed change* and so on. Some types of problems were far more common (e.g., occurring over 10 times per 1,000 textbook problems) while others were rare (e.g., occurring only once or not at all per 1,000 textbook problems). In a subsequent study (Mayer, 1982b), subjects were asked to read and recall a series of story problems. High-frequency problems were recalled much better than low-frequency problems. In addition, errors in recall of low-frequency problems tended to convert them to higher frequency problems.

These results would be expected if subjects assimilate the information to preexisting schemata of problem types.

Implications

The acquisition of skill in solving algebraic story problems involves, among other things, the ability to recognize problem types. Although instruction generally emphasizes computing the correct answer, a major area of difficulty seems to be in problem representation. One implication of this section is that students need practice in how to represent story problems. This need is not served by curricular materials in which all the problems on a page are the same type and are solvable by the same set of operations. Instead, examples of instructional techniques aimed at teaching problem representation include asking students to draw or select a picture corresponding to the problem, asking students to delete irrelevant information and underline essential information, and asking students to sort problems according to type.

IX. SUMMARY

This chapter has explored five representative areas of the mathematics curriculum: counting, arithmetic computation, arithmetic application, algebraic computation, and algebraic application. For each area, examples of research have been presented in order to show how cognitive research and the mathematics curriculum are related.

Traditionally, the mathematics curriculum has been viewed as a series of behaviors to be acquired by the learner. In contrast, cognitive research has provided new ways of describing "what is learned"—including techniques for representing and planning—as children develop competence in mathematics. It is hoped that this chapter will serve to continue the fruitful interaction between those interested in cognitive psychology and those interested in the mathematics curriculum. In particular, this chapter is based on the idea that cognitive psychologists can benefit from the challenges posed by the need to provide mathematics instruction to children, and mathematics education can benefit from the new ways of describing mathematics learning offered by cognitive psychologists.

ACKNOWLEDGMENTS

The author appreciates the assistance of Barbara Patterson, Assistant Superintendent for Instruction, Goleta Union School District, Goleta, California. The author also appreciates the assistance of the Curriculum Library, University of California, Santa Barbara.

REFERENCES

Ashcraft, M. H., & Battaglia, J. (1978). Cognitive arithmetic: Evidence for retrieval and decision processes in mental addition. *Journal of Experimental Psychology: Human Learning and Memory, 4,* 527–538.

Ashcraft, M. H., & Fierman, B. A. (1982). Mental addition in third, fourth, and sixth graders. *Journal of Experimental Child Psychology, 33,* 216–234.

Brown, J. S., & Burton, R. R. (1978). Diagnostic models for procedural bugs in basic mathematical skills. *Cognitive Science, 2,* 155–192.

California State Department of Education. (1980). *California assessment program: Student achievement in California schools:* Sacramento: Author.

California State Department of Education. (1981). *Catalog of instructional materials in mathematics.* Sacramento: Author.

California State Department of Education. (1982a). *California assessment program: Student achievement in California schools.* Sacramento: Author.

California State Department of Education. (1982b). *Mathematics framework for California public schools.* Sacramento: Author.

Carpenter, T. P. (1980). Heuristic strategies used to solve addition and subtraction problems. In R. Karplus (Ed.), *Proceedings of the fourth international conference for the psychology of mathematics education.* Berkeley: University of California.

Comprehensive test of basic skills: Preliminary technical report. (1982). Monterey, CA: McGraw-Hill.

Fuson, F. C. (1982). An analysis of the counting-on solution procedure in addition. In T. P. Carpenter, J. M. Moser, & T. A. Romberg (Eds.), *Addition and subtraction: A cognitive perspective.* Hillsdale, NJ: Erlbaum.

Fuson, F. C., & Hall, J. W. (1982). The acquisition of early number word meaning: A conceptual analysis and review. In H. P. Ginsburg (Ed.), *The development of mathematical thinking,* (pp. 49–107). New York: Academic Press.

Fuson, K. C., Richards, J., & Briars, D. J. (1982). The acquisition and elaboration of the number word sequence. In C. Brainerd (Ed.), *Progress in cognitive development: Vol. 1. Children's logical and mathematical cognition.* New York: Springer-Verlag.

Gagne, R. M. (1968). Learning hierarchies. *Educational Psychologist, 6,* 1–9.

Gagne, R. M., & Briggs, L. J. (1974). *Principles of instructional design.* New York: Holt.

Gelman, R. (1980). What young children know about numbers. *Educational Psychologist, 15,* 54–68.

Gelman, R., & Gallistel, C. R. (1978). *The child's understanding of number.* Cambridge, MA: Harvard University Press.

Ginsburg, H. P. (1982). Introduction. In H. P. Ginsburg (Ed.), *The development of mathematical thinking.* New York: Academic Press.

Goleta Union School District. (1978). *Mathematics continuum.* Goleta, CA: Author.

Greeno, J. G. (1980). Some examples of cognitive task analysis with instructional implications. In R. E. Snow, P. Federico, & W. E. Montagu (Eds.), *Aptitude, learning, and instruction* (Vol. 1, pp. 1–21). Hillsdale, NJ: Erlbaum.

Greeno, J. G., Riley, M. S., & Gelman, R. (1978). *Young children's counting and understanding.* Paper presented at the annual meeting of the Psychonomics Society, San Antonio, TX.

Groen, G. J., & Parkman, J. M. (1972). A chronometric analysis of simple addition. *Psychological Review, 79,* 329–343.

Hinsley, D., Hayes, J. R., & Simon, H. (1977). From words to equations: Meaning and representation in algebra word problems. In M. A. Just & P. A. Carpenter (Eds.), *Cognitive processes in comprehension* (pp. 89–106). Hillsdale, NJ: Erlbaum.

Klahr, D. R., & Wallace, J. G. (1976). *Cognitive development: An information processing view*. Hillsdale, NJ: Erlbaum.

Markman, E. M. (1979). Classes and collections: Conceptual organization and numerical abilities. *Cognitive Psychology, 11*, 395–411.

Mayer, R. E. (1981a). Frequency norms and structural analysis of algebra story problems into families, categories, and templates. *Instructional Science, 10*, 135–175.

Mayer, R. E. (1981b). *The promise of cognitive psychology*. San Francisco: Freeman.

Mayer, R. E. (1982a). Different problem solving strategies for algebra word and equation problems. *Journal of Experimental Psychology: Learning, Memory and Cognition, 8*, 448–462.

Mayer, R. E. (1982b). Memory for algebra story problems. *Journal of Educational Psychology, 74*, 199–216.

Mayer, R. E., Larkin, J. H., & Kadane, J. (1984). A cognitive analysis of mathematical problem solving ability. In R. Sternberg (Ed.), *Advances in the psychology of human intelligence* (Vol. 2, pp. 231–273). Hillsdale, NJ: Erlbaum.

Paige, J. M., & Simon H. A. (1966). Cognitive processes in solving algebra word problems. In B. Kleinmuntz (Ed.), *Problem solving* (pp. 51–119). New York: Wiley.

Resnick, L. B. (1982). A developmental theory of number understanding. In H. P. Ginsburg (Ed.), *The development of mathematical thinking*, (pp. 109–151). New York: Academic Press.

Resnick, L. B., & Ford, W. (1981). *The psychology of mathematics for instruction*. Hillsdale, NJ: Erlbaum.

Riley, M. S., Greeno, J. G., & Heller, J. I. (1983). Development of children's problem solving ability in arithmetic. In H. P. Ginsburg (Ed.), *The development of mathematical thinking* (pp. 153–196). New York: Academic Press.

Siegler, R. S., & Robinson, M. (1982). The development of numerical understanding. In H. W. Reese & L. P. Lipsitt (Eds.), *Advances in child development and behavior* (Vol. 16). New York: Academic Press.

Soloway, E., Lochhead, J., & Clement, J. (1982). Does computer programming enhance problem solving ability? Some positive evidence on algebra word problems. In R. J. Seidel, R. E. Anderson, & B. Hunter (Eds.) *Computer literacy* (pp. 171–185). New York: Academic Press.

Thorndike, E. L. (1922). *The psychology of arithmetic*. New York: Macmillan.

Trabasso, T. (1977). The role of memory as a system for making transitive inference. In R. V. Kail and J. W. Hagen (Eds.), *Perspectives on the development of memory and cognition* (pp. 333–36). Hillsdale, NJ: Erlbaum.

Weaver, F. J. (1982). Interpretations of number operations and symbolic representations of addition and subtraction. In T. P. Carpenter, J. M. Moser, & T. A. Romberg (Eds.), *Addition and subtraction: A cognitive perspective* (pp. 60–66). Hillsdale, NJ: Erlbaum.

6

Science

MARCIA C. LINN
Lawrence Hall of Science
University of California
Berkeley, California 97420
and
Weizman Institute of Science
Rehovot, Israel

I. THE NEED FOR SCIENCE CURRICULUM REFORM

It is now almost universally acknowledged that science education must be rejuvenated to serve the needs of American society. The National Commission on Excellence in Education (1983), in its well-publicized document, concludes that our nation is at risk:

> We report to the American people that while we can take justifiable pride in what our schools and colleges have historically accomplished and contributed to the United States and the well being of its people, the educational foundations of our society are presently being eroded by a rising tide of mediocrity that threatens our very future as a nation and as a people. (p. 5)

The commission challenges U.S. citizens to work toward educational reform to create what they call a "learning society": a society which is committed to a system of education that allows all members the opportunity to stretch their minds to full capacity to *think* effectively. One essential aspect of meeting this challenge involves reform of science curricula in light of recent advances in psychological research.

The National Science Board (NSB) Commission on Precollege Education in Mathematics, Science and Technology in its comprehensive report calls for "sweeping and drastic change" (1983, p. v) to provide the "new basics" in mathematics, science, and technology. The new basics "include communication and higher problem solving skills and scientific and technological literacy—the *thinking* tools that allow us to understand the technological world around us" (p. v). The NSB commission points

155

out that the new basics are needed by *all* students, and that, to accomplish this objective, new curricula must be developed.

Strong evidence for the need for rejuvenation in science education comes from the results of the National Assessment of Educational Progress. Tests which measure science knowledge have revealed how little information many learners acquire and have drawn attention to individual differences in attainment. There has been a steady decline in science achievement scores in the United States. For example, 17-year-olds, as measured by NAEP in 1969, 1973, and 1977, demonstrated seriously diminished science achievement. In addition, large numbers of 17-year-olds do not possess the thinking skills required to draw inferences from written materials or to solve multistep mathematical problems (NAEP, 1978a, 1978b, 1979a, 1979b, 1979c, 1979d, 1983).

Another reason for the need to rejuvenate science curricula is that the proliferation of scientific information has changed the nature of the field. Fensham and Kornhauser (1982) report that the first million entries in Chemical Abstracts took 32 years to accumulate while the second million accumulated in the last 2 years. The next generation of science curricula must help learners access, organize, and effectively utilize this vast amount of information. This proliferation of knowledge gives strong motivation to curriculum designers to seek assistance from psychologists and educators who are also addressing issues of knowledge acquisition, knowledge organization, and problem solving.

Thus, there has been a definite decline in student attainment of scientific understanding at the same time that the knowledge to be acquired has increased. To create a society which can provide scientific leadership, make responsible decisions in the voting booth, and offer equitable opportunities for all learners, we must make substantial changes in how science is taught. Resources available to those responding to this crisis include recent advances in psychological research which suggest how science curricula could be improved. This chapter suggests how these advances can be used to rejuvenate science curricula to meet the needs of society.

II. A SCIENCE OF SCIENCE EDUCATION

This is not the first time, nor is it likely to be the last time, that observers of science education in America call for reform. Now, however, an emerging *science of science education* based on these recent advances in psychological research could make this reform dramatic. First, knowledge proliferation in science education corresponding to that described for chemistry has given new urgency to our quest to understand how students learn. Second, new methodological tools have enabled researchers to address previously inaccessible questions. Before considering the implications of the emerging science of science education for curriculum design, this chapter provides a historical perspective on advances in psychological research and discusses the advantages and pitfalls of the new methodological tools. Following this discussion, the remainder of the chapter focuses on implications of recent research for curriculum design.

A. Advances in Psychological Research

1. Processing Capacity

One area where psychological research offers promise is in identifying parameters of human performance which can be reliably measured and which can explain behavior in a variety of situations. For example, researchers have sought to estimate how much information reasoners can process simultaneously, a factor referred to as *processing capacity*. Miller (1956) initially identified the magic number 7, plus or minus 2, as the number of "chunks" which adults can process simultaneously. Subsequently, Mandler (1967) developed a different definition and identified processing capacity as 5. Recently, Simon (1974) has suggested another definition which places special emphasis on the time required to memorize a chunk. All of these investigations reinforce the notion that humans have limited processing capacity. Learners tend to reformulate instructional materials which exceed their processing capacities in ways which may lead to misconceptions or to no learning at all. Thus, important advances in describing processing capacity have implications for curriculum reform.

2. Problem Solving

A second area where the emerging science of science education offers implications is in reconceptualizing the nature of reasoning strategies in problem solving. Reasoning strategies are the processes used to solve scientific problems.

Historically, Piaget described stages of reasoning such as *concrete operations* and *formal operations* to characterize strategies leading to valid inference in problem solving in all subject matter domains. Formal reasoners can, for example, control variables to achieve causal inference (reasoners use the controlling variables strategy when they design experimental conditions to change only the variable under investigation and keep all others the same). Formal reasoning was seen as the culmination of the development of problem-solving ability. Many science education researchers and curriculum developers viewed Piaget's stages of concrete operational and formal operational thought as characterizing strategies governing scientific reasoning (e.g. Lawson, 1983; Lawson, 1985).

Recently, a change has occurred in how problem solving performance is viewed. Piagetian theory placed major emphasis on valid inference, de-emphasizing the role of subject matter knowledge. Recent research (Linn, 1983) suggests that most rules for valid inference are strongly tied to the subject matter of the problem. New candidates for subject matter inde-pendent reasoning strategies called metareasoning strategies have received attention and will be described later. A reasonable body of research, also to be discussed suggests that subject matter knowledge strongly influences whether or not reasoners use what Piaget called concrete and formal rea-soning.

As has been discussed extensively, there is doubt about the existence of the qualitatively different stages which Inhelder and Piaget (1958) de-scribed (e.g., Furby, 1980; Siegler, 1981). Researchers have found that, although performance on Piagetian tasks correlates with performance on other scientific tasks, successful solution of one Piagetian task appears neither necessary nor sufficient for success on another which seemingly requires the same logical strategy (Carey, 1985; Linn, 1982). Furthermore, performance on Piagetian tasks correlates closely with measures of general ability (Humphrey & Parsons, 1979; Linn & Swiney, 1981) suggesting that Piagetian tasks measure the gradual acquisition of more powerful reasoning strategies rather than the abrupt change from one strategy to another.

Recent research contributes to a redefinition of what have been his-torically viewed as problem-solving strategies. Piagetian theory, with its emphasis on valid inference, has predominated in the past. Metareasoning, defined as the ability to reason about one's own reasoning, now appears to offer greater promise. Recent detailed analysis of scientific problem solving (e.g., Clement, 1982; Eylon, 1979; Greeno, 1978; Larkin, 1981; McDermott, Piternick, & Rosenquist 1980; Schoenfeld, 1985) suggests examples of metareasoning strategies. Greeno (1978) suggests that a rea-soning approach called *strategic planning* is central to scientific problem solving. Strategic planning refers to the ability to consider and combine known information to solve a multistep problem such as combining axioms and theorems to design a geometric proof. Strategic planning can be seen as metareasoning in that reasoners must consider various approaches be-fore selecting a promising one. Another aspect of metareasoning is the *testing* of the selected approach to see if it meets the reasoner's needs or if another option should be generated. The method used for testing depends on the subject matter. The propensity to engage in testing may be less subject matter specific. Both planning and testing involve the learner in reflection about the solution to a problem. Both can be invoked at the discretion of the problem solver.

3. Intuitive Conceptions

A third area where psychological research contributes to the emerging science of science education is in the study of how learners construct views of scientific phenomena. Piagetian research drew attention to certain intuitive conceptions but sought to explain them in terms of the previously discussed stages. Current research focuses more on the content of conceptions in each subject matter area than on the similarities across subject matter. In addition, current research reveals that intuitive conceptions tend to be held by adults as well as children, contrary to Piagetian theory. Recent research reveals that reasoners construct views of natural phenomena which they bring to their science classes (e.g., Driver, 1983; Linn, 1983; Resnick, 1983). Reasoners hold conceptions which can be referred to as intuitive conceptions. These are logically consistent and strongly held conceptions which differ from conceptions held by experts. For example, many seventh- through twelfth-grade reasoners believe that the weight of a metal object determines how much liquid it displaces and strongly defend this view (Linn & Pulos, 1983b). The view of the world constructed by the reasoner has been extensively researched and has important implications for curriculum design, as will be discussed (Linn & Siegel, 1983; Stevens, Collins, & Goldin, 1982).

The emerging science of science education, therefore, is characterized by advances in understanding processing capacity, problem-solving strategies, and intuitive conceptions. Later sections of this chapter discuss the impact of these advances on current understanding of the *state of the reasoner* (di Sessa, 1981; Larkin, McDermott, Simon, & Simon, 1980; Linn & Pulos, 1983a, 1983b; Sternberg, 1982), the *mechanisms which govern change* in reasoning (Linn & Eylon, 1983; Linn & Siegel, 1983; Reif & Heller, 1982), the *delivery of instruction* using new technology (Sleeman & Brown, 1982), and the *equity of educational outcomes* (Klein, 1985; Linn & Petersen, 1986).

B. Methodological Issues

The science of science education involves several new methodologies. As new techniques become available, methodological concerns are raised. However, it would be unwise to overshadow the creativity of researchers by criticism of methods. Often valid conclusions can be recognized because they occur in differing methodologies, even when they are only partially supported within each methodology.

The increased concern of researchers with the impact of processing capacity and the role of subject matter knowledge reflects a corresponding increase in methods for characterizing and analyzing such information (Ericsson & Simon, 1984). Some important issues in employing these methodologies are discussed in this section.

1. Protocol Analysis

One methodology for investigating the role of subject matter knowledge in problem solving is *protocol analysis*. Many researchers have respondents think aloud while they solve problems. The researcher then attempts to describe a model of how the reasoner solved the problem by analyzing the resulting protocol. Such an approach has yielded much useful information about problem solving. However, this approach also yields a large amount of data per respondent, thereby necessitating studies with small numbers of subjects. In addition, analysis requires a great deal of experimenter judgment. Because a small number of subjects are used and because the experimenter's judgment is required to analyze the results, these studies might lack generalizability.

Another possible methodological problem with using thinking-aloud protocols concerns the processing requirements. Some respondents to thinking-aloud experiments appear to be very fluent and may be able to produce their thoughts verbally without employing a great deal of their processing capacity. Other respondents, however, may need to use all of their processing capacity to think and therefore have difficulty incorporating thinking aloud into their problem-solving activities. This is especially problematic for young subjects who may have limited processing capacities as well as limited availability of verbal formulas for presenting their thoughts. Thus, in interpreting the results of protocol analyses one needs to consider whether the added requirement that one think aloud might have interfered with problem solving.

The demand features of the thinking-aloud environment may also interfere with the validity of the resulting protocol. Presumably the respondent in a thinking-aloud situation wishes to appear intelligent to the experimenter. The subject may therefore spend more time planning the solution to the problem and may ask more questions before moving ahead than he/she would characteristically do in an autonomous problem-solving situation.

Another issue concerns the selection of problems. Problems must be selected not only to demand appropriate reasoning strategies but also to allow analysis of the contribution of subject matter knowledge. Reasoners investigating similar phenomena often use extremely different problems (e.g., Clement, 1982; di Sessa, 1981; McDermott et al., 1980). Each group identifies intuitive conceptions: Some are at the level of expectations about how objects behave, while others reflect models of the physical world. Problems may also differ in their problem-solving requirements. Some problems simply do not require planning, and therefore investigations that use them fail to assess that skill (Linn, 1985). Although hardly a new concern in science education research, selection of problem features and of response requirements deserves serious attention. (See Linn, 1977, for a discussion of these issues in a different context.)

2. Comparisons of Experts and Novices

A prevalent methodology in research on problem solving concerns the comparison of experts and novices. Comparison of groups is a common technique for identifying potentially meaningful variables in a new field. This technique has offered insight (e.g., Adelson, 1985; Larkin et al., 1980). Nevertheless, results of these studies must be viewed with caution. Experts differ from novices on many factors besides expertise. For example, they usually differ in age and if they differ in age they probably also differ in the character of the learning experiences which they have received. When experts and novices are asked to solve the same problems, often one group is solving familiar problems, while the other group is solving unfamiliar problems. Thus, it is important to validate findings from expert–novice studies by means of other investigations.

3. Knowledge Representation

An important aspect of current research in psychology relevant to physical science curriculum design concerns how knowledge might be represented. Questions about the representation of knowledge are largely unresolved. Some researchers use computer representations such as production systems, nomological nets, or hierarchical trees. Sometimes these representations are chosen because they are ideally suited to the problems, but at other times they are chosen because they suit the available technology. Computer models can impose on researchers certain constraints which stem from technology rather than from theory, as many commentators on artificial intelligence have noted (e.g., Boden, 1977; Pylyshyn, 1978).

The purpose of a knowledge representation clearly influences its form. Production systems, which are sets of "if . . . then" associations, have been popular for developing computer models which perform as expert problem solvers and as computer tutors (Anderson, 1985). These models, however, are poor representations of human problem solving. Clancey (1982, 1983), had difficulty converting a production system into an intelligent tutor because although the production system could solve the problems, it did not solve them in a manner similar to that used by human problem solvers. Clancey concluded that human problem solvers used loosely structured associations to search their knowledge base rather than using a production-system type organization. Clancey was able to better understand human problem solving by developing a model which characterized the loosely structured associations (Clancey, 1984). in contrast, Anderson sought to teach the production rules to students.

Similar findings are reported in studies of expertise in chess playing. Chase and Simon (1973a, 1973b) and others studying expertise in chess have identified how experts recognize patterns and use them to generate just a few moves. The expert then selects from among this small number of moves by analyzing the consequences of each. This approach is considerably different from an exhaustive search of all the possibilities. Exhaustive search is not efficient even for computers in chess problem solving. However, it turns out to be sufficient for expert performance on many of the problems in the problem-solving literature. In spite of the efficiency of this procedure for the computer, since it does not mimic the procedure used by the individual its usefulness for understanding human problem solving and for curriculum design must be carefully evaluated.

4. Level of Analysis

A large body of recent psychological research relevant to science education operates primarily at the very detailed level of analysis of solutions to individual problems. The detailed level of analysis is reflected in protocol analysis of individuals solving problems and in attempts to model knowledge representations. In contrast, many science education researchers have examined correlations between individuals' performance on science problem-solving tasks and their other attitudes and aptitudes.

The usefulness of combining an information-processing approach and a human-abilities approach to understanding learning has been discussed by Cronbach (1957, 1975). The human-abilities approach has demonstrated that scientific problem solving is strongly related to general ability constructs such as fluid ability and crystallized ability. These findings appear useful in investigating possible aptitude–treatment interactions (Doyle, 1983; Snow, 1976). In contrast, they appear to shed little light on the processes which reasoners employ when solving a specific problem (Kyllonen, Woltz, & Lohman, 1982; Linn & Pulos, 1983a, 1983b; Webb, 1985). Thus, it appears that the stable characteristics of individuals, which can be measured using standardized tests of general ability, general anxiety, and general attitude toward science, correlate with performance on scientific tasks but do not predict specific performance in learning situations. These stable characteristics may govern the acquisition and use of metareasoning strategies more than the selection of subject matter knowledge for a given problem. Curriculum developers need to know both the specific features of instruction which will foster problem solving and the characteristics of learners likely to profit from it.

In summary, recent advances in psychological research reflect corresponding advances in methodology. The new methods offer promise but also raise some concerns. When interpreting research for curriculum designers, one must consider these issues.

III. PSYCHOLOGICAL RESEARCH RELATED TO CURRICULUM DESIGN

The emerging science of science education offers useful implications for science curriculum design. Four aspects of psychological research relevant to science curriculum design as mentioned previously are discussed in this section: the state of the reasoner, the mechanisms governing change in reasoning, the delivery of instruction, and the equity of educational outcomes. This discussion focuses on implications and is not intended as a review of the literature. The research studies described are illustrative of relevant issues rather than representative or exhaustive.

A. State of the Reasoner

The state of the reasoner refers to the knowledge, beliefs, and capabilities of the reasoner. Recent psychological research has been concerned with comparison of reasoners at different states, such as comparisons of experts and novices, to determine which aspects of the reasoner's state change as learning progresses. Characterizing the state of the reasoner at the start of a science class, the observed final state of the reasoner, and the desired final state of the reasoner will help those designing science curricula.

Two aspects of the state of the reasoner are central to curriculum design. First, the reasoner's available problem-solving strategies deserve consideration. Second, the view of natural phenomena constructed by the reasoner in terms of intuitive conceptions must be considered. These aspects can characterize the initial state and the desired final states for reasoners.

1. Problem-Solving Strategies

The reasoner's state includes a repertoire of problem-solving strategies. Piagetian theory suggests that strategies for valid inference develop as the reasoner gets older. Valid inference occurs intermittently; even logicians sometimes reason "illogically" in solving abstract problems such as Wason's selection task (Wason & Johnson-Laird, 1972). In contrast, young children often reason validly when assessing, for example, fairness of foot races and illogically in many other content areas. Much Piagetian-based research, starting with the first replication of Inhelder and Piaget's (1958) studies of adolescents conducted by Lovell (1961), indicates that valid reasoning occurs infrequently and that reasoners correctly use valid reasoning strategies only for certain subject matters and in certain contexts.

Role of Processing Capacity. Several research traditions suggest that the fundamental characteristic of development is the increase in processing capacity rather than an increase in the repertoire of reasoning strategies. A number of theorists (Case, 1974, 1980; Fischer, 1980) have argued that the intermittent employment of logical reasoning stems from processing-capacity limitations in the learner. Case (1974) demonstrated that 8- and 9-year-old subjects could employ formal reasoning strategies, which Piaget had hypothesized were acquired only during adolescence, if the strategies were taught in such a way that limited processing capacity was required for their employment. Similarly, Scardamalia (1977) demonstrated that increasing the processing-capacity demands of tasks involving controlling variables by increasing the number of variables to be considered simultaneously resulted in age-related changes in ability to solve the problems. She demonstrated that as children got older they could solve problems with more variables and that the relationship between age and number of variables controlled is strikingly consistent.

Thus, the application of logical strategies may be constrained by available processing capacity. The challenge to the educator (Case, 1975) is to develop instructional procedures which allow reasoners to solve problems using their available processing capacity. In particular, teachers might supply problem-solving strategies which allow logical reasoning with limited processing capacity.

Metareasoning Strategies. Recent research suggests that metareasoning strategies are important components of problem solving (Brown & Palincsar, 1985; Sternberg, 1982). Metareasoning is the capacity to reason about one's own reasoning. Metareasoning includes the ability to assess and revise one's own understanding. Brown and Palincsar (1985) found that students comprehend text better when taught to regularly verify their ideas about the meaning of each passage.

To understand a reasoner's state of metareasoning it has been effective to compare how experts and novices solve problems. As discussed in the methodology section, this approach has both strengths and weaknesses.

Recent research focusing on states of reasoning has compared experts and novices to attempt to understand strategies which differentiate these two groups.

Chi, Feltovich, and Glaser (1980) asked expert and novice physicists to categorize physics problems. They found that novices tended to rely on the superficial features of the problems, possibly because they lacked appreciation of what information was relevant for solving the problem, while experts tended to categorize problems using the essential information required to generate a solution. The *cues* reasoners use to select problem solutions appear to become more relevant to the solution as expertise increases.

Gains in ability to categorize problems by factors relevant to solution could be viewed as metaknowledge relevant to planning. Larkin (1983a, 1983b) argues that experts have planning knowledge not held by novices, knowledge which facilitates their problem solving. Experts in the Chi, Glaser, and Rees (1981) study appeared to spend a reasonable time in this sort of planning.

Experts appear to develop skill at metareasoning, or the ability to plan their problem-solving aproach as the result of experience (Larkin et al., 1980). Much research suggests that this knowledge is tacit. That is, experts have difficulty describing their own planning processes. An interesting question for researchers to investigate has been whether making this knowledge explicit fosters effective planning.

Planning becomes more important as individuals gain expertise based on increased knowledge (Larkin et al., 1980). In order to access a larger knowledge domain, experts need a procedure for selecting the appropriate information. As discussed previously cueing of solution procedures can be either effective or superficial. Gains in planning involve gains in recognizing which features of the problem to consider.

Role of Subject Matter Knowledge and Context. Logical reasoning occurs infrequently in problem solving, possibly because it is inextricably bound to the subject matter and context of the scientific problem (Carey, 1985; Griggs, 1983; Linn, 1983; Linn & Swiney, 1981). To investigate content effects, Linn and Swiney (1981) studied the "bending rods" task which was first introduced by Inhelder and Piaget (1958). Linn and Swiney established which variables in the bending rods problem the reasoner considered to be important for the solution. They then asked reasoners to conduct experiments using the bending rods apparatus and demonstrated that reasoners tend to control the variables which they think are important, illustrating the role of subject matter knowledge in problem solving.

Another demonstration of the role of subject matter knowledge comes from Tschirgi (1980), who differentiated *sensible reasoning* from Piagetian *logical reasoning*. Whereas Linn and Swiney (1981) investigated knowledge about the problem variables, Tschirgi investigated knowledge and beliefs about the experimental outcome. She asked elementary-age subjects to design experiments to investigate the effects of variables which influence certain outcomes, such as variables which influence how good a cake tastes. She found that, when designing experiments to determine what variables influence whether or not a cake tastes good, her respondents tended to confound their experiments. They designed their experiments in such a way that the resulting cake would definitely taste good. Tschirgi described this as sensible reasoning because the reasoners included in their experimental design the commonsense idea that a cake ought to taste good. These reasoners incorporated their expectations about the reasoning situation into their problem solutions. They expected that they were to achieve "good" outcomes rather than to really investigate the role of each variable.

The context in which problem solving takes place can also influence reasoning performance. Reasoners may perform differently in a school context from in a home context. Linn, de Benedictis, and Delucchi (1982) demonstrated the effect of context on reasoning by comparing a scientific context to a consumer context. Linn et al. (1982) found that reasoners tended to accept claims in advertisements. When Linn et al. (1982) asked reasoners to plan experiments to investigate whether these claims were true, reasoners generally designed relatively unrigorous investigations. They designed less rigorous investigations for the consumer context than for the scientific context. For example, reasoners controlled fewer variables in the advertising context than in the scientific context.

These results all point toward the need to include processing capacity, subject matter knowledge, and context in our view of problem solving. It seems reasonable to assume that metareasoning can become subject matter and context independent as a result of numerous experiences. Reasoners may initially fail to identify which information is subject matter specific and which is not. By solving many problems in different domains, expert reasoners come to be at least tacitly able to use the subject matter–independent procedures effectively in new problems (Clement, 1982). Curricula can make matter–independent features explicit and can also provide diverse examples which illustrate which problem-solving procedures generalize from one subject matter to another.

2. Intuitive Conceptions

It is helpful to expand our conceptualization of the initial state of the reasoner to include the intuitive conceptions of natural phenomena which learners construct. Recent research demonstrates that reasoners do hold intuitive conceptions of scientific phenomena. Intuitive conceptions are consistent ideas reliably held by the reasoner, which differ from scientific conceptions held by experts. Reasoners appear to construct a view of natural phenomena from personal experience guided by analogical reasoning which is reflected in alternative conceptions about all aspects of science. Interestingly, the alternative conceptions held about a given topic such as electricity generally fall into only a few categories (Cohen, Eylon, & Ganiel, 1983) and occur consistently in studies of different age respondents (Andersson and Karrquist, 1982; Driver, 1983).

An example of an intuitive conception occurs in reasoning about displaced volume (see Figure 1). Adolescent respondents, when asked to predict the relative amount of liquid that a submerged aluminum cube and a submerged steel cube of equal volume will displace, frequently respond that the heavier cube will displace more liquid (Linn, 1983). Close to 50% of 12- to 16-year-olds use an inaccurate rule based on weight for this problem (Linn & Pulos, 1983b; Pulos, de Benedictis, Linn, Sullivan, & Clement, 1982). When probed, reasoners explain that the weight of an object generally influences experimental outcomes such as how far an object rolling down an inclined plane hits another object. By analogy, they suggest, weight also influences displacement.

Other commonly observed intuitive conceptions include Aristotelian ideas about mechanics in general (Champagne, Klopfer, & Anderson, 1980; Wilkening, 1981) and about curvilinear motion in particular (Caramazza, McClosky, & Green, 1981; McClosky, Caramazza, & Green, 1980), conceptions of the earth as being round like a pancake (Nussbaum & Novick, 1976), and conceptions of electricity as a liquid (Driver & Erickson, 1983). Many of these intuitive conceptions are held by a large percentage of the population, including adults. Both Linn and Siegel (1983) and Stevens, Collins, and Goldin (1982) provide extensive lists of intuitive conceptions.

The universality of intuitive conceptions both within age cohorts and across the life span is noteworthy. Di Sessa (1981) analyzes conceptions about a series of natural phenomena and notes that the range of intuitive conceptions is small but that the frequency of responses which differ from those held by experts is high. Linn and Pulos (1983b) report that for certain balance-beam problems an additive rule is more commonly selected than the correct multiplicative rule. At least in theory, reasoners could choose from among a wide range of intuitive conceptions. In practice, many reasoners appear to construct the same intuitive conceptions.

In the case of predicting displaced volume, for example, the weight of the object is its salient feature for many reasoners. They use their subject matter knowledge about weight to develop their intuitive conception. They

1. Blocks *A* and *B* are the same size. Block *B* weighs more than Block *A*

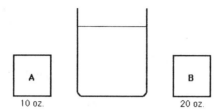

Which block will make the water go up higher?

    Block *A*

    Block *B*

    Both the same

2. Block *C* and *D* are the same size. Block *C* weighs more than Block *D*.

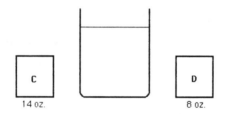

Which block will make the water go up higher?

    Block *C*

    Block *D*

    Both the same

Fig. 1.   Items from the predicting displaced volume task.

are much less likely to develop conceptions based on the shape of the object or on the material of the object. In addition, processing capacity may limit the range of conceptions, since reasoners may tend to select conceptions which have only a few variables rather than multiple variables and may tend to consider single variables rather than interacting variables to explain the outcome.

Acquisition of Intuitive Conceptions. Intuitive conceptions characterize the responses of scientists and nonscientists alike to a wide range of scientific problems. All reasoners appear to construct these conceptions. Factors which contribute to this situation include processing-capacity limitations, availability of alternatives, and lack of prerequisite knowledge.

Limited processing capacity, as defined previously, no doubt contributes to the development of intuitive conceptions in both scientists and nonscientists. When the conceptions of experts are too complicated to fit into the processing capacity of students or of adults who lack prerequisite knowledge, intuitive conceptions may emerge. Reasoners may acquire intuitive conceptions about scientific phenomena because instruction overloads their processing capacity and they are forced to select a subset of the presented information and use it to solve problems. For example, many have commented that students learn from textbook examples rather than from other information in textbooks.

Eylon and Helfman (1985) and Eylon and Reif (1984) investigated how reasoners use information in the text and in examples when learning physics. They found, consistently with other research (e.g., Mayer & Greeno, 1972), that students failed to learn from text alone, were able to solve problems similar to the examples they received, and tended to overgeneralize the examples they received to nonisomorphic problems, thereby performing rather poorly on nonisomorphic problems. Thus, respondents relied on the examples and appeared to pay little attention to the text which accompanied the examples. Students might have benefited from instruction which emphasized metaknowledge about testing isomorphisms between examples and new problems.

In a related study, Eylon (1979) demonstrated that instruction in *analogy formation* does help reasoners form conceptions. In her study, physics students received either (1) examples, (2) textbook descriptions of how to solve the problem, (3) instruction in how to test the effectiveness of an analogy between one problem and another, or (4) a combination of these. Her results suggested that instruction in how to test analogies helped learners form accurate conceptions. These results indicate that learners may benefit from explicit instruction in how to test the isomorphism between the problem and the example they choose, as will be discussed in the section on mechanisms of change.

Eylon (1979) and Eylon and Helfman (1985) illustrated one way that reasoners form intuitive conceptions. They showed that reasoners fail to learn from text and depend instead on the examples. By overgeneralizing examples to new problems, reasoners may gain additional ideas which differ from those held by experts.

These studies illustrate how reasoning progresses. Using analogies, reasoners can construct a view of a natural event with a limited amount of information. Reasoners with limited subject matter knowledge can use an analogical reasoning approach to attempt, often with success, to solve problems. The ability of reasoners to employ analogies to solve problems may convince observers that they are using subject matter knowledge which they actually have not acquired.

Analogical reasoning may provide a partial explanation for the low achievement test scores reported by NAEP and others. If reasoners employ analogies widely, as research suggests, then achievement tests which emphasize information as it is presented in the text may fail to measure most of what the learner acquires. These results are consistent with responses of physics instructors to the behavior of their pupils during problem-solving sessions: They are universally amazed at how *little* the students know about the subject matter (Larkin, 1981).

Power of Intuitive Conceptions. Intuitive conceptions tend to resist change. Reasoners do not easily abandon their points of view. These conceptions are a central part of the reasoner's initial state. For example, Smith (1980) reported an interview with an 8-year-old. The respondent indicated that wood floats and metal sinks. The interviewer asked what the local ferry boats were made of; the respondent said they were made of metal. Then the interviewer asked how the boats could float if they were made of metal. After some thought, the respondent replied, "I was wrong, the ferry boats are made of wood." This student denied an accurate recollection to maintain his conception about what floats and what sinks.

Research in the displaced-volume task described earlier revealed a similar response (Linn, 1983). One student, having predicting that the steel cube of the same volume as the aluminum cube would displace more water than the aluminum cube, was dismayed to observe that both displaced the same amount. He quickly accused the experimenter of cheating, saying, "You tricked me, you brought magic water."

Di Sessa (1983), studying adults' descriptions of what happens when the air intake valve of a vacuum cleaner is blocked, reported yet another example of respondents' altering their recollections to support their inaccurate conceptions. Di Sessa's respondents often accurately recollected that the motor went faster when the valve was blocked. However, those who used a "work" analogy based on the notion that the vacuum works harder when it has to pick up more dirt sometimes altered their recollection and responded that, after thinking it over, they thought the motor slowed down when the valve was blocked because it was not "working."

Insight from Philosophy of Science. In characterizing the state of the reasoner, Linn and Siegel (1983) argued that Lakatos's (1972) distinction between the *hard core of ideas* and the *protective belt of ideas* might have analogies with the system of intuitive conceptions which reasoners develop. Lakatos described the hard core of ideas in a given subject matter domain as those ideas which are unresponsive to data. In the history of science, scientists have persisted in believing the hard-core ideas, even when evidence contradicting these ideas was available. In contrast, Lakatos described the protective belt of ideas as consisting of ideas which are readily changed to defend the hard core.

Reasoners also appear to have ideas which resist change and ideas which are readily modified. In the examples we mentioned, reasoners changed ideas which they considered peripheral to their main argument and maintained their hard core of ideas. In the ferry boat example, the reasoner was willing to modify his recollection of what the ferry boat was made of in order to protect his hard-core idea that metal does not float. In the displaced-volume task example, the reasoner was willing to question the properties of water rather than give up his belief that weight influences displacement. In the vacuum cleaner example, reasoners were willing to modify their recollections of changes in the behavior of the motor in order to support their ideas about "work."

Evidence for the persistence of hard-core ideas in intuitive conceptions of scientific phenomena greatly enhance our understanding of the state of the reasoner. The reasoners' state includes not only the conceptions of scientific phenomena but also ideas about which aspects of the conceptions are central to the argument and which are peripheral. Reasoners hold on to some ideas which they appear to view as unalterable by data.

If students have ideas which they consider unalterable by data, science educators who provide excellent contradictions to students' alternative conceptions are likely to experience frustration. Even contradictions which are seemingly matched to the learners' initial state may fail to change the students' reasoning. Driver (1983) provided numerous examples of this frustration. It seems clear that intuitive conceptions characterized by a hard core of ideas are an important aspect of the state of the learner. Curriculum designers must incorporate this understanding into curriculum materials in order to enhance student understanding of scientific phenomena and avoid teacher frustration. Suggestions are offered in the section on mechanisms of change.

The analogy between Lakatos's philosophy of science and reasoners' intuitive conceptions can be pursued further. Lakatos (1972) has stressed that scientific thought progresses even when the hard core of ideas is later shown to be wrong. Lakatos differentiates between a progressing research program and a degenerating research program. According to Lakatos, a progressing research program is one which predicts novel facts. In contrast, a degenerating program fails to predict novel information. Lakatos shows that, in the history of science, research programs have been followed as long as they predict novel information, even though they also make false predictions.

Linn and Siegel (1983) suggested the value of an analogy between Lakatos's (1972) ideas about groups of scientists and our understanding of the behavior of individual learners. They proposed that the individual reasoner's performance in a given content domain can be characterized as following a progressing or a degenerating research program, depending on whether the reasoner's ideas can predict novel facts. Reasoners appear to find this criterion adequate as evidenced by the examples cited—predicting displaced volume and explaining the operation of a vacuum cleaner. Individuals appear to accept conceptions which account for some of the events in the content domain but not others. The metaknowledge which reasoners might use to test their ideas and decide whether their conception accounts for *enough* of the events they observe deserves serious attention in science curricula.

Multiple Conceptions. Reasoners often hold more than one conception for essentially the same phenomenon. By "the same phenomenon" is meant the actions and interactions of a set of variables. Reasoners seem to select different conceptions for events governed by essentially the same variables.

For example, in the problem of predicting displaced volume, when experimenters asked reasoners to predict the amount of sawdust displaced by styrofoam shapes buried in the sawdust, reasoners tended to pay less attention to the weight of the objects and more attention to the space that the objects take up (Sinclair, 1980). Presumably, in this situation, cues about the weight of the objects are less salient than they are when metal cylinders are immersed in water. Di Sessa (1983) found that physicists who reason accurately about the concept of work in solving textbook physics problems sometimes fail to apply their knowledge of that concept when confronted with his vacuum cleaner problem. Thus, selection of a conception is often *cued* by the subject matter and context of the problem presentation rather than by the essential variables. Reasoners may construct approaches for solving problems based on superficial features of the situation rather than on the essential elements of the problem. Educators can help students overcome this tendency by emphasizing the essential elements of problems and by presenting numerous examples in which the central features are the only consistencies between problems.

Extensive study of multiple conceptions for a problem with the same essential structure is found in the work of Wason and Johnson-Laird (1972) and Griggs and Cox (1982) on the selection task. In this task the subject matter appears to cue selection of a solution strategy. In the abstract content presentation, the reasoner is confronted with four cards, each with an A or B on one side and a 1 or 2 on the other side. The respondent is asked to turn over the card or cards which will test a rule. The rule is "If there is an A on one side, then there is a 2 on the other side." This problem is very difficult; even logicians have trouble with it. In contrast, Griggs and Cox used more readily understood subject matter. They prepared cards which indicated on one side whether the individual was drinking beer or coke and on the other side whether the individual was age 16 or age 22. Respondents were asked to indicate which card or cards they would turn over to test the rule "If the individual is drinking beer, then the individual must be over 21." This problem is considerably easier than the problem with abstract content. The subject matter in the drinking-age problem appears to cue selection of an approach based on reciprocity of age and beverage consumed, while the abstract condition appears to cue a form of conditional reasoning and to allow reasoners to spend time considering whether there might be an A on the other side of a card with a "1" on it.

Thus it appears that reasoners hold multiple conceptions for problems with the same underlying logical structure. The subject matter and context of a reasoning problem cues selection of a conception for viewing the problem and ultimately facilitates or inhibits solution of the problem.

3. Summary

The state of the reasoner, as emphasized in Piagetian theory, now requires elaboration. Subject matter knowledge and reasoning context interact with valid reasoning, casting doubt on the centrality of Piagetian reasoning strategies in student performance.

Perhaps the most important aspect of the state of the reasoner for curriculum developers is that reasoners generally come to science classes with well-developed ideas about natural phenomena referred to as alternative conceptions. These subject matter–specific ideas are strongly held and require creative response on the part of science educators.

Metareasoning strategies, or reasoning strategies which are independent of subject matter, constitute another important aspect of the state of the reasoner. Developing metareasoning skill, including skill in planning problem solutions and testing the effectiveness of possible solutions, offers promise as an objective of science instruction.

B. Mechanisms of Change

Mechanisms which govern changes in conceptions constitute a crucial but as yet largely unexplored area of research. Many have called for investigation of mechanisms of change in reasoning, although few have studied these mechanisms. This chapter refers to mechanisms of change as procedures or characteristics of the learning environment that lead to changes in the learner's conceptions of scientific phenomena.

Perhaps the most important issue in curriculum design concerns mechanisms governing changes in conception. As numerous unsuccessful training studies attest (e.g., Keating, 1979; Levin & Linn, 1977; Linn, 1980), the mechanisms which govern changes require greater clarification. All researchers considering mechanisms of change agree that an effective mechanism must take into consideration the initial state of the reasoner. As the discussion has illustrated, several aspects of the learner's initial state deserve serious consideration. First, any mechanism of change must consider the limitations of the learner's processing capacity. Second, the learner's subject matter–specific problem-solving strategies determine how he/she incorporates new information. Third, both the availability of mathematical reasoning strategies and the propensity to use them will influence performance. Fourth, the intuitive conceptions the learner brings to science class must be considered. If a learner has a conception for a particular problem, then mechanisms of change must address the hard core of ideas and the protective belt of ideas held by that learner. Since many questions about the state of the reasoner remain unanswered, investigations of mechanisms of change are largely speculative.

Historically, mechanisms of conceptual change have received limited attention. For example, Piagetian theory postulates assimilation and accommodation as the mechanisms of change. This theoretical perspective is far too vague to be employed in curriculum design. Another example is found in the many textbooks which implicitly assume that reasoning changes will result from the presentation of clearly integrated, logically presented subject matter material. Recent understandings about how reasoners construct views of natural phenomena and tenaciously defend them demonstrate that reasoners do not incorporate new information which is at variance with the conceptions they already hold. In fact, as suggested the prevalence of intuitive conceptions about much physical science subject matter may account for the low performance of students on tests such as the National Assessment of Educational Progress.

Whereas mechanisms of changing intuitive conceptions, especially those that are strongly held, have received limited attention from researchers, such mechanisms have been considered in philosophy of science. Philosophers of science have been concerned with the mechanisms which govern change in the reasoning of groups of scientists working in a particular knowledge domain. Although many of the concerns of philosophers of science focus on procedures used by groups of scientists to understand scientific phenomena, their studies raise issues that might also be addressed by researchers considering how to foster conceptual change in individuals or in classroom groups of students.

1. Elaboration of Subject Matter Knowledge

Frequently reasoners fail to solve problems because they lack relevant subject matter knowledge. An efficient mechanism of change is to elaborate subject matter knowledge as long as the new knowledge does not contradict hard core ideas. Reasoners then use available logical reasoning strategies in conjunction with the new subject matter knowledge to solve the problem. Champagne, Klopfer, and Gunstone (1982) have demonstrated how knowledge elaboration can result in successful physics problem solving. In another example, Linn, Clancey, Dalbey, Heller, and Reese (1983) investigated how reasoners learn to program in PASCAL. They found that reasoners frequently behave as if constructions using DO . . . UNTIL are equivalent to those using FOR . . . WHILE. However, reasoners change their ideas quickly when the differences between the two constructions are explained.

Processing Capacity. The learners' processing capacity places a constraint on the amount of information that can be considered at any one time. Instruction which teaches reasoners how to solve problems using their limited processing capacity has the potential for changing reasoning. Instruction which fails to consider the learners' processing capacity and presents so many conceptions that learners experience an overload of information cannot succeed and will tend to encourage formation of intuitive conceptions.

Knowledge Organization. To use subject matter knowledge, learners must be able to locate relevant information when solving problems. When new knowledge is taught through elaboration it is also possible to elaborate the organization of subject matter knowledge. Many have argued that a hierarchical organization of knowledge can facilitate learning.

An intervention study by Eylon and Reif (1984) illustrates the role of knowledge elaboration and of hierarchical knowledge organization in physics problem solving. Eylon and Reif compared performances of college students receiving one of three treatments. The *hierarchical treatment* provided knowledge at two levels of detail: an overview followed by detailed elaboration of the overview. The *single-level treatment* provided only the detailed elaboration of the problems. The *intensive single-level treatment* provided a double presentation of the single-level treatment. Eylon and Reif evaluated these treatments using *local* tasks which required no reorganization of the information in the detailed elaboration and *complex* tasks which required reorganization of the information in the detailed elaboration. All treatment groups performed equally well on local tasks. The researchers found that treatment had an effect and interacted with ability on complex tasks: High-ability students in the hierarchical and intensive single-level treatments out-performed those in the single-level treatment, and medium-ability students in the hierarchical treatment out-performed medium-ability students in the other treatments. Independent of treatment, low-ability students performed poorly, solving an average of fewer than 50% of the complex problems correctly. It appears that hierarchical information facilitates performance of medium-ability students, while high-ability students can infer the knowledge they need from information given at a single level. These results are congruent with those of Mayer (1979) for prose learning and show that the logical organization of knowledge in instruction influences performance.

In a second experiment, Eylon and Reif (1984) investigated the effect of two alternative hierarchical organizations of the same physics information. Their results were as expected: Subjects performed better on problems requiring the information emphasized in the hierarchical organization they received. These results are congruent with those of Shavelson (1973a, 1973b), who showed that reasoner's knowledge structures were the same as those which they encountered in the instructional materials.

Instruction emphasizing knowledge organization appears to influence problem solving because it makes the information relevant to solving a particular problem readily available to the learner. Thus Eylon and Reif (1984) demonstrated that hierarchical knowledge organizations which are congruent with the problem-solving situation result in better problem solving than irrelevant knowledge organizations.

If, as argued earlier, strategies for valid inference are strongly tied to subject matter knowledge, then instruction emphasizing both might be helpful. Linn, Clement, Pulos, and Sullivan (1982) investigated how instruction in problem solving and in subject matter knowledge influenced reasoning performance. The subject matter knowledge training consisted of five class sessions, adapted from the Health Activities Project (1980), on factors influencing blood pressure. All participants made substantial gains in knowledge about blood pressure. The problem-solving training consisted of a 40-minute individual session during which participants learned how to set up controlled experiments using familiar variables. The problem-solving training culminated in a requirement, met by each participant, to accurately state the controlling variables strategy in their own words. The training was evaluated by asking participants to design and criticize experiments about blood pressure and experiments about bending rods.

The blood pressure–subject matter knowledge training fostered good performance on problems with blood pressure subject matter. The problem-solving training combined with blood pressure–subject matter knowledge training further enhanced performance on problems with blood pressure subject matter and also fostered good performance on problems with bending rods subject matter.

Analysis of individual responses revealed that the blood pressure–subject matter knowledge training increased the number of variables each participant considered, while the problem-solving training increased the likelihood of participants' verbally producing the controlling-variables strategy to solve the problems. Furthermore, improved performance on problems with previously unfamiliar variables (concerning blood pressure) did not result from problem-solving training, but resulted only from blood pressure–subject matter training. Thus, Linn, Clement, Pulos, and Sullivan (1982) showed that subject matter and problem-solving training have somewhat separate roles in fostering effective performance.

In summary, as long as instruction does not question hard-core ideas as defined in the previous section or exceed processing capacity, reasoners' problem-solving effectiveness is likely to increase as a result of elaboration of subject matter knowledge. As the studies previously discussed suggest, this process is successful because training makes explicit the subject matter knowledge relevant to the problem solution. As these studies illustrate, subject matter knowledge, knowledge of the hierarchical relationships between subject matter concepts, and valid strategy knowledge can all lead to increased reasoning performance. As these studies also reveal, the determination of which knowledge will be relevant to which type of problem requires careful analysis.

2. Intuitive Conceptions

As discussed above, contradiction of reasoners' intuitive conceptions generally results in reasoners' protecting their hard core of ideas and altering their protective belt of ideas. Mechanisms which govern change in conceptions must respond to this situation.

Progressing Research Program. One response to contradiction is to modify some ideas while retaining others. Reasoners may protect their hard core of ideas by using their protective belt of ideas. Logical defense of the hard core of ideas has the potential for fostering what might be called a *progressing research program*. Reasoners following a progressing research program modify their ideas to account for contradictions and defend their hard core as long as it predicts *some* novel facts. For example, in the case of contradictions to ideas about predicting displaced volume, reasoners may consider variables associated with the size of the object, such as its height, width, circumference, and cross section. Second, reasoners may modify the criteria which govern application of ideas as a result of contradiction. Some reasoners choose not to focus on weight when the weight of the two solids is equal. Linn and Pulos (1983b) demonstrated that many solvers of the problem in predicting displaced volume had two categories of responses—one category for problems in which the weight of the two solids was equal and a second category for problems in which their weight was unequal. These reasoners differentiated a single weight-based conception of displacement into two conceptions. Thus, reasoners who protect their hard core of ideas may identify new variables and use them to partition the instances under which their hard-core ideas are invoked.

Cueing a New Solution. Another response to contradiction is governed by a mechanism called *cueing*. As discussed previously, reasoners may entertain several alternative conceptions for problems with the same essential features. The subject matter or other superficial information may cue the reasoner to invoke a certain conception. A change in reasoning could result if the cues which reasoners attend to are changed. The reasoner might then select a different conception. As noted earlier, Chi et al. (1980) demonstrated that experts use different cues from novices to solve the same problem. One way to enhance the likelihood of conceptual change would be to influence the cueing process.

Reasoners may identify *new* cues for selecting a solution when they respond to contradictions. When reasoners choose to apply an intuitive conception to only a limited number of the instances of a problem (such as only cases when weight is unequal), they are changing their ideas. Instruction which encourages learners to alter their protective belts might indirectly increase the importance accorded to a variable which could cue selection of a new solution strategy.

Evidence for cueing of solutions as a mechanism of change comes from a study by Linn, Delucchi, and de Benedictis (1984). Students received contradictions to their notions about the role of weight in predicting displaced volume. When students were asked to explain how they came to change their conceptions, many students who changed to a volume rule from a weight rule indicated that they had always believed in a volume rule and had not changed their ideas. These respondents may have selected a conception which they had available but which had not been cued previously. They had the information necessary to form an accurate volume-based rule for predicting displaced volume: They understood the principle of conservation of liquid, they knew that the volume of metal does not change when immersed in water, and they could add volumes together. The many contradictions to their weight rule may have cued an available but less salient conception based on volume.

Cueing can succeed when reasoners have alternative conceptions for the same problem. Thus, part of a cueing-based mechanism of change includes making sure the reasoner has some alternatives. Instruction which increases the pool of conceptions available to the reasoner may facilitate this process. For example, Burbules and Linn (1984) investigated the role of what they called *alternative generation* in fostering conceptual change. Alternative generation consisted, for example, of helping reasoners identify the variables and possible hypotheses about predicting displaced volume. After these had been identified, reasoners then responded to contradictions about their weight rules for predicting displaced volume. For some respondents, the alternative generation activity facilitated conceptual change. Presumably reasoners are more likely to change their conceptions when they have additional options. In many cases, as in the Burbules and Linn (1984) study of predicting displaced volume, in which reasoners spontaneously generated a volume rule after numerous contradictions, the alternatives already exist. In other cases, however, reasoners may not be aware of alternative conceptions for a particular problem. In these cases instruction which emphasizes alternative generation may be effective.

3. Metareasoning

Research suggests that expert problem solvers use metareasoning skills to solve problems more effectively than novices. This is consistent with the theoretical model of planning put forth by Wilensky (1983) and with writing on planning by Hayes-Roth (1980). One mechanism of change that would foster problem solving would be to increase metareasoning about selection of problem solutions. Increased metareasoning skill might facilitate conceptual change.

Clancey's (1983) research on medical problem solving stresses the centrality of metareasoning in problem solving. He postulated that what he described as "weak associations between observed data and bottom line conclusions" controls problem solving. He suggested that reasoners engage in testing and data acquisition until they are satisfied. The criteria for the termination of testing determine the efficacy of the solution. Clancey argued that a large body of subject matter knowledge is used to test whether the diagnosis is correct after the diagnosis is hypothesized. Elstein, Shulman, and Sprafka (1978) in their book on medical problem solving lent support to this observation by demonstrating that expert physicians consider only a few diagnoses for a given set of symptoms (although many diagnoses could be considered) and then test their ideas. Similarly, Chase and Simon (1973a, 1973b) revealed that chess experts have a repertoire of "patterns" of chess moves. Expert chess problem solvers first use these patterns to determine a few alternative moves, and then they use their subject matter knowledge to test the alternatives more thoroughly. Thus, good problem solvers appear to have both the ability and the inclination to test initial problem solutions. Testing allows them to discard poor ideas and to pursue good ones.

Good problem solvers have good planning skills. Researchers such as Reif (1986), Larkin et al. (1980), Reif and Heller (1982), and Champagne, Klopfer, and Gunstone (1982) have investigated use of planning in solving mechanics problems. Larkin modeled the problem-solving procedures used by experts and novices. Her model, based on protocol analyses, provides an explicit definition of planning, as she defined it, and suggests that experts engage in more planning than novices. If planning can be explicitly taught, reasoners may spend more time planning and, as a result, solve problems more effectively. However, as Linn (1985) reported, instruction intended to foster planning may be resisted by students. In contrast, Clancey, in teaching PASCAL, found that requiring planning fostered problem solving.

Further evidence for the role of metareasoning in conceptual change comes from Clement (1982), who asked expert scientists to solve physical science problems outside their domain of expertise. These reasoners used metareasoning strategies to test their ideas. They explicitly described both the ideas they used to investigate the problems and the mechanisms they used for testing their ideas. For example, one of Clement's subjects, trying to develop an analogy between the expansion of a spring and the flexibility of a rod, talked about the spring as being composed of a series of very short rods. After testing, he abandoned this idea and sought a different one which was based on the amount of material in the spring.

Planning may be related to the cueing process described above. The planning processes which experts appear to use more than novices may include determining which cues should be used for selecting a solution. Novices are far less likely to engage in such planning, possibly because they may have fewer candidates for cues. Instruction which increases alternatives and encourages use of the metareasoning processes of planning and testing might facilitate conceptual change.

Evolution of Ideas. Curriculum materials can help learners by encouraging them to consider more cues before selecting a solution and by helping them generate additional conceptions for a problem. Until learners have experienced a reasonable number of problems, they will lack criteria for differentiating relevant from irrelevant cues.

Philosopher of science Toulmin (1972) applied an evolutionary metaphor to the survival of ideas. Toulmin argued that the fittest ideas survive while others eventually become extinct. Evidence that reasoners entertain multiple conceptions for the same problem suggests that the survival of certain conceptions could be described by the same metaphor. Refinement of the metareasoning strategy of testing could be seen as fostering selection of the most effective cues. Instructional procedures which emphasize the diversity of views held by reasoners and which encourage reasoners to test their views would seem to foster the evolution of better ideas.

4. Summary

In summary, mechanisms which govern changes in reasoning are available but require better understanding. Mechanisms which elaborate subject matter knowledge succeed in extending the subject matter understanding of reasoners as long as they are logically consistent with the reasoners' view. These mechanisms fail to change strongly held conceptions. Contradiction, the most widely used mechanism, also generally fails to change strongly held ideas. Instead, a mechanism based on cueing of solution strategies, combined with increased metareasoning skill, offers promise.

To help students construct productive science concepts, researchers concur that covering a few science topics in depth rather than many in a fleeting fashion will have a more lasting impact. Researchers and educators alike note that students can "learn more by learning less." Such coverage makes it possible for instructors to link new ideas to related ones and establish which ideas are encompassing and which are specific.

C. Delivery of Instruction

Delivery of instruction refers to all the characteristics of instructional programs, including the subject matter selected and the methods for presenting the subject matter to students. Historically, there has been controversy between *direct instruction* and *discovery learning,* with direct instruction referring to the explicit presentation of facts and processes in science, and discovery learning referring to the presentation of opportunities for learners to discover important scientific principles by interacting with scientific material.

Delivering instruction which reflects both the initial state of the reasoner and the known mechanisms of conceptual change will greatly enhance student learning. Identification of initial states and mechanisms of change suggests how instruction should be designed; the mode of delivery of scientific information in science classes requires sensitivity to the response of the learner. Even the best instruction will fail if the learner is uninterested and resists learning.

1. Direct and Discovery Learning

A main controversy in science education has focused on the advantages of direct versus discovery-oriented instruction (Welch, 1979). The mechanism of change referred to as *elaboration* characterizes direct instruction, and much of the recent textbook material in science education has taken this approach. As previously emphasized, reasoners *can* acquire subject matter knowledge, knowledge about hierarchical relationships among information, and knowledge of valid strategies from elaboration or direct instruction. Reasoners can efficiently incorporate this information into their knowledge structure as long as it is consistent with the conceptions that they hold about the problems being studied and does not exceed their processing capacity. Direct instruction may not be successful when the information being presented contradicts information held by the reasoner, because changing strongly held conceptions requires other instructional procedures.

The direct instruction approach often treats the act of scientific discovery as a unique, unusual, and infrequent event. Students learning science, however, are engaged constantly in the act of discovery, in that they are discovering for themselves principles which were previously discovered by other scientists. Students in a direct instruction format frequently fail to appreciate the analogy between their own acts of discovery in science learning and the acts of discovery in the history of science. They may find science boring and irrelevant. They may see science as an accumulation of information and fail to learn the metareasoning skills of planning and testing.

Discovery learning, in contrast to direct instruction, encourages students to figure out scientific principles on their own. Discovery learning is frequently associated with a hands-on approach in which students can conduct experiments in order to identify scientific principles. Understanding of what factors cue selections of conceptions for scientific phenomena (as discussed in the section on mechanisms of change) may result. Students are likely to use and refine testing skills. The most frequent criticism of discovery learning is that it is inherently time consuming. Obviously a student using only discovery learning would complete his or her education prior to reaching any modern scientific understanding. On the other hand, discovery learning is often exciting and can result in students' gathering information which they personally find useful. Such learners are likely to feel *responsible* for their learning and motivated to form accurate conceptions.

Although discovery learning is inefficient for imparting large amounts of information, it is potentially the best approach for helping students gain metareasoning skills and deep understanding. In discovery learning, students get practice in selecting approaches to problems. They often get feedback showing that their approaches are unsuccessful, and they then seek a different approach until they find a solution to the problem. Thus, the students actively practice the skills embodied in planning for the solution of a problem. They experience the process of generating alternatives, testing them, generating more alternatives, and testing again. They may generate the alternatives essential for conceptual change, as emphasized in the section on mechanisms of change. They do this in an independent and autonomous fashion, which is, therefore, likely to be available when solving naturally occurring problems.

Optimal instruction probably includes a balance between direct and discovery learning. Researchers have referred, for example, to *directed discovery,* in which reasoners are directed to engage in discovery learning in areas in which they are most likely to encounter experiences which change their alternative conceptions and increase their understanding of scientific discovery. Burton and Brown (1982) suggested that new technological tools such as computer tutors might provide more efficient presentation of directed-discovery experiences than has been possible in the past. Papert in *Mindstorms* (1980) stressed that computer learning environments such as LOGO allow reasoners to rapidly develop ideas which would take years to develop in traditional classroom situations. Linn, Fisher, Dalbey, Mandinach, and Beckum (1982) suggested that the precise and interactive nature of the computer learning environment fostered development of planning skills.

In contrast, attempts to validate these suggestions about LOGO or to implement discovery-learning experiences (Leron, 1983; Linn, 1980, 1985; Pea and Kurland, 1984) have suggested that the picture is considerably more complex. Undirected discovery, as numerous educators have documented, infrequently yields the sort of understanding which educators would prefer. In the history of science, when large numbers of scientists investigated problems, only a small number of discoveries resulted; in classrooms, when a large number of students investigate scientific phenomenon, very frequently only a small number of discoveries result.

For example, LOGO offers students the opportunity to discover how to solve problems using a computer. Some users, however, appear to give the computer haphazard instructions and to be pleased when things happen on the screen. These users fail to benefit from the precise feedback available because they do not have precise expectations. They learn that the software responds, but they do not learn how to get the computer to solve their own problems. Furthermore, they fail to use the metareasoning skill of testing their problem solution and responding to feedback.

The design and impact of directed discovery requires careful thought. Students may avoid discovery and simply enjoy the environment. Although directed discovery can attempt to make students focus on discovering ideas which the instructor knows are important, these may be discoveries of no interest to the learner. Students who "suffer" through undirected discovery and identify a principle which eluded them at first sometimes gain insights which do not come when directed discovery is implemented (Salomon, 1979; Snow, 1976). Furthermore, procedures for directing students to gain the most useful insights are not well established. To better understand this dilemma, this chapter considers delivery of instruction in conjunction with the learners' processing capacity, subject matter knowledge, intuitive conceptions, and metareasoning.

2. Processing Capacity

A series of studies have emphasized that processing capacity constrains reasoning. Direct instruction can respond to this situation by presenting information that does not exceed the processing capacity of the learner. Case (1975) illustrated procedures for presenting subject matter knowledge and conceptual understanding within the capacity of the learner.

Discovery-learning environments may foster construction of conceptions that differ from those held by experts because limited processing capacity constrains how much information the student considers. Guided discovery learning can address this problem by encouraging learners to consider relevant information and avoid irrelevant information. Intelligent tutoring systems which attempt to model the reasoning processes of the learner (e.g., Sleeman & Brown, 1982) might go further and provide specific contradictions to unproductive intuitive conceptions as well as encourage consideration of other options for problem solution. Thus one role for guided discovery is to foster effective use of limited processing capacity.

3. Subject Matter Knowledge

Subject matter knowledge is an important element in physical science instruction. Direct instruction is quite successful in imparting superficial subject matter knowledge as long as the knowledge does not contradict intuitive conceptions already held by the learner. Some learners, however, resist this form of instruction. Most learners forget what they learn by memorization because they fail to understand the implications of the information.

The question is what and how much to teach. One hypothesis to explain the decline in science achievement tests scores is that teachers require students to memorize unintegrated bits of information rather than helping them learn to use information to solve problems. As scientific knowledge proliferates, information selection becomes a bigger and bigger issue. It might be argued that reasoners will benefit more from instruction in procedures for locating information than in acquisition of a large number of facts, that they will learn more by learning less. Thus, in deciding which subject matter knowledge to impart, instructional designers need to consider the availability of the information in some resource accessible to the learner and the skills needed to use the information.

As a number of studies previously reported suggest, the organization of subject matter knowledge is critical for later information retrieval (Eylon, 1979; Eylon & Reif, 1984). Direct instruction in knowledge organization as reflected in the studies of Eylon and Reif (1984) can be successful. Shavelson (1973b) argued that learners acquire knowledge structures which the teacher or text presents. Thus, a component of direct instruction can and should be an explicit emphasis on organization of subject matter knowledge.

One feature which differentiates high- and low-ability students is their capacity to organize on their own the knowledge presented. A number of studies comparing high- and low-ability students suggest that high-ability students often impose their own organization on knowledge, whereas medium- and low-ability students demonstrably benefit from having a knowledge organization presented to them (Doyle, 1983), Thus, to serve medium-ability students, instructional delivery should emphasize knowledge organization. On the other hand, high-ability students either may not benefit from instruction emphasizing knowledge organization or may have a limited learning experience because the imposed knowledge structure prevents them from developing their own (Snow, 1976).

4. Intuitive Conceptions

As discussed previously, reasoners construct a view of natural phenomena which they bring to science classes. Intuitive conceptions are an important element of physical-science-knowledge acquisition which can be featured in instruction. Individual learners construct conceptions before they receive science instruction and are able to learn to test these conceptions in a discovery environment. Instruction can capitalize on alternative conceptions by asking students to compare their ideas. The learners' metaknowledge about problem solving may increase as a result of such discussion.

In the attempt to change strongly held intuitive conceptions, direct instruction, even with concrete examples of contradiction, may well fail. The examples of ferry boats and magic water cited earlier illustrated that contradiction is not sufficient to change strongly held ideas. Mechanisms of change based on the availability of alternatives and on cueing can be facilitated by guided discovery learning and depth of coverage of science topics. Effective instruction must offer optimal alternatives for the learner and must encourage students to change the cues used to select problem solutions.

To provide reasoners with alternatives to their own ideas, instructors can have students compare their ideas about the same phenomenon (Lockhead, 1985; Webb, 1985). A study of predicting displaced volume by Burbules and Linn (1984) revealed that learning often occurs when two students are asked to resolve differences between their conceptions. Similarly, group instruction methods demonstrated by Nussbaum and Novick (1982) illustrated the advantage of student discussion. When learners are confronted with the ideas of their peers, they frequently engage in negotiations which result in modifications of their own alternative conceptions.

To change cues used to solve problems, guided-discovery activities which emphasize new cues are useful. For example, in one study, contradictions to predicting displaced volume were not sufficient to change the cues reasoners used, so in transfer items they reverted to previous ideas (Burbules & Linn, 1984). In another study (Linn, Clement, Pulos, & Sullivan, 1982), students learned both alternatives and new cues and succeeded in acquiring new conceptions.

5. Metareasoning

The ultimate objective in fostering conceptual change is to instill in learners the ability to reason about their reasoning process. This ability allows reasoners to test their intuitive conceptions and to understand the processes which they use to select conceptions. Direct instruction, to facilitate metaknowledge about reasoning, must require students to review and revise their ideas.

It appears extremely difficult to teach students metareasoning skills which they can transfer to new knowledge domains. One problem might be that students cannot separate the problem-specific information from the strategies they are using—strategies that are actually independent of content and context—because those strategies seem always closely bound to the subject matter knowledge. Thus students may have difficulty recognizing metareasoning strategies. One approach to fostering meta-knowledge appears to be to provide numerous instructional experiences in a variety of subject matter domains and to continuously point out metareasoning strategies. This approach might help students recognize the metareasoning strategies which they have acquired.

Discovery learning can potentially encourage development of metareasoning skill. Reasoners probably construct intuitive conceptions in informal learning environments which resemble discovery-learning settings. Given appropriate metareasoning skills, learners can also discover the inadequacy of their conceptions by seeking feedback. Given the tenacity with which learners hold on to their intuitive conceptions, however, unless discovery-learning settings are augmented with some instruction in metareasoning it may take considerable time before learners recognize that their alternative conceptions fail to predict novel events. If classroom instruction which involves discovery also recognizes that intuitive conceptions have frequently been acquired and that the best approach to a particular problem may be cueing learners to select solution strategies, then the students may gain metareasoning skill.

6. Summary

In summary, direct instruction and discovery learning both have a place in the science education curriculum. Discovery learning acknowledges the importance of metareasoning skill and encourages students to become autonomous learners. In contrast, direct instruction can provide students with the large body of well-integrated scientific knowledge required by those who are to make expert contributions to scientific fields. Combining discovery learning and direct instruction can provide a balance. Overemphasis of either side will lead to incomplete understanding of scientific problem solving and ultimately will detract from the important societal objective of providing scientifically literate as well as scientifically expert individuals.

D. Equity of Educational Outcomes

Concern with equity of educational outcomes has permeated American education and is a tenet of the constitution. Thomas Jefferson stated, "I know no safe depository of the ultimate power of the society but the people themselves; and if we think them not enlightened enough to exercise their control with a wholesome discretion, the remedy is not to take it from them but to inform their discretion." Initially this dictum was interpreted as a mandate for providing the same educational opportunities for all segments of society. With increased educational and psychological research came the realization that equitable outcomes may result when different students receive different forms of instruction (Cronbach & Snow, 1977). This realization has led psychological researchers to investigate the conditions under which different learners are likely to master a particular subject matter area.

Concern for equity of educational outcomes includes consideration of appropriate outcomes for individual learners as well as consideration of appropriate levels of societal attainment. Thus we are concerned both with the attainments of individuals and with the distribution of those attainments across groups in society. Of particular concern is the distribution of proficiency in science across males and females and across minority groups.

Curriculum design plays an important role in fostering equity of educational outcomes. Psychological research offers some insights into the means by which curriculum designers can have impact on educational equity.

1. Levels of Achievement

Science-knowledge attainment is declining and is distributed unequally. Some variability is useful; other variability is undesired and undesirable.

As an example of the general decline, it has been noted that recently a dwindling number of individuals have become expert or scientifically literate in physical science. Of special concern has been a decline in achievement among the most able students (Branscomb, 1983; Franz, Aldridge, & Clard, 1983).

The other concern is the distribution of science knowledge. Although differences in science knowledge between males and females and between high and low socioeconomic groups are often documented (Chipman, Brush, & Wilson, 1985; Miller, Suchner, & Voelker, 1980), they are not readily explained. Research reports that males have greater expertise than females in science and that those from high socioeconomic groups have greater science achievement than those from low socioeconomic groups. (Linn, & Petersen, 1985a, 1986; Stage, Kreinberg, Eccles (Parsons), & Becker, 1985). This inequitable distribution of science knowledge has implications for vocational success: The segments of the population which, as a group, achieve less in science are also likely to acquire fewer highly paid science-related positions.

Both the decline in achievement and the inequitable distribution of knowledge present potential dangers to society. Those who lack scientific literacy may become disenchanted with science and thus not encourage the achievements of others. Worse, individuals may come to fear scientific and technological advances and interfere with the acceptance of new ideas and of new technologies.

Role of Experience. An important factor contributing to the unequal distribution of science knowledge among precollege students is unequal *experience* with physical science–based activities. Such experiences seem essential for fostering metareasoning strategies. Of the potential explanations for inequality, difference in experience is the most readily addressed by educational programs.

A variety of research documents different levels of experience with science. In general, females have less experience with science than do males (Linn & Petersen, 1986; Petersen, 1982). In informal settings, females are less likely to visit science centers, to have science-related hobbies, or to engage in science-related activities with their parents. In school settings, females are less likely than males to participate in advanced mathematics and science courses (Armstrong, 1979). Economically advantaged youngsters are more likely to participate in informal learning experiences in science than are economically disadvantaged youngsters. For example, the economically advantaged are more likely to visit science museums, to have science-related activities and books in their homes, and to attend science camps (Estavan, 1983). Similarly, the economically advantaged are more likely to pursue mathematics and science courses at advanced levels (Armstrong, 1979).

As one might expect, experience with science-related activities is linked to science achievement. For example, Linn and Pulos (1983a, 1983b) found that a background of courses in mathematics and science was the most important factor influencing the performance of students tested on Piagetian science-related reasoning problems. (Other factors measured included three aspects of spatial ability and four aspects of general ability.) Although causal relationships between all the varied science experiences and ultimate science achievement have not been well established, the correlation between courses in science and science achievement is reasonably high.

Role of Ability. It has been suggested, but not substantiated, that gender differences in science performance may be influenced by gender differences in certain abilities (e.g., Benbow & Stanley, 1980). Spatial ability is the most commonly mentioned factor, but no mechanism linking spatial ability and scientific reasoning has been established.

Linn and Petersen (1985b) conducted a "meta-analysis" of gender differences in spatial ability. They compared the types of spatial ability which showed gender differences to the types of science tasks which showed gender differences. They found that gender differences were observed primarily in forms of spatial ability not commonly associated with science achievement. In particular, they found some gender differences in the ability to estimate how nearly horizontal or vertical was a rod in a tilted picture frame (the Rod and Frame Test) and in the ability to rapidly rotate a figure through space in a task called *mental rotations*. On mental rotations very few subjects make errors in selecting the correct alternative although there is reasonable variability in the amount of time taken to select an alternative. In contrast, Linn and Petersen found almost no gender differences on tasks which require the analytic ability to combine spatially presented information in solving complex problems (called *spatial visualization tasks*). Thus gender differences in spatial ability were most common on tasks which required specialized spatial skills and were least common on tasks which required the sort of analytic abilities used in science problem solving. The speculation that gender differences in spatial ability might account for gender differences in science problem solving is not supported.

Role of Interest. The teaching of science may create unnecessary *barriers* to participation for some students. In particular, emphasis on mathematics or the "scientific method" may dissuade some students from participating, and irrelevant curricula may dissuade others. Science curriculum designers will encourage the participation of as wide a range of students as possible if no artificial barriers are included.

Recently, a number of researchers (e.g., Ridgeway, 1983; Rowe, 1983) have called on curriculum developers to carefully reconsider mathematics requirements for precollege science instruction. Scientists point out that important science content can be taught without mathematics, thus increasing the number of potential students for science courses. If mathematics is not a prerequisite for learning science content, then making mathematics a barrier may artificially dissuade students from the study of science. Furthermore, students who study science in courses requiring limited mathematics may come to recognize the importance of mathematics and may ultimately study mathematics because they need the information to continue their study of science.

Many individuals have come to believe that science is identified with the scientific method of valid inference rather than with important discoveries and creative insights. The emphasis on logical reasoning in science may create an unnecessary barrier to participation in science. To avoid this barrier, curriculum designers are encouraged to capitalize on the nature of scientific discovery. Curricula which point out the analogy between the student's mastery of new material and the scientist's mastery of new problems will do a great deal towards broadening the students' view of science.

In summary, differential experience is the most readily addressed explanation for inequality in science achievement. Curriculum designers can, in part, remedy differential experience by providing curricula which encourage all students to participate in science-related experiences. Modification of science curricula to encourage more students to participate in entry-level courses and to ensure that those courses are relevant to learners would certainly help.

2. Desired Outcomes

The desired outcomes from precollege science education are difficult to establish. Much has been written on the nature of scientific literacy (e.g., National Commission on Excellence, 1983; National Science Board, 1983). A policy on equitable science attainment must include consideration of the distribution of knowledge in society, of the needs for public information in a democracy, and of individual needs for satisfaction in vocational and personal activities. Furthermore, implementation of such policies is constrained by our limited understanding of mechanisms governing change in reasoning. All of these concerns occur in conjunction with rapid proliferation of science knowledge and with rapid technological advances.

Of particular concern has been the desire to encourage individuals to become expert in science. The National Commission on Excellence in Education has suggested that we greatly increase the number of science courses required in high school and modify the content to better serve society. As the quote from Jefferson eloquently stated, democracy cannot function without an informed public. The best assurance of intelligent decision making in science policy comes from informing the public so that they have sufficient knowledge to participate in these decisions. Curricula must, however, be relevant to the needs of learners if the public is to become "informed." Current materials seem unsuited to this task. More instruction using available materials is unlikely to achieve the desired learning society. Deeper coverage of a few topics is much more promising than fleeting coverage of many.

Rapid Technological Advance. Rapid scientific advance is a major factor in the growth and development of modern nations. Our science curricula need to encourage some individuals to participate in this important technological progress and others to foster their achievements. Science curricula can prepare individuals to cope with rapid change in science knowledge. Only if these changes are welcomed and encouraged can we expect to create a society which takes pride in the scientific accomplishments of its experts and continues to produce such experts. Citizens are repeatedly asked to participate in policy decisions concerning new scientific advances such as genetic engineering or computerized record keeping. Furthermore, many jobs require employees to change functions with the advent of new technology. Science curricula that prepare individuals to cope with these advances are needed.

Many students complete their last science course in about the ninth grade; their knowledge is likely to be out of date by the time they complete high school. As the popularity of recent magazines such as *Science 86, Discover,* and *High Technology* has revealed, individuals in our society recognize that they need to maintain their expertise in science as knowledge advances and technologies are refined. Our educational programs need to pave the way for this continuing educational activity. Science curricula must not only prepare students to deal with current science information but also instill in them both the interest and the ability to cope with new advances in scientific knowledge.

Individual satisfaction from the study of science often results when individuals can see the advantages of their learning in the solving of real-world problems. An example is cardiopulmonary resuscitation, which has been widely taught and has the potential for increasing societal health. In addition, science courses provide information about hazards such as dangerous chemicals and about the optimal responses to hazards, such as the use of appropriate antidotes. The relevance of such learning for students is clear and may encourage participation in science courses.

In summary, the preferred scientific accomplishments for reasoners in our society are difficult to pinpoint, but some important considerations can be identified. First, science curricula can alert students to the wide range of options available for gathering scientific information such as periodicals, science centers, and computerized data bases. Second, since our society is experiencing rapid change in scientific knowledge and frequent breakthroughs in physical science understanding, it is important to prepare individuals to solve new real-world problems as they arise. Third, to foster personal satisfaction and societal well-being, science instruction can provide information in areas such as health and safety, which are relevant to the individual. Fourth, instruction which introduces new technologies and new advances can emphasize the job opportunities in these areas and thus encourage participation in science-related vocations.

3. Procedures for Achieving Equity

Perhaps the single most effective way to foster equitable outcomes from science instruction is to encourage effective instruction. All learners profit from good teaching. Those who have difficulty may profit *only* from good instruction. Others may learn in spite of mediocre instruction.

Different forms of instruction may be required to bring different learners to the same level of achievement. In particular, individuals who lack experience in science may need instruction which provides that experience. Some learners may require discovery learning while others may require a great deal of explicit instruction. Research on aptitude–treatment interaction is central to equity of educational outcomes (Cronbach & Snow, 1977).

For example, a dilemma in using elaboration as a mechanism of change to achieve equity of outcomes concerns the role of explicitness. Explicit instruction concerning how to solve a scientific problem often results in excellent problem solving but may not generalize to other related problems and may not be recalled if the problem is encountered at a later time. For some learners, explicit instruction may be counterproductive. As Doyle (1983) reveals in a comprehensive review, high-ability learners are likely to learn more and to retain it for a longer period of time if they are required to discover the solution to problems on their own. In contrast, some students may not be able to discover these solutions on their own and are likely to profit from explicit instruction in how to solve the problems. Curriculum designers using formative evaluation activities might find it particularly useful to pay attention to the role of explicitness as it interacts with general ability.

Reasoners who hold intuitive conceptions about an area require different forms of instruction from those who hold incomplete conceptions. Great inequities can result if elaboration is used for all learners when some of these learners hold intuitive conceptions and therefore fail to benefit from elaboration. In order for instruction to achieve equity of educational outcomes, careful diagnosis of the initial state of the learner is essential, and instruction which matches the learner's initial state is needed.

4. Summary

In summary, science curriculum design can play a role in the achievement of equity in science learning. Curricula which take into consideration the existing achievements of reasoners have greater potential for bringing all reasoners to appropriate achievement at the end of their schooling.

To achieve equity of educational outcomes, it is especially important to insure that students do not avoid the study of science because of artificial barriers. Barriers such as advanced mathematics requirements or emphasis on the "scientific method"—barriers which are not central to expertise in science—should be carefully reviewed. Precollege science curricula have as a primary purpose the presentation of scientific information that will serve reasoners throughout the life span. In addition, they have the purpose of enticing students to study science. If these courses succeed, they will greatly enhance the scientific literacy of our society.

Science curricula which prepare students to deal with advances in science throughout their life span need to emphasize metareasoning skills. These skills will enable students to become autonomous learners. One vehicle for insuring that reasoners continue to incorporate new advances in science into their reasoning is the public science center. These centers and other sources of science information can help to remedy intuitive conceptions about new advances in scientific phenomena and can ultimately create a citizenry educated to deal intelligently with science policy issues.

IV. CONCLUSIONS AND IMPLICATIONS

The "rising tide of mediocrity" described in the report of the National Commission on Excellence in Education (1983) must be reversed. To substitute excellence for mediocrity a change in both the quality and the quantity of instruction is required. Our nation's schools can create a learning society and can teach the "new basics." Such a change requires a concerted and thoughtful effort at curriculum reform. The emerging science of science education can have a lasting impact on science curriculum design provided that recent research findings are considered by those developing the curricula.

Schooling is a complicated interdependent combination of forces. To achieve lasting change in education, it is necessary to influence the curriculum, the teachers, the students, the administration, the community, and the political decision makers who set policy and provide school funding. Here we focus specifically on curriculum design. In order for modifications of curriculum programs to have an impact on students, however, all aspects of schooling must be considered.

A. Qualitative Change in Science Curriculum

Recent psychological research suggests that qualitative changes in science curricula will be effective. Science instruction can encourage students to be autonomous learners. In particular, it is suggested that emphasis on deeper coverage of topics and on discovery learning in the design of curricula will produce a larger number of citizens and scientists who appreciate acts of discovery and who understand some of the phenomena which contribute to scientific creativity and insight.

Discovery plays an important role in scientific problem solving and is especially relevant to the solution of everyday scientific problems which learners are likely to encounter after they have completed their last science course. Individuals who have the capability of intelligently employing metareasoning strategies to solve naturally occurring real-world problems will meet the demands of the National Commission on Excellence for a learning society.

For example, to achieve a learning society, instruction can emphasize that contradiction is not sufficient to change the conceptions held by individuals. Reasoners who are themselves aware that contradictions will not necessarily change their intuitive conceptions are better able to learn from new experiences.

Autonomous learners can gain additional information after they have completed their last science courses. Instruction which emphasizes discovery of new ideas, which helps learners gain feedback about their ideas, and which encourages them to assess their own conceptions is likely to produce citizens who continue to learn in the future.

B. Quantity of Science Instruction

As the preceding discussion of psychological research illustrates, reasoners come to science classes with conceptions about natural phenomena which are relatively resistant to change. Without intensive and innovative educational efforts, these intuitive conceptions are likely to persist into adulthood. It is clear that to change conceptions already held by individuals requires a reasonable amount of instructional time and deep coverage of science topics. In the past, science education has not received sufficient time or deep enough coverage to reliably modify the intuitive conceptions held by learners. An increase in the quantity of science instruction seems appropriate in light of the proliferation of science knowledge and in light of our increased understanding of how reasoners change their conceptions.

Mathematics instruction not only takes up a great portion of precollege instruction time but also involves a reasonable amount of repetition of the major concepts involved. For example, students are introduced to division first with whole numbers without remainders, then with whole numbers with remainders, then with fractions, etc. Thus the main concept of division is presented many times in the curriculum. Students who initially have intuitive conceptions about division ultimately overcome those misconceptions. In contrast to mathematics instruction, science instruction frequently lacks repetitiveness. Science instructors often introduce a concept and assume that students have acquired it without either checking to see if that is the case or offering an extension of the concept in a new domain in subsequent instruction. It would seem useful to intensify the science curriculum in order to emphasize a small number of conceptions and to present those conceptions in a variety of domains. In this way, intuitive conceptions might eventually be replaced by conceptions held by expert scientists.

Thus, both the quality and the quantity of science instruction need to be modified in order to respond to the crisis in science education. Qualitatively, science instruction could incorporate a deeper emphasis on the problem-solving processes which characterize scientific discovery in a single domain. Quantitatively, science instruction could increase the intensity and frequency with which science concepts are presented in the curriculum.

C. Implementation of New Curricula

Advances in psychological research reveal ideas which generally resonate with the knowledge of expert science teachers. The most thoughtful teachers will have expertise which reflects the findings of recent psychological research and prompts them to choose curricula based on these findings.

As recent psychological research reveals, expertise is not always accompanied by explicit understanding of the procedures which are used to display that expertise. Many expert teachers may be unaware of the procedures they use to achieve educational outcomes. They may have tacit knowledge of their expertise which has not been made explicit. An important approach for incorporating the findings of recent psychological research into the practice of teachers is to encourage expert teachers to make their expertise explicit and then to relate the explicit reports of those expert teachers to relevant psychological investigations. Some successful professional development programs such as the Bay Area Writing Project (Gray & Mayers, 1978) employ this approach.

Teachers who have conceptions about educational practice which differ from those of expert teachers are likely to hold them tenaciously, just as students hold intuitive conceptions of scientific phenomena. The same notions which apply to changing students' conceptions of scientific phenomena can also be applied to changing teachers' ideas about instruction. It is useful to identify the intuitive conceptions that teachers have. It is important to recognize that contradiction may be an inappropriate vehicle for changing those conceptions and that metareasoning skills will allow teachers to autonomously regulate their own learning. Finally, professional development programs which provide numerous opportunities for consideration of alternative instructional approaches are most likely to succeed.

D. Response to the Crisis

Response to the crisis in science education requires a concerted, thoughtful, and innovative approach. The participation of curriculum developers, teachers, school administrators, students, and parents is essential for the success of this endeavor. The emerging science of science education provides some interesting opportunities for fostering both qualitative and quantitative change in science instruction. Certainly quantitative change without qualitative change is unlikely to achieve the objectives which all the various commissions studying recent trends in science education have described as essential.

Acknowledgments

This chapter was drafted while Linn was a Fullbright professor abroad at the Weizman Institute of Science. Support from the Fullbright program and the Weizman Institute is appreciated. Partial support from the National Science Foundation under grant SED-81-12631 is gratefully acknowledged. Any opinions, conclusions, or recommendations are those of the author and do not necessarily reflect the views of the National Science Foundation.

A portion of this chapter was presented at the 1984 American Educational Research Association Meeting and at the 1984 National Association for Research in Science Teaching Meeting, New Orleans.

REFERENCES

Adelson, B. (1985). Comparing natural and abstract categories: A case study from computer science. *Cognitive Science, 9,* 417–430.

Anderson, J. R. (1982). Acquisition of cognitive skill. *Psychological Review, 89,* 369–406.

Anderson, J. R. (1985, April 26) Intelligent tutoring systems, *Science, 228,* 456–462.

Anderson, B., & Karrqvist, C. (1982). Light and its properties (EKNA Report No. 8). Molndal, Sweden,: University of Gothenburg.

Armstrong, J. M. (1979). *A national assessment of achievement and participation of women in mathematics.* Denver, CO: Education Commisssion of the States.

Benbow, C. P., & Stanley, J. C. (1980, December). Sex differences in mathematical ability: Fact or artifact? *Science, 210,* 1262–1264.

Ben Zvi, R., Eylon, B., & Silberstein, J. (in press). Structure and process in chemistry: the concepts and their conception. *Journal of Chemical Education.*

Boden, M. A. (1977). Artificial intelligence and natural man. New York: Basic.

Boswell, J. (1957). *Boswell's life of Johnson.* London: Oxford University Press.

Branscomb, L. M. (1983, September). High school physics—Why doesn't somebody do something? *Physics Today,* pp. 9, 106–107.

Brown J. S., & Palincsar, A. S. (1985, April). "Reciprocal Teaching of Comprehension Strategies: A Natural History of One Program for Enhancing Learning," *Center for the Study of Reading, 334.*

Burbules, N. C., and Linn, M. C. (1984). Response to contradiction: Scientific reasoning during adolescence. (Adolescent Reasoning Project Report). Berkeley: University of California, Lawrence Hall of Science.

Burton, R. R., & Brown, J. S. (1982). An investigation of computer coaching for informal learning activities. In D. Sleeman & J. S. Brown (Eds.), *Intelligent tutoring systems* New York: Academic Press.

Caramazza, A., McCloskey, M., & Green, B. (1981). Naive beliefs in "sophisticated" subjects: Misconceptions about trajectories of objects. *Cognition, 9*, 117–123.

Case, R. (1974). Structures and strictures: Some functional limitations on the course of cognitive growth. *Cognitive Psychology, 6*, 544–573.

Case, R. (1975). Gearing the demands of instruction to the development capacities of the learner. *Review of Educational Research, 45*, 59–87.

Case, R. (1980). Intellectual development from birth to adulthood: A Neo-Piagetian interpretation. In R. Siegler (Ed.), *Children's thinking: What develops?* Hillsdale, NJ: Erlbaum.

Champagne, A. B., Klopfer, L. E., & Anderson, J. H. (1980). Factors influencing the learning of classical mechanics. *American Journal of Physics, 48*, 1974–1979.

Champagne, A. B., Klopfer, L. E., Desena, A. T., & Squires, D. A. (1981). Structural representations of students' knowledge before and after science instruction. *Journal of Research in Science Teaching, 18*, 97–111.

Champagne, A. B., Klopfer, L. E., & R. F. Gunstone (1982). Cognitive research and the design of science instruction. *Educational Psychologist, 17*, 31–53.

Chase, N., & Simon, H. A. (1973a). The mind's eye in chess. In W. G. Chase (Ed.), *Visual information processing*. New York: Academic Press.

Chase, N., & Simon, H. A. (1973b). Perception in chess. *Cognitive Psychology, 4*, 55–91.

Chi, M. T. H., Feltovich, P. J., & Glaser, R. (1980, May). Categorization and representation of physics problems by experts and novices. *Cognitive Science, 5*, 121–152.

Chi, M. T. H., Glaser, R., & Rees, E. (1981, May). Expertise in problem solving (Tech, Rep. No. 5). Pittsburgh: University of Pittsburgh, Learning Research and Development Center.

Chipman, S. F., Brush, L. R., & Wilson, D. M. (1985). *Women and mathematics: Balancing the equation*. Hillsdale, NJ: Erlbaum.

Clancey, W. J. (1982). Tutoring rules for guiding a case method dialogue. In D. Sleeman & J. S. Brown (Eds.), *Intelligent tutoring systems*. New York: Academic Press.

Clancey, W. J. (1983). The epistemology of a rule-based system: A frame-work for explanation. *The Journal of Artificial Intelligence, 20*, 215–251.

Clancey, W. J. (1984). Acquiring, representing, and evaluating a competence model of diagnostic strategy. In M. Chi, R. Glaser, & M. Farr (Eds.), *The nature of expertise*. Hillsdale, NJ: Erlbaum.

Clancey, W. J., & Buchanan, B. G. (1982). Exploration of teaching and problem-solving strategies, 1979–1982 (Heuristic Programming Project No. 82-8). Stanford, CA: Stanford University.

Clancey, W. J., Shortliffe, E. H., & Buchanan, B. G. (1979). Intelligent computer-aided instruction for medical diagnosis. *Computer Application in Medical Care, 3*, 175–183.

Clement, J. (1982). *Spontaneous analogies in problem solving: The progressive construction of mental models*. Paper presented at the meeting of the American Educational Research Association, New York.

Cohen, R., Eylon, B., & Ganiel, U. (1983). Potential difference and current in simple electric circuits: A study of students' concepts. *American Journal of Physics, 51*(5), 407–412.

Cook, T. D., & Campbell, D. T. (1979). *Quasi-experimentation: Design & analysis issues for field settings*. Chicago: Rand McNally College.

Cronbach, L. J. (1957). The two disciplines of scientific psychology. *American Psychologist, 12*, 671–684.

Cronbach, L. J. (1982). *Designing evaluations of educational and social programs*. San Francisco: Jossey-Bass.

Cronbach, L. J., & Snow, R. E. (1977). *Aptitude Treatment Interactions*. New York: Irvington, 1977.

di Sessa, A. A. (1983). *Phenomenology and the evolution of intuition*. In D. Gentner & A. L. Stevens (Eds.), *Mental models*. Hillsdale, NJ: Erlbaum.

di Sessa, A. (1982). Unlearning Aristotelian physics; A case study of knowledge based learning. *Cognitive Science, 6*, 37–75.

Doyle, W. (1983). Academic work. *Review of Educational Research, 53*, 159–199.

Driver, R. (1983). *The pupil as scientist?* Milton Keynes, England: Open University Press.

Driver, R., & Erickson, G. (1983, April). *The study of students' conceptual frameworks in science: Some theoretical and empirical considerations*. Paper presented at a symposium entitled "Stability and change in conceptual understanding" held at the annual meeting of the American Educational Research Association, Montreal.

Elstein, A. S., Shulman, L., & Sprafka, P. (1978). *Medical problem sovling: An analysis of clinical reasoning*. Cambridge, MA: Harvard University Press.

Ericsson, K. A., & Simon, H. A. (1984). *Protocol analysis. Verbal reports as data*. Cambridge, MA: MIT Press.

Estavan, L. (1983, October 25). Gender gap: Women behind in computer age, study says. *The Stanford Daily*, pp. 1, 10.

Eylon, B. (1979). *Effects of knowledge organization on task performance*. Unpublished doctoral dissertation, University of California, Berkeley.

Eylon, B., & Helfman, J. (1985). *The role of examples, generalized procedures and ability in solving physics problems* (Tech. Rep. 85/5). Rehovot, Israel: Weizmann Institute of Science.

Eylon, B., and Linn, M. C. (1986). *Science education theory and practice: Implications from three research programs*. (Adolescent Reasoning Project Report). Berkeley: University of California, Lawrence Hall of Science.

Eylon, B., & Rief, R. (1984). Effects of knowledge organization on task performance. *Cognition and instruction, 1*, 5–44.

Fensham, P. & Kornhauser, A. (1982). Challenges for the future of chemical education. In M. Gardner (Ed.), *Sixth international conference on chemical education* (pp. 115–137). College Park, MD: University of Maryland.

Fischer, D. (1980). A theory of cognitive development: The control and construction of hierarchies of skills. *Psychological Review, 97*, 477–531.

Franz, J. R., Aldridge, B. G., & Clard, R. B. (1983, September). Paths to a solution. *Physics Today*, pp. 44–49.

French, A. P. (1958). *Principles of modern physics*. New York: Wiley.

Furby, L. (1980). Implications of cross-cultural Piagetian research for cognitive developmental theory. In S. Modgil & C. Modgil (Eds.), *Toward a theory of psychological development*. Windsor, England: National Foundation for Educational Research Publishing Co.

Galison, R. (1983). How the first neutral-current experiment ended. *Reviews of Modern Physics, 55*, 477–509.

Glaser, R. (1983, June). Education and thinking: The role of knowledge (Tech. Rep. No. PDS-6). Pittsburgh: University of Pittsburgh, Learning Research and Development Center.

Gleick, J. (1983, August 21). Exploring the labyrinth of the mind. *The New York Times Magazine, 6*, pp. 23–27, 83, 86–87, 100.

Gray, J., & Mayers, M. (1978). The Bay Area Writing Project. *Phi Delta Kappan*, pp. 410–413.

Greeno, J. G. (1974). Structural differences between learning outcomes produced by different instructional methods. *Journal of Education Psychology, 63*, 165–173.

Greeno, J. G. (1978). A study of problem solving. In R. Glaser (Ed.), *Advances in instruction psychology*. Hillsdale, NJ: Erlbaum.

Greeno, J. G. (1983). *Skills for representing problems*. Paper presented at the meeting of the American Educational Research Association, Montreal.

Griggs, R. A. (1983). The role of problem content in the selection task and THOG problem. In J. Evans (Ed.), *Thinking and reasoning: Psychological approaches*. London: Routledge.

Griggs, R. A., & Cox, J. R. (1982). The elusive thematic-materials effect in Wason's selection task. *British Journal of Psychology, 73*, 407–420.

Hayes-Roth, B. (1980, December). *Human planning processes*. Santa Monica, CA: Rand.

Heller, J. I., & Reif, F. (1984). Prescribing effective human problem-solving processes: Problem description in physics. *Cognition and Instruction, 1*(2), 177–216.

Hewson, M. G. (1985). Epistemological commitments in the learning of science: Examples from dynamics. *European Journal of Science Education, 7*, 163–172.

Hofstadter, D. R. (1980). *Gödel, Escher, Bach: An eternal golden braid*. New York: Vintage.

Humphrey, L. C., & Parsons, C. K. (1979). Piagetian tasks measure intelligence and intelligence tests assess cognitive development: A reanalysis. *Intelligence, 3*, 369–382.

Inhelder, B., & Piaget, J. (1958). *The growth of logical thinking from childhood to adolescence*. New York: Basic.

Karplus, R. (1977). Science teaching and the development of reasoning. *Journal of Research in Science Teaching, 14*, 169–175.

Karplus, R., & Thier, H. D. (1967). *A new look at elementary school science*. Chicago: Rand McNally.

Keating, D. P. (1979). Adolescent thinking. In J. P. Adelson (Ed.), *Handbook of adolescence*. New York: Wiley.

Kleer, J. de, & Brown, J. S. (1983). The origin, form and logic of qualitative physical laws. *Proceedings of the International Joint Conference on Artificial Intelligence*.

Klein, S., Ed. (1985). *Handbook for achieving sex equity in education*. Baltimore: Johns Hopkins University Press.

Kyllonen, P. C., Lohman, D. F., & Woltz, D. J. (1984). Componential modeling of alternative strategies for performing spatial tasks. *Journal of Educational Psychology, 76*, 1325–1345.

Lakatos, I. (1972). Falsification and the methodology of scientific research programs. In I. Lakatos & A. Musgrave (Eds.), *Criticism and the growth of knowledge*. Cambridge, England: Cambridge University Press.

Lakatos, I. (1976). *Proofs and refutation: The logic of mathematical discovery*. Cambridge, England: Cambridge University Press.

Lakatos, I. (1978). The methodology of scientific research programs. New York: Cambridge University Press.

Larkin, J. (1981, June). Cognition of learning physics. *American Journal of Physics, 49*, 534–541.

Larkin, J. H. (1983a). A general knowledge structure for learning or teaching science. In A. C. Wilkinson (Ed.), *Computers and cognition*. New York: Academic Press.

Larkin, J. H. (1983b). Spatial reasoning in solving physics problems (C.I.P. No. 434). Pittsburgh: Carnegie-Mellon University, Department of Psychology.

Larkin, J., McDermott, J., Simon, D. P., & Simon, H. A. (1980, June). Expert and novice performance in solving physics problems. *Science, 208*, 1335–1342.

Lawson, A. E. (1983). Predicting science achievement: The role of developmental level, disembedding ability, mental capacity, prior knowledge and beliefs. *Journal of Research in Science Teaching, 20*, 117–129.

Lawson, A. E. (1985). A review of research on formal reasoning and science teaching. *Journal of Research in Science Teaching, 22*, 569–617.

Leron, U. (1983). *Some problems in children's LOGO learning*. Haifa, Israel: Univeristy of Haifa.

Levine, D. I., & Linn, M. C. (1977). Scientific reasoning ability in adolescence: Theoretical viewpoints and educational implications. *Journal of Research in Science Teaching, 14*, 371–384.

Linn, M. C. (1977) Scientific reasoning: Influences on task performance and response categorization. *Science Education, 61*, 357–363.

Linn, M. C. (1980). Teaching children to control variables: Some investigations using free choice experiences. In S. Modgil & C. Modgil (Eds.), *Toward a theory of psychological development within the piagetial framework*. Windsor, England: National Foundation for Educational Research Publishing Co.

Linn, M. C. (1982). Theoretical and practical significance of formal reasoning. *Journal of Research in Science Teaching, 19*, 727–742.

Linn, M. C. (1983). Content, context, and process in adolescent reasoning. *Journal of Early Adolescence, 3*, 63–82.

Linn, M. C. (1985). The cognitive consequences of programming instruction in classrooms. *Educational Researcher, 14*(5), 14–29.

Linn, M. C., Clancey, M., Dalbey, J., Heller, J., & Reese, P. (1983). *Acquisition of programming skill*. Berkeley: University of California, Lawrence Hall of Science.

Linn, M. C., Clement, C., Pulos, S., & Sullivan, P. (1982, November). *Logical vs. sensible reasoning: An instruction based investigation* (Adolescent Reasoning Project Report). Berkeley: University of California, Lawrence Hall of Science.

Linn, M. C., & Dalbey, J. (1985). Cognitive consequences of programming instruction: Instruction, access, and ability, *Educational Psychologist, 20* (4).

Linn, M. C. de Benedictis, T., & Delucchi, K. (1982). Adolescent reasoning about advertisements: Preliminary investigations. *Child Development, 53*, 1599–1613.

Linn, M., Fisher, C., Dalbey, J., Mandinach, E., & Beckum, L. (1982). *ACCCEL Proposal—Demands and cognitive consequences of computer learning*. Berkeley: University of California, Lawrence Hall of Science.

Linn, M. C., and Petersen, A. C. (1985a). Facts and assumptions about the nature of sex differences. In S. Klein (Ed.), *Handbook for achieving sex equity in education* (pp. 53–77). Baltimore: Johns Hopkins University Press.

Linn, M. C., & Petersen, A. C. (1985b). *Gender differences in spatial ability: A meta-analysis. Child Development, 56*, 1479–1498.

Linn, M. C., & Petersen, A. C. (1986). A meta-analysis of gender differences in spatial ability: Implications for mathematics and science achievement. In J. S. Hyde & M. C. Linn (Eds.), *The psychology of gender: Advances through meta-analysis* (pp. 67–101). Baltimore: Johns Hopkins University Press.

Linn, M. C., & Pulos, S. (1983a). Aptitude and experience influences on proportional reasoning during adolescence: Focus on male–female differences. *Journal for Research in Mathematics Education, 14*, 30–46.

Linn, M. C., & Pulos. S. (1983b). Male–female differences in predicting displaced volume: Strategy usage, aptitude relationships, and experience influences. *Journal of Educational Psychology, 75*, 86–96.

Linn, M. C., Pulos, S., & Gans, A. (1981). Correlates of formal reasoning: Content and problem effects. *Journal of Research in Science Teaching, 18* (5), 435–447.

Linn, M. C., & Siegel, H. (1983). Post-formal reasoning: A progressing research program. In M. Commons (Ed.), *Models of post formal reasoning*. New York: Praeger.

Linn, M. C., and Swiney, J. (1981). Individual differences in formal thought: Role of expectations and aptitudes. *Journal of Educational Psychology, 73,* 274–286.

Lochhead, J. (1985). Teaching Analytic Reasoning Skills Through Pair Problem Solving. In Susan Chipman (Ed.), *Thinking and Learning Skills* (Vol. 1, pp. 109–131). Hillsdale, NJ: Erlbaum.

Lovell, L. (1961). A follow-up study of Inhelder and Piaget's *The growth of logical thinking. British Journal of Psychology,* 143–153.

Mandler, G. (1967). Organization and memory. In I. W. Spence & J. R. Spence (Eds.), *The psychology of learning and motivation.* New York: Academic Press.

Mayer, R. E. (1979). Qualitatively different encoding strategies for linear reasoning premises: Evidence for single association and distance theories. *Journal of Experimental Psychology: Human Learning and Memory, 5,* 1–10.

Mayer, R. E., & Greeno, J. G. (1972). Structural differences between learning outcomes produced by different instructional methods. *Journal of Educational Psychology, 63,* 165–173.

McCloskey, M. Caramazza, A., & Green, B. (1980). Curvilinear motion in the absence of external forces: Naive beliefs about the motion of objects. *Science, 210,* 1139–1141.

McDermott, L. C., Piternick, L. K., & Rosenquist, M. L. (1980). Helping minority students succeed in science: I. Development of a curriculum in physics and biology, II. Implementation of a curriculum in physics and biology, III. Requirements for the operation of an academic program in physics and biology. *Journal of College Science Teaching, 9,* 201–205, 261–265.

McDermott, L. C., Rosequist, M. L., Popp, B. D., & Zee, E. H. van. (1983, April). *Identifying and overcoming student conceptual difficulties in physics: Student difficulties in connecting graphs, concepts and physical phenomena.* Paper presented at an invited symposium during the annual meeting of the American Educational Research Association, Montreal.

Michotte, A. (1963). *The perception of causality.* New York: Basic.

Miller, J. D. (1956). The magic number seven plus or minus two: Some limits on the capacity of human processing. *Psychological Review, 63,* 81–97.

Miller, J. D., Suchner, R., & Voelker, A. M. (1980). *Citizenship in an age of science.* New York: Pergamon.

National Assessment of Educational Progress. (1978a). *Three national assessments of science: Changes in achievement, 1969–77.* Denver: Education Commission of the States.

National Assessment of Educational Progress. (1978b). *Science achievement in the schools: A summary of results from the 1976–77 national assessment of science.* Denver: Education Commission of the States.

National Assessment of Educational Progress. (1979a). *Three national assessments of science. 1969–77: Technical summary.* Denver: Education Commission of the States.

National Assessment of Educational Progress. (1979b). *Attitudes toward science: a summary of results from the 1976–77 national assessment of science.* Denver: Education Commission of the States.

National Assessment of Educational Progress. (1979a). *Mathematical application 1977–1978 Assessment.* Denver: Education Commission of the States.

National Assessment of Educational Progress. (1979d). *Mathematical knowledge and skills: Selected results from the second assessment of mathematics.* Denver: Education Commission of the States.

National Assessment of Educational Progress. (1983). *The third national mathematics assessment: Results, trends, and issues.* Denver: Education Commission of the States.

National Commission on Excellence in Education. (1983). *A nation at risk: The imperative for educational reform.* Washington, DC: U.S. Government Printing Office.

National Science Board Commission on Precollege Education in Mathematics, Science and Technology. (1983, September). *Educating Americans for the 21st century.* Washington, DC: U.S. Government Printing Office.

Newcombe, N., Bandura, M. M., & Taylor, D. G. (1983). Sex differences in spatial ability and spatial activities. *Sex Roles.*

Nisbett, R. E., Zukier, H., & Lemley, R. E. (1981). The dilution effect: Nondiagnostic information weakens the implications of diagnostic information. *Cognitive Psychology, 13,* 248–277.

Norman, D. A., & Rumelhart, D. E. *Explorations in cognition.* San Francisco: Freeman, 1975.

Nussbaum, J., & Novick, S. (1976). An assessment of children's concepts of the earth utilizing structured interviews. *Science Education, 60,* 535–550.

Nussbaum, J., & Novick, S. (1982). Alternative frameworks, conceptual conflict and accommodation: Toward a principled teaching strategy. *Instructional Science, 11,* 183–200.

Palmer, S. E. (1980). What makes triangles point: Local and global effects in configurations of ambiguous triangles. *Cognitive Psychology, 12,* 285–305.

Papert, S. (1980). *Mindstorms,* New York: Basic.

Pea, R. D., & Kurland, D. M. (1984). On the cognitive effects of learning computer programming. *New Ideas Psychology, 2*(2), 137–168.

Petersen, A. C. (1982, January). *In biological correlates of spatial ability and mathematical performance.* Invited presentation in a symposium at the annual meeting of the American Association for the Advancement of Science, Washington, DC.

Physical Science Study Committee. (1964–1966). *Introductory physical science.* Englewood Cliffs, NJ: Prentice-Hall.

Pulos, S., de Benedictis, T., Linn, M. C., Sullivan, P., & Clement, C. (1982). Modification of gender differences in the understanding of displaced volume. *Journal of Early Adolescence, 2,* 61–74.

Pylyshyn, Z. W. (1978). Computational models and empirical constraints. *The Behavioral and Brain Sciences, 1,* 93–127.

Reif, F. (1981, May). Teaching problem solving—a scientific approach. *The Physics Teacher. 19,* 210–316.

Reif, F. (1986). Interpretation of scientific or mathematical concepts: Cognitive issues and instructional implications (Office of Naval Research: Report No. CES-1). Berkeley: University of California.

Reif, F., & Heller, J. I. (1982). Knowledge structure and problem solving in physics. *Educational Psychologist, 17,* 102–127.

Reif, F., & John, M. St. (1979, November). Teaching physicists' thinking skills in the laboratory. *American Journal of Physics, 47,* 950–957.

Resnick, L. B. (1983, April). Mathematics and science learning: A new conception. *Science, 220,* 477–478.

Ridgeway, D. (1983). *Personal communication.* Berkeley: University of California, Lawrence Hall of Science.

Rowe, M. B. (1983). Science education: A framework for decision makers. *Daedalus, 112*(2), 123–142.

Rumelhart, D. E., & Norman, D. A. (1983). *Representation in memory* (Tech. Rep. No. NR 667-473). San Diego: University of California, Institute for Human Information Processing.

Salomon, G. (1979). *Interaction of media, cognition and learning.* San Francisco: Jossey-Bass.

Scardamalia, M. (1977). Information processing capacity and the problem of horizontal decalage: A demonstration using combinatorial reasoning tasks. *Child Development, 48*, 28–37.

Schoenfeld, A. H. (Ed.). (1985). *Mathematical problem solving*. Orlando, FL: Academic Press.

Science Curricula Improvement Study (SCIS). (1970, 1972). Chicago: Rand McNally.

Shavelson, R. J. (1973a). Learning from physics instruction. *Journal of Research in Science Teaching, 10*, 101–111.

Shavelson, R. J. (1973b). Some aspects of the correspondence between context structure and cognitive structure in physics instruction. *Journal of Educational Psychology, 63*, 225–234.

Siegler, R. S. (1981). Developmental sequences within and between concepts. *Monographs of the Society for Research in Child Development, 46*.

Simon, H. A. (1974, February). How big is a chunk? *Science, 183*, 482–488.

Simon, H. A. (1980). The behavioral and social sciences. *Science, 209*, 72–78.

Simon, H. A. (1981). *The sciences of the artificial* 2nd ed. Cambridge, MA: M.I.T. Press.

Sinclair, H. (1980). *Reasoning and development*. Talk given at the meeting of the International Congress for Mathematics Education, Berkeley.

Sleeman, D. (1982). Assessing aspects of competence in basic algebra. In D. Sleeman & J. S. Brown (Eds.), *Intelligent tutoring systems*. New York: Academic Press.

Sleeman, D., & Brown, J. S. (Eds.). (1982). *Intelligent Tutoring Systems*. New York: Academic Press.

Smith, J. (1980). *Personal communication*. Paper presented at the Search for Excellence in Science and Mathematics (SESAME) Seminar.

Snow, R. E. (1976). Research on aptitude for learning: A progress report. *Review of Research in Education, 4*, 50–105.

Stage, E. K., Kreinberg, N., Eccles (Parsons), J., & Becker, J. R. (1985). Increasing the participation and achievement girls and women in mathematics, science, and engineering. In S. S. Klein (Ed.), *Handbook for achieving sex equity through education* (pp. 237–238). Baltimore: Johns Hopkins University Press.

Sternberg, R. J. (1982). Reasoning, problem solving, and intelligence. In R. J. Sternberg (Ed.), *Handbook of human intelligence*. New York: Cambridge University Press.

Stevens, A., Collins, A., & Goldin, S. E. (1982). Misconceptions in students' understanding. In D. Sleeman & J. S. Brown (Eds.), *Intelligent tutoring systems*. New York: Academic Press.

Toulmin, S. (1972). *Human understanding: An inquiry into the aims of science*. Princeton, NJ: Princeton University Press.

Tschirgi, J. E. (1980). Sensible reasoning: A hypothesis about hypotheses. *Child Development, 51*, 1–10.

Wason, P. C., & Johnson-Laird, P. N. (1972). *Psychology of reasoning: Structure and content*. Cambridge, MA: Harvard University Press.

Webb, N. (1985). Cognitive requirements of learning computer programming in group and individual settings. *American Educational Data Systems Journal, 18*, 183–184.

Weiss, I. R. (1980). *Report of the 1977 survey of science, mathematics, and social studies education*. Research Triangle Park, NC: Center Triangle.

Welch, W. W. (1979). Twenty years of science curriculum development: A look back. In D. C. Berliner (Ed.), *Review of research in education* (pp. 282–308). Washington, DC: American Educational Research Association.

Wilensky, R. (1983). *Planning and understanding*. Reading, MA: Addison-Wesley.

Wilkening, F. (1981). Integrating velocity, time, and distance information: A developmental study. *Cognitive Psychology, 13*, 231–247.

7

Social Studies

JAMES F. VOSS
Department of Psychology
University of Pittsburgh
Pittsburgh, Pennsylvania 15260

I. INTRODUCTION

Psychology and education have been living together for many years. At times it has seemed as though a marriage would be forthcoming; at other times each has functioned as if the other did not exist. In recent years, however, the relationship has once again been drawing closer, and in large part this trend has been due to the increasing interest of cognitive psychologists in complex mental processes. Especially important has been the study of psychological phenomena within the context of specific subject matter domains such as mathematics, physics, and social sciences, and the study of cognitive skills such as comprehension, writing, and problem solving. It is of course argued, or at least hoped, that such research will lead to a better understanding of the processes of learning as well as to the improvement of instruction in the respective domains. Indeed, the existence of the present volume attests to this belief (or hope).

Despite their increasing interest in the educational process, most psychologists are not well acquainted either with the curricula or with the teaching and administrative components of elementary and secondary education. Because of this, the first part of this chapter contains a discussion of such factors as are found in relation to the teaching of social studies in the elementary and secondary schools. The reason for providing such information is to help sensitize the actual or potential investigator to problems and issues that are found in social studies instruction below the college level. (As parents, academicians sometimes feel that they know about teaching in elementary and secondary schools because of what they see their children learn or not learn. However, the academician does not always realize the personal bias that may occur in such an assessment, nor is it apparent how constraints of the community, school administration, facilities, teachers, and student population may substantially influence the educational process.)

II. SOCIAL STUDIES AND SOCIAL SCIENCES: CURRICULUM AND INSTRUCTIONAL COMPONENTS[1]

Social Studies Curricula

1. Information Sources

In the 1970s the National Science Foundation sponsored three studies involving the teaching of mathematics, science, and social studies at the K–12 levels. Two of the studies were more traditional in nature, with one (Weiss, 1978) a survey type of study, providing data regarding the courses taught at various levels, the enrollments, the texts employed, the background of teachers, and the difficulties of teaching as indicated by teachers. Also, the roles of the state supervisor, district administrative official, and principal were considered, as well as the extent to which the schools used federal funded programs. A second survey (Wiley, 1977) was basically a compiling and summarization of research papers that were concerned with issues such as those outlined above. The third study was ethnographic in nature, involving a series of case studies (Stake & Easley, 1978). The day-by-day operation of 12 schools was studied, with the schools selected to represent the diversity found in the schools of the United States.

After the publication of the three studies, the National Science Foundation requested that nine organizations respond to the findings of the studies with brief reports, which were published in Rutherford (1979). In addition, a report was published by the Social Science Education Consortium of Boulder, Colorado, which was concerned with some controversial issues involving the National Science Foundation and curriculum development (Wiley, 1976). Except where indicated, the information presented on curriculum and instruction in this chapter is drawn from these works.

2. Curricula

The K–6 curricula of social studies, even with some changes, has been reasonably stable. While specifics are difficult to determine, the subject

---

[1]The terms *social studies* and *social sciences* are generally not used interchangeably; the latter expression especially embraces a particular approach to curriculum content. This issue is discussed in greater detail in the chapter.

matter covered through Grades K–6 typically moves from local concerns to more general issues. Indeed, themes for the topics covered over the K–6 period have included "Expanding Horizons" or "Expanding Environments." At the first two grade levels, the family and local community have been the subject of concern. By Grade 3 there typically is a greater emphasis upon the community, and by Grade 4 the emphasis is further broadened, with world geography a frequently taught topic. Grade 5 tends to emphasize U.S. history, and Grade 6 the Western Hemisphere. There are of course variations in the topics that are covered, such that one program may endeavor to show cultural similarities and differences more than other programs.

The average time per day spent in teaching social studies in Grades K–3 (21 min) and 4–6 (34 min) is roughly equivalent to that spent in science instruction (17 and 28 min, respectively), but less than that spent in mathematics (41 and 51 min, respectively) and in reading (95 and 66 min, respectively).

The curriculum of Grades 7–12 has some variation across schools, but there is nevertheless considerable consistency. By far the most frequently offered course in these years is U.S. history. For Grades 7–9, of the total number of social studies offered, 34% of the courses are in U.S. history, 18% in social studies, 7% in state history, 6% in civics, 6% in world geography, and 29% in other courses. For Grades 10–12, 27% of the courses are in U.S. history, 10% in world history, 7% in psychology, 7% in American culture or contemporary issues, 6% in U.S. government, 5% in economics, and 38% in other courses. The category of "other courses" includes sociology, anthropology, law, Afro-American studies, black history, or courses on special topics. Incidentally, classes average about 25–30 students.

With respect to state requirements, for Grades 9–12, 2% of the states require less than one year of social studies, 17% require one year, and 68% require more than one year. Interestingly, only 7% of the states require at least one specific course in mathematics and only 8% require a specific science course, but 83% of the states require a specific social studies course. A course in U.S. history is required in 68% of the states, a U.S. government course is required in 32% of the states, and a course in the history of the particular state is required in 20% of the states. In addition, six states require a course in consumer education, and instruction in the "free enterprise system" must be incorporated into the social studies curriculum in 14 states. Finally, in order to compare the relative enrollments found in various social studies courses, national enrollments for a given year (1976–1977) for Grades 10–12 were estimated as follows: U.S. history, 4 million; world history, 2 million; and U.S. government, 1.6 million. Psychology, sociology, economics, and anthropology enrollments ranged from approximately 575,000 to 750,000 each. Black studies and anthropology each had approximately 90,000 students and law approximately 65,000. There has been a tendency for courses such as economics, psychology, sociology, and anthropology to be offered with greater frequency, but this trend has apparently diminished. One of the problems with such offerings is the number of teachers available that are qualified to teach such courses, an issue that leads to the next topic.

3. The Teacher

Social studies teachers at all grade levels have about the same number of years of teaching experience (approximately 11). In addition, the higher the grade level taught, the more likely it is that the teacher will have earned a degree beyond the bachelor's (K–3, 23%; 4–6, 33%; 7–9, 51%; 10–12, 58%).

The ratio of male to female teachers changes substantially over grade level (K–3, 3% male; 4–6, 19% male; 7–9, 62% male; 10–12, 75% male). (These figures are roughly comparable to the equivalent data for mathematics teachers and science teachers.)

The most commonly employed classroom techniques are, in order of decreasing frequency, discussion, lecture, and student reports on projects. In addition, there is relatively frequent use of audio-visual aids.

The issue of teacher qualifications, as defined by formal training, is of special interest. The information previously presented indicated that a substantial number of social studies teachers have advanced degrees. But one may ask whether the advanced degree is in the specific subject matter the instructor is teaching or in some other field. (The master's degree, of course, may be in a field other than the particular subject matter, e.g., in educational administration.) While data are not available on this issue, i.e., in what fields advanced degrees were taken, Wiley (1977) did summarize a number of studies that were concerned with the extent to which the teachers' formal training was related to what they were teaching. While the data in some studies are from the 1960s and early 1970s, the studies provided evidence which supported some rather surprising conclusions. In a relatively large number of cases, social studies teachers did not meet minimum state requirements with respect to courses they had taken in the subject matter they were teaching. For example, in one state 18% of the teachers were deficient in the state's U.S. history requirement, 36% did not meet the European history requirements, and 81% did not meet the geography requirements. In another state 46% of the teachers of world history had majored in fields other than history or social science. Indeed, it was reported that teachers frequently were assigned to teach courses in areas in which they did not have specific training. For example, athletic coaches with little formal training in social studies were sometimes asked to teach social studies courses because of the need to complete their course load.

Turning now to teacher concerns, teachers were polled with respect to the areas in which they felt they needed assistance. A particular set of needs of social studies teachers was that of obtaining information about instructional materials, learning new teaching methods, and learning about and using "hands-on" material. In other words, teachers felt they needed more specific instructional information. Teachers also were asked the extent to which they found particular sources of information useful. The most useful source for teacher learning is other teachers, with 58% of K–3 social studies teachers indicating other teachers as "very useful" and approximately 45% responding in this manner for Grades 4–12. Principals were regarded as "very useful" by only 26%, 28%, 19%, and 15% of the social studies teachers over Grades K–3, 4–6, 7–9, and 10–12 respectively. Over the same grade levels, local subject matter specialists or coordinators were judged as "very useful" by 28%, 17%, and 11% of the teachers respectively. State personnel received "very useful" ratings from approximately 5% of the teachers over all grade levels. On the whole, the findings thus suggest that administrative officials at all levels are not viewed as especially helpful to teachers. Finally, college courses were judged "very useful" by 46%, 37%, 34%, and 34% of the teachers respectively, and local in-service courses received similar ratings. Interestingly, journals and other professional publications received "very useful" ratings from 39%, 47%, 42%, and 45% of the teachers respectively.

Teachers were also given a list of factors that they felt might influence instruction, and they were asked to judge whether each factor was a "serious problem," "somewhat of a problem," or "not a significant problem." Those factors receiving the highest percentages of "serious problem" or "somewhat of a problem" ratings were inadequate student reading abilities, lack of material for individualized instruction, insufficient funds for purchasing equipment and supplies, student belief that the subject is less important than other subjects, and lack of student interest (Morris & Garcia, 1982).

The information presented thus far primarily consists of results obtained by the National Science Foundation (NSF) studies. One of the commentaries on the NSF findings that were published in the Rutherford (1979) volume was by Shaver, Davis, and Helburn (1979), and the comments of these authors are now discussed.

Shaver et al. (1979) considered one particular conclusion of the Stake and Easley (1978) research to be quite important, namely, that the role

of the teacher is central (Superka, Hawke, & Morrisett, 1980). Thus, what
and how well the individual learns is taken to be a function of the teacher's
beliefs, knowledge, training, and ability to produce learning in the classroom. Another point noted by Shaver et al. is that classes are usually
taught in a manner that is heavily textbook oriented, with the course content by and large presumed to be that which is written in the text(s). The
textbook is thus somewhat of an "authority figure." Still another point
made by Shaver et al. is that teachers, while concerned for young people,
feel that students learn in order to receive grades and/or approval, and it
is not commonly assumed among teachers that students are intrinsically
motivated. Moreover, teachers tend to take the view that instruction involves the dissemination and acquisition of subject matter, and there is
little emphasis upon the development of critical thinking and scientific
inquiry. As pointed out by Shaver et al., such an approach to instruction
is not surprising when one considers the type of training most teachers
receive, i.e., doing assignments and learning the subject matter of a course
with little experience in research and critical activity.

Shaver et al. (1979) also pointed out that instruction typically involves
a "middle class" type of socialization which emphasizes the work ethic
as well as an attempt to be sure the child acquires "American values."
In one sense then, as Shaver et al. pointed out, all social science teachers
"indoctrinate" students, and in doing so they expose their own systems
of values to the students.

With respect to the extent to which controversial issues are considered,
Shaver et al. (1979) pointed out that since textbooks are regarded as au-
thoritative and since most often they are written in such a way as not to
produce controversy or confrontation, the text is conducive to helping
avoid controversy in the classroom. Furthermore, more or less in support
of this view, the previously described survey research indicated that
teachers feel that dealing with controversial issues does not constitute "a
serious problem."

A particularly interesting point made by Shaver et al. (1979) is that while
teachers hold the view that the school constitutes a means by which socialization occurs and subject matter contents are acquired, they view the
university academic community as being out of touch with the problems
of teachers. Thus, teachers feel that parents and other teachers may have
a substantial effect upon what is done in the classroom, but that the university academic community per se has little effect, except for textbooks
written by professors and specific courses taken by teachers.

4. Summary

As noted previously, the purpose of including the description of the
social studies curriculum and teacher characteristics in this chapter is to

provide the reader with information about the nature of social studies instruction at the precollege level. A number of additional issues could have been included and, in particular, data the present writer would have liked to find are those indicating how many classroom sessions are lost because of assemblies, pep rallies, and participation in extracurricular activities such as student government, sports, debate, and cheerleading. While such data are perhaps tangential to the objectives of the present chapter, they would nevertheless have provided a special touch of realism with respect to school environments.

The material presented thus far suggests that the "improvement of instruction" is not a simple matter, especially in the field of social studies. What complicates things for the well-intended university professor who is attempting to improve instruction via research is that the environment found in colleges and universities is in fact essentially a different culture from that found in the elementary and secondary schools and that in the latter, a number of variables other than those directly concerned with the learning of the subject matter per se may influence learning and instruction. To improve instruction in social studies thus means that the investigator needs to confront basic issues that are raised in such instruction, or at a minimum be aware that such issues exist. Given the perspective provided by the information presented thus far in this chapter, an analysis of social studies instruction is now presented which is based upon concepts taken from contemporary research in problem solving.

III. SOCIAL STUDIES INSTRUCTION: A PROBLEM-SOLVING APPROACH

A. A Problem-Solving Model

For the purposes of the present chapter, social studies instruction is considered within a general problem-solving framework. While problem solving has been interpreted within the framework of various theories (Mayer, 1977), the present analysis involves use of the information-processing model of problem solving (Newell & Simon, 1972).

The information-processing interpretation of problem solving, as adapted for the purposes of the present chapter, may be examined in relation to four components: the goal(s); the initial state of the individual solving the problem, i.e., what the individual brings into the problem-solving situation in terms of knowledge and motivation; the constraints, i.e., those factors operating in the particular problem-solving situation which in some way constrain the analysis and/or solution of the problem; and the solution process itself, which basically consists of the individual moving from his or her initial state to the goal. A more detailed description of these four components as found in the classroom situation is now presented.

Figure 1 presents a diagram of the components as found in the instructional context. The reader is asked first to refer to the boxes labeled *goals*. As noted, the primary instructional goals are to determine the contents and skills of instruction and to help produce student learning, which consists of acquiring the respective contents and skills. In addition, the teacher has the goal of assessing how readily the contents of the course are acquired and how effective are the methods of teaching. The primary student goal is presumed to be that of learning the contents and skills. Students at the elementary and secondary levels generally have little to say about what contents and skills should be acquired in a particular course, but *determination of contents and skills* is listed because the student sometimes is able to pursue a particular interest via an individual report or project.

There is a particularly interesting point to note about the instructional goals, namely, that the previously mentioned findings rather clearly show that teachers are generally concerned about the *learning of* and *learning about* goals but seem to have little to say about the *determination of* goals. Instead, determination of what is taught tends to be dictated largely by textbook contents. (This issue is considered in greater detail later in this chapter.)

The reader is now asked to refer to the boxes labeled *initial state*. The teacher comes into the instructional situation with a number of characteristics and attributes including knowledge and skills, values, and motivation. The student comes into the instructional situation with essentially the same set of traits, although the specific components of each are of course usually quite different for students and teachers. *Classroom position* refers to the difference in social settings, i.e., in general, the teacher is the authority figure and the student is the student. Some teachers may of course consider themselves to be "learning facilitators" rather than "authorities," but, taken as a whole, it seems fair to assume the existence of a more or less traditional teacher–student distinction.

The reader is now asked to refer to the box labeled *constraints*. There are various classes of constraints that impact upon the instructional situation. For the present purposes, only a few are delineated. One is termed *general community*, which refers to the local community as well as to the state and national community. A second is *home relations*, a third *peer and other* (nonpeer but personal) *relations*, and a fourth is *school community*, which refers to the administrative staff and other personnel of the school. The *facilities* constraint refers to the extent to which instructionally related resources are available, e.g., library resources and laboratory, audio-visual, and computer equipment. The final category is *class-*

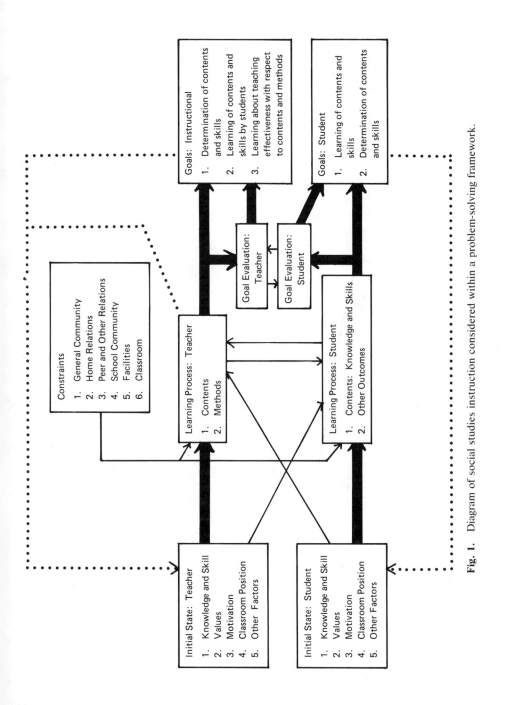

Fig. 1. Diagram of social studies instruction considered within a problem-solving framework.

room constraints, referring to any type of component of the classroom context that may act as a constraint.

One could argue that a number of factors found in the *initial state* boxes really constitute constraints, as, for example, poor teaching skills or poor student motivation. While such an argument is certainly valid, for the purposes of the present explanation it seemed more appropriate to consider such constraints as personal characteristics. Later in the chapter, however, some teacher characteristics are regarded as constraints.

The reader is now asked to refer to the boxes termed the *learning process*. These boxes portray how the learning takes place by the student or teacher, i.e., what happens as the student or teacher moves from his or her initial state to the goal.

As indicated in the diagram, the learning process presumed to take place within the student is being influenced by the student's own characteristics, as well as by the teacher and the constraints. (The heavy line is used to denote the individual moving from the initial state to the goal.) The learning process refers to acquisition of the contents and skills of the course as well to other outcomes, such as attitude regarding the particular teacher and interest in subject matter. In addition, the learning process taking place within the teacher refers to the teacher's opportunity to learn new information about the contents of what is being taught, to learn that some information should be added to or deleted from what is being taught, and to learn about the effectiveness of methods of teaching that are employed.

Finally, one more step is required in the outline of the process portrayed in Figure 1. In many cases, it is quite clear when a problem is solved as, for example, in solving most classroom mathematics problems. But in many other cases, when a problem is solved is much less clear. Problems of the latter type belong to a class referred to as *ill-structured problems* (Reitman, 1965; Simon, 1973; Voss, Greene, Post, & Penner, 1983). The instructional problem portrayed in Figure 1 is ill structured, in the sense that student learning and teacher learning is not self-evident, and some form of evaluation is thus usually employed in order to evaluate the learning that occurs. In the case of student learning, a test is usually given, while a teacher's evaluation of his or her own learning is typically more informal. The *goal evaluation* boxes are inserted in order to take the testing phase into account. As noted, student goal evaluation occurs, and it is assumed that the students compare these results to the original goals. The teacher's evaluation, influenced by the student performance during learning and during student evaluation, is presumed to occur as the teacher considers the course outcomes in relation to his or her original goals.

Finally, the dashed line is used to indicate feedback. Having taught the course, the teacher has had experience which modifies the initial state of the teacher for the next instructional situation. Similarly, the methods employed during classroom intruction may be modified. The student also, it is assumed, has acquired knowledge and skills which modify the attributes of the student's subsequent initial state.

B. Social Studies Instruction and the Problem-Solving Model

In this section the component processes of the problem-solving model are used to analyze social studies instruction.

1. What Are the Goals of Instruction in Social Studies?

As previously mentioned, one of the goals of the instructional process is to determine what it is that should be taught, i.e., what contents and skills students should be expected to learn. This issue is especially important in social studies because there has been considerable disagreement concerning the goals of such instruction. Before this matter is considered in detail, however, some general issues concerning instructional goals are discussed.

It is assumed that instructional goals are hierarchical in nature, with the highest level assumed to be the goals of education per se. The next level is presumed to be related to the broadest outcomes that are desired from instruction in social studies affecting such issues as why there should be a curriculum in the social science area and what should be accomplished within this area. The next lower level is assumed to involve goals related to specific course contents. Thus, a course in U.S. history is presumed to be taught with particular goals in mind. At the next level, it is assumed that within that course there are goals of particular units, and finally, there may be goals for a single day's activity or a part thereof. Thus, in general, the goals of instruction may be viewed as hierarchical with the more global goals occurring at the higher levels and the more specific goals occurring at the lower levels. Figure 2 presents a diagram of the hypothesized instructional goal structure. (An expression used frequently in educational literature is *learning objectives*. This term usually refers to specific goals that are to be accomplished within a particular unit of a course. In this present context such objectives would generally be low-level goals.)

An interesting facet of the hierarchical structural involves the extent to which the levels shown in Figure 2 are explicitly related to each other in actual practice. In general, it may be argued that the lowest levels have the most articulated interaction, i.e., the goals of Levels 5 and 6 are interwoven within the contents of the course while the goals of Levels 4 and 5 are usually less interrelated than are the goals of Levels 5 and 6. Furthermore, while course contents and the major units of a course may

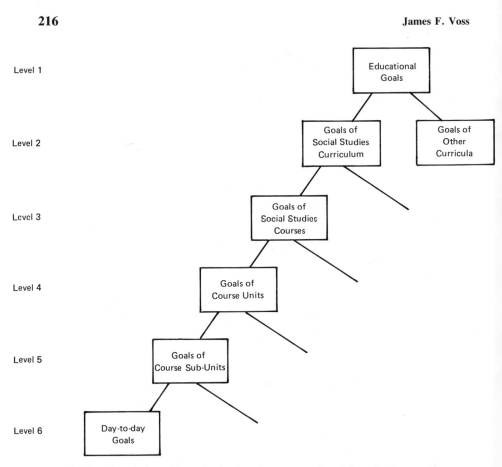

Fig. 2. Description of hypothesized goal structure of social studies instruction.

be shown to be closely related to the goals of the course, the question of how the goals of a particular day's activity relate to the highest level goals is not usually an issue of concern. Instead, it is generally assumed that the contents of the course in some way are helping to achieve the goals of the highest levels.

There is a good reason why lower level goals are often not examined in relation to higher level goals. For one thing, course contents tend to remain relatively stable over time, and with such stability a type of "conventional wisdom" is usually assumed; the subject matter is developed by tradition and by the generally agreed upon idea that experience in the teaching of the subject matter has established the higher level goals. For another thing, the nature of a hierarchical structure discourages examination of the interrelationship of goals. To elaborate, the highest level goals, as previously noted, are usually stated in general terms, and this means that it is both quite easy and quite difficult to relate these goals to lower level goals. It is easy because almost any low-level goal may be shown to be related to a broadly stated high-level goal; it is difficult because to relate a low-level goal to a high-level goal in a reasonably precise manner would necessitate the development of a series of inferences which would require testing to determine their validity. This task is thus not easy; moreover, it probably would be viewed by most people as having "little to do with instruction." Thus, from the teacher's point of view, the more important problem is to attach the task at hand, i.e., how to teach the specific topics to be considered (today) in the classroom, and not to be concerned with how specific topics are related to higher level goals. Furthermore (and this point should not be underestimated), it is generally assumed that the textbook writers must take high-level goals into consideration when they write the text.

Now that the general nature of the goal structure of social science instruction has been considered, the next issue to be discussed is the specific nature of social studies goals, i.e., goals ascribed to Level 2 in Figure 2. Examining the goals of social studies is extremely important, possibly more important than in any other subject matter, because social studies instruction characteristically has had multiple high-level goals, which sometimes produce controversy.

Barth and Shermis (1970) provided an interesting analysis of the goals of the social studies curriculum. They argued that there have been three distinct traditions that have led to the present state of affairs. These traditions are termed *citizenship transmission, social sciences,* and *reflective inquiry.*

The first, citizenship transmission, has as its goal the indoctrination of students with appropriate values and beliefs. Thus, teachers instructing within this tradition may feel it important to emphasize "the rights of the individual," "the importance of loving one's country," or other values and beliefs. Moreover, such instruction may be explicit or implicit, i.e., the teacher may be teaching such values and beliefs without being aware that such teaching is taking place. Thus, as Barth and Shermis pointed out, a teacher may feel that he or she is not actively trying to indoctrinate students, but the teacher may (implicitly) allow students to come away from the course with particular ideas. Similarly, national and community values may be inculcated in instruction. Barth and Shermis also noted that the two methods primarily used within this tradition are persuasion and description, with emphasis, for example, upon how historical phenomena may be interpreted in the context of the tradition.

Barth and Shermis (1970) indicated that the citizenship-transmission tradition has three somewhat questionable assumptions: (1) Good citizenship is developed best by storing up facts, principles, and beliefs; (2) what is valid curriculum in the past is valid curriculum today; and (3) what is considered to be important by a consensus of authorities is a sufficient means to select curriculum, i.e., the values and beliefs subscribed to by a particular set of individuals prescribe curriculum. Finally, Barth and Shermis also pointed out that this tradition assumes that some values are better than others. In summary, this tradition emphasizes the importance of passing on traditional values, or at least passing on those values that are perceived as traditional by a particular segment of the population.

The second tradition delineated by Barth and Shermis, that of considering social studies "social science," has as its goal the acquisition of knowledge for knowledge's sake. In other words, this tradition places a strong emphasis upon subject matter learning. The curriculum within this tradition stresses content, such as one would find in particular social science courses found at the college level. Thus, just as algebra, geometry, and trigonometry provide a basis for college mathematics and high school chemistry provides a basis for college chemistry, so should social studies courses provide a basis for learning in one or more of the college courses of history, anthropology, political science, economics, geography, psychology, and sociology.

The methods employed within the social science tradition are those that would be in general agreement with the nature of teaching usually found in the particular social science disciplines, i.e., using lectures, reading assignments, etc., in order to acquire the subject matter. Barth and Shermis further noted that some individuals had argued that the students should be instructed in the methods used by researchers to acquire such knowledge. Thus, such instruction would include writing research papers or perhaps doing a historical analysis of a particular topic.

The reader may note that the social science tradition differs from the citizenship-transmission tradition in a number of significant ways. Especially noteworthy is the citizenship-transmission goal of value acquisition as contrasted with the social science emphasis upon the description and analysis of phenomena.

The third tradition, that of reflective inquiry, is related to the educational philosophy of John Dewey. This tradition places emphasis upon citizenship, but from a perspective considerably different from that of the citizenship-transmission tradition. In the reflective-inquiry tradition, citizenship is regarded as a process, and not as a system of values and facts per se. Thus, emphasis is placed upon learning about decision making as it takes place in a democracy, and it is therefore important that students receive experience in the processes of such decision making.

The primary method used within this tradition, according to Barth and

Shermis (1970) is *inquiry,* with inquiry referring to addressing problems, considering solutions to the problems, and deciding which solution is most appropriate and why it is so. Moreover, the curriculum contents to a large degree become interdisciplinary within this tradition because the analysis of a particular problem may cut across the lines of traditional disciplines.

One concern that may be raised regarding this tradition, according to Barth and Shermis (1970), is that if the nature of the inquiry guides the selection of the knowledge that is to be used in solving a particular problem, and if the contents of the curriculum are thus problem based, the field of social studies is left without a defined data base. Thus, the reflective-inquiry tradition may be somewhat weak in defining subject matter as well as in establishing principles, data, and theory of the subject matter. More-over, this argument in turn suggests that the reflective-inquiry tradition can readily generate an emphasis upon "method" as opposed to "content" with respect to social studies curriculum. Finally, there is a serious question involving the extent to which decision-making experience in the classroom context transfers to real-world situations, especially when the students may not have acquired knowledge that is relevant to the problems with which they are confronted.

The Barth and Shermis (1970) analysis raises a number of important issues concerning social studies instruction, and two of these are now briefly considered. First, the preceding discussion rather clearly indicates that the goals of the three traditions may be in conflict with each other. In general, the citizenship-transmission tradition emphasizes the trans-mission of a particular set of values and the interpretation of information, e.g., historical information, in relation to such values. The social science tradition emphasizes the development of knowledge and skills with a ten-dency to compare and evaluate positions maintained by advocates of var-ious value systems. The reflective-inquiry tradition, in a sense, considers the acquisition of appropriate decision-making procedures as highly de-sirable, while perhaps having less of an emphasis upon knowledge ac-quisition than the social science tradition and even the citizenship-trans-mission tradition. Given this state of affairs, it is clear that there is the potential for conflict in lower level instructional goals because of a desire to incorporate some aspects of the goals of two or more of the traditions.

A second issue raised by the Barth and Shermis (1970) analysis involves the relationship of social studies instruction in K–12 to the undergraduate curriculum or even the graduate curriculum in one of the social sciences. What is particularly interesting is that only the curriculum emphasized by the social sciences tradition provides any substantial continuity between K–12 and college. The contents taught within the framework of the citi-zenship-transmission tradition may involve the teaching of U.S. history, but the emphasis is not the same as one would expect in a similar course taught in a social science tradition. Indeed, if a U.S. history course is taught in the context of the citizenship-transmission tradition, it should come as no surprise that when students take university courses (and especially graduate courses) they may have a "rude awakening" with respect to what they previously had learned. Indeed, when value transmission is emphasized in K–12, issues and events that are embarrassing to the values being transmitted may be avoided. Also, in relation to the K–12 and college continuity issue, it is worth noting that courses taught at the secondary level in fields such as psychology and economics often provide little continuity with college courses as, for example, in psychology, in which only "adjustment" may be considered, or in economics, in which only "the free enterprise system" may be discussed.

It may of course be argued that because everyone does not attend college, continuity with college instruction should be on an equal level with or perhaps even secondary to other goals, such as good citizenship. While this argument has some validity, it must be pointed out that if continuity is not regarded as especially important, social studies stands as unique among subject matter curricula, for in virtually every other academic discipline, what is taught in K–12 is regarded as basic to subsequent study in the particular subject matter. In addition, even if one argues that good citizenship should be a goal because everyone does not attend college, there is the real question of whether good citizenship is best developed within the citizenship-transmission tradition.

2. What Are the Goals of Students?

The problem-solving analysis as diagrammed in Figure 1 raises the issue of student goals. Perhaps somewhat surprisingly, little information is available regarding what students think they should learn and, in particular, learn in the area of social studies. For present purposes we may assume that the goals of many students involve grade achievement more than an understanding of the content per se. Students thus would be expected to accept low-level instructional goals because of their relationship to course accomplishment and grades. Also, some students may essentially not accept even low-level goals because of a general dislike of school, a dislike of the course contents, or a lack of stimulation (the course is not sufficiently challenging). Other students, however, may be quite interested in the course and have the goal of acquiring the course contents and even relating the contents to world events.

3. What Does the Teacher Bring into the Classroom?

This question, in addition to being considered in part in the earlier sections of this chapter, is discussed in the section on constraints.

4. What Does the Student Bring into the Classroom?

There can be little doubt that the knowledge and skills that the individual brings into the classroom situation are indeed critical to what the individual is going to learn. While it is beyond the scope of this chapter to provide an extensive analysis of the characteristics of the learner and how such characteristics are similar or different at various grade levels, there are a number of points that may be briefly considered. While some of these assertions are obvious, it nevertheless is worth articulating them because of their relevance to instruction issues.

1. Younger children are more capable of dealing with concrete than with abstract concepts, and they are especially adept in dealing with those concepts with which they have had direct contact. Applied to social studies, this means that the younger child is more likely to understand ideas related to his or her immediate environment. Indeed, as previously noted, the social studies curriculum of the primary grades emphasizes the family and immediate community.

2. The intelligence of children at any grade level (considering intelligence in relation to the ability to learn) varies considerably. Thus, for a topic in U.S. history such as the Civil War, the issues considered may be the factors leading to the war, the military as well as the politico-economic events of the war, and the conclusion and immediate aftereffects of the war. A student may be able to receive a passing grade in the course by being able to describe a number of things about these events. Another student, however, may be able to generalize what was learned and, for example, be able to consider how some of the factors involved in the Civil War may be seen in relation to broader questions such as the relative power of the federal and state governments. Thus, while each student may pass a course in U.S. history, what each "understands" about U.S. history may be quite different.

3. As individuals mature, differences in experience increase, often dramatically, so that there is increasing diversity in terms of what individuals bring into the classroom situation. Some schools, for example, may have individuals who are living in economically deprived conditions and who have never traveled outside of their own immediate community, while at the same school other individuals may not only have taken trips outside of their own community, but also have traveled to other states, other regions of the United States and of North America, and even other parts of the world. Such differences, of course, also exist within homes in the same general community.

4. Given the experience that there is an increasing diversity in intellectual development, it is clear that what different individuals bring into the classroom is indeed, in many cases, marked by wide variation. While

it is no doubt true that in some communities, schools have considerable student homogeneity, it also is true that among other schools, especially those in urban areas, there is considerable diversity.

5. Prior courses in social studies play a role in what the individual brings into the classroom situation, but how important such experience is to learning in the subsequent classes is not clear.

5. What Are the Major Constraints That Exist in the Instructional Context?

The constraints that exist in social studies instruction may be classified in a number of ways. For present purposes three categories are delineated, namely, teacher related, personal, and curricular.

One quite obvious set of constraints involves the intellectual capabilities and limitations of the teachers as well as the teaching skills that the teachers may or may not have. In addition, especially in social studies, particular viewpoints of teachers may serve as constraints. As an example, the extent to which teachers are willing to consider a controversial issue may vary considerably, especially if the issue is controversial in the context of the local community.

Some of the information presented earlier in this chapter points to at least one serious teacher-related constraint, namely, that in a relatively large number of cases, teachers may have little training in the subject matter they are teaching. While some training in U.S. history seems to be reasonably widespread, social studies teachers, taken as a whole, often have not formally studied to any substantial degree in areas such as political science, economics, sociology, and anthropology. Since it may be assumed that teaching generally is more effective when one knows the subject matter (knowledge of subject matter may be regarded as a necessary but not sufficient condition for good teaching), and since knowing the subject matter relates at least in part to formal training, it seems reasonable to ask why the formal background of social studies teachers is relatively weak.

There are at least two reasons that may be offered for this state of affairs. First, critics of the training provided by schools of education would be quick to point out that such schools emphasize methods more than content and that this emphasis leads prospective teachers to take methods courses at the expense of taking courses in the particular subject matter in which they are going to teach. In other words, because the total number of courses to be taken is more or less specified, the number of required courses in education makes it difficult for the student to take specific social science courses.

A second reason why social studies teachers may not have substantial training in the related academic disciplines is more subtle and is related to the nature of the knowledge domain per se. This reason is that the social studies curriculum, by and large, does not tend to be cumulative; social studies courses tend to have more breadth than depth. This is important with respect to the teaching of social studies because it enables a teacher with little background to step in to a social studies course and teach it because the prior knowledge of social studies required to teach the course is minimal. In contrast, teachers having little training in mathematics are not usually asked to step into a trigonometry course because they may not be sufficiently conversant with algebra and geometry. Thus, because the need for prerequisite knowledge is not extensive in social studies, teachers not well trained in the area may be assigned to teach such courses.

Finally, there is one other issue involving teacher-related constraints to consider, even though it is probably beyond the scope of this chapter. This issue is the extent to which the individuals who become teachers have the abilities and potential to become highly effective teachers and how teacher selection, in the sense of who is likely to become a teacher, may be modified so that the profession attracts individuals having strong capability and potential.

It seems to be clear from test results such as those found on the SAT examination that individuals choosing to become elementary or secondary school teachers have the lowest set of test scores of students entering any professional school, and it also seems clear that the teachers who leave the field for better paying positions are by and large among the more effective teachers. But why do these things occur? One answer is simply that the status and prestige accorded to elementary and secondary school teachers in American society is quite low. Certainly this statement is supported by data on the level of salaries received by primary and secondary school teachers. In this writer's opinion, there is one change that would provide for a higher quality of teaching, although it would take at least a generation to take effect. It is a major increase in teacher's salaries—at least a doubling of current salaries—with the possibility of further increase if the teachers are highly effective. In the long run, this action would, one hopes, influence highly capable individuals to select teaching as they make their vocational choices, and, more importantly, it wuld help to raise the general prestige level of the elementary and secondary school teacher. It should be noted that the idea is not simply to give merit raises, although rewarding good performance would also be important. Instead, the basic idea is to upgrade the prestige and status enjoyed by primary and secondary teachers, and in the American society this means more money. (The idea of raising teaching quality in the primary and secondary schools via large salary increases was first suggested to the present writer in a speech made · by Robert Maynard Hutchins, then chancellor of the University of Chicago and one of the foremost proponents in his time of the responsibility of schools for intellectual development.) However, such a salary change is highly unlikely, unless it were to be subsidized by the federal government. In most cases, K–12 teacher salaries are tied directly to local votes, and people simply would not vote for tax increases to cover such wage changes. Indeed, individuals strongly objecting to the quality of teaching would perhaps be the first to vote against such salary increases. Thus, the present writer is not optimistic when it comes to improvement in instruction via the selection process, because the basic problem is societal and the system as it stands does not really provide for the opportunity to make the appropriate changes.

These remarks must be qualified in two respects: First, there are of course highly qualified and competent teachers currently teaching, and this point is acknowledged. Second, to improve teaching at the elementary and secondary levels, changes other than salary increases would also be of importance, e.g., increasing the number of courses taken by teachers in the subject matter in which they teach.

The term *personal constraints* refers to characteristics of individuals with whom the student or teacher comes into contact. Thus, the student interacts with peers, as well as with older and younger individuals, and the resulting influences may place constraints, perhaps indirectly, on the learning situation. The home environment is no doubt highly influential. Similarly, teachers interact with their peers as well as with the administrative and supportive staff of the school, and such interaction can influence the instructional process. Thus, the support given by the principal to a particular teacher, or the lack thereof, may have repercussions in the classroom.

Another set of constraints is curricular. Such constraints include the contents of textbooks and the availability and use of resource materials in the library and classroom. These factors become more important when viewed in relation to the previously made point that teachers tend to teach from the text, with the text serving an authority role.

One could of course ask how good the current textbooks are. As legitimate as this question is, it is beyond the scope of the present chapter. Indeed, evaluation of social studies texts is at least as difficult as evaluation of other texts because of the questions about the goals of social studies instruction. However, one comment is in order. Because of the way in which texts are written and published, it would be expected that the changes that occur when new texts are written (or previously published texts are revised) are relatively minor, and that larger and perhaps more innovative changes in text contents are not frequent. This is because publishers want text writers to write what the potential adopters want, and in general what the potential adopters want is that they already have, spiced of course by the "latest research findings." (The study of textbook adoption is in itself an interesting process, especially with respect to where the responsibility lies, e.g., at the district level and/or state level.) Texts which change contents drastically thus do not stand much chance of acceptance. Indeed, this rather conservative approach to innovation is no doubt part of the reason why teachers consider other teachers (not textbooks) as their major resource for improving their instructional skills.

6. How Does the Student Go from the Entering Knowledge State to the Goal?

With respect to the question of how learning of social studies subject matter is presumed to take place, one finds relatively little study of the acquisition of social studies material per se. However, findings do suggest the following tentative conclusions:

1. As previously indicated, a number of methods are used in the instructional process, with lecture, discussion, and reports being predominant. Existing practice thus presumes that learning, as related to classroom instruction, takes place via the application of traditional teaching methods.

2. Tests given in the classroom, so far as it can be determined, include most of the standard methods of testing.

3. At a more theoretical level, the learning process is generally viewed as the accumulation of knowledge with little emphasis upon utilization of knowledge. Social studies thus tend to be taught as somewhat isolated from application and from other subject matter. Furthermore, as pointed out by Shaver, Davis, and Helburn (1979), critical thinking is not emphasized.

7. How Does the Teacher Go from the Entering Knowledge State to the Goal?

This process has received little formal attention. While a teacher may be able to articulate the methods of teaching that are being employed (although two teachers may not do the same thing when they both say they are using a particular method), the data are minimal with respect to how teachers assess what they have learned about the methods they have employed. Transient data on this issue probably exist in the teachers' coffee rooms. Indeed, the idea of teacher learning in the classroom has simply been a neglected area of study.

*8. How Are Students Evaluated, and How Does the Student
   Interpret This Evaluation in Relation to Goals?*

As previously stated, student evaluation takes place via the use of standard testing procedures. The extent to which students relate test results to their goals is of course open to question. In general, it may be assumed that students have particular expectations regarding their own performance and that the test results do or do not confirm such expectations. How realistic the expectations are as well as the reliability and validity of testing procedures are issues beyond the scope of this chapter.

C. Social Studies Instruction Revisited

The issue addressed in this section is what, if anything, research in psychology (especially in cognitive psychology) may have to say about instruction in social studies. This matter is discussed via reconsideration of the problem-solving analysis previously described, although only three components of the analysis are considered, namely, the goals of social studies instruction, what the student brings into the classroom situation, and how the student goes from the initial state to the goal. Only these three issues are discussed because of their direct relevance to the position being developed.

Before these topics are taken up, two preliminary comments are in order. First, the focus of discussion will not be upon what psychological research may have to say about learning and instruction in general, but instead will be upon such processes as they occur in social studies. Second, as previously mentioned, an extremely important aspect of social studies instruction is that of the instructional goals. But psychological research has little to say, at least directly, about what the goals of social studies should be. Yet it is not only essential but critical that the instructional goals be determined, because the goals of social studies that one adopts are intimately related not only to the content but also to the method of instruction. (The one thing psychological research may have to say about the goals of social studies instruction is that people tend to learn most effectively when they are motivated to learn and interested in the subject matter, and this in all likelihood occurs because such factors produce a type of processing which provides for better learning.) Thus, the present writer feels that it is necessary to consider the instructional goals of social studies in some detail. The reader is therefore forewarned that while the comments regarding social studies goals may seem to be somewhat off the point of relating psychological research to social studies instruction, the position taken here is that the goals must be considered. The means cannot be considered independently of the ends, and considering only the means and not the ends leads to a content-free methods approach to instruction which is less than fruitful.

1. What Are the Goals of Social Studies Instruction?

Two assumptions are made with respect to this question. One is that learning is basically goal directed. This assumption is meant to imply that learning generally takes place when instructional goals are well articulated and when these goals are accepted by the learner. Due to individual differences in ability, interest, and experience, however, the extent to which such goals are accepted and the extent to which such acceptance influences motivation would be expected to vary from person to person. The second assumption, which is basic to the position being developed, is that instructional goals and curriculum contents in social studies should be based upon an analysis of contemporary needs, both theoretical and practical. This assumption requires further consideration.

The most theoretically important issues in social studies are presumed to be defined by the research of the field and the social science courses offered at universities. If one uses this criterion, then courses at the secondary level should have as one of their goals the development of an understanding of concepts and principles of such courses. Thus, at the secondary level, a course in economics should include a discussion of the basic principles of micro- as well as of macroeconomics, and not be simply a course on "the free enterprise system." Similarly, a course in psychology should include basic issues of learning, perception, and motivation, and not be just a course emphasizing "adjustment." The assumption thus is made that one goal of social studies instruction should be to develop an understanding of the basic concepts and principles of the particular subject matter.

The idea that the goals of social studies instruction should be guided by contemporary practical needs explicitly assumes that social studies are different from other academic disciplines in that in the social studies area, cultural values, in one way or another, are part of the subject matter. Because of this, the study of issues of practical significance is designed to accomplish two things, namely, to provide the student with the opportunity to learn about important societal issues, i.e., become knowledgeable, and to help the student learn how to evaluate the positions taken on such issues.

Finally, it would be anticipated that the goals of theoretical significance and of practical significance could be shown in fact to be interwoven; the study of the significant practical problems often becomes one facet of more general issues, and the general issues usually constitute basic theoretical problems.

The position that significant theoretical and practical issues should be included in the social studies curriculum constitutes a type of integration of the three traditions previously mentioned. The concern with theoretically significant issues is in clear agreement with the social science tradition in that social studies are viewed as a type of introduction to the college-level curriculum, much in the same way as other academic disciplines. The concern with issues of practical significance is related to the reflective-inquiry tradition in that specific problems are isolated and solutions are to be developed and evaluated. The proposed position differs from the reflective-inquiry tradition, however, in that the proposed position emphasizes the development of one's knowledge base and consideration of theoretical and practical issues in relation to such knowledge, and does not emphasize social studies as a method of gaining experience in the solving of problems in a democracy. The current position is also related to the citizen-transmission tradition in that cultural values are presumed to emerge during the course. However, the two positions differ considerably in that the citizen transmission presumes a set of "true" values to be transmitted, while the present position is concerned with the evaluation of values and with considering how alternative value systems may deal with a particular problem.

One of the issues that is raised by the present position is that of controversy, and it is this writer's opinion that this issue must be met head-on. As previously stated, it seems reasonably clear that, like it or not, social studies are somewhat different from other academic disciplines with respect to their likelihood of controversy. While the biological sciences may contain some topics which produce controversy, evolution or genetic engineering for example, the field of social studies, by the nature of the case, tends to contain large bodies of subject matter about which there may be substantial disagreement. Moreover, it is this writer's opinion that one of the major weaknesses of social studies instruction and curriculum content has been this potential for controversy.

What has been taught, by and large, is what has been "safe." Certainly teaching U.S. history and how "our country has developed" has largely been done without extensive questioning of values and their application. Indeed, a course may be taught in which American ideals are emphasized, but the ideal of everyone's having equal opportunity has been considered only recently in relation to blacks and American Indians. Not only has U.S. history been generally taught so as to be "safe," but another major component of social studies, geography, has also generally been a "safe" topic. Adding to U.S. history and geography the topic of world history, which is largely void of contemporary controversy because it is "in the past," one finds the social studies curriculum indeed to be quite "safe." Similar arguments could be made for what is taught in economics and psychology. Indeed, if one questions whether "safety" is really a major factor in curriculum inclusion, then one may consider what sometimes happens when it is suggested that topics such as sexual education, including birth control, are to be introduced into the curriculum. In other words, issues that have a high probability of producing controversy have generally not been included in the social studies curriculum because of a mostly implicit but sometimes explicit tendency to avoid such issues. Correspondingly, what has been included in the courses are basically "safe" contents. (The reader is referred to a paper by Wiley, 1976, which provides a commentary on the fate of an NSF-developed curriculum called "MAN: A Course of Study" or "MACOS." In the commentary the author discusses how a movement, led by congressmen, was undertaken to reject this social studies curriculum.)

The point is not that a teacher should seek out controversial issues or should by design try to undermine existing beliefs and values and/or be "sensationalistic" in teaching. Rather, an analytic approach is needed in the social studies in which issues of theoretical and practical significance are analyzed and discussed in the context of existing literature—not a "compounding of ignorance" discussion, but an informed analysis based upon data and theory.

The problem with the practice of teaching what is "safe," which typically goes hand in hand with a nonanalytic approach to social studies, is that such teaching is theoretically and practically superficial. It is theoretically superficial because issues tend to be not considered at all or not considered in depth, and thus causal factors of phenomena tend to be neglected; it is practically superficial because it does not really equip the student with means of understanding his or her environment—its sociological, psychological, economic, political, and cultural components. It would seem that a goal of social studies instruction should be to produce an in-depth understanding of these factors as they operate in society. Indeed, if one wants to advocate the view that an important goal of social studies is to pass on the cultural values of a democratic society, then perhaps the first values that should be passed on are that a democracy presumes an informed public, and that to be informed requires knowledge and the ability to use such knowledge in the making of decisions. Thus, if individuals are to make intelligent decisions based upon considered judgment, then the goal of the instructional process should be to provide an opportunity for growth in knowledge development and knowledge utilization.

The National Commission on Excellence in Education (1983) recommended that social science teaching be emphasized, especially advocating instruction in economics. The present position is that this recommendation does not go far enough. Basically, in this writer's opinion, the social studies curriculum should address at least the following issues, primarily because these issues are of such importance in contemporary society that a theoretical as well as practical understanding is critical:

1. Instruction should be given in the field of economics, both microeconomics and macroeconomics, because of their theoretical importance and because of the need that each person understand more about economic issues facing today's society, issues which probably will become more important in the future. Such issues include international trade (including the importance of foreign markets and the effects of foreign producers' selling on the American market), unemployment (with emphasis upon factors contributing to unemployment), taxation, and energy consumption.

2. A study of the U.S. government should be made, with emphasis upon (a) its structure and function and (b) its history, in reference to both its strengths and weaknesses. While such topics are usually covered in the curriculum, there sometimes is a need to consider in more detail some of the practical issues such as the role of lobbying, the growth of bureaucracy, and other components of government function. Of importance would be the study of the powers that reside in the three branches of government and how these have evolved and been interpreted. Furthermore, the understanding of the society-shaping Supreme Court decisions, one would think, would be something that every U.S. citizen should have.

3. The curriculum, within the context of world history and/or political science, should provide for an in-depth study of the historical impact of cultures upon the contemporary world scene. This work should lead to consideration of such issues as (a) problems related to the Middle East, including the role of the cultural and religious history of the area; (b) a study of the Soviet Union in relation to its cultural development, as well as the study of socialism as found in the People's Republic of China and the Eastern-Bloc countries; (c) a study of the nature of, and problems involved in, Third World development. Some courses in "world cultures" do cover issues such as these, but there is a pressing need to develop a better understanding of such matters because they increasingly impact upon the lives of individuals.

4. There is a need to enhance knowledge regarding a number of problems confronting society, and these include crime and its prevention, prison reform, drug (including alcohol) abuse, nuclear energy development, and the role of the media in contemporary society. This list of topics is of

course not exhaustive, but these do serve as examples of significant societal issues that should be studied in depth.

It is quite clear, indeed all too clear, that there has been high priority given in education as well as in federal research funding to science and technology, in large part because of the commercial and military benefits that accrue from technological development. At the same time, most of the major problems that dominate the news every day are political, social, economic, and/or personal. While research on physical disease is given high priority and has had somewhat of a "sacred cow" status, developing an understanding of the causes of drug abuse (including the opportunity to profit) is made subordinate to treatment. Understanding the etiology of crime is made subordinate to enlarging police enforcement and increasing prison facilities. Understanding and transmitting information about the economic causes of unemployment are made subordinate to handling reactions to unemployment. Finally, understanding the relationship of the United States to other countries in the world and evaluating the alternative positions that the United States may take are made subordinate to a turning-inward response by which one takes recourse in the rhetoric of "American values" and "American interests."

The position taken in this chapter regarding the goals of social studies is demanding, in that more student study would be necessary than that currently found in social studies. At least two questions may thus be raised about this position, namely, "Are you not expecting too much by advocating that these rather complicated issues be included in the curriculum?" and "Who would teach these courses?"

The answers offered to these questions are as follows: The curricula of mathematics and the physical sciences in many schools are quite demanding, and such courses involve the need to understand relatively difficult concepts and solve reasonably complicated problems. Furthermore, some secondary schools are now offering courses in programming languages, a movement no doubt emanating from the perceived social and vocational need for computer-based skills. Certainly the concepts of social studies would not, in a number of ways, be more difficult to learn than those in mathematics and physical sciences. It is, therefore, on a content basis, difficult to see why such material could not be incorporated into the curriculum. Even in Grades K–6 concepts may be introduced, as they frequently are now, upon which may be built the subject matter of Grades 7–12. Some curriculum restructuring would be required, and new textbooks would need to be written, but these modifications are feasible.

The question of who would teach such courses must be answered by suggesting that while today there are a limited number of qualified individuals who are available, the number could be augmented by modifying the requirements for individuals who are likely to teach social studies, i.e., emphasizing more work in the academic disciplines. Finally, it would be necessary to accept the idea that the social studies curriculum in the elementary and secondary schools would be more challenging and, it is hoped, more rewarding than it is at present.

In sum, the position taken here is that the goals of K–12 social studies instruction, as currently conceived, should be reevaluated and new or modified goals established because of the increasing need that individuals make considered decisions with respect to the problems of today's society. Moreover, the curriculum should be centered upon subject matter of theoretical and practical significance with an in-depth treatment of the subject matter. Indeed, it is not out of place to suggest that human survival may be at stake.

2. What Does the Student Bring into the Classroom?

The question of what knowledge and skills the student brings into the classroom has been a neglected field of study. Moreover, despite the frequently made assumption that learning is cumulative, it is only in recent years that psychologists have begun to study how the individual's existing knowledge within a particular knowledge domain influences the acquisition of new domain-related information (e.g., Spilich, Vesonder, Chiesi, & Voss, 1979) and how domain-related knowledge influences the solving of problems within the particular domain (Chi, Feltovich, & Glaser, 1981; Larkin, McDermott, Simon, & Simon, 1980; Voss, Greene, Post, & Penner, 1983). Such research has shown not only that prior knowledge is indeed quite important, but also that knowledge produces qualitative as well as quantitative performance differences.

Research has also been pursued on the question of what misconceptions individuals have about domain-related knowledge, primarily in the field of physics. Such research has shown not only that individuals have misconceptions about physical phenomena, but also that such misconceptions sometimes persist even after the individuals have taken a course in physics (Larkin, 1980). Indeed, one investigator (White, 1983), has provided evidence indicating that the failure to modify conceptions when taking a course results in part from a lack of complete understanding of the physics concepts considered in the course.

At the time of this writing, there is no similar work in social studies of which this writer is aware, although there has been a substantial amount of research conducted on political socialization. In such work, (e.g., Rodgers & Tedin, 1976) children's ideas of political concepts or institutions have been studied. One would expect that the study of what naive conceptions entering students have about social studies and how instruction is influenced by such conceptions would be a fruitful area of inquiry. Indeed, research by Furth (1980) supports the notion that a child's concept of money changes considerably as the child develops.

In sum, there is much to be learned about the acquisition of social studies concepts and principles and how one's cumulative knowledge develops in the social studies. Moreover, developing an understanding of the cumulative nature of knowledge could quite possibly lead to instructional facilitation.

3. How Does the Student Move from the Initial State to the Goal?

This section is concerned with the learning process, and four topics of potential significance to instruction in social studies are considered, namely, the solving of ill-structured problems, reasoning, comprehension, and controversy.

As previously noted, problems have been classified as well structured or ill structured (Reitman, 1965; Simon, 1973), although when considered in detail the distinction may be difficult to maintain. Well-structured problems are characterized as having well-defined goals, explicitly stated or at least obvious constraints, and well-defined steps that lead to the goal. An example of such a problem would be a river-crossing problem. In this case, a number of missionaries and a number of cannibals are assumed to be on one side of a river which they want to cross. However, there is only one boat, which holds only two people, and at no time may the number of cannibals exceed the number of missionaries on either side of the river. In this problem the goal is explicit (all must cross the river), the constraints are explicit (boat size and relative number of missionaries and cannibals on either side of the river), and the steps involved in solving the problem, while not explicitly presented, are readily derivable (in some way the steps must involve changing the number of missionaries and cannibals on each side of the river via use of the boat). The problem is thus well structured in relation to the goal, the constraints, and the intervening steps.

Ill-structured problems are characterized as having goals that are not well defined, having constraints that are not explicitly stated, and having solutions, or at least potential solutions, which are not readily derivable from the problem statement. Reitman (1965) used the composition of a fugue by a competent composer as an example of an ill-structured problem.

In the present context probably the most interesting fact is that, taken as a whole, the problems of social studies tend to be ill structured. For example, reducing the crime rate within a particular community is a complex, ill-structured problem. The goal is vague: How will crime rate be measured and what will be regarded as a significant reduction? The constraints are not given in the problem statement and must be obtained from memory or from resources such as the library or other individuals who have dealt with the problem. Finally, the steps leading to the solution are neither well defined nor readily derivable.

As one might expect, while the problem solving that occurs in well-defined and ill-defined problems has similarities, there also are marked differences (Voss, Greene, Post, & Penner, 1983; Voss, Tyler, & Yengo, 1983). While previously reported results cannot be considered in detail, some of the findings have distinct implications for instruction in social studies and thus are now summarized. Although the research conducted by Voss, Greene, Post, & Penner did not focus upon how to reduce the crime rate, the findings are discussed in the context of the hypothetical crime rate problem.

Assume that the procedure employed involves asking experts on community crime and people who are novices in this respect to indicate how they would go about solving this problem. Assume further that these individuals are asked to "think aloud" as they are presenting their solutions. Given the question of how to reduce the crime rate in one's community, a hypothetical novice protocol would be expected to have contents somewhat like this: "One could reduce crime by using more police. Maybe they could put more police on duty when crimes are more likely to be committed. One could also reduce crime by having detectives work on identifying people who fence stolen property. More houses should probably have burglar alarm systems. One could consider stopping the sale of handguns. Maybe stores could close earlier in the evening." While this protocol is hypothetical, two characteristics are obvious. First, the protocol is essentially a listing of what things could be done in order to reduce the chances of specific crimes. Second, little has been said about the possible causal factors in producing crime, except for the ideas implied by the statements that crimes include home burglaries and that warning systems may be used to help prevent this type of crime.

Experts, on the other hand, would be likely to respond by first delineating the factors which operate to produce a high crime rate. These factors would probably be viewed as subproblems. The expert would also probably describe constraints under which the problem would need to be solved—budget and staff limitations, ethical and legal limitations (e.g., stopping everyone on the street after dark could not be done). After considering these issues, the expert would state an abstract representation of the problem, e.g., "The problem is really socioeconomic in nature." Subsequently, the expert would probably propose one or possibly two relatively abstract solutions such as providing a socioeconomic environment in which there are more opportunities for jobs. Finally, after proposing the solution, the expert would tend to do three things, each of which is related to justifying the proposed solution. The expert would tell about things the solution would accomplish, would indicate subproblems that could be encountered in trying to implement the proposed solution, and would also try to propose solutions to these problems. Finally, the expert would evaluate these solutions.

What is particularly instructive about the differences between novice and expert protocols is not simply that the expert knows more, but that the knowledge of the expert is organized and is apparently organized in such a way that it is accessible within a number of problem contexts. Indeed, research on expert and novice problem solving in physics has yielded similar conclusions (Chi et al., 1981; Larkin, et al., 1980). Moreover, Voss, Greene, Post, and Penner (1983) reported a study in which undergraduates taking a political science course were given a particular problem both before and after the course. Although the course contents included information germane to the problem, the protocols taken at the two times (the same subjects were involved before and after) were not appreciably different in form or content. The authors were thus led to conclude that while relevant information had presumably been acquired, it was not organized in a way that made it accessible when a problem was presented. The implications of this conclusion are important with respect to the learning process, for they suggest that it is one thing to "learn" or memorize information but that to have such information serve as "working knowledge" requires experience in organization and utilization. Indeed, essentially the same point has been made in relation to research in the domain of physics. In this case it was argued that physics textbooks tend to indicate how equations may be used to solve problems but that they fail to indicate how individuals should know when to use particular sets of equations (Larkin, 1980; Simon, 1980).

The findings just described at least provide support for the proposition that social studies interaction could perhaps benefit from a greater emphasis upon problem solving, but it must be underscored that problem solving in this case does not involve a simple discussion of how to solve a problem (Voss, in press). Instead, it involves considering how to solve a given problem using information the individual has acquired. Thus, problem solving would effectively be used as a learning tool which at least theoretically could be used to help students organize information they had acquired and, it is hoped, to enable them to respond to new problem situations via the development of "working knowledge." What is being suggested is thus that learning to use the knowledge acquired, especially in a variety of contexts, allows that knowledge to "work" for the student. It is not just stored away; it becomes increasingly available for use.

The second aspect of research to be considered is that of reasoning. As noted, the research on social science problem solving (Voss, 1983) provided findings indicating that once a solution is stated, the expert justifies the solution in the three ways previously described. This finding suggests that instruction in social studies could probably be employed more extensively than it is in order to provide experience in developing verbal reasoning skills, and, most importantly, the development of such skills would also serve as a tool to enhance social studies learning. As in the case of problem solving, experience in verbal reasoning should provide for utilization of information in the context of particular issues.

Two facets of the reasoning process warrant special comment. First, emphasizing reasoning, in the sense of providing a rationale for a position, would be expected to have the outcome that the student would develop a sense of evaluating his or her own position rather than simply reacting. Also, by having students question each other, it would probably be possible to develop critical skills to even a greter extent.

A second point is that the topic of reasoning, in one form or another, has been receiving increased attention in recent years in psychological research (e.g., Tversky & Kahneman, 1980). While this research is not reviewed here, it is worth noting that the question of the extent to which individuals are able to provide a reasonable rationale for decisions they have made has been the subject of study (Nisbitt & Wilson, 1977). The findings of these studies point to the importance of both studying reasoning and developing reasoning skills.

The third problem of contemporary psychological research that relates to social studies instruction is the study of comprehension. In recent years there has been substantial research conducted on the processes of reading and comprehension. Of particular note is the fact that while reading is taught at the primary grade levels, the teaching of reading gradually gives way to reading in content areas, and reading skill thus, if appropriately developed, gives way to comprehension. Thus, the study of comprehension in content areas provides an opportunity to study the acquisition of social studies (Herber, 1970; Wade, 1983).

Finally, the fourth aspect of psychological research considered in relation to social studies instruction is that of controversy. The question of whether considering controversial issues facilitates learning has been addressed. (Johnson & Johnson 1979) considered the issue in relation to Piaget's theory (Piaget, 1924/1976) as well as in relation to the position advanced by Berlyne (1965). Basically, Johnson and Johnson argued that controversial issues can be used to facilitate learning because controversy essentially sets up inconsistencies that usually require resolution, and, to resolve the conflict, it is usually necessary to acquire more information. Moreover, Johnson and Johnson cited data that supported these notions.

The four areas of psychological research that have been described suggest that learning may be facilitated in social sciences by employing procedures which emphasize not only that individuals should know more but also that they should learn to use what they know in various contexts, whether the context relates to problem solving, reasoning, comprehension, or dealing with controversial issues. Learning thus is not simply taken to mean that "we know something." Instead, learning is taken to involve the development of a strong knowledge base with the development of skill in the utilization of such knowledge. In this way a "working knowledge" is developed.

IV. SUMMARY

This chapter presented a discussion of psychology and the social studies curriculum. The main points may be summarized as follows: (1) The actual or potential investigator of processes involved in learning and instruction as found in social studies should be aware that learning in this domain is related to a large number of variables, one set of which involves content acquisition per se. In order to sensitize the investigator to the other variables as they are found in K–12 social studies instruction, a discussion of curriculum issues and teacher characteristics was presented. (2) An analysis of social studies instruction was presented based upon the information-processing model of problem solving, with four components being emphasized. These were the goals, the initial state of the teacher and student, constraints, and how learning takes place. The existing state of social studies instruction was then analyzed in terms of the components of the problem-solving analysis. Especially emphasized was the need to reevaluate the goals of social studies instruction. Finally, four sets of findings of contemporary psychological research were considered, and it was pointed out how these findings may be able to make significant contributions to social studies instruction. The four sets of findings involved problem solving, reasoning, comprehension, and controversy.

ACKNOWLEDGMENTS

The preparation of this paper was supported in part by funds provided to the Learning Research and Development Center of the University of Pittsburgh by the National Institute of Education. The opinions reflected in this paper are not necessarily those of either organization. The author wishes to thank Dr. Cathy Cornbleth of the University of Pittsburgh for her assistance in helping him develop an understanding of social studies instruction.

Naturally, if this understanding is found wanting, it is not her fault. The author also wishes to thank Mary L. Means for her comments on a preliminary draft of this manuscript.

REFERENCES

Barth, J. L., & Shermis, S. S. (1970). Defining the social studies: An exploration of three traditions. *Social Education, 34,* 743–751.

Berlyne, D. E. (1965). *Structure and direction in thinking.* New York: Wiley.

Chi, M. T. H., Feltovich, P., & Glaser, R. (1981). Categorization and representation of physics problems by experts and novices. *Cognitive Science, 5,* 121–152.

Furth, H. G. (1980). *The world of grown-ups.* New York: Elsevier.

Herber, H. L. (1970). *Teaching reading in content areas.* Englewood Cliffs, NJ: Prentice-Hall.

Johnson, D. W., & Johnson, R. T. (1979). Conflict in the classroom: Controversy and learning. *Review of Educational Research, 49,* 51–70.

Larkin, J. H. (1980). Teaching problem solving in physics: The psychological laboratory and the practical classroom. In D. T. Tuma & F. Reif (Eds.), *Problem solving and education: Issues in teaching and research* (pp.111–125). Hillsdale, NJ: Erlbaum.

Larkin, J. H., McDermott, J., Simon, D. P., & Simon, H. A. (1980). Models of competence. *Cognitive Science, 4,* 317–345.

Mayer, R. E. (1977). *Thinking and problem solving: An introduction to human cognition and learning.* Glenview, IL: Scott, Foresman.

Morris, J. E., & Garcia, J. (1982). Social studies in rural America. *Social Education, 46,* 115–120.

National Commission on Excellence in Education. (1983). *A nation at risk: The imperative for educational reform.* Washington, DC: U.S. Government Printing Office.

Newell, A., & Simon, H. (1972). *Human problem solving.* Englewood Cliffs, NJ: Prentice-Hall.

Nisbett, R. E., & Wilson, T. D. (1977). Telling more than we can know: Verbal reports on mental processes. *Psychological Review, 84,* 231–259.

Piaget, J. (1976). *Judgment and reasoning in the child.* (Reprinted from original, 1924). New York: Littlefield.

Reitman, W. (1965). *Cognition and thought.* New York: Wiley.

Rodgers, H. R., & Tedin, K. L. (Eds.). (1976, December). Political socialization: An assessment of theoretical approaches, methods, and findings. *Youth and Society, 8,* 107–207.

Rutherford, J. F. (1979). In *What are the needs in precollege science, mathematics and social science education? Views from the field* (Document No. SE 80-9). Washington, DC: National Science Foundation, Office of Program Integration, Directorate for Science Education.

Shaver, J. P., Davis, O. L., & Helburn, S. M. (1979). An interpretive report on the status of precollege social studies education based on three NSF-funded studies. In *What are the needs in precollege science, mathematics, and social science education? Views from the field* (Document No. SE 80-9). Washington, DC: National Science Foundation, Office of Program Integration, Directorate for Science Education.

Simon, H. A. (1973). The structure of ill-structured problems. *Artificial Intelligence, 4,* 181–201.

Simon, H. A. (1980). Problem solving and education. In D. T. Tuma & F. Reif (Eds.), *Problem solving and education: Issues in teaching and research* (pp. 81–90). Hillsdale, NJ: Erlbaum.

Spilich, G. J., Vesonder, G. T., Chiesi, H. L., & Voss, J. F. (1979). Text processing of domain-related information for individuals with high and low domain knowledge. *Journal of Verbal Learning and Verbal Behavior, 18,* 275–290.

Stake, R. E., & Easley, J. A., Jr. (1978, January). *Case studies in science education* (Report to the National Science Foundation on Contract No. C7621134). Urbana-Champaign: University of Illinois at Urbana-Champaign, Center for Instructional Research and Curriculum Evaluation and Committee on Culture and Cognition.

Superka, D. P., Hawke, S., & Morrisett I. (1980). The current and future status of the social studies. *Social Education, 45,* 362–369.

Tversky, A., & Kahneman, D. (1980). Causal schemata in judgments under uncertainty. In M. Fishbein (Ed.), *Progress in social psychology* (pp. 49–72). Hillsdale, NJ: Erlbaum.

Voss, J. F. (1983). Problem solving and the educational process. In R. Glaser & A. Lesgold (Eds.), *Handbook of psychology and education.* Hillsdale, NJ: Erlbaum.

Voss, J. F., Greene, T. R., Post, T. A., & Penner, B. C. (1983). Problem solving skill in the social sciences. In G. H. Bower (Ed.), *The psychology of learning and motivation: Advances in research theory* (vol. 17, pp. 165–213). New York: Academic Press.

Voss, J. F., Tyler, S., & Yengo, L. (1983). Individual differences in the solving of social science problems. In R. Dillon & R. Schmeck (Eds.), *Individual differences in cognition* (pp. 205–232). New York: Academic Press.

Wade, S. (1983). A synthesis of the research for improving reading in the social studies. *Review of Educational Research, 53,* 461–497.

Weiss, I. R. (1978, March). *Report of the 1977 national survey of science, mathematics, and social studies education* (Report to the National Science Foundation on Contract No. C7619848). Washington D.C.: Research Triangle Institute, Center for Educational Research and Evaluation.

White, B. Y. (1983). Sources of difficulty in understanding Newtonian dynamics. *Cognitive Science, 7,* 41–66.

Wiley, K. B. (1976). *The NSF science education controversy: Issues, events, decisions.* Boulder, CO: ERIC Clearing House for Social Studies/Social Science Education, and Social Science Education Consortium.

Wiley, K. B. (1977). *The status of pre-college science, mathematics, and social science education: 1955–1975: Vol. 3. Social science education.* Boulder, CO: Social Science Education Consortium.

8

Art

SUSAN C. SOMERVILLE
and JEFFREY L. HARTLEY
Department of Psychology
Arizona State University
Tempe, Arizona 85287

This chapter deals with the implications of current evidence about children's cognitive development for curriculum design in the arts. However, we do not undertake a complete examination of this question. The focus is on children's drawings and in fact on the drawings of quite young children, for the most part. Our first interest is in the cognitive strategies which children employ when they draw and in how these strategies change with age. The strategies pertain to developmental changes occurring universally in young children rather than to individual differences between children in the extent of their creative skills. Of central importance are the developments occurring immediately before and after children enter school for the first time. This is partly because a great deal of evidence has become available recently about children of this age and partly because the first entry into school occurs at a crucial point in children's artistic development. Most of the evidence we discuss concerns children's production of drawings rather than their appreciation of the work of others. However, when we examine the educational implications of cognitive developmental work, we incorporate ideas stemming from studies of children's artistic appreciation as well.

A second question, which is as important as the first, is that of children's drawings as artistic endeavors. Only recently have developmental psychologists begun to investigate the aesthetic and artistic aspects of young children's drawings. Some of their investigations of these aspects have important implications for curriculum design in the arts. Therefore, we include theoretical ideas and empirical evidence about the aesthetic aspects of early development in our discussion of the way children draw and appreciate drawings. In fact, we concentrate for some time on the concept of individual artistic styles and the question of whether children possess

241

and develop styles of their own. The notion of individual styles lies at the heart of both the expert's and the layman's ideas about art and artists. We argue that it can be as useful in studies of the work of young children as it has always been in evaluating the work of adults. This question of style, in conjunction with more traditional questions about the spatial and cognitive abilities implicated in the drawings of young children, leads us next to the step of considering what kinds of early educational experiences in the arts might be of most benefit to children. The educational implications which we discuss also pertain primarily to drawing. At times we point to parallels with developments and education in other branches of the arts, but the theoretical and empirical evidence which we consider is almost all concerned with drawing.

Before turning to details first of the developmental work and then of the implications of this work for early education, it is worthwhile to consider more generally the importance of pictorial activities for both children and adults. People have a universal interest in pictures, maps, and other methods of depicting the world. Pictures and maps are valued both as aesthetically pleasing creations and for the information and ideas which they convey. The conventions involved in pictorial forms of representation are complex and the question of whence they arise an extremely important one. Psychologists have found that the conventions which we use reflect our cognitive structuring of experiences of objects and events (e.g., Hochberg, 1978). Kennedy (1983; Kennedy & Fox, 1977; Kennedy & Heywood, 1980) has suggested, on the basis of the perception of pictures by the blind, that at least some knowledge of the conventional system of graphic depiction is innate and that the system is accessible not just through vision but also through touch. For example, both blind and sighted people tend to assume that a narrow line in a drawing represents the edge of something, rather than a boundary separating different regions of a single entity. Pictorial displays offer a powerful and congenial way for people to convey information and ideas. This appears to be so partly because we tend to mold our pictorial systems to fit the way in which we understand the world.

If it is true that our systems of pictorial representation reflect our cognitive structuring of the world, then the question of how children acquire such systems becomes a particularly intriguing one. It is certainly not true, for example, that children have to be coaxed or goaded into learning to make pictorial representations. Nor is it true that their learning of these systems has to wait until a relatively late stage in development. Very young children spontaneously develop an interest in depicting the world, and the developmental steps through which their methods of graphic representation pass are intriguing (e.g., Gardner, 1973, 1980; Kellogg, 1969;

Lark-Horovitz, Lewis, & Luca, 1973). From an educational point of view, it is important to ask what processes or strategies the child uses when drawing, what changes occur in these strategies, and when and how these changes occur. Do the changes reflect and depend on changes in the child's growing understanding of the world? If they do, what is the best way for children's education in methods of pictorial representation to proceed? The answers to these questions must form an essential basis for the design of early education in the graphic arts.

Aside from the question we have raised about the dependency of graphic skills on cognitive development, the question of how best to devise methods of instruction in pictorial representation is particularly interesting for at least two further reasons. First there is the problem, brought to our attention by the quality of primitive art and to some extent by the art of young or exceptional children (e.g., Arnheim, 1972; Gardner, 1980; Selfe, 1977), of whether or not instruction in the arts is necessary or even beneficial (e.g., Gardner, 1976; Shulman, 1978). Second, the multifaceted nature of graphic skills in particular and of representation in general introduces complexities into the question of what is required of an instruction program. In order to instruct or guide children in the development of graphic skills one must understand how their knowledge of different systems or modes of representation is derived. For example, children develop knowledge of both cartographic and pictorial systems (Davis & Fucigna, 1983) just as they develop knowledge of both literal and metaphorical modes of language use (e.g., Winner, 1979; Winner, Blank, & Miller, 1983). It is important to know whether their knowledge of the different systems develops separately, or whether one is an offshoot of the other and therefore materializes at a somewhat later point. Even if the developmental evidence turns out to be sufficient only to raise and not to provide answers to such questions, the questions must nevertheless be considered in designing early curricula for the arts.

As a preliminary illustration of the relevance of these questions for children's art let us consider several drawings by children aged between 5 and 7 years (Figure 1). This 2- or 3-year period, incidentally, is the time in which young children's creative abilities are thought to reach a kind of peak (Gardner, 1980). The first point is that many drawings at this age reveal that the child has a sense of how to assemble or compose elements to form a picture. Figure 1a shows a 5-year-old's drawing of a human figure on the horizon; the sense of balance in this drawing is elegant in its simplicity. More complex compositions by children of about the same age also show balanced placement of parts on the page, as is illustrated by the drawing of a space station shown in Figure 1c. Golomb (1981) has suggested that there are limitations to the kinds of balance achieved by

Fig. 1. (a) Upper left, person on horizon by girl 5 years old; (b) center left, space station by boy 7 years old; (c) lower left, house and family by girl 5 years old; (d) upper right, instructions for building a tree house by boy 7 years old; (e) center right, map of Canada and United States by boy 6 years old; (f) lower right, the planets by boy 7 years old.

children younger than 8 years, but her evidence came from drawings of subject matters which were suggested to the children by an adult rather than being of their own choice. Whether this would matter to their compositional approach is not known.

The second point is that the predominantly pictorial representations we have discussed differ from drawings made at the same age to convey information of a more diagrammatic nature. This is clear, for example, if we compare the drawings in Figures 1b and 1d, both by the same child. In Figure 1d the diagrammed steps in the construction (and eventual use) of a tree house are presented in separate, numbered "frames," and the action of climbing to the house is indicated by arrows rather than movement. Similar to this diagram are the maps by two different children shown in Figures 1e (the United States and Canada) and 1f (the planets). Both maps concentrate on the itemization of parts or elements rather than on the composition of these elements into a pictorial whole. This indicates that quite young children are capable of using different representational methods for different purposes. It may also be true that when children begin to acquire these different systems they do not keep them entirely separate. This is suggested by the drawing shown in Figure 1e, in which a cow is suspended between the differentiated region of southern states (where the child lived) and an undifferentiated Canada, bringing about an unconventional combination of pictorial and maplike qualities in the same drawing.

Recent studies have begun to provide insight into children's early systems of graphic representation. It has been found, for example, that children follow certain cognitive rules or strategies when they produce drawings of various types (e.g., Freeman, 1980; Goodnow, 1977; Van Sommers, 1984). The philosophical and psychological issues involved in a cognitive approach to the arts are complex and are by no means resolved (e.g., Arnheim, 1969, 1972; Gardner, 1977; Gombrich, 1961, 1972; Goodman, 1976, 1977, 1978; Langer, 1942, 1957; Olson, 1978; Silvers, 1978). Nevertheless, there is undeniably a cognitive component to the production and appreciation of works of art. Particularly in the case of young children, whose cognitive skills and strategies differ from those of adults, any means of gaining insight into these cognitive processes is valuable. Most investigators who have adopted a cognitive approach to children's drawings have examined such aspects as the representation of spatial relations (e.g., Piaget & Inhelder, 1967; Willats, 1977a, 1977b) or the strategies involved in graphic production (e.g., Freeman, 1980; Goodnow, 1977; Phillips, Hobbs, & Pratt, 1978; Van Sommers, 1984). These studies have provided only indirect information about aesthetic aspects of children's art. Although aesthetic aspects such as a sense of balance or harmony, the use of expressive qualities, and the development of individual styles have been discussed in many different contexts (e.g., Arnheim, 1969; Edwards, 1979; Gardner, 1980; Gardner, Wolf, & Smith, 1982; Lark-Horovitz et al., 1973; Schaefer-Simmern, 1948), until recently there has been little systematic investigation of these aspects (cf. Winner, 1982).

The questions and issues which we have outlined are taken up in more detail in the next four sections of the chapter. Because it has been a some-what neglected aspect of investigations of children's drawings and because we want to emphasize its importance, the concept of artistic style is ex-amined in the first section, which develops an approach to the study of individual styles in both children and adults. In the next section we turn to the more traditional areas of developmental investigation—the changes with age in children's graphic skills and strategies. Then the third section integrates the evidence derived from traditional areas of investigation with evidence from our own studies of children's individual drawing styles. The final section draws on all of this information about both cognitive and aesthetic aspects of the development of graphic skills to arrive at implications for curriculum design in the early school years.

I. THE CONCEPT OF STYLE

In both the appreciation and the mastery of artistic ability the concept of style is important. Developing artists are encouraged to search for a style that will distinguish them from others; the work of new artists is evaluated and understood in terms of its origins in and/or its departures from stylistic traditions; and an ability to recognize and appreciate the major stylistic categories into which we place works of art is required of all students. And yet an artistic style is something which is very difficult to define. In fact, the very concept of style itself is an elusive one.

There are several reasons for this. First, although it is tempting to think of style as just one aspect of a work, more careful analysis shows it to be inextricably bound up in all the aspects of that work. A commonly accepted view is that there are three major components of style: expression (or intended meaning), form (or technique), and subject matter (Finch, 1974; Gardner, 1980; Goodman, 1976, 1978; Silvers, 1981). For example, Goodman (1978) argued that "style comprises certain characteristic fea-tures both of what is said and how it is said, both of subject and of wording, both of content and of form" (p. 27). Second, the concept of style refers not to a static, clearly defined entity, but to something that is continually changing or evolving with time (Arnheim, 1981). In Kubler's (1967) view, "styles . . . are neither perpetual nor in random change. Being in change, however, their identity is in doubt at every instant" (p. 845). Thus an adequate conceptualization of style must incorporate principles or processes which generate changes at the same time as they preserve the structure and functioning of the artist's activity as a whole. Finally, although style is certainly part of what makes the works of an artist or of a school distinctive, not all of the distinctive properties of works of art are stylistic. The authenticity of a Gauguin painting could, in principle, be determined just as well by a chemical analysis of the paint as by an appeal to stylistic properties.

These properties of the concept of style are similar to the properties of other concepts which have been studied by psychologists. In particular, the way in which we think of paintings as belonging to a stylistic category is similar to the way in which we think of the members of semantic and natural categories such as animals (Henley, 1969), vegetables (Brown, 1978), and games (Wittgenstein, 1953). These are categories that philosophers and psychologists have come to regard as *ill defined*. This term is used to distinguish them from categories that are *well defined* in the sense that there is at least one defining characteristic shared by all members of the category (e.g., Neisser, 1967). Two implications for the knowledge or acquisition of a category follow if it is well defined. First, whether or not a particular item is a member of the category can be decided unambiguously by determining whether or not it possesses the defining characteristic(s). Second, a person's knowledge of the category does not change as he or she becomes acquainted with more and more of its members. For example, the concept of a red triangle is not subject to modification by the addition of previously unseen instances.

The concept of an ill-defined category, by contrast, has been shown to evolve and change as a person encounters new members (Homa, Rhoads, & Chambliss, 1979). It is also distinct from a well-defined concept because there is no feature or combination of features shared by all of its members and because, as a consequence, the membership of items cannot be determined unambiguously. For example, no perceptual or functional characteristics are common to all pieces of furniture, and there are items in every household which are viewed possibly as furniture, possibly not (e.g., a piano). The most extensive studies of ill-defined categories have dealt with concepts derived from abstract shapes such as dot patterns and irregular polygons (e.g., Homa, 1978; Homa, Sterling, & Trepel, 1981; Posner & Keele, 1968, 1970; Rips, 1975) or with natural and semantic categories (e.g., Rosch, 1975, 1978; Rosch & Mervis 1975; Rosch, Mervis, Gray, Johnson, & Boyes-Braem, 1976). However, it has also been argued that ill-defined categories provide an appropriate conceptual approach to artistic styles (Hartley & Homa, 1981; Hartley, Somerville, Jensen, &

Eliefja, 1982; Neisser, 1967). This argument is supported both by an examination of the concept of style itself and by empirical studies of adults' acquisition of stylistic concepts (Hartley & Homa, 1981; Rush & Sabers, 1981).

Knowledge of the style of a given artist or school is derived through experience with a collection of works. A number of different positions could be adopted on the perceptual and cognitive processes involved in its derivation and on the exact form which the derived knowledge might take. For example, there is evidence to support the notion that knowledge of ill-defined categories is based on the abstraction of prototypes (e.g., Homa et al., 1981; Rosch, 1978), that it is based on the perceived relations (e.g., similarities) between exemplars (e.g., Brooks, 1978; Medin & Schaffer, 1978; Tversky, 1977), or that it is based on the abstraction of features common to category members (e.g., Barresi, Robbins, & Smith, 1975). It is not clear, however, that these differing conceptions are necessarily mutually exclusive (see, e.g., Rosch, 1978). For the present purposes they will be regarded as providing alternative or possibly complementary accounts of the major characteristics of ill-defined categories. These major characteristics are what is most important to the explication of the concept of an artistic style.

The first major property of an artistic style is the absence of a defining feature or combination of features shared by all of the works in that style. Some works may share one feature while others share another one or more, and these sets may be partially overlapping, leading to a structure which is like that of "family resemblances" (Rosch & Mervis, 1975; Wittgenstein, 1953). Further, the features or combinations of features that are important to the style are those that serve to distinguish the style most sensitively from others. These points are emphasized in Goodman's (1978) analysis of the concept of style, in which he argues that "some properties may be only usual rather than constant features of a given style; and some may be stylistically significant not through appearing always or even often in the works of a given author or period but through appearing never or almost never in other works" (p. 34).

Goodman's view of the concept of style is similar to Rosch's (1978) analysis of both real-world and artificial categories, in which she argues that there is a "human tendency once a contrast exists to define attributes for contrasting categories so that the categories will be maximally distinctive" (p. 37); it is also similar to Tversky and Gati's (1978) contention that people tend to organize sets of stimuli into clusters so as to "maximize the similarity of objects within the cluster and the dissimilarity of objects from different clusters" (p. 91). The preconceived similarities between objects and indeed the features that are useful for distinguishing members of one category from another will also vary according to the overall context within which categorical judgments are made (Goodman, 1972; Tversky & Gati, 1978). If we consider several artists from the impressionist school, for example, the stylistic concepts that would be used to distinguish the works of individual impressionists would differ from those which would be used to distinguish those artists, as a school, from other schools. Thus a style is not a property of the works themselves, but represents the conceptual groupings of the works that are relevant to that style (Goodman, 1978). Silvers (1981) has argued that stylistic concepts refer not just to the works but also to the artist, period, or school which they exemplify. However, whether there is a connection between style and the character or personality of an artist is a matter of considerable debate (see O'Hare, 1981).

A further important characteristic of ill-defined categories relevant to the notion of style is that their members vary in representativeness. Central, or typical category members are those which are readily judged to belong to the category, judged to be good examples of the category, judged to be similar to many other category members, and also found to share a variety of features with other members of the category (e.g., Rosch, 1978). Their judged resemblance to members of other categories is low, as is their likelihood of being included as members of other categories. In addition to these highly representative members, ill-defined categories contain peripheral, atypical members that differ from the typical ones in all the above respects. It follows from this that, by contrast with well-defined categories, ill-defined categories have unclear boundaries, and the membership of outlying, atypical members is always in doubt (cf. Wittgenstein, 1953). This makes the notion of ill-defined categories particularly applicable to styles, because the style of an artist at a particular time may, for example, be in the process of evolving from the style of an earlier or contemporary artist, or even from the same artist's own style in a former period.

There have been several empirical studies of adults' ability to learn the individual styles of recognized artists (Hartley & Homa, 1981; Rush & Sabers, 1981; Walk, Karusaitis, Lebowitz, & Falbo, 1971). Hartley and Homa presented adults who had no formal training in the appreciation of art with varying numbers of paintings by Matisse, Manet, and Renoir. After learning to categorize these paintings correctly according to artist, the adults were tested on their ability to categorize previously unseen works by the same artists. Several aspects of the findings supported the notion that adults abstracted ill-defined stylistic concepts from the paintings they saw. First, their ability to recognize new works increased as they were given experience with a greater number of examples of the artists' work. Second, some new drawings by each artist were recognized better than others, suggesting variations in typicality. Third, new drawings were sometimes attributed to the wrong artist, suggesting that the boundaries between stylistic concepts were vague. Finally, when the adults were asked to make similarity ratings of all possible pairs of the paintings, some paintings were rated as more similar to those of another artist than to others by the same artist. Together these findings indicated that the adults' stylistic concepts did not consist of a particular feature or combination of features which could be found in all and only the paintings of a given artist; that is, their concepts could not be described as well defined.

Rush and Sabers (1981) showed adults who were taking classes in art five paintings each by Manet, Degas, Renoir, and Toulouse-Lautrec. Half of the adults were told only the artists' names as they viewed the paintings, and the other half were given a brief verbal description of the style of each artist in addition to the names. For example, for Manet the description was "His work is austere and deliberate, without shadows and with little depth" (p. 32). Rush and Sabers next asked the adults to judge previously unseen paintings by the same artists and found no differences between the judgments made by those who had been given verbal descriptions and those who had not. It can be inferred from this that the stylistic concepts abstracted from the paintings were not changed or made more precise by the provision of particular ready-made rules. However, it is not possible to distinguish between a number of interpretations of why this was the case. For example, perhaps the adults lacked the ability to apply the rules to the paintings that they saw, or perhaps the rules did not add to the insights gained spontaneously through viewing the initial paintings.

The adults' stylistic concepts were assessed by asking them to judge the likelihood that the previously unseen paintings (10 by each of the four artists) were the work of Manet. Rush and Sabers found that these likelihood judgments were higher, on the average, for paintings by Manet than for those by any of the other artists. They were lowest for Lautrec, indicating that his style was seen as most distinct from that of Manet. Thus over all, the adults were able to distinguish the styles of the three other artists from that of Manet. However, there were some individual paintings by Manet that were consistently judged as unlikely to be by him, some that received a wide range of likelihood ratings, and some that were consistently judged as certain to be his work. That is, Manet's paintings varied considerably in the degree to which they typified the adults' concepts of his style. The next important point is that there were paintings by Degas and Renoir judged (at least by some adults) as likely to be the work of Manet. So we can conclude that the stylistic concepts for these three artists did not possess definite boundaries. There was apparently a clearer boundary between Manet and Lautrec, because all of Lautrec's previously unseen paintings were consistently rated as unlikely to be the work of Manet. Overall, the findings of this study were similar to those of Hartley and Homa (1981), and they supported the notion of artistic styles as ill-defined concepts. Rush and Sabers concluded that each painting contained "some mix of distinctive features, rather than all those associated with any painter's style"(p.30).

In summary, we have suggested a conceptual approach to artistic style which is based on several philosophical and psychological investigations of ill-defined concepts. We have placed emphasis on the concept of style because it seems capable of encompassing many different aspects of children's graphic activity. The aesthetic aspects of their drawings must certainly enter into style, as must the strategies they use in the formation of lines and shapes to convey objects and expressive qualities. In other words, content, form, and intended meaning can all be incorporated in the notion of style in children's drawings, just as they can for the work of adult artists. Our next step is to examine the implications of this approach to the concept of style for two major areas of educational interest. The first is the development of artistic ability in young children. The second is the acquisition of knowledge about art and its appreciation by both children and adults.

II. ARTISTIC DEVELOPMENT IN YOUNG CHILDREN

Developmental psychologists traditionally have not been concerned with the aesthetic or artistic aspects of children's representations of the world (in graphic or other forms). Instead, they have emphasized the symbolic skills required by the creation of drawings, sculptures, poems, or play events (e.g., Piaget, 1954; Smith & Franklin, 1979; Werner & Kaplan, 1963). Studies of children's graphic skills have been used, for example, as indices of general intellectual development (Harris, 1963), although the validity of this approach has been questioned on several grounds (Freeman, 1977; Goodnow, 1977; Kellogg, 1969; Yule, Lockyer, & Noone, 1967). Children's understanding of various methods of representing spatial relations has also been assessed by examining the drawings that they produce (or select) to depict shapes, objects, or scenes (e.g., Golomb, 1981; Kosslyn, Heldmeyer, & Locklear, 1977; Lewis, 1963; Light & Simmons, 1983; Phillips et al., 1978; Piaget & Inhelder, 1967; Willats, 1977a, 1977b, 1981, 1983). Finally, there have been several investigations of the motor sequences, cognitive strategies, or rules that children develop to guide their graphic productions (Freeman, 1980; Goodnow, 1977; Van Sommers,

1984). These studies are informative about the cognitive underpinnings of children's developing artistic skills. The most basic question which they address is that of the foundations or origins of representational drawing.

A. The Origins of Symbolic Representation

The commonly accepted view of how representation begins has been that children initially produce graphic products as an unplanned by-product of motor activities with a pencil or crayon (e.g., moving it back and forth, or in a circular path, or jabbing it repeatedly on a page). For example, Kellogg (1969) has argued that children's early scribble patterns (produced from about 1½ or 2 years) take a number of regular forms and are gradually transformed into distinguishable shapes and then into various complexes (e.g., the mandala) that eventually form the building blocks of the earliest representational drawings (at about 3 or 4 years). Similarly, Gardner (1980) has emphasized that the 1- to 2-year-old's interest is in the contrasting motor activities that produce dots, smooth lines, or jagged patterns, rather than in the products of those motions on the page. Although there are occasional earlier signs, "the linkage of the world of graphic activity to the universe of experience does not occur until the age of three" (Gardner, 1980, p.46). In this respect, children's graphic skills have been said to lag behind developments in play, block building, and the creation of stories or musical tunes. Whereas these other activities are used to signify events in the real world as soon as the the capacity for symbolic activity is attained (i.e., at about 18 to 24 months of age; cf. Piaget, 1951, 1954), "the forms that are drawn remain just forms, still unconnected to the world of objects and experiences beyond" (Gardner, 1980, p. 45). However, in the light of several recent studies this view now seems a controversial one.

Golomb (1981) has questioned whether representational drawings are produced only after the mastery of various nonpictorial patterns and shapes has occurred. In a study in which 2- to 7-year-olds were asked to draw human figures, animals, a tree, a house, and other items, Golomb found that 39% of 2-year-olds produced at least one representational drawing (most often a human) and that the 3-year-olds were able to comply with a variety of representational requests. These representational drawings, in common with those of the older children, were marked by characteristic preferred orientations for different items (e.g., sideways and horizontal for a snake, front facing and upright for a human). Golomb therefore argued that children are aware of the representational possibilities of graphic activity at a very early age and that "objects in the real world rather than . . . practice with designs determine the selection of representational forms and models" (p.41).

This position is also supported by the work of Freeman (1977, 1980), who found that 2-year-olds, if asked, were able to make appropriate additions to a partially drawn human figure to represent, for example, an ear or a nose. However, these same children were unable to initiate complete representational drawings of a human figure on their own. Matthews (1983) has argued on the basis of detailed consideration of the drawings of several 2-year-olds (interpreted with the help of contextual and verbal information) that even at this young age the child's graphic products represent actions and the figurative appearances of objects. Although it is extremely difficult to obtain conclusive evidence about the precise beginnings of representation in drawings, it seems likely that children are sensitive at least to the potential for differential representation of different objects soon after they begin to place marks on the page.

Gardner and his colleagues (Gardner, 1983; Gardner & Wolf, 1983; Wolf, 1983) provided new insights into the early development of symbolic skills through a longitudinal study of 9 children over a period of 6 years, beginning at the age of 1 year. The investigators assessed these children's developing use of seven different symbol systems at very frequent intervals. The seven symbol systems were "language (particularly story telling and metaphor), symbolic play, two-dimensional representation, three-dimensional representation (primarily block-building), bodily expression, music and number" (Gardner, 1983, p. 4). They then analyzed and compared developments occurring within these different systems and postulated three successive "waves of symbolization" beginning approximately 1 year apart, the first at the age of about 2 years.

They suggested that the first wave depends on the child's early capacity to structure his or her experience with the world in terms of events, and is signaled by the child's use of language and symbolic play to represent this structured knowledge. At this early stage there is somewhat inappropriate transfer of this type of symbolization to other systems; for example, the child may use a marker to enact the action of "driving" across the paper when asked to draw a picture of a truck. The second wave of symbolization involves an important step for graphic representation, because the patterns or spatial properties of events or displays which the child experiences are now mapped onto the symbolic system. Now an object such as a truck will be represented by a closed shape, perhaps with additional shapes for the wheels. These mappings are restricted to elementary topological features of the spatial relations (cf. Piaget & Inhelder, 1967) and do not include precise representations of the relative sizes, numbers, or interval properties of items belonging, for example, to an ordered series. In a third wave of symbolization, beginning at about 4 years, the child begins to represent metric properties such as the relative sizes of objects and the intervals between notes in a musical scale (Wolf, 1983).

In summary, in the period from 2 to 4 years the child is engaged in an effort to connect the forms and marks that he or she can produce to the subject matter of his or her world. As N. R. Smith (1979) has pointed out, this struggle to achieve a balance between the potentials of the artistic materials and the intended portrayal of a subject is common to the work of all artists, be they children or adults. At about 4 years of age the child enters a period of artistic productivity that is unparalleled by any other developmental period in its exuberance and air of mastery (Gardner, 1980). In the next several years the child acquires, modifies, and perfects an impressive repertoire of strategies for graphic and other forms of representation. The next section examines the developments which occur during this remarkable period, dealing first with the cognitive rules and strategies and then with the aesthetic aspects.

B. Representational Strategies in the Young Child

A detailed examination of the burgeoning literature on children's early representational strategies is beyond the scope of this section. In keeping with the conceptual approach we outlined, our principal aim is to present findings that establish that young children command graphic skills sufficient to form a basis for individual styles. We therefore select studies and evidence of particular relevance to this question. A second criterion used in our selection is that the studies should provide insight into cognitive or aesthetic knowledge that is important in the artistic education of the young child. The first three sections describe the cognitive and the fourth the artistic developments.

1. Parts and What They Represent

Children's earliest representational drawings are composed of parts, each represented by a line or shape. An encircling shape is often used to signify the collection of various parts into a whole. The most famous of children's early representations are the "tadpole" figures in which a closed, irregular shape has certain features contained inside it and others extending outward. These are perhaps the earliest representations of human and other animal forms. There have been arguments about the interpretation of tadpole figures: Some investigators have seen them as revealing children's insensitivity to the spatial relations between body parts (e.g., Piaget & Inhelder, 1967), while other investigators have argued that they represent more global visual concepts of the body (Arnheim, 1974). Goodnow (1977) has drawn attention to the great variety of shapes, line forms, and connections between them that children use in these early representations of the human figure. By presenting human figures that are partially drawn and asking young children to add to them, several investigators have also shown that the placement, size, and orientation of new parts will be influenced by the positions, relative sizes, and other features of the parts which are already present (e.g., Freeman, 1975, 1980; Goodnow, 1977; Goodnow & Friedman, 1972).

Interpreters of these early representational attempts have tended to fall into two camps, one emphasizing the cognitive deficits or limitations in information-processing capacity that might lead to missing or strangely connected parts (e.g., Freeman, 1980), the other stressing that the drawings represent visual concepts and should not be misconstrued as attempted "copies" of an original form (Arnheim, 1974; Golomb, 1981). The same issue has arisen in studies of children's reproductions of geometric shapes and of three-dimensional objects such as houses or cubes. Early investigators in this area interpreted children's failures to produce accurate copies as indicative of deficiencies in their understanding of spatial relations (e.g., Lewis, 1963; Piaget & Inhelder, 1967). More recently, however, researchers have been concerned to emphasize that drawings cannot be taken as direct indicators of children's knowledge of spatial relations (Kosslyn et al., 1977) or of their knowledge of how to transform two- and three-dimensional relations in the real world into a two-dimensional graphic representation (Phillips el al., 1978; Willats, 1981, 1983).

For example, Phillips et al. (1978) found that 7-year-old children copied the same two-dimensional pattern differently under conditions where it was seen as representing a three-dimensional object (cube) and conditions where it was seen as a two-dimensional pattern of lines. Thus the children's concepts of what the drawing was intended to represent (i.e., its denotational purpose) had a distinct effect on the copies they made. Somewhat paradoxically, their copies more accurately reflected the Euclidean relationships between lines when the drawing was not seen as a cube. In their copies of the cube children introduced "distortions," perhaps in order to denote the fact that a cube would normally rest flat on a surface rather that standing on one corner. In a different study which supports this interpretation, Willats (1981, 1983) has argued that the drawings of various three-dimensional solids by 5- to 11-year-olds illustrate the parallel development of two systems of representation. The first (*transformational*) system governs the transformation of one set of spatial relations into another and is relatively independent of what the elements in the drawing might stand for. For example, there are a number of projection systems which a person might use to transform a three-dimensional set of relations into a two-dimensional set. The second (*denotational*) system is concerned with what type of element can stand for what, that is, with rules governing the denotation of parts of an object or scene by lines, shapes or regions in a drawing. For example, a line can conventionally be used to denote an edge or crack, but not a boundary between colors (Kennedy, 1983). Willats found that in a denotative sense the young child initially uses two-dimensional regions of a drawing to denote three-dimensional objects, and lines to represent surfaces (Willats, 1981, 1983). He also found that, with development, changes occur both in the projection system used to transform spatial relations (Willats, 1977a, 1977b) and in the denotational correspondences found in the drawings.

One of the most dramatic changes in the drawings of young children is the change from the separate placement of adjoining or collected parts to the execution of a single-outline figure.Drawings of the human figure in which a single contour combines two or more parts of the body into one begin to appear at 5 or 6 years and are most common in the drawings of children at about the age of 7 years (Goodnow, 1977). There is a similar developmental change from the use of separate lines to the use of a continuous line when children copy a many-sided shape such as a square. Goodnow pointed out that this change from the production of separate parts to the execution of an all-embracing line represents a major intellectual as well as artistic step because "the child must mentally have constructed not simply a list of parts but a number of interacting relationships between them" (1977, p. 35). She also examined the planning and production problems that result from the adoption of a single-outline strategy. For example, if the single outline includes arms and five fingers for each hand, it is inevitable (due to problems of motor control) that the fingers and perhaps the arms as well will become out of proportion with the rest of the body. Goodnow argued that as a consequence of these production problems the hands and even the arms are sometimes omitted from young children's outline drawings of a human figure. She also made the important point that these omissions and/or exaggerations of regions of the body have been misinterpreted by adults as indicating, for example, that the child is preoccupied with certain parts or functions.

2. Sequences and Rules Governing the Placement of Parts

The first group of production rules or strategies dealt with what the parts in a drawing might represent. A second type of representational strategy prescribes sequential steps or placement rules which govern the composition of separate parts into a unified whole. Goodnow (1977) reported one study in which 50 out of a total of 79 "tadpole" drawings by 3- to 5-year-olds were executed in the order "circle, some face details, then legs" (p. 56). In 21 of these 50 drawings the child then stopped, producing a figure without arms. However Goodnow (1977), Freeman (1980), and Bassett (1977) have all reported departures from this top-to-bottom ordering, in addition to the many cases of conformity. Similarly, there are particular patterns followed by many young children in the execution of a sun with radial lines, or in the copying of letters and letter like forms (Goodnow, 1977; Goodnow & Levine, 1973). Furthermore, the preferred patterns tend to change with age, for example, from a right-to-left to a left-to-right order for drawing two arms or two legs (Goodnow, 1977), or from a shape-copying strategy that minimizes the ambiguity about where to start each line to one in which all verticals are drawn top to bottom and all horizontals left to right (Ninio & Lieblich, 1976). Children's differential tendencies to use strategies such as these are likely to lead to discernible differences between the drawings of one child and another. Because no strategy is followed universally, there will be differences between children of the same age as well as differences between younger and older children. These differences provide a plausible foundation for the development of individual artistic styles in young children.

A series of intricate investigations by Van Sommers (1983, 1984) has revealed a great deal about the cognitive and motor sources of regularities to be found in the drawing actions of children and adults. One of his studies provided detailed documentation of some individual strategies employed by 20 children aged 5 to 6 years. Each child produced at least 10 drawings of each of 12 objects (some from life, some from memory) over a period of several months. The objects drawn from life included a pair of scissors, a light bulb, and a tennis shoe; those drawn from memory included a bicycle, a television set, and a baby in a pram. The strokes used by each child to execute each drawing were recorded on videotape, and the production sequences were then analyzed in detail. Van Sommers found evidence that individual children evolved and retained a distinctive graphic "schema" for organizing the parts of their drawings of each different object (e.g., for one child the bicycle might consist of three major parts—the two wheels and the frame). For each object there was a "strong family resemblance amongst the productions of a single child" (Van Sommers, 1983, p. 7). He also found a great deal of variation in the order in which the major and minor parts of the drawings of the same object were executed by a given child on different occasions, despite the similarities between the finished products. For example, the order and direction in which the same lines were drawn were not constant across successive drawings of the same object, and there were small additions and deletions made to the drawings on different occasions. Thus the consistency over time in each child's portrayal of the same object could not be accounted for by the repeated use of a fixed sequence of motor movements. Instead, the

child used an extremely flexible production process to arrive at a representation which was generated by a structured graphic schema. For example, from a detailed examination of one 6-year-old's repeated drawings
of a clear light bulb, Van Sommers drew the conclusion that "the whole
process of depicting the lamp is a mosaic of graphic devices developed
and mobilized in various combinations throughout the sequence" (1984,
p. 219). These findings strongly suggest that the young child is a master
of rather than a slave to the idiosyncratic sequencing strategies which he
or she may adopt when depicting a particular subject.

Young children also show an awareness of various rules governing the
placement of one part of a drawing in relation to others. Preschoolers will
avoid placing hair on a head if it threatens to cross the figure's arms, even
to the point of drawing a hat instead (Goodnow, 1977). Goodnow suggested
that for the young child it is important for each part to preserve its own
boundaries. Winner (1982) has pointed out that even when the young
child's drawings do not portray spatial relations between the parts with
accuracy, there is a "visual logic" to the placement of parts on the page:
"The layout of forms on the page creates an ordered and balanced two-
dimensional composition" (p. 152). This aspect of young children's placement of parts is perhaps most striking in certain types of drawings of
three-dimensional objects which do not represent overlap or occlusions,
but lay out the various sides of the object as flat, two-dimensional shapes.
Goodnow (1977) referred to these as "aerial perspective" drawings, Willats
(1981) as drawings with "oblique" projection rules, and Kosslyn el al.
(1977) as "diagrammatic" layouts of the object. Arnheim (1974) has emphasized the artistic merit and acceptability (especially in non-Western
cultures) of such two-dimensional compositions that are not drawn from
a consistent viewpoint.

When young children do depart from a strategy involving the segregation
of the parts in their drawings, they often produce so-called transparency
drawings (e.g., a person's legs are "seen" through the clothing, or the
contents of a house "seen" through the wall). In these drawings the occluded and occluding parts are overlaid on one another, again creating an
unusual visual effect that has also been sought by adult artists (Winner,
1982). A variation on drawings with overlay are those in which parts of
the foreground are "cut away" to enable objects which would be occluded
to be shown. An illustration of this is provided by the drawing of a sailboat
and some fish by a 7-year-old boy, shown in Figure 2, in which the ocean
is cut away to reveal the boat, which in turn has a transparent side through
which details of the cabin interior can be seen. This drawing also illustrates
the use of multiple perspectives in the same drawing: the fish are seen
from above and the boat from the side, while the small representations
of the skipper, the crew, and the helm are drawn from the front.

Fig. 2. Drawing of a sailboat and fish by a boy 7 years old, illustrating cut away parts, transparency, and the use of multiple perspectives.

Children's strategies of placing parts of a drawing in a segregated arrangement or overlaid upon each other or with sections cut away to reveal what is behind are eventually replaced by attempts to capture three-dimensional spatial relations using a variety of perspective cues. Willats (1977a, 1977b) has found that children progress through a number of stages of perspective representation, several of which do not correspond to the conventional system that was devised at the time of the Renaissance and is now accepted as "realistic." He suggested that the developmental progression occurring between 5 years of age and late adolescence illustrates children's changing cognitive attempts to solve the perspective problem. Children do not simply copy the accepted representations they see around them, although their later attempts at solution are apparently influenced by the conventional system.

There are other types of placement rules that young children follow, for a time, in their drawings. These rules complement and interact with those described. For example, some time after the child produces drawings in which each item has a separate place but in which there is no overall coordination of spatial relations between the items, drawings with a groundline appear (e.g., Goodnow, 1977; Kellogg, 1969). Objects are now related to one another by being drawn on or above the groundline, often in a no-man's land between one line for the ground and another for the sky. Eventually these two lines become one, making a dividing horizon between earth and sky (typically with the two regions colored differently) and creating depth effects not present in younger children's representations (Winner, 1982).

Another family of placement rules concerns the orientation of objects and their parts with respect to each other and to the page (Freeman, 1980; Goodnow, 1977). For example, the young child considers that the eyes of a human face should not be centered in the head, but should be closer to one edge with the body attached to the outside of the opposite edge. A 4- or 5-year-old's tendency to follow this rule can lead to figures drawn upside-down or floating sideways on a page, constrained by the initial placement of the eyes (Goodnow & Friedman, 1972). Even children older than this have difficulty with the angular relations between parts of a drawing. The well-known examples of chimneys drawn perpendicular to roofs or trees drawn perpendicular to the sides of a hill are difficult to interpret. They may perhaps illustrate children's early tendencies to adopt a local or internal frame of reference rather than an external, absolute one (e.g., Freeman, 1980; Piaget & Inhelder, 1967) and/or their biases toward perpendicularity and the bisection of angles in their drawings (Bremmer & Taylor, 1982; Ibbotson & Bryant, 1976; Perner, Kohlmann & Wimmer, 1984). Alternatively, they may reflect quite different concerns, such as that the chimney should have two equal sides and thus conform to a good shape.

The discussion of rules and principles for drawing to this point has assumed that there is a single graphic system of representation to be acquired by the child. The situation is actually more complex than this, as is seen in the next section.

3. Different Representational Systems

Children must become acquainted with a number of different conventional systems governing which particular marks or shapes can stand for what in a drawing. For example, when used in different contexts a wavy line can represent a water surface (see Figure 2), the smoke emanating from a chimney, or, in a metaphorical way when drawn behind a figure, movement (see Figure 1b). Similarly a rectangular shape can represent the walls of a house or can be used to separate one step from the next in a diagrammatic account of house building (see Figure 1d).

Davis and Fucigna (1983) have suggested two major developmental steps in the young child's mastery of different representational systems. First, by the age of about 4 or 5 years the child has mastered the basic distinctions between the methods of representing depth or motion in different symbol systems (e.g., block building, drawing, gesture). Whereas a 2-year-old "drawing" a car might "drive" the marker across the page (i.e., use a gesture), a 5-year-old draws the shape for a car, with lines to represent the movement. And whereas a 3-year-old might turn the page over to draw the back of the house on the other side (a method reminiscent of block building), a 5-year-old depicts the whole house on one side. However, Davis and Fucigna argued that within any given symbol system, such as drawing, the 5-year-old does not distinguish between the different "channels" which the activity of representation may take. Although children at this age show some awareness that marks on the page are sometimes pictures, sometimes maps or diagrams, and sometimes written stories or lists, their own attempts to produce these different representations are unsuccessful imitations that do not follow the accepted conventions. For example, a 5-year-old's maps are pictorial rather than designed to convey information about spatial landmarks and their layout (see also Goodnow, 1977).

It is not until the second step occurs at the age of about 7 or 8 years that the child realizes that an X is sufficient to represent a house on a map, but not in a picture, or that an aerial perspective is appropriate for a map, a frontal perspective for a picture. These developments in the graphic system are paralleled by differentiations occurring within other symbol systems: For example, language skills may be channeled toward either an eye-witness account or a story version of the same events.

Goodnow (1977, 1978) has interpreted similar developmental changes as indicative of children's progressive mastery and modification of various equivalence relations. She argued that the child initially establishes very simple equivalences, such as that a closed shape can represent a person, an object, or perhaps a sound. These basic equivalences are gradually modified to produce, for example, animals that are human equivalents with longer ears and/or with a different orientation of parts on the page, or to produce maps which are constructed by the assembly of a number of different shapes (see Figure 1e). Of particular interest are the developmental changes Goodnow (1978) found in the modifications that children introduce to convey movements of various kinds. In this study, when 5-to-10-year-olds were asked to draw a person bending to pick up a ball or a person running fast, the younger children made at most a few simple modifications to their customary (upright, stationary) "equivalents" for the human figure. For example, the "bending" figure remained upright and front-facing, with an arm elongated to make contact with the ball, or modifications to the person were avoided entirely by simply enlarging the ball so that it touched the hand. As they became older, children were more likely to modify the person to show bending at the neck, waist, and/ or knee, different positioning of the arms, and an overall side view of the person. Similar developmental changes were found in the additions (e.g., "streaming" lines) and modifications (limb orientation, bending, etc.) that the children used to portray a figure running fast.

In summary, these studies have revealed a great deal about the varied, continually changing strategies for graphic representation with which young children work. There is ample evidence in these studies to explain the child's own enjoyment of and fascination with graphic activity. There is also sufficient indication that a variety of rules and techniques might be employed differently by individual children to warrant an investigation of individual styles. We consider this question of children's individual styles in the context of a more general consideration of children as artists.

4. Young Children as Artists

Whether the drawings and other products made by a young child should be regarded as the work of an artist is a debatable matter. The opinion one adopts will depend on the criteria one uses to define the process of artistic creation, and it is not clear that a definite set of criteria can be found (Winner, 1982). For example, if we suggest that artistic activity consists of the creation of things of beauty, we confront the problem that not all works of art are beautiful and, conversely, not all things of beauty are art. Furthermore, not all works of art are created intentionally by an artist. A piece of driftwood found on the beach may function as art, although not created as such. Finally, although we may be able to agree that a work of art is art when it functions as a symbolic object, again we face the difficulty that not all symbols are art (Goodman, 1976; Langer, 1957, Olson, 1978).

Goodman's (1977) analysis of artistic symbols changed the question "What is art?" into the question "When is art?" and suggested a number of symptomatic features that would be found in symbolic objects functioning as art. These symptoms include *relative repleteness*, in which many different aspects of a work are significant for its symbolic functioning, and *exemplification*, in which the work of art literally or metaphorically exemplifies something through its possession of certain properties. Goodman (1978) argued that these and other characteristics of works of art focus attention on the symbol rather than on its referent(s): "We cannot merely look through the symbol to what it refers to as we do in obeying traffic lights or reading scientific texts, but must attend constantly to the symbol itself as in seeing paintings or reading poetry" (p. 69).

Working from these notions of what works of art entail, Gardner (1982) suggested a definition of what it means to be an artist: "Goodman's artistic creator is the individual with sufficient understanding of the properties and functions of certain symbol systems to allow him to create works that function in an aesthetically effective manner—works that are replete, expressive, susceptible to multiple readings, and the like" (p. 61). Gardner (1973, 1980) also considered the nature and development of children's artistic abilities and addressed the question of whether the young child can be regarded as an artist. As far as graphic skills are concerned, he concluded that the real "flowering" of the child's art occurs between 5 and 7 years. Although the basic capacity for symbolic activity is acquired several years earlier, it takes some time for the child to understand and master the use of graphic forms to represent aspects of the world. There are parallel developments in other symbolic domains and so, even as the child appears at this time to be a youthful artist, he also may lay claim to be a young musician, dancer, or storyteller (Gardner, 1980, p. 98; see also Gardner & Winner, 1982).

Gardner (1980) also stipulated that certain qualifications should be made to the notion that the young child is an artist. He suggested that although "the 5- to 7-year-old has achieved some formal aspects of drawing—as well as an appreciation of the fact that drawing may be used to represent aspects of the world" (Gardner, 1980, p. 218), there are limitations to the extent to which children's drawings function as symbols. Young children are less deliberate and less conventional than adults in their attempts to express meanings through art and are also less aware of the success or failure of their drawings in conveying ideas to others (Korzenik, 1977). For these reasons, Gardner (1980) suggested that they are capable only of "first-draft artistry" as compared with the more directed, revised, and assessed artistry of an adult.

Carothers and Gardner (1979) investigated 7- to 12-year-olds' sensitivity to a number of aesthetic qualities in specially prepared drawings. For example, children were asked to complete (or to choose a completing part for) a drawing in which the lines used were uniformly either thin or thick. They found that the completions which were drawn (or chosen) by 7-year-olds did not vary as a function of the overall quality of the drawings, whereas those drawn or chosen by the 12-year-olds did. This suggested a limited awareness among young children of the techniques through which certain aesthetic effects might be achieved. These findings do not necessarily imply that young children would be unable to devise their own methods of expressing various feelings, moods, or ideas in spontaneous drawings. The difficulty with using the child's own drawings, however, is that an adult looking at the drawings might read expressive qualities into them when no such qualities were intended by the child (cf. Winner, 1982).

There have in fact been relatively few studies of the expressive or communicative properties of young children's drawings as seen through the eyes of the beholder. Individual writers with a special interest in children's art have often argued that it has artistic merits (e.g., Arnheim, 1969; Edwards, 1979; Gardner, 1980; Lark-Horowitz el al., 1973; Mendelowitz, 1963; Schaefer-Simmern, 1948). On the other hand, some writers have expressed opposition to this view and have even found the lack of precision and clarity in children's drawings to be extremely unattractive (e.g., Montessori, 1918, reported in Read, 1945; see also Gardner, 1980; Kellogg, 1969).

One question that can be asked of someone who looks at drawings, independently of evaluative issues, is whether a number of drawings are recognizably the work of the same artist. Several authors have chronicled the development of graphic ability in individual children across a period of months or years (e.g., Eng, 1931; Gardner, 1980; Goodnow, 1977; Van Sommers, 1984, and some have drawn attention to stylistic differences between specific individual children both in drawing (Gardner, Wolf, & Smith, 1982) and in symbolic play (Wolf & Gardner, 1979). Others have reported a conviction, based upon their experience with large numbers of children in an educational setting, that young children do exhibit individual styles or approaches to drawing (e.g., Lark-Horovitz et al., 1973; Mendelowitz, 1963). Stacey and Ross (1975) asked 6-year-old children to make drawings of six different subject matters on one occasion and then to make them again, under varying instructions, 1 month later. When children were instructed on the second occasion to draw from memory, and to make their picture the same as before, adults were able to match the pairs of drawings by the same child with high levels of accuracy. When the instruction was to make the second picture different from the first, the pairs of drawings were less recognizable by adults as the work of the same child.

Hartley et al. (1982) and Somerville (1983) conducted a series of experiments designed to provide evidence about the individual artistic styles of three young children. These experiments required adults to make a number of different judgments about the children's drawings. The children were not exceptional in their drawing abilities, and the adults did not have any special expertise or interest in children's art. These studies used procedures analogous to those which have been used to investigate ill-defined categorical concepts and were thus derived, in part, from the notion of style discussed in Section I. The findings of these experiments are considered in the next section.

III. EVIDENCE FOR INDIVIDUAL STYLES IN YOUNG CHILDREN

The reasoning behind the studies of children's artistic styles conducted by Hartley et al. (1982) and Somerville (1983) was similar to that in studies of the acquisition of other concepts (e.g., Hartley & Homa, 1981; Homa, 1978; Posner & Keele, 1968, 1970). Suppose that an adult has been given experience with a number of exemplars of each of a number of categories. If the adult has formed a general concept for each category, this will be reflected in his or her ability to categorize previously unseen exemplars at levels significantly better than would be expected by chance. To the extent that the "old" learned exemplars and the "new" exemplars which are identified correctly do not share a small number of identifying features, it can be argued that the adult has derived concepts which are ill defined and abstract. Our studies of children's styles employed the category abstraction paradigm, outlined above, in addition to several other procedures that were designed to investigate adults' perceptions of children's drawings. The first step in these studies was to obtain sets of drawings from a number of children that would permit appropriate tests for the presence of individual styles.

A. Individual Styles of Three 5-Year-Olds

Hartley et al. (1982) initially obtained 20 or more drawings from each of three children, one girl (artist C) and two boys (artists A and B), drawn over a period of 2 to 3 months when the children were about 5 years old. A shape-copying task (from Piaget & Inhelder, 1967) was used to establish that the children were not widely disparate in their levels of graphic skills. The drawings were all made on the same type of paper, using a standard set of eight markers. From the total collections obtained, a set of 15 was selected for each child. These sets were chosen to exemplify, as far as possible, a similar range in the use of color, the choice of subject matter, and the complexity of the drawings for each child. The drawings were photographed so as to edit out obvious identifying features such as signatures. A set of comparable drawings made by other children of about the same age was obtained for use as distractor drawings in the experiments.

In a preliminary experiment, adults were asked to rate the similarity of every possible pair of drawings generated from the total set of 45 (15 by each child). The ratings were made on an 11-point scale from 0 (extremely similar) to 10 (extremely dissimilar). The adults were given no information about the children who produced the drawings and in fact were not told how many children were involved. Their ratings indicated that it was not the case that all the drawings by one child were very similar to one another and very dissimilar to those of the other two children. Two types of scores were derived from these ratings for the drawings by each artist. One was the average similarity rating for pairs of drawings in which both were by a given artist (the "within-artist rating"); the other was the average similarity rating for pairs of drawings in which one was by a given artist and one was by another artist (the "between-artist rating"). The mean within-artist rating was significantly lower than the mean between-artist rating for artists A and C, but not B. This indicated that for two of the children there was a tendency for the same-artist pairs to be seen as more similar than the between-artist pairs. However, the size of the difference between the mean ratings was small—less than 1 point on the 11-point scale for each artist—indicating that the drawings of one child were certainly not completely distinguishable from those of the others. This supported the notion that if adults were to learn the children's styles, the concepts on which they would have to rely would be ill-defined rather than clear-cut ones.

In a series of category-abstraction experiments, groups of adults learned to classify varying numbers of drawings by each of the three children according to artist. They were then tested on their ability to classify previously unseen drawings by each of the children and by other children (the distractors). In the test phases the adults were told that there would be equal numbers of drawings by artists A, B, C, and "other" (i.e., by none of the three they had learned). The learned and previously unseen drawings used in these experiments were taken from the sets of 15 for each artist and the distractor set.

Hartley et al. (1982) found that adults' classifications of new drawings by artist A and C were consistently better than would be expected by chance, if they had learned to classify six or nine drawings by those artists in the learning phase. There was less evidence that adults could recognize new instances of the work of artist B, although some groups of subjects who had learned nine exemplars performed better than would be expected by chance. Adults also recognized a greater number of individual new drawings by artists A and C than by artist B. This suggested that whereas the adults may have abstracted stylistic concepts for artists A and C their recognition of new drawings by B might have rested on the resemblance of those new drawings to specific learned exemplars.

We obtained further evidence that the adults in our experiments may have attained abstract concepts of styles for artists A and C, but not for B, by looking at their choices of prewritten style descriptions for the artists. At the conclusion of the learning and testing phases in one experiment we asked the adults to sort through a set of nine brief descriptions of styles in order to select one for each of artists A, B, and C. These descriptions used abstract adjectives and phrases and were devoid of references to specific forms, colors, or subject matter that the children may have chosen. Briefly, the descriptions, which were intended to be accurate ones for each of the artists, depicted the styles of A, B, and C, respectively, as reflecting "unpredictability, imagination, moodiness . . . a fanciful, mad-scientist view of the world"; "clarity, determination, rigidity . . . a literal, down-to-earth view of the world"; and "humor, repetitiousness, sociability . . . a simple, sugar-and-spice view of the world" (Hartley et al., 1982, p. 1207). The other six descriptions were written as plausible descriptions of the work of a child of this age, but were nevertheless distinct from each of the three above.

The adults' selections of style descriptions were significantly better than would be expected by chance for artists A and C, but not B. That is, they tended to agree with the essentially subjective views of the authors about the descriptions which were most appropriate for artists A and C. The same adults were also asked to guess the sex and to estimate the age of each artist at the conclusion of the experiment. Significantly more adults than would be expected by chance decided correctly that artists A and B were male and that C was female. On the average they judged that C was older than B who was older than A. In fact the ages of A, B, and C when the initial sets of drawings were collected were 55, 66, and 60 months, respectively, so that these judgments were accurate only with respect to the age of artist A relative to the others.

These findings supported the conclusion that at least two of the three 5-year-olds exhibited individual drawing styles which were recognizable to adults. The next question was whether the styles would remain recognizable as the children grew older and their graphic techniques and predilections changed.

B. Consistency of Individual Styles across a 2-Year Period

We used the same drawing materials as before and obtained new sets of drawings from artists A, B, and C in a second and again in a third collection period. The second collection period was approximately 9 months after the first drawings had been obtained (artists A, B, and C were thus 64, 75, and 69 months of age, respectively), and the third collection period was approximately 12 months after that (artists A, B, and C were 71, 87, and 81 months old, respectively). The same procedures for ensuring the overall comparability of three selected sets of 15 drawings (one for each artist) were followed in Collections 2 and 3 as had been followed in the first collection. A second and a third set of 15 comparable distractor drawings were also obtained, all from one child (a boy), who was aged 67 months in the second collection period and 79 months in the third.

We conducted a new series of category-abstraction experiments in order to examine whether adults who had learned to classify drawings from the first collection period could recognize which artist had drawn which drawings from the second and third periods. These experiments used the same procedure of a learning phase followed by transfer phases. The evidence that adults could recognize later drawings which they had not seen before was stronger and more consistent across experiments for artists A and C than for artist B. The findings obtained in three experiments extending across collection periods, of which one was reported by Hartley et al. (1982) and two by Somerville (1983), are now examined in some detail.

In all three experiments, a group of adult subjects learned to categorize nine drawings by each of artists A, B, and C from the first collection period. Then, in a first transfer phase common to all experiments, they were tested on their ability to categorize six "new" (previously unseen) drawings from the same period by each of the artists. The transfer phases which followed the first one were different in each experiment. In Experiment 1 (Hartley et al., 1982) there was a second transfer phase in which 30 adults categorized 10 new drawings by each of artists A, B, and C from the second collection period. In Experiment 2 (Somerville, 1983) there was a second transfer phase in which 45 adults categorized 15 new drawings by each artist from Period 2, followed by a third transfer phase in which the same adults categorized 15 new drawings by each artist from Period 3. Experiment 3 (Somerville, 1983) eliminated the potentially problematic fatigue and interference effects associated with the succession of three transfer phases in Experiment 2. Two separate groups each comprising 42 adults participated in Parts a and b of Experiment 3. In Experiment 3a the second transfer phase was identical to that of Experiment 2; in Experiment 3b it was identical to the third transfer phase of Experiment 2. Each transfer phase in each experiment included distractor drawings equivalent in number to the number by each of the artists. Thus it could be assumed that the probability of correct assignment of any new drawing to A, B, C, or "other," by chance, was .25 in each transfer phase.

In the first transfer phase of each experiment, adults were significantly more successful than would be expected by chance in their categorizations of new drawings by artists A and C, but not B. In the second transfer phases requiring categorizations of drawings from Period 2 (Experiments 1, 2, and 3a), adults were again consistently above chance for A and C, but not B. The adults' performance on drawings from the third period was better when those drawings were categorized in a second (Experiment 3b) than in a third (Experiment 2) transfer phase. In the former case adults were significantly above chance in their categorizations for all three artists, in the latter case only in their categorizations of drawings by artist C. These findings suggested that there was considerable continuity in the children's styles, over time, at least for artists A and C. This was particularly impressive because of obvious changes in the sophistication and compositional qualities of the drawings with age. These changes are illustrated in Figure 3, which contains a pair of drawings of the same (or very similar) subject matter by each artist, one taken from Period 1 and one from Period 3 in each case.

For the most part, the adults' categorizations of new drawings by artist B were not correct significantly more often than would be expected by chance. This cannot be taken as evidence that his drawings lacked a recognizable style, however, because it is possible that if adults were given more experience with examples of his work they might succeed in recognizing new ones. It is also worth considering whether his drawings might have been particularly confusable with those of one of the other artists. To examine this possibility and to provide more insight into the children's styles as perceived by adults in these experiments, we examined the adults' categorizations of individual new drawings by each child. Assuming that the probability of assigning any drawing to any category by chance was .25, we identified the new drawings which were assigned to artist A, B, C, or "other" by more adults than would be expected by chance in each transfer phase of each experiment. The number of assignments required to reach significance (at the 5% level, using the binomial theorem) was 12 of 30 subjects in Experiment 1, 17 of 45 in Experiment 2, and 16 of 42 in Experiments 3a and 3b.

Table 1 shows the significant assignments of new drawings from the first collection period to artists and to "other." Four of the six new drawings by artist A were assigned to A by at least three of the four groups of adults. One of the remaining two was assigned by one group to A and by the other three to "other"; the other drawing was not consistently assigned to any category by any group. There was only one instance of consistent assignment to another artist (artist B). Four of the six new drawings by artist C were assigned to C by all four groups; one assigned to C by two groups and to "other" by two; and one to C by one group,

Fig. 3. Pairs of drawings from the first (left side) and third (right side) collection periods for the three artists: upper row, Artist A, plane with pilot (Periods 1 and 3); center row, Artist B, train (Period 1) and car (Period 3); lower row, Artist C, person in rain (Periods 1 and 3).

TABLE 1

Assignments to Artists of New Drawings from the First Collection Period

Experiment number[a]	A. Drawings by Artist A					
	$^A4$ bird	$^A9$ diver	$^A5$ camel	$^A12$ king's house	$^A15$ "phose" machine	$^A3$ fish
1	—	A***	A*	A**	A***	A**
2	—	A***	O***	A**	A*	A*
3a	—	A***	O**	A***	O*	A*
3b	—	A***	O**	A**	A***	B**

	B. Drawings by Artist B					
	$^B14$ dinosaur	$^B10$ two dogs	$^B5$ camper	$^B15$ crabs	$^B12$ bedroom	$^B1$ cow
1	—	—	O**	O**	O**	—
2	B**	—	B**	O**	O**	O**
3a	B**	—	O*	O***	O***	—
3b	—	—	O**	O***	A*	O*

	C. Drawings by Artist C					
	$^C14$ road suns	$^C6$ girl	$^C11$ cat	$^C12$[b] person horizon	$^C5$ tree house	$^C8$[c] person rain
1	C***	C***	C***	C***	C*	C**
2	C***	C***	C***	C***	—	O*
3a	C***	C***	C***	C***	—	O**
3b	C***	C**	C***	C***	O**	C*

Note. A, B, C, and O indicate that a drawing was assigned to Artist A, B, C, or "other," respectively, by significantly more subjects than would be expected by chance (— indicates no significant assignment of a drawing); binomial tests, chance probability of assignment to any category = 0.25: *p < .05; **p < .01; ***p < .001.

[a] Experiment 1: Hartley et al. (1982), Experiment 3, $N = 30$; Experiment 2: Somerville (1983), Experiment 4, $N = 45$; Experiments 3a and 3b: Somerville (1983), Experiment 5, Group 1 and Group 2, respectively, $N = 42$ in each.

[b] This drawing is shown in Figure 1(a).

[c] This drawing is shown in Figure 3.

to "other" by one, and not assigned consistently by the other two. Of the six new drawings by artist B, by contrast, only one drawing was assigned to B by more than one group—two groups assigned it correctly, but two did not assign it consistently to any category. For the most part the new drawings by artist B were judged consistently to be by "other" children. There was just one instance of assignment to another artist (artist

A). These findings are remarkable because they show that there was little confusion of the artists in the adults' assignments of new drawings from Period 1. This is not to say that drawings by one child were never assigned to another, but that such misclassifications were not consistent across adults. The adults' low overall performance on artist B was not due to a tendency to assign his drawings to one or both of the other artists. Instead, the adults judged his drawings to be different from those by all three children that they had seen.

Tables 2 and 3 contain similar information about the adults' assignments to categories of 15 new drawings by each child from Periods 2 and 3, respectively. There were fewer instances of consistent assignments of drawings to any category for these collection periods. Nevertheless, if we consider just the assignments of new drawings by artists A and C, in both periods, a large proportion of the significant assignments made were to the correct artist. There was also, however, an increased tendency to assign drawings by each of these artists erroneously to B (more so than to each other). If we next consider artist B, the majority of the significant assignments of his Period 2 drawings were to "other" (similarly to the findings for Period 1), but for his Period 3 drawings there were more correct assignments to B than to any other category (including "others"). These findings suggest that when adults attempted to adjust the stylistic concepts they had formed to accommodate changes with age they could not do so without creating some overlap between the categories for each of the artists. However, their stylistic concepts for artists A and C remained more distinct from each other than they did from the B category. The better-than-chance assignments of new drawings by artist B from Period 3 (made by adults in Experiment 3b) were possibly due to a tendency to "guess" B more frequently when the drawings were quite different in overall appearance from those that were learned. However, when we corrected the scores on Period 3 drawings by artist B for guessing, for this group of adults, they remained significantly above chance expectancy (Somerville, 1983).

C. Adults' Concepts of the Children's Styles

There were several sources of evidence that the adults in these experiments derived concepts of the children's styles that were relatively ill defined and abstract, at least for artists A and C. First, the adults were able to recognize new drawings from Period 1 which covered quite a range of subject matter (see Table 1). The recognizable new drawings for each artist also varied in their use of color, form, and compositional techniques. Furthermore, for both A and C some new drawings were recognized more consistently (within and across groups of adults) than others. This sug-

Assignment to Artists of New Drawings from the Second Collection Period

Experiment number[b]	Drawing number[a]														
	1	2	3	4	5	6	7	8	9	10	11	12	13	14	15
A. Drawings by Artist A															
1[c]	A***	—	—	—	A***	—	—	—	A**	—	··········	··········	··········	··········	··········
2	A***	—	B*O*	A**	A***	—	B*	A*	A**	A**	O*	C***	—	O*	C*
3a	A*	—	O**	B*	A***	—	B*	A**	—	A**	O*	—	—	O**	A*B*
B. Drawings by Artist B															
1[c]	O*	—	B†	A†B†	O**	B***	—	B**	O**	—	··········	··········	··········	··········	··········
2	O***	—	—	A**	O**	B*	C*	B***	O**	—	O**	O**	—	—	—
3a	O*	O**	O*	—	O***	—	—	B***	—	O*	O***	—	—	—	O**
C. Drawings by Artist C															
1[c]	C**	C**	—	—	O***	C***	—	—	C**	C***	··········	··········	··········	··········	··········
2	C***	C***	A*	B**	O***	—	C*	B*	B***C*	C***	B*	—	O***	—	O*
3a	C***	C***	C*	B**	O***	—	—	B*	B**	C**	—	—	O***	B*	—

Note. A, B, C, and O indicate that a drawing was assigned to Artist A, B, C, or "other," respectively, by significantly more subjects than would be expected by chance (— indicates no significant assignment of a drawing); binomial tests, chance probability of assignment to any category = 0.25. †p = .05; *p < .05; **p < .01; ***p < .001.

[a] The titles of drawings 1–15 by Artist A, in numbered order, were the following: plane with pilot; machine with plugs; two motorcycles; Easter bunny and tree; people and wires; dragon; sky ride, San Diego Zoo; foot with machine; spaceship; people in shower; birthday cake on table; man on TV; kangaroos and tree; lots of plug-ins; a girl. The titles of drawings 1–15 by Artist B, in numbered order, were the following: seashells under water; birds and road; palm tree in wind; plane, house, and flowers; starfish in water; babysitter; leopard with trees and clouds; two tigers; basketball court; ice-cream van and boy; bunk bed; laundry room; airplane; candlestick; clothes closet. The titles of drawings 1–15 by Artist C, in numbered order, were the following: two girls at table; swing set and tree; bedroom furniture; bird in cage; ghosts; two dogs and girl; dragon; boat in water; house; tree and flowers; rocket; car and boat; blowing cloud; cars on road; mountains and sea.

[b] Experiment 1: Hartley et al. (1982) Experiment 3, N = 30; Experiment 2: Somerville (1983), Experiment 4, N = 45; Experiment 3a: Somerville (1983) Experiment 5, Group 1, N = 42.

[c] Drawings 11–15 were not included in the transfer phase in Experiment 1.

TABLE 3

Assignment to Artists of New Drawings from the Third Collection Period

Experiment number[b]	Drawing number[a]														
	1	2	3	4	5	6	7	8	9	10	11	12	13	14	15
A. Drawings by Artist A															
2	—	B**	A**	A**	B**	—	B**	—	A**	—	B*	O*	A***	C*	A**
3b	—	—	A**	—	—	O*	A*	—	A***	—	A*	—	O*	—	—
B. Drawings by Artist B															
2	—	—	C**	B***	O**	B*	B***	—	B*	A**	—	B**	—	—	—
3b	O*	—	C***	B**	—	—	B**	C***	B**	A*	O**	O**	B*	—	—
C. Drawings by Artist C															
2	O**	A*C*	B*	C***	C*	C*	B*	—	C***	B*	B*	C*	—	—	B**O**
3b	O*	C*	—	—	C*	—	—	A*	C**	—	—	C***	—	—	O*

Note. A, B, C, and O indicate that a drawing was assigned to Artist A, B, C, or "other," respectively, by significantly more subjects than would be expected by chance (— indicates no significant assignment to a drawing); binomial tests, chance probability of assignment to any category = 0.25; $*p < .05$; $**p < .01$; $***p < .001$.

[a]The titles of drawings 1–15 by Artist A, in numbered order, were the following: cat and bowl; car; plane with pilot (shown in Figure 3); table tennis match; house on hill; fish underwater; man with tent and campfire; cars on road; Indian rugs; rocket; haunted house; table and chandelier; plane; house and tree; sailboat and fish (shown in Figure 2). The titles of drawings 1–15 by Artist B, in numbered order, were the following: desk; furniture in room; roundabout and sun; car (shown in Figure 3); truck; cowboy shooting; cowboy on horse; plane, house, and flowers; Rubik's cube on chair; strawberry; boy at desk; football game; two boys kicking; guinea pig; football. The titles of drawings 1–15 by Artist C, in numbered order, were the following: two cars; person in rain (shown in Figure 3); playground; girl with dog and sun; Halloween house; furniture in room; fire truck; lion; birthday party and people; ambulance and people; boat with people; two planes, sun, and people; house and motorcycle; witch and cauldron; two cars and bird.

[b]Experiment 2: Somerville (1983), Experiment 4, $N = 45$; Experiment 3b: Somerville (1983) Experiment 5, Group 2, $N = 42$.

gested that they were more typical of these children's styles than other drawings, in that they shared a greater variety of features with other exemplars. Less typical drawings, which may have shared relatively few identifying features with other exemplars, were less likely to be consistently recognized as belonging to the style. Finally, indirect evidence that the adults' correct classifications of new drawings did not depend on the presence of one or more defining features was provided by their success on drawings from Periods 2 and 3. Across the 2-year period between Collections 1 and 3 there were dramatic changes in each child's drawings, exemplifying many of the changes in strategies discussed in Section II. Thus it is unlikely that recognition of a new drawing from Period 3 would occur because of a close resemblance to a specific learned drawing from Period 1.

The pairs of drawings of similar subject matter from Periods 1 and 3, shown in Figure 3, are relevant to this point. The drawing of a plane with a pilot by artist A in Period 1 was a member of the set of nine learned drawings for that artist. The adults in both Experiment 2 and Experiment 3b recognized the drawing of a plane with a pilot from Period 3 at levels significantly better than would be expected by chance (see Table 3). However, although the subject matter was identical in these two drawings by artist A, there were marked differences between the two drawings in the use of graphic techniques and in overall expressive quality. The results were similar for the illustrated pair of drawings by artist B. The drawing of a train from Period 1 was included in the learned set, and the Period 3 drawing of a car was recognized at levels significantly above chance by the adults in Experiment 2 and Experiment 3b. Again the continuity in subject matter was offset by the marked differences in the line quality, texture, and mood of the drawings. It should be noted that a simple explanation in terms of subject matter cannot account for these results. Cars and planes were drawn about equally often by all three artists in Period 3, and not all cars were attributed consistently to artist B (in Table 3 see, e.g., Drawing 8 by artist A and Drawing 15 by artist C), nor were all planes attributed consistently to artist A (e.g., Drawing 13 by artist A, Drawing 8 by artist B, and Drawing 12 by artist C). This means that other characteristics of the drawings, instead of or in addition to their subject matter, must have been important in determining the attributions to artists that were made by the adults.

The fact that considerations other than subject matter must have been influential is further illustrated by the results pertaining to the pair of drawings by artist C, each entitled "person in rain," shown in Figure 3. Each of these drawings was in a transfer set (see Tables 1 and 3). There were two groups of adults who were tested on their recognition of both new drawings (in Experiment 2 and Experiment 3b). The adults in Experiment 2 assigned the Period 1 drawing to "other" and the Period 3 drawing to both A and C; those in Experiment 3b assigned both new drawings correctly to artist C. Thus, although there may have been some subjects who used subject matter to make decisions about both of these drawings, it is likely that other considerations contributed to the variety of assignments that were made (see also Experiments 1 and 3a in Table 1).

In summary, adults who learned to classify a relatively small number of drawings by each of three 5-year-olds showed evidence of attaining abstract stylistic concepts, at least for two of the three children. These stylistic notions enabled them to recognize previously unseen drawings collected not only when the children were the same age, but also when they were 9 and 21 months older. Evidence that the adults' recognition of new drawings depended on abstract concepts rather than on resemblances between particular drawings was provided by the diversity of new drawings recognized, by the fact that some drawings were recognized more readily than others, and by adults' ability to select appropriate abstract descriptions of these two children's styles from a set of nine descriptions.

IV. EDUCATIONAL CONSIDERATIONS

The preceding discussions of the concept of style, of artistic development in young children, and of adults' perceptions of young children's styles have implications for art education, at least in the early school years. We have reviewed evidence which suggests that children begin to attempt graphic representations of the world between 2 and 3 years of age and that, in the course of the next 2 or 3 years, individual children gain sufficient mastery of graphic techniques and methods of expressing meaning to produce drawings that reflect recognizable individual styles. The mastery of these graphic and expressive methods has been seen to involve the progressive use of relatively complex, flexible rules or strategies for the production and composition of drawings. We have also suggested that young children's artistic styles exhibit a structure similar to that of adult styles and that this structure can best be understood as analogous to the structure of ill-defined semantic or natural categories. Clearly there are many issues in the education of adults and older children for which these empirical and conceptual findings have, at best, only indirect relevance. Thus our consideration of educational issues does not attempt to be comprehensive, and even in the case of the education of young children only the most directly relevant questions are addressed.

We first examine contrasting approaches to curriculum design in the arts and suggest contributions that might be made by investigations of young children's strategies and styles. Then we address more specific issues concerned with the provision of experiences conducive to the production and appreciation of graphic representations by the young child. As we have done throughout the chapter, we focus primarily on graphic skills, although many of the issues may also apply to education in the arts more generally.

A. Contrasting Views of Curriculum

There is every reason to be cautious in the application of knowledge from any academic discipline to curriculum design. The rational procedure of specifying clear educational goals and then implementing techniques known to achieve them is rarely attainable in any field, for a variety of conceptual and practical reasons. Where cognitive psychology is concerned, there have been attempts to apply knowledge to education in two distinct ways. First, such knowledge has been used to supply a working definition of educational goals themselves, for example, in the specification of a series of developmental steps or stages through which the person should pass as a result of instruction. A well-known example of this type of application specifies the attainment of Piagetian stages as the goal of educational programs (at various levels) in the sciences (see, e.g., Kuhn, 1979). The second type of application is more process oriented, attempting to devise classroom, computer-based, or other procedures through which educational goals may be reached.

A third possible view, perhaps more tenable for education in art, is that the conceptual and empirical findings of cognitive psychology can inform and contribute to the establishment of educational goals and procedures without making exact prescriptions in either case. Zernich (1981) has advocated such a role for the models of cognitive-developmental stages and progressions put forward by Piaget (1950) and Flavell (1972). But there are others who encounter serious difficulty with the notion that cognitive psychology can be applied to art education, arguing, for example, that "the psychologist's interest in learning the truth about the evolution of mental operations simply does not coincide with the educator's interest in learning about humanity and the world through making and looking at art" (Feldman, 1981, p. 137).

Feldman (1981) has isolated four major types of approach to curriculum design in the arts, emphasizing, at the same time, that in practice there is much intermixing to be found. The four approaches are those based on technical knowledge and procedures, on psychology (including developmental stage theories), on anthropological and historical aspects of art, and, finally, on aesthetics. In Feldman's view "it is overwhelmingly the technical curriculum that is practised in school art programs" (1981, p. 149), at the expense of broader, more meaningful conceptions of the arts; this concern is shared by Eisner (1980; 1982). For Feldman, the solution is to be found in a broadly defined "aesthetic curriculum" that would recognize the importance of both artistic form and aesthetic experience and focus on both the cognitive and affective components of "intense perception of the relations between form and experience" (1981, p. 148).

Although Feldman is inclined to doubt the potential of cognitive psychology as a contributor to the "aesthetic curriculum," others have argued that an understanding of human cognitive processes is essential to the design of an adequate art curriculum (Eisner, 1982). Eisner specifically advocated that educators should adopt a "wide view" of curriculum, based on an understanding of "the forms of thought through which conceptualization in general occurs and the means humans use to represent what they have conceptualized to others" (1982, p. 21). In his view, the prevailing emphasis on assessment and accountability in schools and on technical means of achieving goals (specified, in turn, by assessment procedures) has combined with the lowering of the professional responsibility of teachers to produce narrow, inappropriate conceptions of curriculum. Eisner argued that the wider view of curriculum, appropriate not only to the arts, should be one which incorporates knowledge of the variety of representational systems and modes which man creates and uses. He argued, further, that it should be the professional role of the teacher and of educational administrators to design and evaluate curriculum goals, methods, and assessment procedures. These professional functions can be performed adequately, he suggested, only by educators who are sensitive to the development and functioning of representational systems.

In his analysis of representational systems, Eisner (1982) drew a contrast between two major types. The first type encompasses the formalized, rule-governed forms of representation that constitute the current backbone of curriculum development in the "basics" (reading, writing, and mathematics) and are also adopted quite frequently in areas such as science, social studies, and geography. The second type includes the less well-defined, "figurative" forms of representation, vital to metaphoric, poetic, and other aspects of language use and, more generally, to the arts. Eisner (1982) referred to these two types of representational systems as two "syntaxes," emphasizing the possibilities of precision, correctness, paraphrase, and translatability in the former, rule-governed type, as against the elusive, idiosyncratic, and inherently ambiguous meanings captured by the second, figurative type. In the early school grades, according to

Eisner, the emphasis is almost exclusively on rule-governed representations, that is, on the correct, conventional approaches and answers to problems in arithmetic, spelling, grammar, and reading. More emphasis is needed on the role of judgment, imagination, and interpretive skills in the understanding of linguistic, scientific, and artistic material. In fact, in Eisner's view the most adequate educational methods would be those permitting movement back and forth from one type of representational approach to the other.

Eisner's broad division of representational systems into two types provides a useful framework for considering developmental changes in knowledge. It has been argued that young children possess an intuitive understanding of metaphoric and poetic language use (e.g., Chukovsky, 1968; Winner, 1979), of the intonational patterns and rhythms of language (Peters, 1977), of musical patterns and forms (Bamberger, 1978), of certain properties of the number system (Gelman & Gallistel, 1978), and of graphic representational methods (e.g., Arnheim, 1969; Gardner, 1980). In each case, these intuitive understandings predate the acquisition of formalized, conventional systems of representation. One might be tempted to conclude that the role of the educational system should be to move the child away from his or her early intuitive understandings in the direction of more formalized knowledge. However, it is a serious oversimplification of development to view the young child's intuitive approaches as ones that should be dislodged and supplanted by later acquisitions. For example, Bamberger (1978) has demonstrated the importance of continually coordinating young children's intuitive musical ideas and representations with the formal standardized ones which are normally taught. Not to do so, she argued, would be at the risk of extinguishing the capacity for music making. It is easy to envisage similar kinds of interference with the propensity to create poetry, pictures, or mathematical ideas which might occur at the hands of narrowly conceived, formal instruction programs. In fact, Kellogg (1969) has concluded in no uncertain terms that "the demand for a restricted kind of pictorialism in school art is one important influence that causes children to give up or to do poorly in art or to succeed by restricting their art formulas to those which adults appreciate" (p. 157).

Of what do the intuitive understandings of the young child consist? This is a question to which cognitive psychological investigations such as those reviewed in earlier sections might provide at least part of the answer. And if such intuitive knowledge is to be incorporated in the basis for curriculum design, it is essential to comprehend that knowledge as fully as possible. In the next two sections we examine, with educational concerns in mind, two complementary areas of young children's developing knowledge of graphic representation. The first area is the capacity to produce graphic representations, and the second is the capacity to perceive and appreciate the styles of graphic representations created by others.

B. Children's Graphic Production

There has been something of a revolution in our thinking about young children's drawings, akin to the vast changes in our understanding of their language which have been brought about by studies of their early speech (e.g., Brown, 1973; Bruner, 1974; Halliday, 1975). Researchers who are in sympathy with Arnheim's (1969) conviction that visual thinking is underemphasized in Western cultures, as a result of these cultures' preoccupation with linear, verbal forms of thought, have made several attempts to reveal the structure and sophistication of visual knowledge. To underscore the fact that visual knowledge involves a representational system of equal importance to language, language has often been used either explicitly or implicitly as a metaphor for the new conceptual approaches to graphic representation.

The first example is the work of Goodnow and others (Goodnow & Levine, 1973; Ninio & Lieblich, 1976) in which the authors have spoken of the rules that guide the young child's production of various forms as "syntactic" rules, amounting to a "grammar of action." By this they mean that the child may try to draw letter like forms, for instance, using a series of strokes starting in a particular place (e.g., the top left corner) and drawing verticals first (top to bottom) and horizontals next (left to right). Many of the typical errors made by young children when they draw letters can be explained by their tendency to use rules of this type. As a second example, Willats (1981) has argued, by direct analogy with language acquisition, that the "errors" to be found in children's developing graphic representations are brought about by the application of certain rules for transformation or denotation. His evidence came from an analysis of developmental changes in children's attempts at two-dimensional representations of three-dimensional objects or scenes. Finally, efforts to understand the cognitive strategies or visual "schemata" that generate the flexible but rule-governed graphic productions of the child (e.g., Freeman, 1980; Golomb, 1981; Goodnow, 1977; Van Sommers, 1984) bear a strong resemblance to accounts of the child's developing grammatical competence in language. Generating a variety of sentences which are semantically and/ or syntactically related requires cognitive skills similar to those required for the generation of related drawings. The importance of these analyses for education is that they have demonstrated that the child's intuitive knowledge about graphic representation embodies some understanding of the use of rules or generative schemes. It is this aspect of children's intuitive understanding which it is important to recognize in designing more formal instruction.

However, children's intuitive graphic knowledge consists of more than just "syntactic" production rules, and the educational implications are correspondingly more subtle and complex. To extend the language analogy, there are also semantic, narrative, and more general pragmatic aspects to children's early graphic skills. We argue that this is manifested, in part, in the discernible individual styles of the 4- to 7-year-old. However, before examining evidence about school-age children, we first discuss the earliest semantic and communicative aspects of graphic activity, because it is here that the educational process must begin.

At a very early age the young child understands that communicative acts can be performed by drawing (e.g., Gardner, 1980; Winner, 1982). This is indicated by the verbal labels given to scribbles, dots, and other products of motor activity. These acts seem analogous to the child's primitive speech acts that serve various communicative purposes prior to the acquisition of grammatical linguistic knowledge (e.g., Dore, 1975; Halliday, 1975). Gardner (1980) has also pointed out the similarity between the 2-year-old's tendency to engage in sequences of loosely connected drawing activities and the tendency to rehearse and embellish a repertoire of verbal forms.

Many investigations have attested to the adult's sensitivity to early linguistic communications by the child and to the importance of this sensitivity for language acquisition (e.g., Bruner, 1974; Ratner & Bruner, 1978; Trevarthen, 1979). A particularly informative example, for the present discussion, is Mervis and Canada's (1981; see also Mervis & Mervis, 1982) study of mothers' behavior in relation to their children's early semantic categories. Over a period of 9 months Mervis and Canada observed mothers' tendencies to accept, reject, or attempt to modify their infants' overgeneralized uses of words (e.g., *truck* for any vehicle, *ball* for any round object). They found that mothers initially accepted and encouraged their children's use of terms to refer to "child-basic" categories, that is, to categories that did not correspond to any groupings of items that would be made by an adult. One child, for example, used the word *ball* to refer to a round candle, a wooden bead, and an unshelled walnut. Mervis and Canada found that at opportune moments in later play interactions with their children the mothers attempted to relabel these objects with their "adult-basic" names (e.g., *candle*), but if the children rejected the new labels the mothers reverted to the child-basic usage themselves. Mervis and Canada concluded that the mothers played an essentially supportive role in their children's lexical acquisitions. The generation, differentiation, and revision of categories was under the control of the conceptual system of the child, not the adult.

There have been no comparable enquiries into the capacity an adult might have to interpret, respond to, and interact with a very young child in a graphic exchange. Gardner (1980) observed that a kind of contagion occurred between his own motor movements with a pen and those of his son at the age of 20 months. That is, the two of them tended to copy and extend the jabbing or circling motions made by the other to produce marks on the page. However there have been few systematic investigations of early communicative activity using graphic representation. Matthew's (1983) analysis of what 2-year-olds are attempting to represent in their drawings, Golomb's (1981) demonstration that 3- and to some extent 2-year-olds respond differentially to differing requests for representational drawings, and Freeman's (1977) evidence that 2-year-olds can add parts appropriately to human figure representations constitute a beginning in this regard.

Even where children at a somewhat more advanced age are concerned, the attention given to the semantic or communicative aspects of their drawings has still been sparse. N. R. Smith (1979) described a 4-year-old's step-by-step forging of the connections between forms and intended meanings in a single drawing of an airplane. Gardner (1980) examined the progressions over several years in young children's portrayals of their favorite subject matter; for one child the subject matter was Batman and related characters, and for another it was horses. Gardner, Wolf, and Smith (1982) drew attention to the fact that two children of the same age may use graphic activities in quite different communicative ways. They contrasted the drawings of one $3\frac{1}{2}$ year-old, for whom the lines on the page conveyed everything that was intended, with the drawings of another for whom the graphic forms were merely part of an overall communicative act, forming an accompaniment or "backdrop" to verbal, narrative activities. Again, there has been little systematic investigation of the potential for communicative graphic activity between adult and child in the period between 2 and 4 years, that is, in the period when a basic mastery of graphic forms is achieved. This is in stark contrast with language skills, where much is known about the child's early semantic, pragmatic, and communicative competence (e.g., Ervin-Tripp & Mitchell-Kernan, 1977; Snow & Ferguson, 1977). A more complete understanding of what children mean to convey in their first years of graphic activity would undoubtedly provide better foundations for instruction in the early school years.

More evidence is available about the expressive and communicative aspects of drawings by the 4- to 7-year-old. In the first place, we know that the child of this age has a reliable method of generating representations of the human figure, including methods of adjusting aspects such as the size and orientation of the whole or the parts to be consistent with other constraints in the drawing (e.g., Freeman, 1980; Goodnow, 1977). We also know that there are some types of modification of basic forms (e.g., changes designed to portray movement) that the young child attempts only infrequently in drawing. When they are attempted, it is also likely to be by the use of unconventional methods. This is reminiscent of young children's early attempts at difficult linguistic transformations and inflections. Earlier we discussed evidence which shows that young children make diverse but consistent attempts at drawings of the same subject matter (e.g., a bicycle) over a period of months (Van Sommers, 1984). These attempts are reminiscent of the young child's exploration of the semantic relations between words which have long been acquired, but whose meanings and whose use in different contexts are still capable of elaboration and change (Bowerman, 1978). These parallels between the early development of graphic and linguistic skills suggest that we might discover quite a lot about how children learn to draw by examining how they learn to use other representational systems such as language. In fact, as we mentioned earlier, Gardner and his colleagues (Gardner, 1982; Gardner & Wolf, 1983) have begun to unravel the complex relationships between early developments in a number of symbolic systems.

The next important point about developments in the early school years is that there is an interplay between the rules available for generating forms, on the one hand, and the types of meanings or expressive qualities that the child wants the drawing to have, on the other. It is particularly striking that the 7-year-old will produce quite different copies of the same configuration of lines when those lines represent a three-dimensional object (a cube) as against a two-dimensional pattern (Phillips et al., 1978). These findings suggest that there are certain meanings or ideas connected with a cube, such as the fact that it will sit flat on a surface rather than balancing on one corner, which the child seeks to incorporate in a representation, even though this may interfere with the reproduction of lines and angles which could otherwise be represented accurately (as a "pattern").

Willats' (1981, 1983) studies have also drawn attention to the fact that the drawings of young children are determined by rules for simply denoting or referring to certain features (edges, surfaces, etc.) in addition to rules for transforming spatial relations in the external world into spatial relations on the page. In young children's first attempts at maps and diagrams there is a similar tendency to do more than represent just the spatial relations between elements or the temporally ordered steps in an assembly. In a map, for example, the drawing may also represent events on a journey from one place to another or may include a pictorial display of landmarks that could be denoted adequately in a nonpictorial way (Davis & Fucigna, 1983; Goodnow, 1977).

These findings, taken as a whole, suggest that the young child's intuitive understanding of graphic representational methods includes not only rule-governed or conventional aspects (e.g., a line can represent an edge or a path on a map) but also figural, expressive aspects (e.g., a cube is a solid object, which rests in certain positions). There is also evidence to suggest that each child evolves his or her own characteristic ways of achieving a marriage between rule-governed production techniques and the meanings or expressive qualities which he or she intends the drawings to have (N. R. Smith, 1979; Van Sommers, 1984). This is also shown, indirectly, by the finding that young children exhibit individual styles, recognizable to adults, and by the further finding that traces of a child's style at 5 years of age may be apparent in drawings which are made up to 2 years later (Hartley et al., 1982; Somerville, 1983). There is, of course, the problem that a child at this age may not be aware of, or able to assess, exactly what his or her graphic representations convey to others (Gardner, 1980; Korzenik, 1977). And the complementary problem is that what adults read in a drawing by a young child might not necessarily have been intended (Winner, 1982). In principle, at least, the interpretive difficulties of the adult can be overcome by more sensitive investigations of the young child's representational systems, such as those which we discussed in Section II.

Eisner (1976) suggested that there has been a pervasive tendency to underestimate what children entering school are capable of learning, in the arts as well as in other disciplines. Kellogg (1969) argued that educators have tended to create a gulf between child art and adult art, placing too great an emphasis on the teaching of conventional methods of pictorial representation to the child. Traditionally, in her view, the assumption has been that it is desirable to replace the child's intuitive methods of graphic representation with the more conventional, pictorial representations that are preferred by adults. In fact, Kellogg (1969) considered that "among those art educators concerned with elementary school programs, the importance of pictorialism is stressed to a degree that amounts almost to a repudiation of possible esthetic values in child art" (p. 148).

A more adequate understanding of young children's representational systems has been provided by Kellogg's (1969) extensive observations and categorizations of early graphic products and by the subsequent research which her analyses did much to inspire. Although our understanding of the intricacies of these representational systems and their development is by no means complete, there is sufficient information about the typical strategies, rules, and aesthetic concerns of the young school-age child to form a basis for the design of instruction in graphic production. It seems reasonable to hope that instruction designed with children's intuitive representational systems in mind might mitigate the loss of enthusiasm and creative spontaneity that often occurs in the early school years (e.g., Gardner, 1980; Winner, 1982).

However, art education for the young child does not consist solely of instruction in production. An inseparable part of the ability to produce graphic and other representations is the ability to perceive form, meaning, and aesthetic qualities in the works of others (cf. Gardner & Wolf, 1979). The studies which we discussed in the preceding sections are all concerned with children's graphic production. But there is also some conceptual and empirical evidence available about the acquisition and appreciation of stylistic concepts. In the final section we examine the educational implications of several studies of the development of style perception and of the acquisition of ill-defined concepts. Our argument depends once again on the notion of artistic styles as ill-defined concepts and is that this conceptualization of styles has some powerful implications for the way in which children acquire and can be helped to acquire an understanding of art.

C. Children's Notions of Style

The skills involved in the development of style perception can be understood by considering the culmination of these abilities in the connoisseur. Gardner (1972b) stated that such a person must be able, first of all, to realize that artists "leave their mark" and have characteristic ways of producing art. Second, the connoisseur must be aware of the dimensions that enter into style and be able to search out the relevant values of these dimensions effectively. Finally, knowledge about the characteristics of several styles must be compiled, and this will result in the awareness that different characteristics are diagnostic of different styles. An appreciation of stylistic nuances and the relations between styles thus constitutes the essence of style perception. How are these discriminatory powers acquired by the child?

Developmental differences in sensitivity to style have been investigated using sorting and matching-to-sample tasks. Children have been required to place together paintings by the same artist or have been shown two paintings by a particular artist and asked to choose, from another set, a third by this same artist. Frequently they have also been asked to justify their choices.

Whereas adolescents base their judgments on a combination of several cues, children younger than about 14 years rely primarily on subject matter, seemingly unaware that other factors such as texture or composition might be as important, if not more important, for the definition of an artist's style (Deporter & Kavanaugh, 1978; Frechtling & Davidson, 1970; Gardner, 1970, 1972a, 1972b). However, the results of several studies involving carefully designed training procedures have shown that even 6-year-olds can learn to use cues other than subject matter in order to detect styles. This means that preadolescents are certainly not incapable of perceiving stylistic features, even though they often may not attend to them spontaneously.

Gardner (1970) rewarded 7- and 10-year-olds for sorting paintings according to style and found that a majority of even the youngest subjects could reliably sort by style on a posttest. Silverman, Winner, Rosenstiel, and Gardner (1975) replicated this finding with 10-year-olds by training them to attend to several factors of potential importance to the definition of styles. Furthermore, Gardner (1970) found that when the distracting aspect of subject matter was removed (either by using abstract work or by holding subject matter constant), even 6-year-olds showed some evidence of style sensitivity in a matching-to-sample task. An important adjunct finding in Silverman et al.'s (1975) study was that training the children in sensitivity to style had an effect on the children's own drawings, leading to more varied use of color and texture than before.

The implication of these studies is that even children of elementary school age are capable of perceiving stylistic relations, although they may often choose to focus instead on subject matter when grouping works of art. Their tendency to focus in this way has typically been attributed to the perceptual salience of subject matter for this age group, but it could also reflect, among other things, the children's initial conceptions about how art is produced. There is some evidence to suggest that 4- to 7-year-old children are unaware of or at least relatively naive about the creative processes involved in art. Gardner, Winner, and Kircher (1975) questioned children of this age about the process of artistic production and found that very few seem aware even that cognitive or perceptual skills are entailed. When asked how one could tell who created a certain painting, the children typically gave reasons unrelated to style (e.g., "ask someone," "you saw him do it"). It has also been shown that a young child will accept, for example, the similarity in dress between a sea captain and a policeman as sufficient evidence that they were drawn by the same artist (Deporter & Kavanaugh, 1978). It seems possible that children's initial intuitive ideas about art do not rely on the concept of style, even though with training or special comparisons of examples they can be helped to perceive stylistic relations.

With development, children's awareness of the process of artistic creation gains in sophistication. Older children understand the importance of cognitive activity and the contributions of formal training to the process of artistic creation, and they can focus on the medium, independently of the content, as a source of expression (Gardner et al., 1975). With increasing age, children become better able to recognize and appreciate the viewpoint of the artist, considering both the subjective intentions and creative decisions involved in producing art (D'Onofrio & Nodine, 1981). This increased awareness undoubtedly refines the child's concept of what a style is and how it may vary. And this, in turn, can lead the child to look for a variety of dimensions when involved in a style-learning task.

Of course factors other than a relatively unsophisticated conception of the process of artistic production may contribute to the 4- to 7-year-old's limited understanding of style. Young children use relatively inefficient scanning patterns when looking at a picture (Mackworth & Bruner, 1970), and this means that their extraction of information from paintings might be rather unsystematic and incomplete. We also know that children sometimes respond impulsively in matching and other tasks, with little reflection on the alternatives that are presented (Gardner, 1970; White, 1970). When they are asked to compare complex stimuli, young children seem to respond on the basis of their overall perceived similarity rather than on the basis of their variation along independent dimensions (Kemler & Smith, 1978; L. B. Smith, 1979; Smith & Kemler, 1977). This suggests that they might find it difficult to isolate a number of different features relevant to the perception of style. A finding which supports this indirectly is that young children have difficulty in perceiving the relations between diverse members of a class (Rosch et al., 1976; Saltz, Soller, & Sigel, 1972).

The role that education can play in the growth of stylistic sensitivity is perhaps attenuated by these developmental limitations. Certain abilities that potentially contribute to a mature form of style perception may follow a developmental course which is more or less unaffected by educational intervention. The abilities to make complex perceptual discriminations and to consider the stylistic influences of independent dimensions systematically and simultaneously, for example, may not be amenable to training or acceleration. However, even if this is true (and as we will see there is certainly room for doubt), on the more positive side there is evidence to suggest that most of the age-related differences in these abilities have dissipated by about 8 or 10 years of age (Kemler & Smith, 1978; Rosch et al., 1976).

Contrary to the impression one might gain from the studies we have mentioned that there may be insuperable developmental limitations, the results of several other studies suggest that young children's ability to discriminate stylistic features may be enhanced substantially through the provision of appropriate experiences. The results of the training studies mentioned earlier have shown specific ways in which young children can benefit by being made aware of the dimensions on which paintings vary. Silverman et al. (1975) trained 10-year-olds to pair works of art according to style and found that the children's approaches to this task changed in a regular fashion as time went on. Their initial misconceptions and reliance on subject matter were gradually replaced by choices based on a different single factor (e.g., whether the paintings were light or dark). The most successful and advanced approach, which the children adopted eventually, was a multidimensional one in which they tallied the number of similar features which pairs of the paintings shared and matched those with the highest tally. Gardner (1972a) obtained results which were similar to these using a sort-by-style task. He found that 7- to 10-year-olds successfully decentered from subject matter in the process of sorting and eventually sorted paintings together because they considered them to share "family relations." The children would say, for example, that two pictures seemed to "make a family" (Gardner, 1972a, p. 612) and would rely on a variety of features when attempting to relate the paintings to each other.

There is a similarity between these children's stylistic conceptions and some of the philosophical and psychological descriptions of the structure of categories that we have discussed (Rosch & Mervis, 1975; Wittgenstein, 1953). More specifically, the children's ideas mirror the notion of artistic styles as ill-defined concepts (Hartley & Homa, 1981; Hartley et al., 1982). The results of the studies by Gardner (1972a) and Silverman et al. (1975) are important because they suggest that preadolescents are capable of recognizing the family resemblance structure which is inherent in a style and that the learning of this complex structure can be facilitated through training.

Gardner (1972b) has also obtained evidence that by the age of 7 a child has intuitively sensed stylistic distinctions even though the word *style* may still be foreign. A first grader may notice, for example, that the drawings of houses by different people are reliably different and that the same person can draw many different subjects in related ways. Contained in this realization are the rudiments of style sensitivity, and it is reasonable to suppose that this age group in particular might benefit from exposure to different styles. That is, the 7-year-old's intuitive comprehension of the existence of individual styles could perhaps be fostered and expanded into a more elaborate understanding of styles and their structure. Even in the case of adults who are versed in the appreciation of art, Goodman (1978) has drawn attention to the conceptual benefits of attempting to comprehend a new style: "The less accessible a style is to our approach and the more adjustment we are forced to make, the more insight we gain and the more our powers of discovery are developed." (p. 40). How might a curriculum best be designed to nurture this type of growth in young children?

Eisner's (1982) argument that the predominant syntax (i.e., manner of relating the parts in a representation) involved in artistic creation is a figurative one has direct implications for understanding the process of style learning. The rules in a figurative syntax are implicit and subject to much more idiosyncratic interpretation than are those for rule-governed areas such as mathematics. An artist who wishes to create a work in a given style is aware of certain conventions of the style, though they may not be catalogued. According to Eisner (1982), "the rules are embedded in previous work. Anyone who wishes to produce similar work must observe those 'rules' " (p. 64). And the resulting productions, rather than being correct or incorrect, are better or worse solutions to the problem of creating "in that style." Similarly, a person seeking to recognize a style must recognize the effects of its production rules (e.g., the tendencies to use certain brushstrokes and textures).

Eisner's (1982) concept of a figurative syntax is compatible with the cognitive psychologist's concept of a ill-defined category. Ill-defined categories have been characterized as having vague boundaries, with category members differing in how well they represent the category, and with no verbalizable definitions of the category able to be derived (e.g., Mervis & Rosch, 1981). In Eisner's view, a figurative syntax consists of a loose set of unstated rules that narrow rather than dictate the possible range of exemplars of a particular representational approach (e.g., to the creation of art or poetry). These two theoretical approaches, despite the fact that they pertain to different subjects, have similar implications for the learning of stylistic concepts. Both indicate the importance of exposure to examples and of the concomitant abstraction of information that links them together. Because of the compatibility of these two approaches to style, the findings of psychological research on the learning of ill-defined concepts can be used to generate some specific curricular guidelines for education in art.

The category abstraction paradigm, which was discussed in Section III, has provided the greatest body of evidence regarding the learning of ill-defined concepts. Although the findings obtained with the use of this paradigm apply primarily to artificial visual stimuli (e.g., dot patterns) some of them have been replicated directly with paintings (Hartley & Homa, 1981). In any case it can be argued that the findings are applicable to style learning, at least in a general way, simply because styles are ill-defined categories. The first dependable finding in studies of category abstraction is that the greater the number of exemplars encountered during learning, the better able a person is to classify other members of the category (Bengston, Schoeller, & Cohen, 1978; Goldman & Homa, 1977; Homa, 1978; Homa & Chambliss, 1975; Homa, Cross, Cornell, Goldman, & Schwartz, 1973; Homa & Vosburgh, 1976; Omohundro & Homa, 1981). However, in an educational setting, as in the laboratory or indeed in our everyday experiences of art, there will always be limitations to the number of examples that can be seen. So the important question becomes one of the guidelines a teacher might use to select the most effective subset of an artist's works to be shown to the child.

The first important point is that it has been found that categorical concepts are more accurate and more easily derived if the examples encountered initially are typical rather than atypical ones (Hull, 1920; Mervis & Pani, 1980). In addition, it has been shown that following this establishment of a core concept, it is best for the learner to encounter a broad sampling of the category (Goldman & Homa, 1977; Homa & Vosburgh, 1976). It has been found that the learner can recognize new exemplars better with broad sampling than with experience limited to typical members of the category, and also that after broad sampling the learner's categorization of new exemplars remains stable for a longer period. Experience with a variety of exemplars apparently allows the learner to discern the features that are most typical of the category, in addition to providing more adequate information about the overall structure of family resemblances within that category.

The second important point is that the learning of an ill-defined concept is also better the larger the number of contrasting categories included in the learned material (Homa & Chambliss, 1975). In other words the learner benefits by finding out more about what is *not* in the category. Even though the boundaries between each of the learned categories remain vague, certain features will serve to distinguish any given category from the others. In the case of young children, extensive experience in the discrimination of categories may be necessary to enable them to arrive at useful distinguishing features. And it will almost certainly be difficult for the child to grasp that different styles can be distinguished even when there is considerable doubt about the category membership of some items. A particularly interesting illustration of this was provided by Andersen (1975), whose study of young children's language showed that the process of coming to understand that there is only a vague boundary between the semantic categories of "cup" and "glass" may extend over several years. The youngest children (who were about 3 years old) seemed unaware, for example, that there were some articles which might equally well be referred to as a "cup" or "glass." However, Andersen's study simply looked at the labels which children gave to a whole variety of drinking vessels (and at their justifications of those labels), without attempting to lead the children toward a more adequate understanding of the complexity of the categorical distinctions involved. We are concerned here with the possibility of leading young children toward just such an understanding of stylistic categories, and the findings of the studies of category abstraction discussed above suggest at least some general principles which might be taken into account in designing curricula for the acquisition of these concepts in the early school years.

V. SUMMARY

Education in art is an area in which curriculum design should, ideally, be based on the intuitive understandings and the enthusiasm for creating representations which are shown by the young child. There are many cognitive strategies and expressive skills embodied in the graphic productions of the child both before and as he or she enters school. We have reviewed research that reveals the intricacies of the cognitive strategies that young children use to generate drawings, as well as the evolution of these strategies with age. We have also reviewed evidence suggesting that young children use distinctive representational strategies and adapt them to particular subject matters in such a way as to result in individual artistic styles, recognizable to an adult. The implication of this research is that, at least in the early school years, the curriculum should take into account the cognitive and expressive methods already apparent in a child's art when it prescribes programs for the development of rule-governed strategies, on the one hand (e.g., strategies for perspective representation, or cartographic conventions), and for the development of figurative, "semantic," or stylistic aspects of graphic production, on the other. Children's intuitive understandings provide an adequate foundation for both forms of representational skill. Conceivably, instruction programs that are connected more directly with the child's intuitive understandings might be able to counteract, to some extent, the movement away from spontaneity and toward conventionality that has often been observed in children's art in the early school years (e.g., Gardner, 1980). This is not to suggest that the learning of conventional representational systems is unimportant, but rather that the less rule-governed aspects of children's intuitive graphic skills should be nurtured at the same time.

The notion that artistic styles can be conceptualized as ill-defined concepts has proven useful in two distinct ways. First, it has contributed to our understanding of children's individual styles. Second, it has suggested processes that may contribute to children's developing appreciation of artistic qualities in the works of others. It would be informative to investigate the convergence of these two areas by examining children's perceptions of the differences and commonalities between their own artistic styles and those of their peers. Informal observations suggest that young children engage in such comparisons spontaneously and that the comparison process may generate both innovations to their existing styles and greater stylistic awareness. Research dealing with adults' knowledge of ill-defined and semantic concepts has suggested the importance of making comparisons and contrasts across categories for a more adequate understanding of what the concepts entail. Moreover, the processes of judgment, discrimination, and comparison involved in the discernment of artistic styles and in the creation of works of art constitute valuable educational experiences in and of themselves (Eisner, 1979, 1982; Goodman, 1978). The research we have reviewed concerned both with children's developing conceptions of art and with young children's individual artistic styles strongly suggests that these experiences should be given greater emphasis in designing curricula for the early school years.

REFERENCES

Andersen, E. S. (1975). Cups and glasses: Learning that boundaries are vague. *Journal of Child Language*, 2, 79–103.

Arnheim, R. (1969). *Visual thinking*. Berkeley: University of California Press.

Arnheim, R. (1972). *Toward a psychology of art*. Berkeley: University of California Press.

Arnheim, R. (1974). *Art and visual perception*. Berkeley: University of California Press.

Arnheim, R. (1981). Style as a Gestalt problem. *The Journal of Aesthetics and Art Criticism*, 39, 281–289.

Bamberger, J. (1978). Intuitive and formal musical knowing: Parables of cognitive dissonance. In S.S. Madeja (Ed.), *The arts, cognition and basic skills* (pp. 173–213). St. Louis: Cemrel.

Barresi, J., Robbins, D., & Smith, K. (1975). Role of distinctive features in the abstraction of related concepts. *Journal of Experimental Psychology: Human Learning and Memory*, 1, 360–368.

Bassett, E. M. (1977). Production strategies in the child's drawing of the human figure: Towards an argument for a model of syncretic perception. In G. Butterworth (Ed.), *The child's representation of the world* (pp. 49–59). New York: Plenum.

Bengston, J. K., Schoeller, J., & Cohen, S. J. (1978). On conceptualizing an artistic style: How critical are examples? *Studies in Art Education*, 20, 49–55.

Bowerman, M. (1978). Systematizing semantic knowledge: Changes over time in the child's organization of word meaning. *Child Development*, 49, 977–987.

Bremner, J. G., & Taylor, A. J. (1982). Children's errors in copying angles: Perpendicular error or bisection effect? *Perception*, 11, 163–171.

Brooks, L. (1978). Nonanalytic concept formation and memory for instances. In E. Rosch & B. B. Lloyd (Eds.), *Cognition and categorization*, (pp. 169–211). Hillsdale, NJ: Erlbaum.

Brown, R. (1973). *A first language: The early stages*. Cambridge, MA: Harvard University Press.

Brown, R. (1978). A new paradigm of reference. In G. A. Miller & E. Lenneberg (Eds.), *Psychology and biology of language and thought* (pp. 151–166). New York: Academic Press.

Bruner, J. S. (1974). From communication to language: A psychological perspective. *Cognition*, 3, 255–287.

Carothers, T., & Gardner, H. (1979). When children's drawings become art: The emergence of aesthetic production and perception. *Developmental Psychology, 15,* 570–580.

Chukovsky, K. (1968). *From two to five.* Berkeley: University of California Press.

Davis, M., & Fucigna, C. (1983, April). *Mapping and drawing: Two channels of graphic symbolization.* Paper presented at the biennial meeting of the Society for Research in Child Development, Detroit.

Deporter, D. A., & Kavanaugh, R. D. (1978). Parameters of children's sensitivity to painting styles. *Studies in Art Education, 20,* 43–48.

D'Onofrio, A., & Nodine, C. F. (1981). Children's responses to paintings. *Studies in Art Education, 23,* 14–23.

Dore, J. (1975). Holophrases, speech acts and linguistic universals. *Journal of Child Language, 2,* 21–40.

Edwards, B. (1979). *Drawing on the right side of the brain.* Los Angeles: Tarcher.

Eisner, E. W. (1976). What we know about children's art—and what we need to know. In E. W. Eisner (Ed.), *The arts, human development and education* (pp. 5–18). Berkeley: McCutchan.

Eisner, E. W. (1979). The contribution of painting to children's cognitive development. *Journal of Curriculum Studies, 11,* 109–116.

Eisner, E. W. (1980). Artistic thinking, human intelligence and the mission of the school. *The High School Journal, 63,* 326–334.

Eisner, E. W. (1982). *Cognition and curriculum: A basis for deciding what to teach.* New York: Longman.

Eng, H. (1931). *The psychology of children's drawings.* London: Routledge.

Ervin-Tripp, S., & Mitchell-Kernan, C. (Eds.). (1977). *Child discourse.* New York: Academic Press.

Feldman, E. B. (1981). Varieties of art curriculum. In M. Engel & J. J. Hausman (Eds.), *Curriculum and instruction in arts and aesthetic education* (pp. 131–154). St. Louis: Cemrel.

Finch, M. (1974). *Style in art history.* Metuchen, NJ: Scarecrow.

Flavell, J. H. (1972). An analysis of cognitive-developmental sequences. *Genetic Psychology Monographs, 86,* 279–350.

Frechtling, J. A., & Davidson, P. W. (1970). The development of the concept of artistic style: A free classification study. *Psychonomic Science, 18,* 79–81.

Freeman, N. H. (1975). Do children draw men with arms coming out of the head? *Nature, 254,* 416–417.

Freeman, N. H. (1977). How young children try to plan drawings. In G. Butterworth (Ed.), *The child's representation of the world* (pp. 3–29). New York: Plenum.

Freeman, N. H. (1980) *Strategies of representation in young children.* New York: Academic Press.

Gardner, H. (1970). Children's sensitivity to painting styles. *Child Development, 41,* 813–821.

Gardner, H. (1972a). The development of sensitivity to figural and stylistic aspects of paintings. *British Journal of Psychology, 63,* 605–615.

Gardner, H. (1972b). Style sensitivity in children. *Human Development, 15,* 325–338.

Gardner, H. (1973). *The arts and human development.* New York: Wiley.

Gardner, H. (1976). Unfolding or teaching: On the optimal training of artistic skills. In E. W. Eisner (Ed.), *The arts, human development and education* (pp. 99–110). Berkeley: McCutchan.

Gardner, H. (1977). Senses, symbols, operations: An organization of artistry. In D. Perkins & B. Leondar (Eds.), *The arts and cognition* (pp. 87–117). Baltimore: Johns Hopkins University Press.

Gardner, H. (1980). *Artful scribbles: The significance of children's drawings.* New York: Basic.

Gardner, H. (1982). Nelson Goodman: The symbols of art. In H. Gardner, *Art, mind and brain: A cognitive approach to creativity* (pp. 55–64). New York: Basic.

Gardner, H. (1983, April). *The nature of symbolic skills.* Paper presented at the biennial meeting of the Society for Research in Child Development, Detroit.

Gardner, H., & Winner, E. (1982). First intimations of artistry. In S. Strauss (Ed.), *U-shaped behavioral growth* (pp. 147–168). New York: Academic Press.

Gardner, H., Winner, E., & Kircher, M. (1975). Children's conceptions of the arts. *Journal of Aesthetic Education, 9,* 60–77.

Gardner, H., & Wolf, D. (1979). First drawings: Notes on the relationships between perception and production in the visual arts. In C. Nodine & D. Fisher (Eds.), *Perception and pictorial representation* (pp. 361–387). New York: Praeger.

Gardner, H., & Wolf, D. (1983). Waves and streams of symbolization: Notes on the development of symbolic capacities in young children. In D. R. Rogers & J. A. Sloboda (Eds.), *The acquisition of symbolic skills* (pp. 19–42). New York: Plenum.

Gardner, H., Wolf, D., & Smith, A. (1982). Max and Molly: Individual differences in early artistic symbolization. In H. Gardner, *Art, mind and brain: A cognitive approach to creativity* (pp. 110–127). New York: Basic.

Gelman, R., & Gallistel, C. R. (1978). *The child's understanding of number.* Cambridge, MA: Harvard University Press.

Goldman, D., & Homa, D. (1977). Integrative and metric properties of abstracted information as a function of category discriminability, instance variability, and experience. *Journal of Experimental Psychology: Human Learning and Memory, 3,* 375–385.

Golomb, C. (1981). Representation and reality: the origins and determinants of young children's drawings. *Review of Research in Visual Arts Education, 14,* 36–48.

Gombrich, E. H. (1961). *Art and illusion.* Princeton, NJ: Princeton University Press.

Gombrich, E. H. (1972). The "what" and the "how": Perspective representation and the phenomenal world. In R. Rudner & I. Scheffler (Eds.), *Logic and art: Essays in honor of Nelson Goodman* (pp. 129–149). New York: Bobbs-Merrill.

Goodman, N. (1972). *Problems and projects.* New York: Bobbs-Merrill.

Goodman, N. (1976). *Languages of art: An approach to a theory of symbols.* Indianapolis: Hackett.

Goodman, N. (1977). When is art? In D. Perkins & B. Leondar (Eds.), *The arts and cognition* (pp. 11–19). Baltimore: Johns Hopkins University Press.

Goodman, N. (1978). *Ways of worldmaking.* Indianapolis: Hackett.

Goodnow, J. J. (1977). *Children drawing.* Cambridge, MA: Harvard University Press.

Goodnow, J. J. (1978). Visible thinking: Cognitive aspects of change in drawings. *Child Development, 49,* 637–641.

Goodnow, J. J., and Friedman, S. (1972). Orientation in children's human figure drawings. *Developmental Psychology, 7,* 10–16.

Goodnow, J. J., & Levine, R. A. (1973). The "grammar of action": Sequence and syntax in children's copying. *Cognitive Psychology, 4,* 82–98.

Halliday, M. A. K. (1975). *Learning how to mean.* London: Arnold.

Harris, D. B. (1963). *Children's drawings as measures of intellectual maturity.* New York: Harcourt Brace Jovanovich.

Hartley, J. L., & Homa, D. (1981). Abstraction of stylistic concepts. *Journal of Experimental Psychology: Human Learning & Memory, 7,* 33–46.

Hartley, J. L., Somerville, S. C., Jensen, D. V. C., & Eliefja, C. C. (1982). Abstraction of individual styles from the drawings of five-year-old children. *Child Development, 53,* 1193–1214.

Henley, N. M. (1969). A psychological study of the semantics of animal terms. *Journal of Verbal Learning and Verbal Behavior, 8,* 176–184.

Hochberg, J. (1978). Visual art and the structures of the mind. In S. S. Madeja (Ed.), *The arts, cognition and basic skills* (pp. 151–172). St. Louis: Cemrel.

Homa, D. (1978). Abstraction of ill-defined form. *Journal of Experimental Psychology: Human Learning and Memory, 4,* 407–416.

Homa, D., & Chambliss, D. (1975). The relative contributions of common and distinctive information on the abstraction from ill-defined categories. *Journal of Experimental Psychology: Human Learning and Memory, 1,* 351–359.

Homa, D., Cross, J., Cornell, D., Goldman, D., & Schwartz, S. (1973). Prototype abstraction and classification of new instances as a function of number of instances defining the prototype. *Journal of Experimental Psychology, 101,* 116–122.

Homa, D., Rhoads, D., & Chambliss, D. (1979). The evolution of conceptual structure. *Journal of Experimental Psychology: Human Learning and Memory, 5,* 11–23.

Homa, D., Sterling, S., & Trepel, L. (1981). Limitations of exemplar-based generalization and the abstraction of categorical information. *Journal of Experimental Psychology: Human Learning and Memory, 7,* 418–439.

Homa, D., & Vosburgh, R. (1976). Category breadth and the abstraction of prototypical information. *Journal of Experimental Psychology: Human Learning and Memory, 2,* 322–330.

Hull, C. (1920). Quantitative aspects of the evolution of concepts. *Psychological Monographs, 28,* (1, Whole No. 123).

Ibbotson, A., & Bryant, P. E. (1976). The perpendicular error and the vertical effect. *Perception, 5,* 319–326.

Kellogg, R. (1969). *Analyzing children's art.* Palo Alto, CA: Mayfield.

Kemler, D. G., & Smith, L. B. (1978). Is there a developmental trend from integrality to separability in perception? *Journal of Experimental Child Psychology, 26,* 498–507.

Kennedy, J. M. (1983). What can we learn about pictures from the blind? *American Scientist, 71,* 19–26.

Kennedy, J. M., & Fox, N. (1977). Pictures to see and pictures to touch. In D. Perkins & B. Leondar (Eds.), *The arts and cognition* (pp. 118–135). Baltimore: Johns Hopkins University Press.

Kennedy, J. M., & Heywood, M. (1980). I see what I feel. *New Scientist, 85,* 386–389.

Korzenik, D. (1977). Saying it with pictures. In D. Perkins & B. Leondar (Eds.), *The arts and cognition* (pp. 192–207). Baltimore: Johns Hopkins University Press.

Kosslyn, S. M., Heldmeyer, K. H., & Locklear, E. P. (1977). Children's drawings as data about internal representations. *Journal of Experimental Child Psychology, 23,* 191–211.

Kubler, G. (1967). Style and the representation of historical time. *Annals, New York Academy of Sciences, 138,* 849–855.

Kuhn, D. (1979). The application of Piaget's theory of cognitive development to education. *Harvard Educational Review, 49,* 340–360.

Langer, S. K. (1942). *Philosophy in a new key.* Cambridge, MA: Harvard University Press.

Langer, S. K. (1957). *Problems of art.* New York: Scribner's.

Lark-Horowitz, B., Lewis, H., & Luca, M. (1973). *Understanding children's art for better teaching.* Columbus, OH: Merrill.

Lewis, H. P. (1963). Spatial representation in drawing as a correlate of development and a basis for picture preference. *Journal of Genetic Psychology, 102,* 95–107.

Light, P., & Simmons, B. (1983). The effects of a communication task upon the representation of depth relationships in young children's drawings. *Journal of Experimental Child Psychology, 35,* 81–92.

Mackworth, N. H., & Bruner, J. S. (1970). How children search and recognize pictures. *Human Development, 13,* 149–177.

Matthews, J. (1983, September). *Children drawing: Are young children really scribbling?* Paper presented at the British Psychological Society International Conference on Psychology and the Arts, Cardiff.

Medin, D. L., & Schaffer, M. M. (1978). Context theory of classification learning. *Psychological Review, 85,* 207–238.

Mendelowitz, D. M. (1963). *Children are artists: An introduction to children's art* (2nd ed.). Stanford, CA: Stanford University Press.

Mervis, C. B., & Canada, K. (1981, April). *Child-basic categories and early lexical development.* Paper presented at the biennial meeting of the Society for Research in Child Development, Boston.

Mervis, C. B., & Mervis, C. A. (1982). Leopards are kitty-cats: Object labeling by mothers for their thirteen-month-olds. *Child Development, 53,* 267–273.

Mervis, C. B., & Pani, J. R. (1980). Acquisition of basic object categories. *Cognitive Psychology, 12,* 496–522.

Mervis, C. B., & Rosch, E. (1981). Categorization of natural objects. *Annual Review of Psychology, 32,* 89–115.

Neisser, U. (1967). *Cognitive psychology.* New York: Appleton.

Ninio, A., & Lieblich, A. (1976). The grammar of action: "Phrase structure" in children's copying. *Child Development, 47,* 846–849.

O'Hare, D. (1981). Structure and processes in style discrimination. In D. O'Hare (Ed.), *Psychology and the arts* (pp. 192–210). Atlantic Highlands, NJ: Harvester.

Olson, D. R. (1978). The arts as basic skills: Three cognitive functions of symbols. In S. S. Madeja (Ed.), *The arts, cognition and basic skills* (pp. 59–81). St. Louis: Cemrel.

Omohundro, J., & Homa, D. (1981). Search for abstracted information. *American Journal of Psychology, 94,* 267–290.

Perner, J., Kohlmann, R., & Wimmer, H. (1984). Young children's recognition and use of the vertical and horizontal in drawings. *Child Development, 55,* 1637–1645.

Peters, A. M. (1977). Language learning strategies: Does the whole equal the sum of the parts? *Language, 53,* 560–573.

Phillips, W. A., Hobbs, S. B., & Pratt, F. R. (1978). Intellectual realism in children's drawings of cubes. *Cognition, 16,* 15–33.

Piaget, J. (1950). *The psychology of intelligence.* London: Routledge.

Piaget, J. (1951). *Play, dreams and imitation in childhood.* London: Heinemann.

Piaget, J. (1954). *The construction of reality in the child.* New York: Ballantine.

Piaget, J., & Inhelder, B. (1967). *The child's conception of space.* London: Routledge.

Posner, M., & Keele, S. (1968). On the genesis of abstract ideas. *Journal of Experimental Psychology, 77,* 353–363.

Posner, M., & Keele, S. (1970). Retention of abstract ideas. *Journal of Experimental Psychology, 83,* 304–308.

Ratner, N., & Bruner, J. S. (1978). Games, social exchange and the acquisition of language. *Journal of Child Language, 5,* 391–401.

Read, G. H. (1945). *Education through art* (2nd ed.). New York: Pantheon.

Rips, L. J. (1975). Inductive judgments about natural categories. *Journal of Verbal Learning and Verbal Behaviour, 14,* 665–681.

Rosch, E. (1975). Cognitive representations of semantic categories. *Journal of Experimental Psychology: General, 104,* 192–233.

Rosch, E. (1978). Principles of categorization. In E. Rosch & B. B. Lloyd (Eds.)., *Cognition and categorization* (pp. 28–48). Hillsdale, NJ: Erlbaum.

Rosch, E., & Mervis, C. B. (1975). Family resemblances: Studies in the internal structure of categories. *Cognitive Psychology, 7,* 573–605.

Rosch, E., Mervis, C. B., Gray, W., Johnson, D., & Boyes-Braem, P. (1976). Basic objects in natural categories. *Cognitive Psychology, 8,* 382–439.

Rush, J. C., & Sabers, D. L. (1981). The perception of artistic style. *Studies in Art Education, 23,* 24–32.

Saltz, E., Soller, E., & Sigel, I. E. (1972). The development of natural language concepts. *Child Development, 43,* 1191–1202.

Schaefer-Simmern, H. (1948). *The unfolding of artistic activity.* Berkeley: University of California Press.

Selfe, L. (1977). *Nadia: A case of extraordinary drawing ability in an autistic child.* London: Academic Press.

Shulman, L. S. (1978). Research on teaching in the arts: Review, analysis, critique. In S. S. Madeja (Ed.), *The arts, cognition and basic skills* (pp. 244–262). St. Louis: Cemrel.

Silverman, J., Winner, E., Rosenstiel, A. K., & Gardner, H. (1975). On training sensitivity to painting styles. *Perception, 4,* 373–384.

Silvers, A. (1978). Show and tell: The arts, cognition and basic modes of referring. In S. S. Madeja (Ed.), *The arts, cognition and basic skills* (pp. 31–50). St. Louis: Cemrel.

Silvers, A. (1981). The secret of style. *The Journal of Aesthetics and Art Criticism, 39,* 268–271.

Smith, L. B. (1979). Perceptual development and category generalization. *Child Development, 50,* 705–715.

Smith, L. B., & Kemler, D. (1977). Developmental trends in free classification: Evidence for a new conceptualization of perceptual development. *Journal of Experimental Child Psychology, 24,* 279–298.

Smith, N. R. (1979). How a picture means. In D. Wolf (Ed.), *Early symbolization* (pp. 59–72). San Francisco: Jossey-Bass.

Smith, N. R., & Franklin, M. B. (Eds.). (1979). *Symbolic functioning in childhood.* Hillsdale, NJ: Erlbaum.

Snow, C. E., & Ferguson, C. A. (Eds.). (1977). *Talking to children: Language input and acquisition.* Cambridge, England: Cambridge University Press.

Somerville, S. C. (1983). Individual drawing styles of three children from five to seven years. In D. R. Rogers & J. A. Sloboda (Eds.), *Acquisition of symbolic skills* (pp. 89–96). New York: Plenum.

Stacey, J. T., & Ross, B. M. (1975). Scheme and schema in children's memory of their own drawings. *Developmental Psychology, 11,* 37–41.

Trevarthen, C. (1979). Communication and cooperation in early infancy: A description of primary intersubjectivity. In M. Bullowa (Ed.), *Before speech* (pp. 321–347). New York: Cambridge University Press.

Tversky, A. (1977). Features of similarity. *Psychological Review, 84,* 327–352.

Tversky, A., & Gati, I. (1978). Studies of similarity. In E. Rosch & B. B. Lloyd (Eds.), *Cognition and categorization* (pp. 81–98). Hillsdale, NJ: Erlbaum.

Van Sommers, P. (1983). The conservatism of children's drawing strategies: At what level does stability exist? In D. R. Rogers & J. A. Sloboda (Eds.) *The acquisition of symbolic skills* (pp. 65–80). New York: Plenum.

Van Sommers, P. (1984). *Drawing and cognition.* New York: Cambridge University Press.

Walk, R., Karusaitis, K., Lebowitz, C., & Falbo, R. (1971). Artistic style as concept formation for children and adults. *Merrill-Palmer Quarterly of Behavior and Development, 17,* 347–356.

Werner, H., & Kaplan, B. (1963). *Symbol formation.* New York: Wiley.

White, S. (1970). Some general outlines of the matrix of developmental changes between five and seven years. *Bulletin of the Orton Society, 20*, 41–57.

Willats, J. (1977a). How children learn to draw realistic pictures. *Quarterly Journal of Experimental Psychology, 29*, 367–382.

Willats, J. (1977b). How children learn to represent three-dimensional space in drawings. In G. Butterworth (Ed.). *The child's representation of the world* (pp. 189–202). New York: Plenum Press.

Willats, J. (1981). What do the marks in the picture stand for? The child's acquisition of systems of transformation and denotation. *Review of Research in Visual Arts Education, 13*, 18–33.

Willats, J. (1983, April). *Drawing systems revisited: The complementary roles of projection systems and denotation systems in the analysis of children's drawings.* Paper presented at the Conference on Graphic Representation, University of York.

Winner, E. (1979). New names for old things: The emergence of metaphoric language. *Journal of Child Language, 6*, 469–491.

Winner, E. (1982). *Invented Worlds.* Cambridge, MA: Harvard University Press.

Winner, E., Blank, P., & Miller, C. (1983, April). *Children's understanding of allegory and metaphor.* Paper presented at the biennial meeting of the Society for Research in Child Development, Detroit.

Wittgenstein, L. (1953). *Philosophical investigations.* New York: Macmillan.

Wolf, D. (1983, April). *Event-structures: The first wave of symbolic understanding.* Paper presented at the biennial meeting of the Society for Research in Child Development, Detroit.

Wolf, D., & Gardner, H. (1979). Style and sequence in early symbolic play. In N. R. Smith & M. B. Franklin (Eds.), *Symbolic functioning in childhood* (pp. 117–138). Hillsdale, NJ: Erlbaum.

Yule, Y., Lockyer, L., & Noone, A. (1967). The reliability and validity of the Goodenough-Harris Drawing Test. *British Journal of Educational Psychology, 37*, 110–111.

Zernich, T. (1981). Stage theory and its implications for curriculum development in art education. In M. Engel & J. J. Hausman (Eds.), *Curriculum and instruction in arts and aesthetic education* (pp. 155–161). St. Louis: Cemrel.

9

Music

MARY LOUISE SERAFINE*
Department of Psychology
Yale University
New Haven, Connecticut 06520

I. INTRODUCTION

Despite the fact that music has been a topic of scholarly and scientific inquiry for over 2,000 years, it is a difficult art form to pin down. We can, however, begin with a few observations. No culture exists without music. In the doing of music people engage in a variety of behaviors—composing, performing, and listening. Moreover, the art products they generate in the course of these activities are not random collections of sounds, but rather orderly collections understood by other members of the culture. That is to say, music and "not-music" are clearly distinguishable. Such observations tell us that music is universal, principled, and behaviorally diverse. Yet it is not clear what people are *knowing* or mentally *doing* when they engage in the business of music.

There are a number of unproven hypotheses about this, to be sure. One hypothesis is that people are expressing some ineffable emotion; another is that they are performing mental and motor operations as a result of imitation and reinforcement; another is that they are building mental chains of ever-more-complex structures: assembling tones into melodies, melodies into phrases, phrases into compositions. But these hypotheses are weak as well as unproven. They simply do not tell us what the nature of knowledge in music is like or what forms of mental representation the art form may call upon. What is perceived and stored in memory by people who compose, perform, and listen to music is largely unknown: It may be a symbol system something like musical notation; it may be an assemblage of individual tones; it may be a hierarchic ordering of tones, durations,

---

*Present address: Department of Psychology, Vassar College, Poughkeepsie, New York 12601.

COGNITION AND INSTRUCTION

loudnesses, and so on; or it may be a set of visual, nonmusical images, a pack of muscle movements, or a list of rules.

What is needed to address the topic of curriculum design in music is a theory about musical knowledge. In this chapter I propose a description of musical knowledge, after introducing the research literature in the psychology of music. I then take up educational implications.

II. RESEARCH IN THE PSYCHOLOGY OF MUSIC

The research literature in the psychology of music is older and more vast than is commonly thought. Proper psychological studies begin with Helmholtz (1885/1954) before 1900, and are scattered over hundreds of journals worldwide. Books devoted exclusively to the psychology of music span this century (Mursell, 1937; Seashore, 1938; Revesz, 1953; Lundin, 1967; Farnsworth, 1969; Davies, 1978; Deutsch, 1982). Today at least six journals (in English alone) report only music experiments, and the psychology of music is treated also in foreign journals, the general psychological journals, and journals devoted to all of the art forms. It is possible to give only a brief review here. I discuss first the research on children and then the adult cognitive literature.

A. Research in Children's Musical Ability

Two strands of research on children and music roughly parallel research developments in other areas of psychology: the psychometric testing movement, which lasted roughly from the 1920s to the 1960s, and the neo-Piagetian, developmental movement, which began in the 1960s.

1. The Testing Movement

The literature from the musical testing movement was, and remains, the most powerful influence on both music research and educational practice. For over half a century researchers have been preoccupied with the measurement of musical ability—specifically musical talent and achievement (learning). The goals of this movement parallel those of the intelligence- and achievement-test movement more generally: to define the nature of musical talent, to detect individuals of special, perhaps innate, endowment, and to assess accurately the achievements of musical training. Perhaps a hundred or more tests of musical ability have been developed since the turn of the century. (See reviews by Colwell, 1970; Lehman, 1968; Shuter, 1968; Shuter-Dyson & Gabriel, 1982; Whybrew, 1971.)

Musical talent tests purport to detect those individuals of special, presumably inherited ability, while achievement tests assess the effects of formal training. But in theory and practice it is hard to distinguish talent from achievement; in fact, both types of music tests contain similar items. Both types of tests contain subtests for pitch, melody, rhythm, and meter perception, as well as for other musical factors. Music achievement tests typically contain additional subtests for musical notation, instrument identification, and other information that could only be acquired through learning and not be part of genetic endowment. A brief description of some of the talent and achievement tests will enlighten us on the nature of music research until the recent waning of the music testing movement.

a. Talent Tests. The first music test of any significance appeared in 1919. Designed to measure innate musical potential, Seashore's *Measures of Musical Talent* gained wide recognition among music educators, and was later used even by speech and hearing specialists, telegraph operators, and submarine detectors (Seashore, 1960).

During the two decades prior to the appearance of the battery, most inquiry into the nature of musical talent had involved the "trait approach," i.e., the discovery of the traits or abilities of gifted musicians. There was wide divergence of opinion on the number and relative importance of these abilities, but most authorities held that sensory acuity and memory for sounds were among the most important.

Seashore's tests, revised in 1939 and 1960, were aimed only at sensory capacity: determining whether the second of two oscillator-generated tones differed from the first by being higher or lower (pitch), weaker or stronger (loudness), longer or shorter (time), or same or different (timbre). Seashore himself (1938) acknowledged that sensory capacity was only a necessary, not a sufficient condition for excellence in musicianship. But he claimed that other necessities—aesthetic sensitivity, interest in music, muscular coordination, and so on—could not be measured as accurately as sensory capacity and hence were less useful as predictors of musicianship.

The tests were intended for anyone age 9 years and above, and they were widely used in schools and colleges at least through the 1960s. For nearly half a century, the Seashore test and the raft of similar tests that followed in its wake dominated research programs in both the United States and Britain. Countless studies of predictive validity, restandardization, and intercorrelation with every manner of variable (age, social class, type of instruction, home environment, instrument preference, manual dexterity) were done not just for Seashore's test but for all new tests as they appeared almost annually between the two world wars.

The subsequent tests tampered with Seashore's materials but left perception as the central task. Tests by Kwalwasser and Dykema (1930) had subjects tell whether two items were the same or different: single tones, short piano melodies, various instruments, and rhythmic patterns. In addition, a subtest on "melodic taste" had subjects indicate which of two phrases would better complete a melody.

Wing's test (1939 and 1961), extensively used in British schools, had subjects listen to two melodies and indicate whether they were the same or whether one was to be preferred in terms of rhythmic accent, harmony, loudness, and phrasing. Also a "chord analysis" test had subjects indicate the number of simultaneous tones (one to four) heard in a chord.

Gaston's test (1942 and 1957) consisted of unusual tasks: listening to a single tone followed by a chord and indicating whether the tone belonged in the chord; listening to a melody, comparing it to printed notation, and indicating whether it was the same or different in tones or rhythm; listening to an incomplete melody and indicating whether the final tone should go up or down (from the penultimate tone); and listening to fragments repeated two to six times and determining whether successive repetitions were the same or different in tones or rhythm.

Drake's test (1934 and 1957) asked subjects to listen to clicks from a metronome with a voice simultaneously counting the clicks. When the clicks ceased, the subject was to count at the same rate until told to stop, and indicate the number of counts made to that point. In the musical memory subtest, the subject heard a melody followed by two to seven comparison melodies and indicated whether the latter were the same or different in terms of key, rhythm, or individual tones.

The most recent of the published tests are those by Gordon (1965), widely used in the United States, and by Bentley (1966), more commonly used in Britain.

Gordon's test (1965) requires subjects to listen to two melodies, the second of which contains embellishing tones, and determine whether the second melody would be the same as the first if the added tones were removed. The same task is repeated, not with melodies, but with a cello baseline played as accompaniment to a violin. Additional subtests require subjects to determine whether two melodies are the same or different in tempo and meter and whether one is "better" than the other in terms of phrasing, balance, and style.

Bentley's tests (1966) consists of tasks for pitch discrimination (indicate whether the second of two tones is higher, lower, or the same as the first), tonal memory (indicate whether the second of two melodies is the same as the first and if not, tell which tone has been changed), chord analysis (indicate whether a chord has two, three, or four tones), and rhythmic memory (indicate whether the second of two rhythmic patterns is the same as the first, and if not, tell which pulse has been changed). The test is intended for children as young as 7 years.

It is clear that tests developed after Seashore's were increasingly "musical" rather than "acoustic." They shunned oscillator-generated tones and substituted real musical instruments, usually piano or strings. They favored complex musical contexts such as melodies or rhythmic fragments rather than isolated tones or chords. Some, such as Gordon's, attempted to go beyond discrimination and measure aesthetic judgment and sensitivity.

In part this change was motivated by the antitesting and antiacoustic forces that greeted Seashore's *Measures* as soon as they appeared. Concurrently with his tests, Seashore had propounded a *theory of specifics*: briefly, that musical aptitude consisted of separate, independent abilities that could be isolated and measured in an objective manner. Perceptual acuity and tonal memory were seen as innate (or at least fixed at an early age) and determined by physiological and cognitive limits. Simple hearing, in Seashore's view, was prerequisite to later abilities such as musical understanding, sensitivity, and expression.

Seashore himself acknowledged that a high score on pitch discrimination was not so much an indication of global musical talent as an indication of talent in discriminating pitches. He maintained, however, that since pitch discrimination was necessary to musicianship, it made sense to measure the ability in as pure and isolated a context as possible. He therefore disavowed all attempts to validate his tests against external criteria such as teacher ratings, success in music school, or the rankings of performance judges. Rather, he held that the logical assumption that "perception precedes understanding" was sufficient to prove the validity of his test, as long as the test measured the perceptual abilities in question. That the measurements were accurate was apparent, Seashore said, from the fact that pitch, time, and loudness were isolated and unconfounded by the complexity of real melodies, instruments, and players.

Needless to say, debate ran rampant over such assertions. Seashore's critics, led principally by James Mursell (1937), called his theory *atomistic* and replaced it with a Gestalt approach which Seashore than called the *omnibus* theory. The omnibus theory held that musical aptitude was a general factor rather than a composite of independent, specific factors. Thus tests of musicality should use real music (not isolated tones) and assess musical imagery, musical sensitivity, and interest in music as well as perceptual acuity. In addition, Mursell maintained that specific abilities such as pitch discrimination do not function the same way in pure, isolated contexts as they do in real, complex music. Judging two pitches is not the same as detecting the contour of a melody; judging the loudness of a tone is not the same as being sensitive to the interaction of loudness, tempo, and phrasing in a musical composition. Further, Mursell pointed out that musicians are rarely, if ever, called upon to discriminate two tones 1/100 of a semitone apart in pitch or .05 second apart in duration.

The atomistic versus omnibus controversy was never resolved. Empirical (usually correlational) studies gave no evidence about the validity of the tests that was persuasive to both sides. Seashore's position that external validity was unnecessary counteracted the studies that showed meagre predictive power for aptitude tests in terms of later musicianly success. In any case, measures of success as a musician were hard to come by, since teacher ratings, performance-judge ratings, and music course grades were variable and of doubtful reliability. Moreover, the tasks used on the various tests were so different from each other that intertest correlations, while low, were essentially meaningless.

In spite of these problems, the tests continued to be used to identify school children who would most profitably benefit from music instruction. They also dominated the attention of researchers almost exclusively until the late 1960s. The atomistic versus omnibus controversy persists in our own time in the form of acoustic versus cognitive or contextual views of music, as I take up later.

b. Achievement Tests. In part because of the philosophical and empirical problems with aptitude measurement and in part because of changing political attitudes, attention turned in the post–World War II decades to the measurement of musical achievement rather than aptitude or endowment. In fact, achievement tests used items similar to those of aptitude tests, but their purpose was different: to assess the effects of instruction rather than to identify the specially gifted. For example, Colwell's achievement test (1969b) contained sections on pitch discrimination, as well as interval, chord, meter, and major–minor mode discrimination. In addition, the test measured instrument recognition, feeling for tonal center, style recognition (indicate the probable composer), and ability to read notation.

In contrast, the Aliferis achievement test (1947 and 1954), intended for college students, relied exclusively on the ability to read notation. The Snyder Knuth test (1965) differed from each of these in its use of a musical analogies test (on musical terms) and assessment of harmonization ability, sensitivity to melodic contour, and ability to detect melodic motion by steps, skips, and repeated notes.

To be sure, the music achievement test movement was plagued by as many difficulties as the aptitude movement: Definitions of musical achievement varied widely. Paper-and-pencil tests requiring music listening

ability bore little relation to the ability to play an instrument or compose—
in short, to make music. Moreover, the tests foundered on the task of
assessing the effectiveness of school music programs because the goals
of such programs, even if clear, were seldom in line with the test con-
structors' notions of musical knowledge.

c. Tests and Research. The influence of the testing movement on research on children and music is impossible to exaggerate. The vast majority
of studies either were about the tests (establishing new reliabilities, val-
idities, and norms for special populations) or employed the tests as the
dependent variable in correlational studies of aptitude and achievement.
Time and space do not permit a thorough review of the research here (see
Colwell, 1969a; Shuter, 1968; Shuter-Dyson & Gabriel, 1982), but a sampling of studies will give the flavor of results.

The results of validation studies are difficult to assess, since adequate
measures of musical *behavior* (performance skill, expressiveness, and so
on) are often subjective and unreliable. Moreover, there is no established
theory that would predict which musical behaviors are desirable (artistic).

In one validation study, Bentley (1970) gave formulas for converting
scores on his test (1966) to *musical ability quotients* (MQ), similar to intelligence quotients (IQ) with a mean of 100. Bentley compared test results
to the judgment of auditions by the chapel organist at New College, Oxford,
in a screening of 7- to 10-year-old candidates for the chapel choir. All of
the organist's final selections had MQs of 146 or above, which in Bentley's
view argued favorably for test validity. Rowntree (1970) reported a reliability of only about .60 for Bentley's test, but did show significant correlations with teacher ratings of vocal and instrumental skill.

Lee (1967) found only marginal validity for Gordon's test (1965) among
college music students, since the correlation between test scores and music
course grades was only .38. Lee also provided percentile norms for college
students who were not music majors.

Yoder (1972) found high reliability among college students for Gaston's
test (1957) but could not demonstrate validity by correlation with music
course grades. Nevertheless, music majors scored higher than non–music
majors.

In a study of meagre explanatory power, Bernier and Stafford (1972)
found a correlation between timbre-discrimination ability (using Seashore's
timbre subtest) and preference for instruments with timbres of greater
complexity in sound waves.

Some studies have favored the use of multiple measures as predictors
of musical behavior. Gordon (1968) used a combination of musical aptitude
(his test of 1965), intelligence (Henmon–Nelson Tests of Mental Ability),

and academic achievement (Iowa Tests of Basic Skills) to predict instrumental performance ratings. While his aptitude test was the single best predictor, the highest correlation with performance ratings (.84) was obtained by using all three predictors. In a similar study, Young (1971) found a correlation with performance ratings of .72 for the same variables (although the Lorge–Thorndike test was used for intelligence). Moreover, performance ratings that assessed note-reading ability correlated best with academic achievement, while those dealing with perceptual skills showed highest correlation with the musical aptitude test (Gordon's test of 1965).

The problem with these and similar studies is that neither musical behavior nor musical aptitude–achievement has been precisely defined. Philosophical difficulties abound, as we have seen in the atomistic versus omnibus controversy. The result is that solid research findings are hard to come by. Research results conflict, and studies can be interpreted only within the limited paradigm established by a particular study—the definition of musicality assumed by the test in question, the particular subject sample, and so on.

That interpretations of such research are difficult is nowhere demonstrated more dramatically than in studies of intercorrelation among the tests and correlations between the test scores and other variables. McLeish (1968) reported a positive correlation among three of the musical aptitude tests: Bentley's (1966), Seashore's (1960), and Wing's (1961). But Gordon's test (1965)—one of the best constructed and closest to musical behavior— is uncorrelated with both Seashore's test (Gordon, 1969) and Bentley's test (Young, 1972b). In these studies, even the subtests intended to measure similar elements (pitch, rhythm, etc.) did not intercorrelate.

Studies that sought correlations between musical aptitude and other musical variables were similarly disappointing or uninterpretable. Williams (1972) found that neither musical aptitude (Gordon's test) nor instruction (a music appreciation course) had a significant influence on attitudes toward music. Vaughan and Williams (1971) found no correlation between musical aptitude (Bentley's test) and either musical creativity or creative thinking in general. Moreover, they found little relation between musical aptitude and general intelligence (Henmon–Nelson test). However, using different measures, Whittington (1957) found a modest correlation between musical aptitude (Wing's test) and intelligence (Raven Progressive Matrices), though not between musical aptitude and manual dexterity.

Such results lead to the conclusion that research findings are overpoweringly influenced by the particular music test employed. Each test seems to generate different, even conflicting, research results. Consider the question of whether "culturally disadvantaged" children are deficient in musical aptitude. Gordon (1967), in a study of over 650 seventh graders, found no significant differences in musical aptitude (his test) between disadvantaged students and a heterogeneous sample. Nevertheless, when music instruction is equivalent for both groups, disadvantaged students score lower in music achievement, even though their aptitudes are presumably equivalent (Gordon, 1970a). Thus, so many factors other than aptitude (perhaps cultural differences, attitude, etc.) may influence music achievement that even aptitude-plus-instruction is insufficient in bringing disadvantaged students to the type of achievement obtained by the heterogeneous sample. Moreover, while Gordon had found no differences on his aptitude test between disadvantaged and heterogeneous samples, both Wilcox (1971) and Dawkins and Snyder (1972) found that disadvantaged students score lower than the standardization sample when Seashore's test is used as the measure of musical aptitude.

Thus studies that use the currently available music tests as the main dependent variable have generated conflicting or uninterpretable information with meagre implications for education. Even the studies aimed at instructional practice have not led to convincing theory about music education. Kyme (1967) reported that training for junior high students in music composition, as opposed to more traditional instruction, did not significantly improve scores on a variety of tests, including musical sensitivity. But one would hardly conclude that composition—perhaps the most creative of the several musical disciplines—is unworthy of a place in the curriculum. Moreover, it is impossible to control for countless influential factors in such studies (teacher attitude, materials used, precise content transmitted).

Both Gordon (1970b) and Froseth (1971) showed that students taught by teachers who had knowledge of musical aptitude scores and who adjusted instruction to individual differences achieved more, musically, than did students of teachers with no knowledge of scores. Yet this result leads to no convincing general principle: We do not know whether the greater achievement resulted from some predisposition on the part of the teacher, subsequent adaptation to individual differences, or objective knowledge about the test scores themselves. Perhaps adjustment to individual differences can also be achieved through other means.

Many studies aimed at instructional practice have used such limited manipulations of instruction that they are essentially meaningless for generating educational guidelines. Jeffries (1967) showed that the preferred method of teaching interval discrimination was to present intervals in random order (not in order of difficulty) and to use delayed (not immediate) feedback. His study used a teaching machine and part of Wing's (1961) aptitude test. Peterson (1969) found that scores on a listening-skill test were higher for students taught listening with the visual aid of notation than for those taught without notation. Michalski (1971) found an advantage for programmed instruction on some music tests but not on others.

Such results give us a meagre amount of information about the order of presenting intervals and the benefits of notation, but they do not enlighten us on the more central questions of curriculum and instruction in music: What is the nature of musical knowledge? How is it acquired? Such questions are as taxing in music as they are in other areas of education, but in music they have been especially difficult because there is no established theory about what musical knowledge is.

But one of the stumbling blocks for the musical testing movement was disagreement on this very topic, coupled with the fact that little if any research attempted to test competing theories. Most studies were conducted within the singular paradigm assumed by the test in use. Nevertheless, some general conclusions emerged from the psychometric movement.

d. Summary and Conclusions. The musical testing movement was aimed at data gathering that would speak to five general goals:

1. the establishment of norms for children's musical abilities;

2. the resolution of the nature–nurture controversy with respect to musical ability;

3. the creation of instruments that would predict later musical accomplishment;

4. the investigation of the relationship between musical ability and general intelligence; and

5. the investigation of the relationships between musical ability and abilities in other academic areas as well as in the other arts.

The first goal was accomplished with enormous success. Thousands of children were tested with a vast array of tasks, and the norms were duly reported for age groups ranging from 8–10 years to the college level. It is unfortunate that relatively little is known about children's musical perceptions before the late elementary school years, but the data do show that to some degree children acquire impressive musical skills at least by the third to fifth grade. This is especially impressive since the quantity of school time devoted to music is almost always smaller than that devoted to other subjects. With some qualifications (which I take up subsequently), school-age children can generally determine which of two tones is higher or lower, louder or softer, or longer or shorter. They can tell whether two melodies are the same or different, whether two melodies differ in tempo, rhythm, or meter, and whether a melody has been properly harmonized. The more advanced skills that they acquire include determining the number of tones in a chord, determining whether one melody is a variation of another, judging which of two melodies has the better ending or better phrasing, or, if two melodies differ, telling exactly which tones are different.

Although the research literature is replete with percentile norms for these and similar skills at various age levels, it is difficult to draw the firm conclusion that the concept of melody (or harmony or rhythm or meter, etc.) is generally acquired by a particular age. The reason is that the percentage of children passing or failing a particular task at a certain age depends on the nature of the task and on the nature of the stimulus. For example, younger children generally do better in a simple discrimination task (Are these two the same or different?) than in tasks requiring some other response (Which tones are different? Is it a variation? Should the final tone go up or down? Is the meter duple or triple?). More importantly, the nature of the musical stimulus is a prime determiner of the ease or difficulty of a task. Obviously the more similar two melodies are (the more tones they have in common), the more difficult it will be to discriminate between them. Also, the longer the melodies are, the greater is the memory demand and the more difficult the task. Thus interpreting tables of percentile norms for what children can and cannot do at particular ages is made problematic by the fact that music tests vary enormously in their stimuli. Melodies may range from three to ten tones and last from a few seconds to several in duration. Or the members of a pair of melodies on one test may be substantially similar, hence difficult to discriminate, while the melodies on another test may be more different and easier to tell apart. Indeed, there is no way of quantifying the precise degree to which melodies are similar or different, and professional musicians are themselves in disagreement about the precise way in which melodic, rhythmic, and harmonic factors interact in musical stimuli. Suffice it to say that young children possess the skills described above to some degree when the stimuli in question are relatively unambiguous. In addition, older children do progressively better than younger ones (there appears to be no plateau), and musically trained subjects generally do better than the untrained.

With regard to the second goal, the illumination of the respective roles of "nature" and "nurture" in musical ability, the psychometric data of course provide no easy answer. It is worth pointing out, however, that contrary to popular opinion musical ability is no more a matter of innate potential than is ability in other areas. As in other areas of psychology (most notably general intelligence), research on the question has been plagued by confounding variables. Several researchers have complained that it is precisely the musically talented who tend to seek instruction, hence both innate and learned factors have had their influence on a person by the time his musicianship has developed and can be measured. No person is know to have become an accomplished musician by dint of talent alone and without the aid of instruction, just as certainly as seemingly equivalent environments still give rise to differences in musical ability, presumably owing to innate potential. I forego a full discussion of the issue here, except to say that both innate and learned factors play a role in developing musicianship and to point out that in any case the delineation of musical talent from general intelligence has been problematic, as I take up later.

The third and perhaps most important goal of the testing movement was the creation of instruments that would predict later musical achievement. In part this goal was inspired by the assumption that whenever the financial resources for school music programs are limited, they should be spent on nurturing the talented few, those most likely to reap the benefits of instruction and perhaps become musicians. Thus for many years school systems used music aptitude tests as screening procedures for students' admission to individual instruction and extracurricular activities such as band, orchestra, and chorus. More recently, and especially in the United States, music tests have been promoted as a means of helping teachers meet individual needs in areas that need work (harmony, melody, etc.) rather than as a means for excluding students from instruction. Probably the earlier use of tests resulted in receipt of instruction by those students who had superior sensory acuity, without adequate justification for the assumption that such students would be the only ones capable of musical achievement.

Indeed, the long-range predictive validity of the tests has been problematic. No one doubts that, at least on a conceptual level, there exists a factor called *musical talent* which plays a role in later musicianly achievement. But the difficulty comes with the attempt to correlate test scores with other measures of external musicianly behavior, especially over the long term. Teacher ratings and ratings by performance judges have been used with minimal success (reliabilities are often low), and most studies have made no attempt to collect longitudinal data beyond 1 to 3 years at best. More importantly, so many factors other than talent are responsible for musical achievement that it has been impossible to clarify the contribution of any single factor; for example, general intelligence, perseverance, interest in music, and access to and quality of training undoubtedly play a role.

One of the best known longitudinal studies, conducted in the 1930s, typifies these problems. For over 10 years Stanton monitored the progress of conservatory students at the Eastman School of Music (see discussion of this project by Lundin, 1967). She attempted to predict the likelihood of graduation from the school on the basis of several of Seashore's *Measures of Musical Talent,* an intelligence test, a case history, and an additional test of tonal imagery. On the basis of these predictor variables, subjects were categorized in terms of the likelihood of their graduation: "safe," "probable," "doubtful," and "discouraged." The results showed that graduation rate in each of the groups was 60, 42, 33, 32, and 17% respectively, which lends moderate support to her predictive measures. Unfortunately (and amazingly), no attempt was made to delineate the respective contributions of musical talent and general intelligence to the predictive category assignments. In fact, the research reports contained no precise account of how the category assignments were made. Thus, while the predictions were somewhat successful and undoubtedly were so in part because of the talent measures, we cannot know what portion of the variance was accounted for by talent and what part by general intelligence and other factors. In summary, long-range predictions of musical achievement on the basis of talent measures alone have remained difficult.

Delineating the relationship between musical ability and general intelligence, the fourth goal of the psychometric movement, has remained similarly problematic. Some 50 studies using various music and intelligence tests have been reported, but research results conflict dramatically (see review by Shuter-Dyson & Gabriel, 1982). For example, correlations between intelligence and various subtests of the Seashore *Measures of Musical Talent* range from −.38 to .58. Seashore's Consonance subtest correlated .38 with intelligence in one study, −.38 in another, and 0 in yet another, even with similar sample sizes drawn from the same population type (college students). Gordon's test (1965) is reported to have somewhat more stable correlations with intelligence, ranging from .17 to .48 for the various subtests and with no substantial differences in correlations with verbal as opposed to nonverbal intelligence. In a useful review of the literature on this issue, Shuter-Dyson and Gabriel (1982) included a table that lists over 150 correlation coefficients (for separate musical subtests) culled from studies of musical ability and intelligence done from the 1920s to 1970s. The table reveals that nearly two-thirds of the correlations are below .30. Only 12% of the correlation coefficients equal or exceed an absolute value of .40, but these may be either positive or negative and range from −.60 to .58. Perhaps more important is the fact that no discernable trends emerge for separate musical factors or subject populations. Subtests for pitch, rhythm, harmony, melody, etc., do not appear to be differentially correlated with intelligence in any consistent way. Nor does subject sample appear to be a decisive factor; the range of correlations is disturbingly broad whether the subjects are adults or children. Thus the relationship between musical ability and general intelligence, as measured by the available tests, is simply unknown at this time.

Investigation into the relationship between musical ability and other art forms or academic subjects has been similarly disappointing. Again Shuter-Dyson and Gabriel (1982) provided a review of the 20 or so studies that have sought correlations between musical ability and achievement in the following areas: reading, writing, spelling, foreign language, mathematics, art, poetry, and prose. With only scattered exceptions, the data show that none of the popular notions about the musically talented—that they are better at language, mathematics, or other arts—are supported by evidence. Correlations between musical ability and other areas tend to be insignificant or else significantly positive but low—most often below .30 for language-related abilities and even lower (below .20) for other arts and mathematics. Unfortunately, most studies provide no controls for the factor of intelligence; thus a correlation between musical ability and some other area, even when it occurs, may be spurious because intelligence may account for the variance in both variables. It is surprising that so little information is available on the relationship between music and other areas, especially since standardized music tests have been available for over 50 years. Nevertheless, data collected thus far show no strong relationship between musical and other academic or artistic abilities.

Thus the psychometric tradition in music research was aimed at the general goals of providing norms, illuminating the nature–nurture controversy, predicting later achievement, and assessing the relationship between musical ability and intelligence or other achievements. To some degree research in the psychometric tradition continues. But partly as a reaction against the testing movement and partly because of agenda changes in psychology generally, the attention of music researchers switched to different questions in the 1960s. These new questions were directed at more general issues: What cognitive processes underlie the understanding of music? What developmental patterns pertain to such cognitive processes? How is development affected by instruction? I turn now to a review of the neo-Piagetian and developmental literature in music that has been published since 1960.

2. The Developmental Movement

We have seen that problems in the music testing movement stemmed in part from the diversity of opinion on the nature of musical ability and the proper questions about and means of research. One strand of the developmental movement alleviated this problem by adopting the Piagetian framework as its guiding light in forging new musical concepts, tasks, and strategies for research. The other strand of the movement mounted a broader attack on musical development, disavowing both the testing movement and a wholesale application of Piaget's framework to music.

The Piagetian movement in music was started by Pflederer Zimmerman's pioneering work in the early 1960s. In a radical break with the testing movement, she proposed a set of musical concepts based on Piaget's notion of conservation, designed a set of individual interviews for their measurement, and conducted a group of studies to determine age trends and training effects (Pflederer, 1964; Pflederer and Sechrest, 1968a, 1968b; Zimmerman and Sechrest, 1970). This was followed by a spate of studies that sought to refine and validate the idea of *musical conservation* (Botvin, 1974; Foley, 1975; Larsen, 1973; Perney, 1976; Serafine, 1979).

A review and critique of this body of research was given by Serafine (1980). Briefly, *musical conservation* refers to the understanding that, in musical compositions, some elements remain invariant while others change. For example, meter remains the same while rhythm changes; rhythm may remain the same while melody changes; melody may stay the same while rhythm, key, timbre, or accompaniment changes. The notion of musical conservation is an attempt to account for the twin dimensions of fluctuation and stability in real, complex music. Rather than assess individual elements—melody, rhythm, timbre, etc.—the aim is to assess children's understanding of the relationships among two or more elements in an ongoing piece of music.

The findings of this body of literature are difficult to summarize succinctly (see Serafine, 1980), but these are the main results:

1. Musical conservation—that is, the coordination of multiple elements in music—shows a clear age trend, with a plateau reached by the upper elementary grades. Young children (below 7 or 8 years) are generally unable to "conserve" or perceive sameness in a melody if the rhythm or other factors are changed. By the age of 10 or 12 years, however, most children are able to coordinate the several elements of music and to perceive sameness in meter, melody, or rhythm even when other elements are varied.

2. Moreover, the achievement of musical conservation parallels the achievement of conservation in other domains (number, weight, etc.). Serafine (1979) found that the achievement of nonmusical conservation (number, space, weight, etc.) was an even better predictor of meter conservation than was age. Botvin (1974) found evidence that training in melody conservation (with changes of tempo or speed) improved both melody conservation and nonmusical conservation. This is evidence that the achievement of musical understanding is not specific to music, but may be tied to more general cognitive achievements.

3. In general, conservation of melody is more difficult—hence acquired later—when the changes involve rhythm, contour, or mode (major or mi-

nor) than when they involve tempo, timbre, or harmony. Thus a distinction can be made between substantive deformations of a melody, which make conservation more difficult, and deformations which allow the original melody to be perceived easily.

4. With one exception (Botvin, 1974), studies show that short-term training in musical conservation is not effective. Thus the ability may be more a maturational than a learned ability, although the effects of long-term training have not been adequately studied.

The non-Piagetian developmental literature has covered a broader array of topics than musical conservation (see reviews by Dowling, 1982; Gabrielsson, 1981). Research on infants has shown a surprising degree of aural sensitivity even in very young babies. Kessen, Levine, and Wendrich (1979) showed that infants 6 months or younger can learn to match pitches vocally: They imitate or sing the pitches back to the experimenter with a surprising degree of accuracy. Infants are also sensitive to melodies and melodic changes. Using the habituation paradigm, Chang and Trehub (1977) found that babies consider a transposition of key to be "no change" in a melody. That is, the babies did not dishabituate to transpositions, but they did not show a startle response to changes in contour and rhythm. This is a rather adultlike response, since transposition of key essentially leaves all aspects of a melody unchanged except for the pitch on which it is begun.

Davidson, McKernon, and Gardner (1981) investigated song learning in a small sample of preschoolers in a longitudinal study. They identified four stages in the learning of simple children's songs, ranging from the 2-year-old's grasp of words, general phrase lengths, and a bare melodic outline to a stabilized, repeatable version of the song as an adult might sing it.

There is disagreement about when children grasp the idea of tonality in music—the feeling for tonic or key center that undergirds harmonic closure and modulation. Zenatti (1976) reported that acculturation to tonality (and consonance) is conspicuous by age 5, but Funk (1977) reported that tonality is a much later developing phenomenon. Differences in research results are no doubt due to task differences and the precise way the effect of tonality is defined. Funk's research used a modulation-detection task, which may be more difficult than other tasks that measure key center directly.

It is fair to say that research on infants has produced the general finding that their discrimination capacities are impressive, while research on children between 2 and 8 years finds them surprisingly incapable of musical understanding. Funk (1977) reported that discriminating variations on a theme is difficult (80% error rate) for children about 6 years of age. Gardner (1973) reported that children below age 8 discriminate poorly even the global, stylistic features of music, such as those that distinguish baroque music from later styles. The music conservation literature tends to show a lack of conservation of most musical elements before age 7 or 8 years. Gardner (1971) reported substantial difficulty in the imitation of simple rhythm patterns (via pencil tapping) in children below third grade.

At present there are no unequivocal findings about what children can and cannot do in music at particular stages of development, largely because tasks and operational definitions of musical concepts have varied widely. It is clear that musical performance ability may be quite accessible to young children, since some (mostly imitative) methods of instrumental teaching have been successful in teaching even 3- and 4-year-olds to play substantial pieces of music on an instrument. (The widely used Suzuki violin method is a case in point.) But aside from engaging in rote imitative behavior, it is not clear what such children know or understand of music, even while they are able to engage in musical behaviors. There is no research literature at present on what effect this method has on music perception or understanding.

Music research on children beyond the elementary school years is scant at best, consisting mostly of the aptitude and achievement studies already described. The vast majority of work on postchildhood cognition in music has been done on adults. I turn now to a brief overview of that literature.

B. Research on Adult Musical Cognition

The research literature on adult perception and cognition in music is overpoweringly vast. I estimate that there are perhaps a few thousand studies in the entire domain, with perhaps a hundred or more new studies appearing annually. There are two main branches of inquiry: acoustic approaches and cognitive–perceptual approaches. The most recent reviews and compendiums are those by Davies (1978), Deutsch (1982), and Gabrielsson (1981). I mention here only a handful of the myriad topics that have been and still are under investigation. Unfortunately, the research has thus far failed to provide a consistent picture of what the adult mental representation of music is like. No comprehensive psychological theory of music has been put forth, although scholars in the field of music theory have generated some competing proposals (with cognitive overtones) that are drawn from their analyses of musical *compositions,* not human behavior. (I do not cover such theories here, but they include work by Berry, 1976; Forte, 1973; Meyer, 1956; and Schenker, 1935/1979.)

The psychological literature comprises studies of each separate musical element—pitch, melody, harmony, rhythm, timbre, tempo, meter, and register—in addition to general studies of structure, phrasing, expectation, and subjective experience. Of all the musical elements, pitch has been the most exhaustively studied, and the vast majority of musical studies continue to be devoted to this topic. One of the traditional issues is the nature of the relationship between the *experience* of pitch (high versus low) and the physical occurrence of frequencies of vibration (in strings, air columns, and so on). It has been shown that the experience of pitch is affected not only by frequency, but also by loudness, timbre, range, and other factors.

Studies of pitch perception and memory (see Deutsch, 1982, for a review) have addressed countless topics, including how long and under what conditions a pitch can be remembered and compared to a later pitch, what the effects of silence and extraneous pitches are on pitch memory, and so on. Such studies show that pitch memory is a fluctuating thing, highly dependent on the particular nature of the stimulus materials—the nature of the surrounding pitch context, for example.

The capacity of absolute pitch is another topic much studied (see review by Ward & Burns, 1982) and still under debate. Absolute pitch refers to the ability to immediately name a pitch (C, D, E, etc.) without having been given a reference point in advance. Many musicians are reputed to have this ability. It was once believed to be a genetic endowment, but there is now some evidence that it can be acquired by training. If absolute pitch can in fact be acquired, then pitches can be perceived and remembered as stable entities in themselves, irrespective of some figure or context. Its usefulness as a musicianly ability is negligible, however, since isolated pitch naming is seldom, if ever, employed, and the vast majority of musicians spend their lives without this amenity.

Another topic is categorical perception of pitches (see Siegel & Siegel, 1977a, 1977b). Categorical perception refers to the tendency of adult Westerners to perceive pitches—of whatever variable frequencies—in terms of the categories of pitches that compose the diatonic scale (do, re, mi, etc.). If a tone of 440 cycles per second (cps) is normally perceived as A, then a tone slightly off in pitch—such as 441 or 442 cps—will also be perceived as A without sounding particularly unusual. Of course, the perceptual categories in use will vary according to the particular scale to which one has become acculturated. Scales vary enormously from one culture to the next, and no particular fixed frequencies (440 cps, etc.) universally apply to all scales. There is some evidence that musicians, presumably because of their consistent experience with our scalar music, are even more prone to categorical perception than other adults. Thus the particular scale(s) to which we become acculturated can have a decisive effect on how we perceive pitches.

Along the same lines, Krumhansl (1979) has investigated subjects' similarity judgments of pitch after they have heard some specifically tonal context such as a scale. Hearing a scale (do, re mi, etc., to do) causes us to locate stable areas, such as the first, third, and fifth note of the scale (*do, mi, sol*), as well as unstable areas (*re, fa, ti*). (Readers can prove this for themselves by singing a scale to the penultimate note, ti. Stopping there will create a feeling of instability which is resolved only by going on to the final note, do.) Krumhansl found that tones closely related in terms of scale theory, for example Tones 1 and 3, may be perceived as more similar than acoustically closer pitches, such as 1 and 2. This is evidence that the tonal or scalar music to which we have become accustomed is indeed cognitively based on the scale. That is to say, scales do have cognitive reality. (I return later to the more general problem of establishing the cognitive reality of the many concepts about music derived from the field of music theory—such as scales, chords, and melodic and harmonic rules.)

Among the other topics investigated in the field of pitch perception is the problem of octave equivalence. Two tones an octave apart share the same pitch name (A, B, etc.), sound similar, and are functionally equivalent in certain contexts, such as chords. That is to say, a C major chord still "sounds like" C major even when one of its tones is moved by the octave. Again, the idea of octave equivalence is a concept from music theory, and much psychological research has been done to assess the degree to which octaves are in fact cognitively equivalent. Results vary, depending on the subjects and the operational definition of octave equivalence (e.g., see Deutsch, 1972), but the phenomenon has been established with certain qualifications.

Other topics in the field of pitch perception include the question of individual differences in pitch perception (see Shepard, 1981), the problem of consonance and dissonance, and the phenomenon of "streaming" simultaneous pitches. The problem of consonance and dissonance has been studied for over 50 years, generating competing theories about the definition and causes of pleasant–unpleasant simultaneous tones (for a recent study, see Terhardt, 1974). Bregman and his colleagues have investigated the degree to which two tones fuse into a single blending of sound versus the point at which they are "streamed" or heard as two separate entities (for a review, see McAdams & Bregman, 1979). For example, two tones close in pitch will fuse and be perceived as one sound, but tones separated by a certain pitch distance will be perceived as two sounds.

Pitch perception studies represent the best example of acoustic, as opposed to cognitive, approaches to music research. There is great debate about the relevance of acoustics to music, and indeed the acoustic, and even psychoacoustic, literature has yet to generate principles that explain how complex music is perceived or understood. More cognitive approaches have disavowed studies of one or two pitches and instead focused on more complex stimuli—the several pitches of a melody, for instance.

Research on melody predates substantial interest in any other area of music (see Bingham, 1910; M. Meyer, 1900). More recently, Cuddy, Cohen, and Miller (1979) and Cuddy, Cohen, and Mewhort (1981) have been investigating how melodic perception is influenced by the structure of the melody itself and what structural rules in melody might be employed. Tan, Aiello, and Bever (1981) found evidence that harmonic structure influences the way that melodies are divided into subphrases.

Rosner and Meyer (1982) have proposed two *archetypes* of melody that may be operating in our perception of melodic variations on these types. They call the two archetypes *gap-fill* and *changing-note* melodies, and they show evidence that listeners can learn to discriminate and categorize a wide variety of melodies on the basis of these two archetypes.

Dowling (1978), on the basis of several melodic experiments, has proposed a theory of memory for melodies. His claim is that two factors influencing melodic memory are (1) the scale on which the melody is based and (2) the overall contour (shape) or pattern of ups and downs contained in the melody.

Serafine, Crowder, and Repp (1984) have investigated the influence that words have on the memory for melody in songs. They show that words and melody are integrated, rather than separate, in memory representation.

The aforementioned studies represent only a few of the myriad topics under investigation with respect to the tonal (pitch or melody) dimension of music. An equally large number of diverse investigations have been done on the other elements—the temporal dimension (duration and rhythm), loudness, timbre (tone color), and so forth. Two factors account for the absence of a general psychological theory of music thus far. One is that the vast majority of studies have been aimed at only one musical dimension at a time: melody, rhythm, etc. Such studies generate descriptive findings of what listeners can and cannot hear under particular conditions, but no general laws have emerged that cover the many types of musical conditions that are found in complex music. For example, the findings of studies on three-note melodies may differ from studies of six- or nine-note melodies. Moreover, real musical compositions contain melodies much longer than those typically used in experiments, and in real music, melody is always complicated by the vagaries of rhythm, changing timbre, register, loudness, and other factors. Thus far, studies of separate elements have simply been unable to address the problem of interactions among elements as they occur in real music. Even generating a theory about a single element (much less several) has been difficult, because experimental materials vary widely from study to study and are also vastly shorter, simpler, and less affected by the complicating factors that affect real music. Most melody studies, for example, use pure, electronically generated tones of equal duration, loudness, and timbre. While this is necessary to isolate the element of melody, such studies may bear little implication for how listeners perceive real melodies, which contain variable durations (rhythm), loudness, accent, and so forth.

A second factor is that nearly all investigations of music, even the purportedly cognitive as opposed to acoustic ones, have framed their predictions and explanations in terms of the stimulus rather than the listener's cognition. Thus explanations of many pitch and melody findings tend to be only descriptions of the pitch configurations or melodies themselves—that they are based on the diatonic scale, have a particular contour, etc. For example, the assertion that melodies are stored with reference to their scale and contour is not so much an assertion about memory as a description of some features of melody: All melodies embody a scale and have contour.

Such descriptions, when they are based on solid research, serve to verify the cognitive reality of features of music that we may identify simply by observing and reflecting on music itself: We observe contours, scales, rhythms, and so forth, as features or qualities of the melodies we find about us in the musical world. In fact, identifying the features of the music about us is the business of the discipline of music theory. It is from the historical tradition of this field that the concepts of melody, harmony, and scale first arose. Elsewhere (Serafine, 1983) I take up the problem of the reciprocal goals of the field of music theory and a cognitive psychology of music. But suffice it to say here that much research on music thus far, while establishing the cognitive reality of music theory concepts (e.g., scales exist as cognitive entities), has nevertheless failed to go beyond the concepts already identified and establish a psychological theory of music.

For this reason I propose later in this chapter an alternative description of cognition in music in terms of more general cognitive processes—such as temporality, abstraction, and transformation—instead of isolated musical elements such as pitch, melody, and rhythm. First I set the stage for this alternative framework, then describe the cognitive processes and discuss implications for education.

III. THE NATURE OF MUSICAL KNOWLEDGE

That people *know* something about music is a fact gleaned from two forms of evidence: (1) some human behaviors that we can clearly observe—performing, composing, and listening; and (2) the tangible art products that result—namely, musical composition. Neither the behavior nor the products are randomly occurring; they appear to be undergirded by complex and consistently employed musical knowledge.

Musical knowledge is very much like knowledge of a language. It is not like the semantics of a language, for music does not *mean* anything concrete that is agreed upon by all listeners. But music is languagelike, nevertheless. Consider the parallels. Music is universal in at least two senses. No culture is known to exist without it, and nearly everyone acquires or participates in some form of music. Not everyone is a composer or performer, to be sure, but everyone is capable of listening to and understanding some form of music (whatever his or her preference), everyone can distinguish music from noise or other sounds, and everyone can discriminate "our music" from foreign music. In short, music and musical acquisition are universal.

Also like language, music is not fixed, but continually changes. This is sometimes a hard fact to grasp in a peculiar century like our own, in which the Beethoven symphonies, which never change, are played over and over again. But in fact music does change. The music that people listened to in the Renaissance was different from what Beethoven brought along, and after the death of Beethoven we heard Stravinsky and Schoenberg, whose music was far different. Anyone who knows early jazz or early rock knows that it is different—far different—from the jazz or rock of today. Whatever the nature of musical knowledge, it is apparently very adaptable. Within one lifetime we are capable of hearing and understanding a broad range of musics, as long as they are generally within the musical culture, language, or tradition in which we were brought up.

This is far from saying that the particulars of musical understanding are themselves universal. In fact our adaptability to different types of music is limited by culture. Non-Westerners find our music incomprehensible, and vice versa.

But let me clarify the degree to which music is culturally specific, because it is also true that people may to some degree understand music that lies outside their group. Occasionally people listen to foreign musics and seem to understand and enjoy them. There are even composers who claim to have been influenced by the experience of coming into contact with some exotic, non-Western style. But consider the evidence for music's cultural specificity. Music does vary by geographic area and cultural group, and there can be no question about this. Korean music belongs to Korea, and it does not in the least sound like a Beethoven symphony or folk music from Appalachia. Moreover, while people may occasionally listen to foreign music, they do not habitually do so, and they never actually compose in a foreign style. It is even plausible that, in listening to foreign styles, listeners simply impose their own culture's norms on the music at hand. To use the linguistic analogy again, the understanding of foreign music may be like the acquisition of a second language: it never precisely matches the attainments of a native speaker.

So musical does vary from culture to culture, and there is no worldwide musical Esperanto. One learns the musical language of his group: a set of rules, procedures, or axioms that generally apply to his musical culture. We may refer to this musical grammar as a style: jazz and nineteenth-century classical music are both examples of styles. People brought up to understand one or more particular styles have the capacity to understand and respond to new works in that style as they are composed. Composers who work in a particular style create new, slightly different, instances within the same general type: No jazz writer writes the same piece over again, but it still sounds generally like jazz.

A clarification of musical styles or grammars may be helpful at this point. A musical style is represented by a body of compositions that share similar features. For example, the melodies, chord sequences, instruments used, and other features are similar because a particular set of rules or principles is used to compose *and* understand such music. The rules or principles in operation may be implicit; indeed, we do not know and have not catalogued all the principles of all the styles. But many rules can be stated explicitly, and scholars in the field of music theory have been occupied with this task for several hundred years.

An example of a rule would be this: that dominant chords should, in the vast majority of cases, be followed by a tonic chord. This rule is adhered to by much of American folk music, for example, and by European music of the eighteenth century. Such a rule, once acquired even informally by listeners, allows them to understand, make sense of, and develop expectations about what will happen in the course of a composition. In folk music and some other styles, the appearance of a dominant and then a tonic chord gives the listener a strong sense of the "home key" of the piece, and often results in the feeling of closure, finality, and endedness. This rule in folk music is so widespread that, with rare exceptions, every American folksong has at its end a dominant and a tonic chord.

This rule, however, is not adhered to in all styles. In jazz, for instance, dominant chords are followed by nontonic chords. A listener in this style has a different set of expectations about the types of chord sequences he will hear; his understanding of the compositions in this style is based on different rules or principles.

There are countless principles that could be enumerated for any given style. Some principles overlap across closely related styles (say, across folk and rock, or across early and late nineteenth-century "classical" music). No principles are universal across all the music of the world. But listeners who understand and enjoy a particular style of music operate with a set of principles in mind.

Two points about style principles are important. The first is that a musical style and its body of rules are always specific to a particular culture or community. This community consists of the people who compose, perform, and/or listen to the music of that style. Thus style principles are shared knowledge among a group. Both composers and listeners—while their activities may be different—have in common a set of musical-cognitive principles.

Second, the principles may be implicit and informal. The competent listener does not need conscious awareness or formal knowledge about dominant and tonic chords in order to understand or experience the feeling of finality that they engender. He has only to have acquired sufficient experience with multiple instances of the style (compositions) so that the piece of music "sounds ended" when its end is reached. Every adult listener in America knows the difference between the end of a song and its middle (even with the words removed). Only a relative handful know the names and definitions of various chords.

Thus far I have touched tangentially on pivotal issues for education. On the question of what is acquired by competent members of a musical community, I have stated that style principles or rules are acquired whether the behavior in question is composing, performing, or listening. I have alluded to the fact that style principles are acquired by some form of education or experience, although the implicit, informal nature of many such rules makes the nature of education about them a tricky matter. Finally, I have stated that different rules obtain in different styles, which vary by culture or community. This makes the choice of which styles to use for the purposes of schooling an especially troublesome matter. I take up these issues in detail later, but for now it is important to bear in mind the implications of this definition of musical knowledge.

Note that a definition of musical knowledge in terms of implicit stylistic rules is an assertion that such rules are *cognitive:* They describe the cognitive operations that govern composing, performing, and listening, when people engage in those activities. This is a different way of defining the beast called music. It sidesteps a description of the musical stimulus in terms of its elements—pitch, melody, rhythm, and so forth—and instead locates the source of musical understanding in the cognitive life of people who engage in it.

The difficulty with an approach based on style principles is that it is unwieldy. There are countless style principles, many of them unknown or unstated at this time. Were all of them to become known, they would be obsolete in a matter of time, since styles—and thus principles—are always changing. To use the metaphor of language again, a permanent dictionary or grammar book of music is impossible.

Because of this difficulty, I have developed a description of generic cognitive processes that cut across many styles. My description may be conceived as an alternative way of slicing the pie. It rests neither on the elements of the stimulus itself nor on the particulars of any one style: Rather, it rests on a group of processes that appear to be in evidence in many types of music. I give an overview of the processes here, although a detailed description appears in Serafine (1983). An investigation of the development of these processes in children has been under way at Yale, and remains unpublished at this time. Nevertheless, I refer to some preliminary results. (See Serafine, in press.)

IV. SOME PROCESSES OF MUSICAL COGNITION

There are two types of processes in music: temporal processes, which pertain to the immediate experience of succession and simultaneity, and formal, abstract processes which affect the structure and organization of musical experience. A list follows:

A. Temporal processes
   1. Succession
   2. Simultaneity
B. Abstract processes
   1. Abstraction
   2. Transformation
   3. Hierarchical structuring
   4. Closure

A. Temporal Processes

The temporal aspect of music is its fundamental defining feature. It is not a spatial or visual thing, but rather exists in time. Thus one of the fundamental cognitive abilities that children must acquire is to conceive sound along two dimensions, the successive and the simultaneous.

In the successive dimension, the ability required is to group several tones into a unit or motive. Larger units can then be constructed: Motives may be chained one after another in melodies, melodies succeed each other in phrases, and so on. The important point here is that elements (tones, durations, melodies) group themselves successively through time and form a whole. The acquisition of an understanding of the successive dimension in music is responsible for a person's ability to recognize and appreciate what may be considered a musical *theme,* what may be considered a *pattern* (e.g., alternation, repetition), and what may be considered a *phrase*.

In the simultaneous dimension, music involves the co-occurrence of separate elements that form an integrated unit. For example, timbres (of different instruments) blend to create new sounds. Simultaneous melodies interact to create counterpoint (e.g., fugue). In all forms of music except those in which only one tone at a time is heard (e.g., solo singing) the ability to perceive separate sounds heard simultaneously is required.

The temporal processes that I describe—the understanding of succession and simultaneity in music—are not to be taken for granted. They seem obvious enough, but our research thus far indicates that children below the age of 8 years do not show evidence of the perceptual and memory ability that is required to understand music along these dimensions. We have assessed their capacities with a variety of tasks calling for succession and simultaneity in timbre, melody, and rhythm. The temporal dimension appears to develop earliest (by 8 years) for global qualities such as timbre, and later for other elements.

B. Abstract Processes

There are a number of processes beyond the temporal dimensions that appear to be required in many if not all musics, irrespective of style. These are more formal, abstract processes that go beyond the immediate, one-note-after-another dimension of music. My list of such processes is doubtless not exhaustive, but at least the following four processes appear to occur in (and be required to understand) both Western and non-Western music. In our research thus far, the several tasks designed to measure such processes were almost universally passed by adults, even by those without training. However, children did not show evidence of these more abstract processes until age 10 or 12 years.

Abstraction refers to the process by which some aspect of a musical event is removed from its original context, retained, and then applied elsewhere in the course of a composition. For example, in Western music all or part of the tonal pattern of a melody may appear again in another melody, perhaps in the context of a different rhythm. In order for both the earlier and later melodies to be understood as related to each other, the property that they have in common must be abstracted and recognized in both contexts.

Another process is *transformation*. In the course of a composition, relationships among musical events evolve not only from events that share some abstracted (and identical) property, but also from events that are related by one or more transforming operations. The catalog of possible transforming operations is vast, including relative repetition (transformations of mode or key, which are minimal changes), addition (such as embellishment or extension), and substantive transformations (such as inversion, elision, retrograde, and others). The process of transformation calls for understanding the relationship that exists between two parts of a composition where one is derived by a transformation on the other.

A third process is *hierarchic structuring*. A formalization of hierarchic structures in Western tonal music has been put forth by Schenker (1935/ 1979), among others, and there is some evidence for hierarchy in other musics as well. The notion can best be described by example. A melody is organized structurally according to which of its several tones are more or less important in conveying its shape and harmonic functions. In a melody of, say, 10 tones, a few will act as central, pivotal tones for the whole. Often these are the first or fifth tones of the scale from which the melody is drawn, and often such tones are of the longest duration. Several of the other tones will be at a secondary level of importance in indicating shape and harmonic function. Finally, a few tones will be of little importance in the overall shape and function of the melody. Generally such tones act as embellishments to the pivotal tones at the first or second level of importance.

This simple example is meant to convey the notion that competent listeners do not treat the thousands of tones in a composition with equal regard. Rather, some tones are singled out as central, pivotal events in giving the piece its overall shape and effect. The process is hierarchic in that our understanding of complex pieces of music can be described by imagining several successive levels of importance. My own research on this process thus far (unpublished) indicates that even untrained listeners organize melodies in such a way.

The fourth and last process I propose is *closure versus movement*. Every style embodies melodic, harmonic, or rhythmic cues that generate closure, rest, or stasis as well as movement and instability during the course of a composition. The dominant and tonic chord example I gave earlier is from our own music: Tonic chords generate finality or closure; dominant chords signify instability or incompleteness and indicate that something more is yet to come. But regardless of the particular cues for generating closure or instability, one of the cognitive abilities required for understanding music is the awareness that closure and instability obtain in musical compositions.

V. KNOWLEDGE ACQUISITION IN MUSIC

I have described what is acquired in music: a large body of (often implicit) style principles for understanding music, organized by a smaller, overarching set of more general cognitive processes—temporality, abstraction, transformation, and so forth. Note that what is acquired is not a body of music per se, not a group of compositions or a fixed body of songs. We cannot describe musical acquisition in terms of a fixed body of compositions, for this could not account for the fact that educated members of a musical community are able to compose, perform, and/or listen to new pieces of music throughout their lives. Nor can musical acquisition be described in terms of the elements of music—melody, rhythm, etc. Such elements are only a formal description of the musical stimulus itself; they say nothing whatever about the knowledge processes that underlie musical behavior.

The difficult problem remains of how musical knowledge—style principles and more general, overarching cognitive processes—is actually acquired. Since the list of all possible style principles is impossible to enumerate, it is unlikely that they can be tutored in any direct and formal way. It is not even certain that such a direct approach would be desirable. Formal knowledge about style principles (the names and rules for chords, the rules of counterpoint, etc.) is neither necessary nor sufficient for acquiring the implicit musical understandings that all listeners appear to have. Once the implicit understandings have been acquired, formal knowledge about music—the stuff of music theory—is useful and desirable for that portion of the population who may benefit by it, musicians and interested laymen. But for the purposes of forging the general school curriculum, the task at hand is to characterize the acquisition of implicit knowledge of musical style.

I maintain that three factors are responsible for this acquisition: (1) oral transmission, (2) constructive activity, and (3) more general development of the cognitive system.

Knowledge about musical style is acquired principally through oral transmission, or what may be thought of more generally as social interaction. I say this not only because most style principles are unformalized, but also because they are uncaptured by written notation. All of what can be written down about a musical composition—the pitches, durations, meter, and so forth—is but a small capsule of information about how such a piece was intended to be played. Thus most information about style is transmitted from person to person—from teacher to student or from player to player—largely through the playing of music. Teachers demonstrate the style they have come to know as adults to their students. Players demonstrate their ideas about (within) the style to each other. Throughout history and across cultures, the young members or novices of a group acquire information about style from their elders—and the elders acquire it from each other—by playing, singing, and demonstrating the style to each other.

Consider how a teacher might teach a song to children. She teaches them not only the notes and the words, but much more than that, either explicitly or by example: how to soften the ends of phrases; how to slow down at the end; how to hold the last tone longer than the others so that it sounds finished; how to enunciate words, especially in fast passages; how to get faster and slower as well as louder and softer while balancing tempo and dynamics across the whole. Such qualities make the difference between a song worth listening to and one that is not. They can never be learned from a songbook, but must be acquired by person-to-person interaction and demonstration.

Let me anticipate later conclusions about the implications of this oral-transmission theory for education: The stuff of musical knowledge cannot be acquired from textbooks, teaching machines, programmed packages, or computers. Such aids may foster formal, explicit knowledge about music and its elements, but the implicit style principles that govern musical understanding within a culture or community are transmitted socially, from person to person, by demonstration and example.

A second factor in musical acquisition is constructive activity on the part of the learner: the *doing* of music, chiefly composing, performing, and listening. I single out composing as the exemplar of constructive activity and claim that musical composition should occupy the central role in music curricula. I take up this issue later, but for now I emphasize the importance of active, constructive activity in all three areas of musical behavior.

Constructive activity on the part of students can take many forms. Composing a simple song or composition is one, as is generating one's own interpretation of a piece that is already written. Yet another is critical listening as required when, for example, a student might compare two performances of the same piece.

Not all engagements in music are active or constructive. Listening to music, when it is done inattentively or solely for the purpose of passing a music recognition test, is a passive activity. Playing an instrument primarily to reproduce the written notes and without attention to stylistic graces is seldom a constructive activity. Individual composing is not an active process when it is done according to a formula or with musical material highly defined in advance.

A third factor responsible for music acquisition is more general development of the cognitive system. While the particulars of musical style understanding are acquired by experience—through oral transmission and constructive activity—the more generic cognitive processes in music (temporality, abstraction, transformation, etc.) are achieved in large part through normal maturation and development.

These more general processes (temporality, etc.) are not unique to music. They are related to the child's general conception of temporality, development of abstract intellectual skills, and acquisition of knowledge in other formal domains such as mathematics and language.

The developmental literature that I cited earlier, as well as my own recent work, gives evidence that children's acquisition of musical understanding shows a developmental, stagelike trend that parallels trends in other domains (e.g., those studied by Piaget). Cognitive development is in part content specific and in part all of a piece. Music exemplifies this in that it depends both on music-specific acquisitions (especially style acquisition) and on more general cognitive development.

VI. IMPLICATIONS

The design of the school music curriculum is hampererd by severe constraints imposed on no other formal discipline. In the elementary curriculum, music is typically taught for less than one hour per week. In the junior and senior high school it is confined to elective status and to a handful of after-school activities such as chorus, orchestra, and band. Imagine the education that might be had in some other formal discipline, such as mathematics, if instruction were restricted in such a way. We might expect to reap the benefits of a few rudimentary experiences with the subject, but vast segments of the population would remain untutored in the deeper aspects of the discipline.

Such is the case with music. For this reason the principal forces affecting music acquisition—that is, the understanding of musical style—lie outside the domain of schooling. The musical style best understood by American youth is very often contemporary rock, less often jazz, and somewhat less often the "classical" style of eighteenth- and nineteenth-century Europe. The acquisition of such style understanding occurs, as I described, through oral transmission and constructive activity: Young people buy and share records, talk about them, compare different artists, and stay in touch with the latest developments in the style. Those especially committed form rock groups, invent their own songs, rehearse, and hold up their work to the reaction of their contemporaries who are only too eager to make comparisons, form opinions, and adjust their buying and listening behaviors accordingly.

A legitimate and active musical community exists among American youth. The energy (not to mention money) that is spent on incessant, usually informed and critical listening as well as on composing and performing in the rock tradition is impossible to exaggerate. These behaviors parallel those of the adult community: Adults favor one or more musical styles, and they listen, compose, and perform in that style.

Among very young children the unschooled acquisition of music is less noticeable, but nevertheless apparent. Most young children learn simple songs as well as singing and clapping games from their mothers and from each other. They repeat these, teach them to younger children, and over the years develop a repertory of songs.

The point here is that much of music education currently takes place outside of the school. The school curriculum, were it to become more effective in transmitting the musical knowledge of our culture should seek to replicate those forces that are already in effect in the family, the peer group, and the media. Record stores, radio stations, and the people with whom one comes into contact remain the most effective educators of musical knowledge. The school can complement these forces by adding what the school does best—formal tuition—to the cultural influences already in operation.

It was Dewey's *Democracy and Education* (1916) that first proposed this idea: that the route of *formal* education should be guided by what occurs naturally in *informal* education. By this account, the family, the peer group, and the media are not negative or undesirable forces in music education, to be treated as though they were influences to be counteracted or overcome. Rather, they are the very forces that most effectively transmit musical knowledge in all cultures, whatever the state of that musical knowledge may be. This is not to propose a "selling" or "marketing" model for school music programs. On the contrary, our goal should be to glean general principles about the acquisition of music as it occurs informally, and then to attempt to implement those principles within the constraints of the formal school curriculum. In the next section I discuss the implementation of the following general principles: (1) curriculum content based on musical style principles and generic musical-cognitive processes, (2) instructional methods based on oral transmission and constructive activity, and (3) a sequence of content and instruction that conforms to the natural developmental pattern that children undergo. Throughout, I discuss these principles with reference to the three general skill areas that the school should foster: informed *listening* and reflection upon music, *performing* music with the voice or instruments, and *composing,* or the creation of new music.

A. The Content of the Music Curriculum

We may begin by distinguishing two forms of content in the school music curriculum: its *primary content,* by which I mean the information possessed by one who can be said to "really know" music, and its *secondary content,* which may be desirable and useful as an adjunct to primary content, but is neither necessary nor sufficient for it. The primary content of music I take to be the musical style principles and the generic, musical-cognitive processes I identified earlier. The secondary content of music includes (1) symbol systems that merely describe music, such as musical notation; (2) information *about* rather than *in* music, such as the names of scales and chords and facts about music history and famous composers; and (3) the ability to reproduce in performance a fixed repertory of compositions. In the vast majority of school music programs the emphasis has been only on secondary content, and to a large extent primary content has been left to the tutelage of nonschool forces. Let us look closely at the implications of relocating music's primary content to the curriculum of the school.

What children should be taught in school are those activities of mind that characterize a connoisseur of music. Note that I am not advocating that children have thrust upon them the (inappropriate) requirement of adultlike habits in listening, composing, or performing. I am characterizing the "what" rather than the "how" aspect of curriculum, and for that characterization it is important to specify what the idealized end state of musical knowledge is like, toward which education should aim. This end state is characterized by understanding the specific principles on which various musical styles are based and possessing the generic musical-cognitive processes that I described earlier. For example, the ideal student should be able to experience and understand the processes of closure, transformation, abstraction, and hierarchic structuring as they occur in compositions across different styles. Ideally the student should be able to make use of such processes not only in listening but also in his own performing and composing.

Let us consider in depth what the understanding of one of these processes would entail. Closure is a process that occurs in all musical styles. It refers to the fact that, at various points throughout a composition, the several parameters of melody, harmony, rhythm, etc., interact to produce an experience of rest or stasis. The "finished" quality that allows us to know when a composition has ended is a most obvious example, but closure occurs throughout a composition, most notably at the ends of phrases. A person who "knows" closure as it occurs in traditional Western music, for example, would experience rest or stasis when the final tone of a melody settles on the first or third tone of the scale from which the piece is drawn, when the underlying harmony forms a dominant to tonic progression, or when the rhythmic movement stops on a strong beat. What are some things that the ideal student should be able to do if he has acquired an understanding of closure? He should be able to tell when a phrase has ended or is still in progress. He should be able to tell the number of phrases that constitute a simple composition and which ones are "open" or "closed." Our student should be able to describe how the parameters of melody, harmony, etc., create closure in a particular instance (for example, saying that the melody descends to tonic). In performing, the student should show a sensitivity to closure by slowing the tempo slightly at closure points, or perhaps by stressing the final and penultimate tones of a melody. In composing, the ideal student should intentionally design his points of closure and perhaps experiment with alternatives: Is a simple "fade-out" in sound a suitable ending for a piece? What happens when harmony and rhythm are closed, but melody competes with them and sounds "open"?

There are countless ways in which closure is evidenced in musical compositions, and they vary across simple songs, instrumental pieces, folk music, jazz, rock, and the "classical" styles. An inventory of the types of closure that can be explored from kindergarten through high school is beyond our purpose here, but suffice it to say that the acquisition of an understanding of closure, as well as of transformation, abstraction, and the other processes described earlier, is the primary content of the music curriculum.

Consider how this view of content contrasts with other notions about the music curriculum. It contrasts sharply, for example, with those curriculum models aimed primarily at teaching musical notation as if it were music itself. In such programs children might learn modified forms of notation in the early years and gradually progress to "real" notation later on. They might practice drawing clef signs and key signatures, learn mnemonic devices for the names of lines and spaces, and learn to sing melodies using the names of notes (A,B,C or do, re, mi, etc.) instead of words. The acquisition of musical notation is difficult and time consuming. It can occupy years of the music curriculum with only incidental gain in the acquisition of musical-cognitive processes such as the ones I have described. A further drawback is that it emphasizes traditionally notated musics and slights those styles, such as jazz and non-Western musics, for which notation is unavailable or captures only a small part of the style in question.

My proposal for the primary content of the curriculum also contrasts with those programs that emphasize factual knowledge *about* rather than *in* music. By knowledge about music I mean such things as the names of chords, scales, forms, and other concepts from music theory, as well as facts from the history of music such as the titles and composers of famous pieces, biographical details about composers' lives, and the social circumstances affecting music in one historical epoch or another. Such content is less often found in school music programs that emphasize instrumental performance (which I take up later), but it is certainly the rule in those cases where the performance model has been replaced by the model of college-level "appreciation" courses. There is nothing inherently wrong, of course, with teaching students the facts about music that educated persons might be expected to know in our culture, just as there is nothing wrong with knowing musical notation. But to the degree that such content replaces the primary content of music, it endangers students' acquisition of the cognitive processes necessary for understanding the art form.

Yet a third curriculum model with which my proposal contrasts is the performance model of music education. This model is by far the most common in American schools, and its central aim is instruction that leads to the accurate performance, with voice or instruments, of already composed music. In this model children in the early elementary grades learn to sing a large body of songs; in the later elementary years they begin lessons on traditional band and orchestral instruments and may continue singing in larger groups such as choruses. By the secondary school years the curriculum is almost exclusively devoted to large performance ensembles such as chorus, orchestra, and band. Throughout the 10 or 12 years that it takes to develop the hundreds of thousands of high school bands and choruses in America, the goals of this curriculum remain essentially the same: to develop the note-reading skills and muscular coordination that it takes to reproduce pieces of music *already conceived* by professional musicians. There are two senses in which adult, professional musicians have predetermined the music that students emit: Composers have designed and notated the pieces, and teachers or conductors have made performance decisions regarding tempo, dynamics, phrasing, and so on. In such cases it is adults rather than students who are exercising the cognitive processes necessary for making music; students are often engaging only in rote, imitative behavior to perform the music at hand.

My criticism of curricula based on musical notation, facts about music, or instrumental performance is a serious one: that these skills occupy major portions of teaching time at the expense of music's primary content, the cognition entailed in understanding it. It might be objected that many good teachers emphasize musical cognition in their teaching of song singing, music theory, and so on, and that such skills are desirable components of the curriculum. While these objectives have some validity, curricula based principally on secondary content have two drawbacks: they place emphasis on noncognitive acquisitions in the sense I have described them, and they erroneously attempt to teach formal knowledge of notation, music theory, and so on, *before* rather than *after* cognitive understandings have been acquired. To return to the analogy of language, an early focus on notation is like teaching word reading in advance of speech; worse, imitative performance of precomposed music is like the transmittal of a fixed body of sentences.

B. Instructional Methods: Oral Transmission and Constructive Activity

Let us now consider the implications for instruction of a second general principle: that music is transmitted principally through an oral tradition. This is a somewhat difficult notion to grasp, especially so since many other disciplines, such as literature, art, and mathematics, rely on writing, print, or other concrete media to record and transmit achievements in the field. But music is more like dance: The "know-how" that musicians share is still passed from person to person orally and through demonstration. Written notation, in both music and dance, provides only a rough outline about how a piece should be performed. The important information—exactly how a phrase is turned, how parts should be related to each other—is never specified in notation; it is spoken and demonstrated. This point is especially important for all those styles that lie outside the Western classical tradition, which is the only tradition to have attempted systematically to put down its music in writing over the last several hundred years. But the vast majority of world musics are not captured in notation. Even in the West, jazz, rock, and some folk forms remain unnotated except in isolated cases. Even then, the rudiments of pitch and rhythm may be written down, but little or nothing is given about phrasing, vibrato, vocal timbre, dynamics, rhythmic anomalies, and other factors that give such styles their special character. Rather, such factors are part of an oral tradition; they are "recorded" only in memory and are transmitted directly from person to person.

The general implication of this principle of oral transmission is that notation should be de-emphasized as the primary medium with which students interact in the course of making music. Rather, the classroom should become a place where the oral tradition is at work: The teacher performs for students; students perform for the teacher and for each other. The emphasis should be on critical listening, reflection, and discussion of such performances, with musical material stored in memory rather than on paper. For example, suppose a class activity involves composing simple songs. Even young children are capable of this, and with different requirements for length, text, and accompaniment it can be done by students at any age. Each student (or pair or small group) might select a text, generate a song, then perform or even teach it to members of the class. Discussion and subsequent activities should focus on one or more of the generic processes under consideration at the time: closure (How does this song end? How would a different ending affect it?); transformations (Are some motives related to others?); hierarchic structure (What are the underlying primary tones? Could other performers sing only the structure simultaneously with the song itself?). Throughout, discussion should make use of performed demonstrations rather than written notation. A detailing of the specific activities that should compose the kindergarten through 12th-grade curriculum is beyond the scope of this chapter, but the example I have given illustrates the general principle: that the primary medium for instruction should be shared performance, critical listening, and musical interaction with other people, rather than a collective of individuals' interactions with a printed page.

There are other methods of music instruction that similarly de-emphasize notation and stress oral transmission. Principal among these is the so-called Suzuki method of instrumental instruction, which is widely adopted in the United States. In this method, students learn to play pieces on an instrument solely from memory, learning them directly from the teacher. Notation is generally taught only after several years of instruction and not until the student has mastered many pieces. This method exemplifies oral transmission to a laudable degree, but it entails no creative, constructive activity on the part of the student. That is, the student passively learns through rote imitation only pieces that have been previously composed, generally those in the classical tradition. There is no attempt to teach students to generate their own music and to implement the musical-cognitive processes I have described. This brings us to a third and most important principle for instruction: that creative, constructive activity should compose the bulk of what students do in music class. In part the requirement of constructive activity can be met by listening to music (when it is a critical and reflective listening) and by performing it (when the student determines his own interpretation). But the best exemplar of creative activity is composition. *Composition* in the sense in which I use it here is any attempt to generate music anew, whether the music is written down in notation, recorded electronically, or simply stored in one's memory.

Composing for a young child may be simply making up a one-line song or generating a 10-second melody for xylophone. For older students composition may, but does not necessarily, involve notation.

The main reason why instructional methods based on creative composition are not widely used in schools is that they are difficult to implement, especially with standard-sized classrooms of students. What is needed is a curriculum model that emphasizes composing as well as shared performance followed by critical listening and reflection and discussion. At present there is only one model curriculum of which I am aware that exemplifies the principles I have discussed, the Manhattanville Music Curriculum Program (1970). This program is a sequence of individual and group activities for students in kindergarten through 12th grade. It engages students in composing, performing, and listening to music, with a focus on musical concepts somewhat similar to the ones I have described.

An example of an activity for very young children in this program would be the following. Awareness of a basic musical concept, such as *contrast,* is specified as the goal. Children are introduced to and led to discuss the idea of contrast as it occurs in musical settings—loud versus soft, fast versus slow, etc. In pairs or small groups, or perhaps as individuals, students are instructed to create minicompositions, lasting 10 seconds or less, that exemplify a form of contrast. Very young children might be restricted to only one dimension (e.g., loudness), but older children might work with the interaction of loudness and tempo. For example, a young child might create a composition that simply alternates very loud and very soft or perhaps begins very loud and gradually tapers to soft.

The minicompositions that children create are designed for voice (songs) or for whatever instruments are available—"real" instruments, classroom instruments such as bells and cymbals, or homemade instruments from an earlier activity. Each individual, pair, or small group plans and organizes the composition in advance, rehearses it several times, and records a final performance on tape. Perhaps older children will devise a written notation for their composition. The entire class then listens to and discusses each recorded composition, focusing on the nature and use of contrast in each. Finally, the class may listen to and discuss examples of adult compositions (in a variety of styles) that exemplify the same form of contrast—in loudness or tempo, etc.

From this example it can be seen that active, constructive activity is used as the means through which musical concepts are acquired. An experiential base acts as the foundation for the later learning of more formal information about music, such as the conventions of musical notation and the names of particular techniques.

The Manhattanville Curriculum is sequentially organized so that more advanced activities and concepts are learned at each grade level. The central premise at each grade, however, is that constructive activity in group or social settings is the foundation upon which formal information is built. In this curriculum, performing is integrated with creative composition, both of which precede critical listening.

The Manhattanville Curriculum was designed as a classroom-based program. It was not intended for training performance skills on piano, violin, or other orchestral instruments. My opinion is that it remains the best model for classroom-based instruction, but its general principles are not immune to application in settings for individual instruction on conventional instruments. In fact, many instrumental teachers are able to communicate, in individual instruction, more than just the techniques of note reading and holding an instrument: They communicate the principles of style and engender original performance interpretations on the part of their students.

C. Developmental Sequence

A final principle for the design of music curricula is that methods and material should be in harmony with the developmental sequences that children go through. Indeed, it is difficult to imagine how education could proceed in any other way. Yet the difficulty in implementing this general principle is that so little is known about children's musical development, especially by comparison to well-researched domains such as language and mathematics. In the latter areas, for example, we now know a sufficient amount about the linguistic forms and conservation skills in use by young children so that elementary curricula can be structured accordingly. In a similar manner, research on the period of formal operations has influenced secondary school curricula. But no large-scale analogous body of research exists in music. Indeed, the central assumptions of most music programs are those of the strict environmentalist or behaviorist tradition: Whatever is taught is thought to be best done as early as possible.

At the risk of overgeneralizing from too small a data base, I set down here those few principles that might be gleaned from research thus far:

1. Symbolic skills, such as those involved in "real" notation or any written depiction of music, seem best acquired after the period of concrete operations has begun—after the age of 7 or 8 years.

2. Very abstract musical-cognitive processes, such as complex transformations, forms of abstraction, and hierarchic structuring in music, do not seem to be acquired until late childhood—about the age of 10 or 11 years.

3. Surprisingly, skills related to the temporal dimensions of music (succession and simultaneity) do not necessarily precede the above, but seem to be accessible to children at roughly the same age. By the age of 10 or 11 years, most children can be expected to perceive, understand, and remember successive chains of melodic fragments and the kinds of simultaneous combinations described earlier.

4. Similarly, the coordination of two or more musical parameters (melody, harmony, rhythm, etc.) seems to be available to children during the period of concrete operations but not before. For example, musical "conservation" skills such as recognizing the same melody when it occurs with different tempo, timbre, or harmony, seem to be most accessible during this period.

5. Simple discriminations—even fine discriminations of pitch (high–low), dynamics (loud–soft), and duration (long–short), seem to be accessible to children at any age, even before 5 years.

6. The understanding of global, large-scale aspects of musical composition, such as (a) overall style and form and (b) areas of modulation probably is not acquired until after the elementary school years—about age 12 or later.

Note that such principles are indicative only of the specific curriculum content and instructional methods that are appropriate for particular grade levels. For example, very young children cannot be expected to acquire knowledge about large-scale forms and more abstract musical-cognitive operations. This does not imply, however, that the general principles outlined earlier—especially the focus on creative composition—are not applicable to young children. It is a mistake to assume that the requirements of a developmental sequence have been met when children are put through a lockstep sequence of learning pitch discriminations first, then the names of notes, then how to read notation, play an instrument, and so on. Such a sequence is a breakdown of material (and noncognitive materials at that, in the sense I have proposed it) rather than a sequence of how children *acquire* material.

The general principles I have indicated for the design of music curricula imply something of a change in the goals of music programs. One goal, for example, is enabling the student to understand and appreciate new, unfamiliar compositions rather than simply recognizing "famous" pieces. Another general goal is exposing the student to music in many different styles, including popular and non-Western forms, rather than restricting him or her to the standard classical repertory. Yet another, most important goal, is shifting the emphasis to creative composition rather than stressing the reproduction of already composed works.

In summary, I have proposed a description of the content of musical knowledge in terms of the cognitive processes required to understand the musical style(s) shared by a particular culture. Such understanding, I have suggested, is acquired through the activities of social interaction and active engagement with music. My claim is that such content and such activity are the most fruitful agenda for music curricula.

ACKNOWLEDGMENT

The preparation of this paper was supported by a grant from the Spencer Foundation.

REFERENCES

Aliferis, J. (1954). *Aliferis music achievement test.* Minneapolis: University of Minnesota Press. (Earlier verions published 1947, 1949, 1950.)

Bentley, A. (1966). *Measures of musical ability.* New York: October House.

Bentley, A. (1970). A comparison of a musician's assessments with data from the Bentley *Measures of musical ability. Council for Research in Music Education Bulletin, 22,* 17–24.

Bernier, J., & Stafford, R. (1972). The relationship of musical instrument preference to timbre discrimination. *Journal of Research in Music Education, 20,* 283–285.

Berry, W. (1976). *Structural functions in music.* Englewood Cliffs, NJ: Prentice-Hall.

Bingham, W. V. D. (1910). Studies in melody. *Psychological Monographs, 12,* 1–88.

Botvin, G. (1974). Acquiring conservation of melody and cross-modal transfer through successive approximation. *Journal of Research in Music Education, 22,* 226–233.

Chang, H. W., & Trehub, S. (1977). Auditory processing of relational information by young infants. *Journal of Experimental Child Psychology, 24,* 324–331.

Colwell, R. (1969a). *A critique of research studies in music education.* Washington, DC: U.S. Office of Education, Educationl Resources Information Center. (ERIC Document Reproduction Service No. ED 035 100)

Colwell, R. (1969b). *Music achievement tests.* Chicago: Follett Educational.

Colwell, R. (1970). *The evaluation of music teaching and learning.* Englewood Cliffs, NJ: Prentice-Hall.

Cuddy, L. L., Cohen, A. J., & Mewhort, D. J. K. (1981). Perception of structure of short melodic sequences. *Journal of Experimental Psychology: Human Perception and Performance, 7,* 869–882.

Cuddy, L. L., Cohen, A. J., & Miller, J. (1979). Melody recognition: The experimental application of musical rules. *Canadian Journal of Psychology, 33,* 148–157.

Davidson, L., McKernon, P., & Gardner, H. (1981). The acquisition of song. In *Documentary report of the Ann Arbor Symposium* (pp. 301–314). Reston, VA: Music Educators National Conference.

Davies, J. B. (1978). *The psychology of music.* Stanford, CA: Stanford University Press.

Dawkins, A., & Snyder, R. (1972). Disadvantaged junior high school students compared with norms of the Seashore *Measures. Journal of Research in Music Education, 20,* 438–444.

Deutsch, D. (1972). Octave generalization and tune recognition. *Perception and Psychophysics, 11,* 411–412.

Deutsch, D. (Ed.). (1982). *The psychology of music.* New York: Academic Press.

Dewey, J. (1916). Democracy and education. New York: Macmillan.

Dowling, W. J. (1978). Scale and contour: Two components of a theory of memory for melodies. *Psychological Review, 85,* 341–354.

Dowling, W. J. (1982). Melodic information processing and its development. In Deutsch, D. (Ed.), *The psychology of music* (pp. 413–429). New York: Academic Press.

Drake, R. (1957). *Musical aptitude tests.* Chicago: Science Research Associates. (Earlier version published 1934.)

Farnsworth, P. R. (1969). *The social psychology of music* (2nd ed.). Ames: Iowa State University Press.

Foley, E. (1975). Effects of training in conservation of tonal and rhythmic patterns of second-grade children. *Journal of Research in Music Education, 23,* 240–248.

Forte, A. (1973). *The structure of atonal music.* New Haven, CT: Yale University Press.

Froseth, J. O. (1971). Using musical aptitude profile scores in the instruction of beginning students in instrumental music. *Journal of Research in Music Education, 19,* 98–105.

Funk, J. D. (1977). Some aspects of the development of music perception. *Dissertation Abstracts International, 38,* 1919B. (University Microfilms No. 77–20, 301)

Gabrielsson, A. (1981). Music psychology—a survey of problems and current research activities. In *Basic musical functions and musical ability* (pp. 7–80). Stockholm: Royal Swedish Academy of Music.

Gardner, H. (1971). Children's duplicating of rhythmic patterns. *Journal of Research in Music Education, 19,* 355–369.

Gardner, H. (1973). Children's sensitivity to musical styles. *Merrill-Palmer Quarterly, 19,* 67–77.

Gaston, E. T. (1957). *Test of musicality.* Lawrence, KS: Odell's Instrument Co. (Earlier versions published 1942, 1950, 1956)

Gordon, E. (1965). *Musical aptitude profile.* Boston: Houghton Mifflin.

Gordon, E. (1967). A comparison of the performance of culturally disadvantaged students with that of culturally heterogeneous students on the *Musical aptitude profile. Psychology in the Schools, 4,* 260–262.

Gordon, E. (1968). A study of the efficacy of general intelligence and musical aptitude tests in predicting achievement in music. *Council for Research in Music Education Bulletin, 13,* 40–45.

Gordon, E. (1969). Intercorrelations among *Musical aptitude profile* and Seashore *Measures of musical talents* subtests. *Journal of Research in Music Education, 17,* 263–271.

Gordon, E. (1970a). First year results of a five-year longitudinal study of the musical achievement of culturally disadvantaged students. *Journal of Research in Music Education, 28,* 195–213.

Gordon, E. (1970b). Taking into account musical aptitude differences among beginning instrumental students. *American Educational Research Journal, 7,* 41–53.

Helmholtz, H. (1954). *On the sensations of tone.* New York: Dover. (Original work published 1885)

Jeffries, T. B. (1967). The effects of order of presentation and knowledge of results on the aural recognition of melodic intervals. *Journal of Research in Music Education, 15,* 179–190.

Kessen, W., Levine, J., & Wendrich, K. A. (1979). The imitation of pitch in infants. *Infant Behavior and Development, 2,* 93–99.

Krumhansl, C. L. (1979). The psychological representation of musical pitch in a tonal context. *Cognitive Psychology, 11,* 346–374.

Kwalwasser, J. & Dykema, P. (1930). *K-D music tests*. New York: Carl Fischer.

Kyme, G. H. (1967). A study of the development of musicality in the junior high school and the contributions of musical composition to this development. *Council for Research in Music Education Bulletin, 10*, 15–23.

Larsen, R. L. (1973). Levels of conceptual development in melodic permutation concepts based on Piaget's theory. *Journal of Research in Music Education, 21*, 256–263.

Lee, R. E. (1967). An investigation of the use of the *Musical aptitude profile* with college and university freshmen music students. *Journal of Research in Music Education, 15*, 278–288.

Lehman, P. R. (1968). *Tests and measurements in music*. Englewood Cliffs, NJ: Prentice-Hall.

Lundin, R. W. (1967). *An objective psychology of music* (2nd ed.). New York: Wiley.

McAdams, S., & Bregman, A. (1979). Hearing musical streams. *Computer Music Journal, 3*, 26–43.

McLeish, J. (1968). The validity and reliability of Bentley's *Measures of musical abilities*. (1968). *British Journal of Educational Psychology, 38*, 201–202.

Manhattanville music curriculum program. (1970). R. B. Thomas, Director. *MMCP Synthesis: A structure for music education*. New York: Media Materials.

Meyer, L. (1956). *Emotion and meaning in music*. Chicago: University of Chicago Press.

Meyer, M. (1900). Elements of a psychological theory of melody. *Psychological Review, 7*, 241–273.

Michalski, S. F. (1971). Development and evaluation of a visual-aural program in conceptual understanding of the basic elements of music. *Journal of Research in Music Education, 19*, 92–97.

Mursell, J. L. (1937). *The psychology of music*. New York: Norton.

Perney, J. (1976). Musical tasks related to the development of the conservation of metric time. *Journal of Research in Music Education, 24*, 159–168.

Peterson, A. V. (1969). *Melodic listening survey: Exploratory study of listening development in primary and secondary schools*. Washington, DC: U.S. Office of Education. Educational Resources Information Center, 1969. (ERIC Document Reproduction Service No. ED 041 926)

Pflederer, M. (1964). The responses of children to musical tasks embodying Piaget's principle of conservation. *Journal of Research in Music Education, 12*, 251–268.

Pflederer, M., & Sechrest, L. (1968a). Conservation in musical experience. *Psychology in the Schools, 5*, 99–105.

Pflederer, M., & Sechrest, L. (1968b). Conservation-type responses of children to musical stimuli. *Council for Research in Music Education Bulletin, 13*, 19–36.

Revesz, G. (1953). *Introduction to the psychology of music*. London: Longmans Green.

Rosner, B. S., & Meyer, L. (1982). Melodic processes and the perception of music. In Deutsch, D. (Ed.), *The psychology of music* (pp. 317–341). New York: Academic Press.

Rowntree, J. P. (1970). The Bentley *Measures of musical abilities*—A critical evaluation. *Council for Research in Music Education Bulletin, 22*, 24–32.

Schenker, H. (1979). *Free composition* (E. Oster, Trans.). New York: Longman. (Original work published 1935)

Seashore, C. E. (1938). *Psychology of music*. New York: McGraw-Hill.

Seashore, C. E., Lewis, D., & Seatveit, J. (1960). *Measures of musical talents*. New York: Psychological Corp. (Earlier versions published 1919, 1939)

Serafine, M. L. (1979). A measure of meter conservation in music, based on Piaget's theory. *Genetic Psychology Monographs, 99*, 185–229.

Serafine, M. L. (1980). Piagetian research in music. *Council for Research in Music Education Bulletin, 62*, 1–21.

Serafine, M. L. (1983). Cognition in music. *Cognition, 14,* 119–183.

Seraphine, M. L. (in press). *Music as cognition: The development of thought in sound.* New York: Columbia University Press.

Serafine, M. L., Crowder, R. G., & Repp, B. (1984). *Integration of melody and text in memory for songs. Cognition, 16,* 285–303.

Shepard, R. N. (1981). Individual differences in the perception of musical pitch. In *Documentary report of the Ann Arbor Symposium* (pp. 152–174). Reston, VA: Music Educators National Conference.

Shuter, R. (1968). *The psychology of musical ability.* London: Methuen.

Shuter-Dyson, R., & Gabriel, C. (1982). *The psychology of musical ability* (2nd ed.). London: Methuen.

Siegel, J., and Siegel, W. (1977a). Absolute identification of notes and intervals by musicians. *Perception and Psychophysics,* 143–152.

Siegel, J., and Siegel, W. (1977b). Categorical perception of tonal intervals: Musicians can't tell sharp from flat. *Perception and Psychophysics, 21,* 399–407.

Snyder Knuth, A. (1965). *Snyder Knuth music achievement test.* San Francisco: Creative Arts Research Associates.

Tan, N., Aiello, R., & Bever, T. G. (1981). Harmonic structure as a determinant of melodic organization. *Memory and Cognition, 9,* 533–539.

Terhardt, E. (1974). Pitch, consonance, and harmony. *Journal of the Acoustical Society of America, 55,* 1061–1069.

Vaughan, M., & Williams, R. E. (1971). An examination of musical process as related to creative thinking. *Journal of Research in Music Education, 19,* 337–341.

Ward, W. D., & Burns, E. M. (1982). Absolute pitch. In Deutsch, D. (Ed.), *The psychology of music* (pp. 431–451). New York: Academic Press.

Whittington, R. W. T. (1957). The assessment of potential musical ability in secondary school children. *Journal of Educational Psychology, 48,* 1–10.

Whybrew, W. E. (1971). Measurement and evaluation in music. Dubuque, IA: Brown.

Wilcox, R. (1971). Further ado about Negro music ability. *Journal of Negro Education, 40,* 361–364.

Williams, R. O. (1972). Effects of musical aptitude, instruction, and social status on attitudes toward music. *Journal of Research in Music Education, 20,* 362–369.

Wing, H. (1961). *Standardized tests of musical intelligence.* Buckingham, England: National Foundation for Educational Research. (Earlier versions published 1939, 1948, 1957)

Yoder, V. A. (1972). A study of Gaston's *Test of musicality* as applied to college students. *Journal of Research in Music Education, 20,* 491–495.

Young, W. T. (1971). The role of musical aptitude, intelligence, and academic achievement in predicting musical attainment of elementary instrumental music students. *Journal of Research in Music Education, 19,* 385–398.

Young, W. T. (1972a). *Musical aptitude profile* norms for use with college and university nonmusic majors. *Journal of Research in Music Education, 20,* 385–390.

Young, W. T. (1972b). A statistical comparison of two recent musical aptitude tests. *Psychology in the Schools, 9,* 165–169.

Zenatti, A. (1976). Children's esthetic judgment about music consonance, tonality, and isochronism of the rhythmic beat. *Psychologie Française, 21,* 175–184.

Zimmerman, M., & Sechrest, L. (1970). Brief focused instruction and musical concepts. *Journal of Research in Music Education, 18,* 25–36.

10

Reasoning

RAYMOND S. NICKERSON

Bolt Beranek and Newman Inc.
Cambridge, Massachusetts 02238

1. INTRODUCTION

The three Rs—*reading, 'riting,* and *'rithmetic*—have long been recognized to be in some sense basic to all other education. Without a solid foundation in these skills students are bound to be at a serious disadvantage throughout their educational careers and beyond. This is so, of course, because reading, writing, and mathematical skills are so heavily used in other subjects and in life generally in today's world.

If one wanted to add a fourth R to this list of basics, a candidate would certainly be *reasoning.* The ability to reason effectively is no less important to success in school, in the workplace, and in life in general than are reading, writing, and mathematics. In spite of this fact, reasoning is seldom identified as a focus of attention in course curricula.

One must wonder why that is the case. Is it because reasoning is not recognized to be as important as the traditional three Rs? Is it because effective methods for teaching reasoning have not been developed? Is it because reasoning is assumed not to be teachable? Reflection on why reasoning has not been given the same status in educational curricula as have the three Rs leads one to a number of specific questions:

- What is reasoning? What does it mean to be able to reason effectively?
- How effectively do people reason? Why do they not reason more effectively than they do?
- What reasoning skills, or what aspects of reasoning, are amenable to training? Are there any that are not?
- To what extent do typical approaches to education (content and method) facilitate the development of reasoning ability? To what extent do they inhibit it?

343

COGNITION AND INSTRUCTION

• Are there specific teaching methods that are demonstrably effective in enhancing reasoning skills?

• What can the average teacher do in a conventional content course (math, history, language) to promote reasoning and to increase the students' ability to engage in it?

• What can be done to increase the likelihood that reasoning skills that are acquired in the classroom will be applied in everyday life?

• How does the ability to acquire reasoning skills vary with age?

• How important is it to acquire certain reasoning skills at the earliest possible age? How detrimental is it to future cognitive development and intellectual performance not to do so?

The list goes on.

It would be wonderful to be able to write a chapter that answered these questions. This one certainly does not do that. I believe the answers to most of these questions are not yet known, although there are some partial answers and the results of numerous studies that provide clues and guidance for future work. There is, for example, a large literature on reasoning and the closely associated topics of problem solving, decision making, and, more generally, thinking. In particular, there is considerable documentation regarding various ways in which reasoning frequently goes astray (e.g., Johnson-Laird, 1977; Nisbett & Ross, 1980; Slovic, Fischhoff, & Lichtenstein, 1977; Tversky & Kahneman, 1974; Wason, 1977).

Relatively little research has been done on the question of how to teach reasoning. That is not to suggest that reasoning has received no attention in the classroom. There is a long tradition of textbooks and courses in formal logic, typically at the college level. A primary objective of philosophy courses is to motivate students to reason and to give them something to reason about. And one way to view mathematics is as a set of tools for reasoning quantitatively about real or imaginary worlds. But what has been done traditionally by way of developing reasoning ability in the classroom has been done more or less independently of experimental evidence that the traditional approaches work.

There appears to be a growing conviction that traditional approaches to education have been less successful than one would hope in developing students' ability to think (Carpenter, 1980; National Commission on Excellence in Education, 1983; Karplus, 1974; Renner & Lawson, 1973; Tomlinson-Keasey, 1972). Assuming this conviction has some basis in fact, it does not follow that the fault lies with the curriculum. There are plausible reasons other than a faulty curriculum to explain why the system might yield disappointing results in general and fail to develop effective thinking skills in particular—inappropriate teaching methods and failure to test for thinking ability are but two possibilities.

Some researchers and educators apparently believe that curriculum is at least part of the problem, however, because several programs have been developed in recent years to teach cognitive skills, including reasoning skills, and most of them include new curriculum materials. My colleagues and I have reviewed some of these programs elsewhere (Nickerson, 1984; Nickerson, Perkins, & Smith, 1985). The programs that have been developed differ from each other in many ways, including the specific skills they emphasize, the ages of the students for whom they are intended, and the teaching techniques they advocate. Some programs focus on the development of basic cognitive processes (comparing, classifying, inferring) that are assumed to be essential to general intellectual competence; some promote acquisition of skill in the use of certain problem-solving strategies or heuristics; some focus on thinking as subject matter and attempt to help students gain a better understanding of how our minds work and what we can do to make them work more effectively; others have still other foci or emphases. Some evaluative data have been collected on a few of these programs, but much remains to be done in this regard. We must view these efforts as still experimental, but having the potential to yield the kind of data and experience that should facilitate the development of more effective approaches to the enhancement of cognitive skills in the future.

This chapter is motivated by an interest in the question of how to teach reasoning in the classroom and by the belief that the question is an especially timely and important one. It is more in the nature of an essay than a literature review or report of empirical work. Before saying more about its purpose and scope, it is helpful to consider what is meant here by the term *reasoning*.

II. WHAT IS REASONING?

While probably not completely synonymous to most investigators, the terms *thinking, problem solving,* and *reasoning* are closely related, and the sets of activities that they denote overlap with each other considerably. *Thinking* has, perhaps, a somewhat broader connotation than *problem solving* and *reasoning* and encompasses them both. The task domains denoted by *problem solving* and *reasoning,* at least as these terms have been used in the psychological literature, overlap to a very great extent. Most of the tasks that have been studied as problem-solving tasks could just as easily be referred to as reasoning tasks, and conversely. Sternberg (1982) has pointed out the fuzziness of the distinction between reasoning and problem solving this way:

> Certain kinds of problems have been studied under the rubric of "reasoning," others under the rubric of "problem solving," and it seems to be primarily a historical accident whether a given kind has been classified as one, the other, or both. (p. 226)

Perhaps the most noteworthy exception to this generalization is the work that has been done on syllogistic reasoning. Studies of people's ability to distinguish between valid and invalid syllogisms seem to be classified more naturally as studies of reasoning than as studies of problem solving, although even here the distinction is not sharp.

Genus–species definitions typically identify reasoning as a type of thinking in which *inference* plays a central role. English and English (1958), for example, define *reasoning* as

> 1. that form of thinking which finds its completest expression in logical forms (whether the conclusions reached are valid or not). The reasoner is usually aware that a *judgment* (the conclusion) is dependent upon other judgements (the *premises*). 2. problem-solving by means of general principles. (p 443)

The American Psychological Association's *Thesaurus of Psychological Index Terms* (Kinkade, 1974) gives *cognitive processes* and *thinking* as broader concepts under which *reasoning* is subsumed and *inductive* and *deductive reasoning* and *inference* as narrower concepts that are subsumed under it. As related concepts it gives *dialectics* and *problem solving*.

Formal definitions are of limited help in understanding a concept, however, and especially one that is as abstract as this one. Moreover, even cursory perusal of the literature on reasoning reveals that the term is used in a variety of ways. For present purposes, it will be helpful to make two contrasts, one between automatic and deliberate inferencing and another between closed and open-ended problems.

A. Automatic versus Deliberate Inferencing

It is useful to distinguish between inferential processes that are relatively automatic and largely subconscious and those that are involved in deliberate and conscious efforts to "figure things out." The first type of inference is often involved in language understanding. When, for example, one is told that Paul drives to work, one is likely to infer that Paul is the owner of an automobile, as opposed to, say, a bus, a tank, or a moving van. Although language understanding could not occur in the absence of such inferences, we are not very conscious of making them, and it is only in recent years that this type of inferencing has begun to be scrutinized by students of language and linguistic behavior.

The inferencing on which language understanding is so dependent is sometimes referred to as implicit inferencing. We may assume that people differ in their ability to engage in this type of inferencing, and it seems highly likely that such differences are significant determinants of different levels of competence in language usage. There is evidence, for example, that good and poor readers differ in their ability to make implicit inferences (Johnson-Laird, 1985). In particular, good readers are more likely than poor readers to build a representation of the events in a story from which inferences can be made. Moreover, the building of such a representation itself requires the making of implicit inferences from the information that is explicitly contained in the story. Having such a representation, one is in a better position to interpret further information in the story and to integrate it with what one already knows. Johnson-Laird pointed out that if understanding language depends on the ability to make implicit inferences, then an important objective of training is to provide this ability to people who lack it.

The other type of inferencing—deliberate inferencing—is illustrated by the process that a physician uses to diagnose an illness, that a mechanic uses to locate an automotive fault, or that the inimitable Sherlock Holmes engaged in when attempting to piece together the clues to a crime. In this case, the process occurs on a different time scale and is more open to introspection; the reasoner not only is aware of trying to piece a variety of fragments of information together to make sense of them as a whole, but also is able to describe, to some degree, the inferences involved.

The distinction between these two types of inferences should not be drawn too sharply. One can readily think of instances that fall between these extremes, instances in which a person is somewhat aware that inferences are being made but does not have a strong sense of working hard to figure something out. Nevertheless, the distinction is a useful one for present purposes.

Whether the teaching of communication skills such as reading and writing would benefit from greater focus on inferential skills is an important subject for research, but beyond the scope of this chapter. Attention here is focused on the second type of inferencing and on situations involving deliberate and conscious efforts to reason one's way to a certain goal. The goal in such situations may be to judge the plausibility of an assertion, to determine what conclusion should be drawn from the evidence one has on some particular question, to select the most "reasonable" action from among a set of alternatives, or any of a host of other possibilities.

Interest in this type of reasoning dates back many centuries. How it is done and how it might be done better were favorite themes of the Peripatetics during the acme of Greek philosophy. The question of whether the rules of logic as formalized by Aristotle are descriptive of the way people really reason continues to be a controversial one, as does the question of whether the teaching of formal logic in school improves the reasoning ability of students in any practical sense. There seems to be considerable agreement, however, that students sometimes manage to complete many years of formal schooling without acquiring the ability to reason very effectively about complex or perhaps even relatively simple problems.

How could this possibly be the case? Is reasoning impossible to teach, or is the educational system failing in a fundamental way? If the educational system is failing, is it a failure of objectives or a failure of technique? Does the difficulty stem from insufficient commitment to the teaching of reasoning or from the unavailability of effective materials and methods?

B. Closed versus Open-Ended Problems

Research on reasoning has often focused on the process of figuring out the answer to a problem for which all the necessary information is given and the solution can be obtained via a series of inferences. The problems used in this research typically have known, unambiguous answers, and there is little question about whether an answer is correct once it has been found. Examples of problems of this type that one encounters in the literature include the following:

Problem 1. Given that $D = 5$, assign to each of the remaining letters in the following names a number from 0 to 9 such that the addition will be correct:

$$\begin{array}{r} \text{DONALD} \\ + \text{GERALD} \\ \hline \text{ROBERT} \end{array}$$

(from Bartlett, 1958)

Problem 2. A cat, a small dog, a goat, and a horse are named Angel, Beauty, King, and Rover. Read the clues below to find each animal's name.

King is smaller than either the dog or Rover.
The horse is younger than Angel.
Beauty is the oldest and is a good friend of the dog.

(from Midwest Publications, 1981)

Problem 3. You have 12 ball bearings that are visually indistinguishable. Eleven of these ball bearings are equal in weight, and one has a different weight from all the rest. You have a balance scale with which you can tell only whether the material in one container weighs more or less than that in the other. Specify a procedure whereby with three weighings one can identify the ball bearing with the different weight and tell whether it weighs more or less than the others.

(from a "friend")

Each of these problems can be solved with a sequence of deductive inferences. Sometimes it may be necessary to make an inductive leap or to generate a hypothesis for test purposes, but for the most part one can get successively closer to the solution by making explicit the implications of the information in hand. For example, one reasons one's way to a solution of the first problem with a series of inferences of the following sort: inasmuch as D equals 5, T must equal 0; and since there is a carry into the next column, R must be an odd number; further, from the left-most column and the fact that D equals 5, it follows that R must be greater than 5; therefore R must be either 7 or 9; and so on.

This is not to suggest that solving these types of problems is always easy. Such problems can vary in difficulty over a wide range; indeed they can be made as easy or as difficult as one might wish. Problem 2 is considered an easy problem, and most readers will probably find it to be so. It is included here to illustrate the point that even with simple reasoning problems that are solvable by a straightforward sequence of inferences, the role of knowledge of the world and assumptions beyond the information explicitly given in the problem statement may be greater than it appears. Consider the following sequence of inferences involved in solving this problem:

a. Cat is King: because King is smaller than a small dog, and the only thing smaller than a small dog among the alternatives is a cat.

b. Dog is not King: follows from a.

c. Dog is not Rover: inferred from the phrase "either dog or Rover."

d. Dog is not Beauty: inferred from the information that Beauty is a friend of the dog.

e. Dog is Angel: follows from b, c, and d by elimination.

f. Horse is not Beauty: inferred from the information that Beauty is oldest and Horse is younger than Angel, therefore not oldest, therefore not Beauty.

g. Horse is Rover: follows from a, e, and f by elimination.

h. Goat is Beauty: follows from a, e, and g by eliminaton.

While the solution sequence is quite simple, it involves some knowledge and several assumptions. In particular, one must know that among a collection composed of a cat, a goat and a horse, the only thing that could be smaller than a small dog is a cat. Eliminating Rover as the name of the dog requires the assumption that the writer of the problem would not use the expression "either the dog or Rover" if the dog and Rover were the same animal; that is, the reader must give "or" its exclusive meaning. Eliminating Beauty as the name of the dog involves the assumption that one would not be designated as one's own friend. The fact that we make such assumptions spontaneously and are, for the most part, unaware of making them in no way diminishes their importance; and if we were to attempt to program a computer to solve such problems, we would have to be quite explicit about them. Moreover, that assumptions, albeit perhaps unconscious ones, really are involved is illustrated by the fact that in different contexts different interpretations might well be put on the same words. Thus, for example, one would not interpret ''If he lives on Elm Street, he must know either Jim or Jane'' as ruling out the possibility that he knows both.

Problem 3 is included for the reader's enjoyment. It too can be solved unequivocally by a straightforward, but nontrivial reasoning process. The reader who finds this problem difficult may find it helpful to warm up to the task on the following much simpler problem with some similar aspects.

> You have nine ball bearings that are visually indistinguishable. Eight of these ball bearings are equal in weight, and one weighs *less* than each of the others. You have a balance scale with which you can tell whether the material in one container weighs more or less than that in the other. Specify a procedure whereby one can identify the lighter ball bearing with two weighings.

The main purpose of using these examples of reasoning problems is to make the point that the approach that one must take in solving such problems is often clear, and typically when a solution is obtained there is no question as to whether it is in fact *the* solution. Many of the reasoning problems that one faces in everyday life tend to differ in both of these respects. How best to go about trying to solve them often is not clear, and when one believes that one has obtained a solution, one may be less than completely confident that that solution is in fact the correct one; indeed there may be no single correct solution, and the best one can hope to do is to judge to one's own satisfaction whether the solution one has obtained is acceptable. Examples of such reasoning problems are:

• Diagnosing an interpersonal problem in a work, social, or family context, and trying to figure out how to resolve it.
• Weighing arguments, as when trying to decide how to vote on a referendum issue or as a member of a jury.
• Judging the plausibility of claims one reads in newspapers and magazines or hears on radio or TV.

In what follows we shall focus primarily on such ''open-ended'' problems, not because we know well how to deal with them, but because they are so widespread and important in everyday life. Prototypical of these types of problems is figuring out what to believe. Consideration of that problem leads us directly to the task of evaluating informal arguments, inasmuch as such arguments play a central role in establishing and molding beliefs.

III. FIGURING OUT WHAT TO BELIEVE

One of the most fundamental questions relating to reasoning is how people come to believe what they do. A closely related question of considerable practical educational significance is how to increase the willingness and ability of people to base their beliefs on evidence rather than to seek and mold evidence to support their beliefs.

Figuring out what to believe is not the same as figuring out how to defend an existing belief. The former requires reasoning or weighing evidence; the latter involves rationalizing or case building. When one builds a case, one attempts to amass as much evidence as possible in favor of some particular position. Trial lawyers are expected to build cases. A lawyer for the defense is expected to amass as much evidence as possible to establish the innocence of his client; a lawyer for the prosecution is expected to gather and present evidence that will establish the defendant's guilt. The weighing of evidence in this instance is left to the judge or jury. The system is predicated on the assumption that if both parties to a dispute are represented by competent lawyers, each motivated to present those facts that are most favorable to his client's interests, and the evidence that is presented is weighed by an impartial third party, the truth will be revealed.

Often one's task in a reasoning situation is to play all three roles: prosecutor, defense, and judge or jury, as it were. One must gather what evidence one can relative to an issue, independently of which side of the issue the evidence supports, and then weigh all the evidence as impartially as possible in attempting to come to a decision regarding what to believe. This appears not to be something we do naturally and easily. In particular, distinguishing between reasons for one's own beliefs and rationalizations of those beliefs may be exceedingly difficult.

This raises a methodological problem. In trying to discover the reasons for a particular belief held by a specific individual, one may, in fact, discover rationalizations but not recognize them as such. One cannot assume that when a person gives reasons for a belief, as honestly as he can, what he gives are indeed the reasons why he originally arrived at that belief. There is little evidence that our ability to distinguish between what we now consider to be justification for specified beliefs and what caused us to adopt those beliefs in the first place is very good.

Soelberg (1967) has presented some evidence that discovering the reasons for a decision in retrospect can be a very difficult thing to do. When asked why one did X, one is very likely to be able to produce a plausible explanation. It is well nigh impossible to tell, however, whether the "reasons" one identifies in retrospect were in fact operative at the time the decision was made. The desire to appear to be rational, both to others and to ourselves, is undoubtedly a strong one in most of us; we are disinclined to admit that decisions we have made did not have a very rational basis. This is not to suggest intentional dishonesty or deceptiveness. The possibility that we deceive ourselves first and most completely and that we honestly mistake rationalizations for reasons is a highly plausible one.

The generic problem of overriding importance that people have is assuring that some significant fraction of their beliefs that matter corresponds, at least roughly, to the truth. By "beliefs that matter" I mean beliefs that, if untrue, can have harmful consequences. Not all false beliefs are equally consequential, of course. If I come to believe, even for a short time, that I could fly by flapping my arms, the consequences for me personally could be serious indeed. On the other hand, if I believe that stepping on sidewalk cracks must be avoided if I wish to minimize bad luck, the most serious consequence will probably be a somewhat irregular gait when I walk on cement sidewalks.

The evidence is rather compelling that many people hold false beliefs about the behavior of the physical world. Perhaps the best recently documented illustrations of this fact relate to the physics of motion (Caramazza, McCloskey, & Green, 1981; Clement, 1982; McCloskey, 1983). It is not unusual for people to believe, for example, that if a ball on the end of a string is swung in a circle around one's head and the string breaks, the ball will continue in a circular path for some time following the instant of the break. Another common belief is that if one releases a ball from one's hand while walking, the trajectory of the ball's fall to the ground will be a straight line.

One suspects that as research in this vein continues, examples of ways in which commonly held beliefs about the world fail to correspond to reality will multiply. One suspects too, however, that most of these false beliefs will prove to be relatively inconsequential to our ability to cope effectively with the demands of everyday life. The "naive" or "fuzzy" theories of physics that most of us carry in our heads are undoubtedly ill conceived and, in many respects, patently wrong from the point of view of the physicist. For the most part they are not *so* wrong as to put us at great risk in the day-to-day world. (Few of us believe that if one releases a ball while walking it will fly off into space or remain suspended in midair;

most of us believe it will fall relatively quickly to the ground and stay there.) In other words, for the most part, our models of physical reality are, in spite of their deficiencies, sufficiently accurate to permit us to make the kinds of decisions that survival in our day-to-day world requires.

Many of the beliefs that we hold about the world are not the results of conscious efforts to "figure things out." Their development has involved the kind of automatic inferencing that is so critical to language understanding. They have grown out of our direct observations of the world, and, in many cases, we are not even aware of holding them until we are forced to make them explicit in order to answer, say, an experimenter's questions.

In contrast, some of our beliefs are based less on our direct observations of the world than on what we are told by others, either directly or via media such as radio, television, or the printed page. Much of what we are told by others is conveyed by one or another type of *argument*. An argument, as the word is used here, is a set of assertions that is made for the purpose of convincing someone to believe or do something by giving reasons as to why one should. Typically the arguments that we encounter in everyday life are informal arguments; they are not presented as syllogisms or in any other canonical form. Evaluating such arguments often involves deliberate inferencing on open-ended problems. The inferencing is deliberate in that we may have to struggle to try to figure out what to make of the claims that comprise the substance of the argument, and the situation is open-ended in that the truth of these claims, and that of the belief the argument is intended to support, may in many cases be impossible to determine with certainty. Moreover, there can be little doubt that at least some of the beliefs addressed by the arguments we encounter are among those that really matter, because they play significant roles in shaping our behavior toward other individuals, our attitudes toward groups, and our general outlook on life.

IV. EVALUATING INFORMAL ARGUMENTS

The ability to evaluate informal arguments rationally and reasonably must be as important as most other abilities we possess. Improving the ability of students to reason in this way would be a worthy goal of education if only we knew how to achieve it. Unfortunately, not only do we not know how to teach informal reasoning effectively, but there is no generally accepted set of rules by which we can assess the soundness of informal reasoning; indeed, there is not unanimous agreement among investigators of reasoning whether universally acceptable standards of rationality could be developed (Cohen, 1981; Einhorn & Hogarth, 1981; Kyburg, 1983).

In spite of the somewhat discouraging prospects of getting universal agreement soon on what constitutes rationality, there is, I believe a great need to give more attention to the question of how to teach reasoning explicitly in the classroom, and the problem of evaluating informal arguments is central to that question. Presumably, agreement on theoretical issues relating to rationality is not a prerequisite to the improvement of the ability of students to reason effectively about the claims they encounter from all sides in everyday life. In what follows, I try to be more specific about what I mean by *informal argument,* to identify some factors that serve as impediments to our evaluating informal arguments well, and to suggest some principles or strategies, which, if taught, might help us do it better.

An argument is an effort to persuade. An informal argument, or what I have referred to elsewhere (Nickerson, 1986) as a plausible argument, is an effort to persuade that is not constrained by the rules of a formal logic. Structurally, it is helpful to think of an informal argument as being composed of a key assertion and one or more supporting assertions. The key assertion is that which the argument is intended to persuade one to believe; the role of the supporting assertions is to make the key assertion plausible. The key assertion and supporting assertions of an informal argument are analogous to the conclusion and premises respectively of a formal syllogistic argument. I have chosen not to use the terms *conclusion* and *premises* in this context, however, to avoid the suggestion of logical implication. In an informal argument, the key assertion does not "follow from" the supporting assertions in a logical sense, as the conclusion folows from the premises in a valid syllogism. In an informal argument, as the term is used here, the key assertion is (presumably) made more plausible by the supporting assertions, but its certainty is not assured even on the assumption that the supporting assertions are true.

Informal arguments, like formal arguments, can be more or less complete, and more or less complex. Typically they are not complete, however, and in fact usually it is not clear what would constitute completeness or even that the idea of completeness is meaningful. Informal arguments can vary in complexity over an enormous range, from a few simple assertions to the tortuous multivolume briefs that are sometimes prepared for the purpose of establishing the innocence or guilt of a party in a legal proceeding. Here we will be concerned with the kinds of arguments that we are likely to encounter in our daily lives, which are perhaps best illustrated by example.

The following examples are taken from the October 26, 1982, issue of the *Boston Globe* ("Should the," 1982.) The question being addressed is whether or not the death penalty should be allowed in Massachusetts. The question was scheduled to appear as a referendum issue on the ballot in an upcoming election. The following arguments (the length of which had been limited to 150 words) were prepared by proponents of "Yes" and "No" votes respectively.

Argument for:

It is vitally important that we maintain public confidence in the effectiveness of our criminal justice system. People must believe that the system works for them and for the victim . . . and not just for the murderer.

The death penalty is a necessary tool to protect society from cold-blooded murder.

Capital punishment is an effective deterrent. It will save lives. It will prevent convicted murderers from killing again.

Imposed carefully, it is a defense of community values and human life. The value of human life is best protected by clear punishment for those who would destroy it.

Capital punishment is also a matter of justice. Opponents too readily focus on justice only for the murderer and not on justice for the victim.

Our state has the responsibility to protect life and express justifiable moral outrage at particularly atrocious crimes.

Thirty-seven states have laws providing for capital punishment.

Argument against:

There is no blank slate here. Massachusetts had three centuries of tragic experience with the death penalty before its discontinuance in 1947. Hundreds were executed, invariably the poor, the immigrant and the oppressed. History records notorious executions of innocent people.

The death penalty does not deter crime. Countless studies prove this. In fact, executions may cause the murder rate to rise.

Our system does make mistakes, it is not immune from discrimination, it necessarily relies on human testimony and human judgment. When a prisoner is sentenced to life without parole—the penalty for first-degree murder in Massachusetts—an error can be corrected. But one cannot raise the dead.

Restoration of the death penalty will not protect us. It will produce injustice, sow bitterness and division, and divert us from real solutions. It will cheapen the value we place on life itself. It will reverse a half century of progress.

All of us encounter informal arguments from many sources daily: the television, radio, newspapers, magazines, books, employers, friends, family, acquaintances. Most of the arguments we encounter are not as carefully developed as the two examples above. Some of these arguments we find compelling; others we do not.

It is of both theoretical and practical importance to know more than we do about what determines whether or not we find an argument convincing. One suspects that, on the whole, (1) we are less than superb at evaluating arguments objectively, and (2) the fact that we are not better at it than we are has had some highly undesirable consequences for humankind. Any shortcomings we have with respect to our ability to evaluate informal arguments are presumably symptomatic of limitations in the uses of evidence more generally. And, as we have already noted, numerous ways in which we fairly consistently misuse evidence have been extensively documented.

A common set of misuses of evidence that are particularly relevant to the focus of this chapter have been referred to collectively as a *confirmation bias* (Nisbett & Ross, 1980; Snyder & Swann, 1978; Wason, 1974). Simply stated, a confirmation bias is a bias toward interpreting data as being more supportive of a favored hypothesis than they actually are. If the confirmation bias is as prevalent as it appears to be, it may help to explain how it is that large numbers of people come to believe strongly things that (from the point of view of others who do not believe them) are incredible if not bizarre. And indeed an explanation is needed, because the evidence suggests that the human mind is capable of believing just about anything, and at one time or another probably has (Evans, 1973; Gardner, 1957; Medawar, 1979).

One of my favorite examples of gullibility driven by the desire to believe is the account given by MacKay (1842) of the stock speculation mania in Britain in the early eighteenth century. The desire to get rich quickly by speculating with capital was running high, and schemers willing to relieve people of their assets were rising to the opportunity to turn this desire to their own profit. MacKay described numerous investment schemes into which people eagerly put their money with little or no evidence to support the belief that their expectations for large profits were well founded. MacKay's description of a scheme that he viewed as "the most absurd and preposterous of all" and "which showed more completely than any other, the utter madness of the people" is worth quoting at length. The scheme

> was one started by an unknown adventurer, entitled, "A company for carrying on an undertaking of great advantage, but nobody to know what it is." Were not the fact stated by scores of credible witnesses, it would be impossible to believe that any person could have been duped by such a project. The man of genius who essayed this bold and successful inroad upon public credulity, merely stated in his prospectus that the required capital was half a million, in five thousand shares of 100 pounds each, deposit 2 pounds per share. Each subscriber, paying his deposit, would be entitled to 100 pounds per annum per share. How this immense profit was to be obtained, he did not condescend to inform them at that time, but promised that in a month full particulars should be duly announced, and a call made for the remaining 98 pounds of the sub-

scription. Next morning, at nine o'clock, this great man opened an office in Cornhill. Crowds of people beset his door, and when he shut up at three o'clock, he found that no less than one thousand shares had been subscribed for, and the deposits paid. He was thus, in five hours, the winner of 2000 pounds. He was philosopher enough to be contented with his venture, and set off the same evening for the continent. He was never heard from again. (p. 55)

The twentieth-century reader is likely to find more humor than pathos in this amazing story; however, it is not difficult to think of more frightening examples of what a confirmation bias can produce. Nazi Germany and Jonestown come immediately to mind.

It is easy to criticize people for holding beliefs that appear to us to be strange or unfounded. Sometimes we find such beliefs amusing, and may, in less gracious moments, poke fun at them. What we are likely to overlook is the fact that all of us are capable of holding—and in fact probably do hold—beliefs that appear peculiar or unfounded to others. Moreover, partiality toward evidence that supports beliefs we favor can be very subtle and need not be deliberate to be effective. An example of a particularly significant and long-term effect of an unwitting confirmation bias is given by Thomas (1979), who pointed out that it was only quite recently that medicine became scientific in its approach. In his words:

> The history of medicine has never been a particularly attractive subject in medical education, and one reason for this is that it is so unrelievedly deplorable a story. For century after century, all the way into the remote millennia of its origins, medicine got along by sheer guesswork and the crudest sort of empiricism. It is hard to conceive of a less scientific enterprise among human endeavors. Virtually anything that could be thought up for the treatment of disease was tried out at one time or another, and, once tried, lasted decades or even centuries before being given up. It was, in retrospect, the most frivolous and irresponsible kind of human experimentation, based on nothing but trial and error, and usually resulting in precisely that sequence. Bleeding, purging, cupping, the administration of infusions of every known plant, solutions of every known metal, every conceivable diet including total fasting, most of these based on the weirdest imaginings about the cause of disease, concocted out of nothing but thin air—this was the heritage of medicine up until a little over a century ago. It is astounding that the profession survived so long, and got away with so much with so little outcry. (p 159)

How is it that useless treatments could persist for so long? One possible partial answer to that question is that people may derive some therapeutic benefits from their *belief* in the effectiveness of a particular treatment, independently of the treatment's objective merits. Another possible explanation involves a misinterpretation of temporal succession as compelling evidence of a cause–effect relationship. One observes that people with a certain type of illness often get better if they are given a certain type of treatment. The inference then is made that the improvement in health is caused by the treatment. What is easy to overlook, and according to

Thomas what generally was overlooked, was the fact that many illnesses, and particularly those that yielded to treatment, were temporary anyway. That is, many people would have gotten better with or without the treatment they received, but the natural tendency of practitioners seems to have been to discount the possibility of spontaneous recovery and to attribute regained health to the remedies they had prescribed.

V. IMPEDIMENTS TO EFFECTIVE REASONING IN THE EVALUATION OF ARGUMENTS

Taxonomies are, at best, convenient ways of organizing ideas and should never be taken very seriously. The world seldom is quite as simply divisible into neat compartments as our penchant for partitioning it conceptually would suggest. Nevertheless, it is useful to distinguish three types of impediments to effective evaluation of informal arguments. For want of better terms, I refer to these as *natural limitations, knowledge impediments,* and *attitudinal impediments.*

A. Natural Limitations

Certainly our ability to reason is constrained somewhat by natural limitations. Some of these limitations—fallible memory, inability to think of many things at once—are common to everyone. In addition to the limitations we share, each of us also undoubtedly has his own idiosyncratic natural limitations that may interfere with reasoning in one way or another. I will not dwell on this topic here because I suspect that for the vast majority of people these types of limitations are of less consequence than the others, and we know less well how to deal with them in any case.

B. Knowledge Impediments

Some people believe that if one is smart enough one need not know very much to get along in the world. Perhaps this view has some merit. Cleverness undoubtedly has great survival value. It is not difficult to think of situations in which a quick wit would have greater utility than a large amount of factual knowledge. In general, however, knowledge is an essential component of effective reasoning, and there is no substitute for it. Elsewhere (Nickerson, 1986) I have distinguished three types of knowledge that seem important to reasoning: *topical knowledge, procedural knowledge, and self-knowledge.* It may be helpful to use the same distinction here.

1. Topical Knowledge

Among other things, reasoning has to do with judging the plausibility of assertions, and one cannot judge the plausibility of an assertion about physics or history or economics unless one knows something about physics or history or economics. Moreover, the more one knows about a subject, the more effectively, other things being equal, will one be able to reason about that subject. When two equally intelligent people are engaged in a dispute and one of them is much more knowledgeable about the topic of the dispute than the other, there can be little question that the less knowledgeable person is at a significant disadvantage.

One might protest that this position distorts the meaning of reasoning, that reasoning has to do not with the knowledge one has but with how one uses that knowledge inferentially. But such hairsplitting serves no practical purpose. The less knowledgeable person, though his reasoning be ever so impeccable from a puristic point of view, is very likely to lose the dispute. Another way to make the point is to say that reasoning does not occur in a vacuum. Although logic has to do with the forms of argument as distinct from their content, the arguments one encounters in real life have content as well as form, and being able to judge the truth or falsity of that content, clearly a knowledge-based ability, is essential to effective reasoning in any but the most abstract sense.

Perkins and his colleagues have studied the kinds of difficulties people have in informal reasoning, which "is taken to mean generating arguments to test the truth of propositions, but outside the formalisms of strict deductive or probabilistic inference" (Perkins, 1982, p. 1). Most of the types of problems that were identified were described as problems of inadequate model building, that is, failures to elaborate a model of the situation under consideration. These results are particularly thought provoking in light of Johnson-Laird's (1986) claim that logic alone is neither sufficient nor necessary for a theory of competence that will account for the types of inferences people make, and that there is an alternative conception of competence that supports an alternative and more powerful theory of performance. "Reasoning without logic," Johnson-Laird suggested, "consists of three simple steps: interpret the premises by constructing a model based on their truth conditions, formulate an informative conclusion, and check the conclusion by searching for different models of the premises" (1986, p. 46). How good one is likely to be at model building may well depend somewhat on one's intelligence, but it surely also must depend on one's knowledge about the situation for which the model is built.

The first rule for evaluating informal arguments then is to know something about the topics of those arguments. Moreover, the more one knows about a topic, the better equipped one is to evaluate arguments about that topic. There is nothing quite so certain to render an argument ineffectual as the sure knowledge that a premise or critical supporting assertion is false.

2. Procedural Knowledge

The idea that the lack of topical knowledge can be an impediment to effective reasoning does not carry the implication that much knowledge about a subject suffices to guarantee that reasoning about that subject will be sound. It is certainly possible for a person who knows a lot about a subject to reason poorly about it. Knowledgeability about a subject may lessen the likelihood that one will commit certain types of logical errors in arguments that deal with that subject. That is, one who knows a lot about a particular subject might decide that the conclusion of a formal argument relating to that subject is false, in spite of the fact that the premises are true, simply because he *knows* the conclusion to be false and not because he understands that the argument violates the laws of logic. But topical knowledge is not a guarantee against faulty reasoning and may in some cases facilitate it. It is fairly well known, for example, that people are more likely to judge an invalid syllogism to be valid if they know the conclusion to be true than if they know it to be false (Janis & Frick, 1943; Kaufman & Goldstein, 1967; Morgan & Morton, 1944; Revlin & Leirer, 1978; Wason & Johnson-Laird, 1972). So when one's task is to evaluate an argument with respect to its logical validity, the truth value of the conclusion can in fact impair one's ability to do so.

The role of logic in everyday reasoning is still a much debated subject. Opinions range from those that see logic as the foundation of all valid reasoning, whether or not the rules of logic are explicitly known by the reasoner, to those that see logic and everyday reasoning as quite separate and independent. One may, of course, define reasoning as thinking in accordance with the rules of logic, but this is unsatisfactory for several reasons. First, the definition would be vacuous without a specification of the particular logic to which it refers. A reasonable default assumption, in the absence of a specification, is the formal deductive logic of Aristotle and the Scholastics. But this is at best an insufficient basis for reasoning because it does not accommodate all the forms of inference that would be widely recognized as valid, e.g., the inference from "All A are B or C" to "All A that are not B are C," to borrow an example from Braine (1978). Second, deductive logic does not permit one to go beyond the given. And this makes it insufficient to the demands of reasoning in everyday life. The practical demands of everyday problems require the bringing to bear on them of whatever information one may have that is relevant and helpful in arriving at a solution; deductive logic prohibits the use of any information beyond that contained explicitly in the premises.

Henle (1962) has suggested that many of the "fallacies" that are found in everyday reasoning may not really be the result of faulty reasoning but the result of changes people make in the content of arguments. People may, for example, restate a premise or a conclusion so that its intended meaning is changed. Or they may omit or add premises. The claim has received considerable corroboration in the work of several investigators who have studied the *premise conversion error*, whereby one encodes "All *A* are *B*" as equivalent to "All *B* are *A*" (O'Brien, 1973; Revlis, 1975; Thornton, 1980). When people alter the contents of arguments in such ways, the conclusions they draw may be valid with respect to the altered arguments even if invalid with respect to the original ones. Henle suggested that much of what has been taken as evidence of widespread lack of ability to reason logically may be accounted for in this way.

Whatever one's view regarding the role of logic in everyday reasoning, total lack of knowledge of rules of deductive inference can hardly be considered advantageous. To be sure, if Henle is correct in her claim that people often alter the contents of arguments but then reason logically on the basis of the arguments as altered, this suggests that the need is not so much for teaching the rules of inference as for fostering care in the interpretation of language and sensitivity to the importance of not modifying the content of an argument when evaluating it. For practical purposes, the consequences of violating rules of deductive inference and of modifying the contents of deductive arguments may be the same. In both cases, the result may be the drawing of conclusions that do not follow from the premises *as given*. Also, for practical purposes, the assumption that people understand logic implicitly is somewhat risky in the absence of truly compelling evidence that they do. We should not lightly discard the possibility that among the important impediments to effective reasoning may be a lack of knowledge of the ways in which valid deductive inferences may be drawn and of procedures for checking the validity of instances of such inferences.

In view of our assumption that most of the arguments we encounter in everyday life are informal and have important inductive components, an even more significant impediment to reasoning than lack of knowledge of rules of deductive inference may be the lack of understanding of how to evaluate informal arguments. Unfortunately, here we are in territory that is largely unexplored. While much effort has been put into codifying rules of deductive logic, relatively little attention, by comparison, has been given to the problem of developing effective procedures for evaluating informal arguments. So there is a sense in which lack of knowledge of this type is the norm. This in no way diminishes its importance as an impediment to reasoning.

3. Self-Knowledge

Psychologists have been studying human reasoning for many years. Although our understanding of it is still very limited, some of the knowledge that has been acquired has significant practical implications. It is possible, for example, to identify a variety of specific ways in which our reasoning is often fallacious or deficient, e.g., we often appeal to authority, number, or tradition for justification of beliefs, accept explanations uncritically, confuse naming with explaining, confuse correlation or temporal succession with causation, use analogies as proofs, and so on. While knowledge of the tendency of our reasoning to go astray in specific ways does not assure us of avoiding these problems, lack of that knowledge should make us especially vulnerable to them.

Perhaps more problematic than lack of knowledge about the reasoning limitations or deficiencies that we share with most other human beings is unawareness of those that tend to be most consequential to each of us as individuals. It is in the nature of things that we find it much easier to see the faults or weaknesses of others than our own. Unawareness of one's own particular mix of strengths and weaknesses as a reasoner, however, is itself a weakness that is likely to amplify whatever others exist.

C. Attitudinal Impediments

Perhaps there are no greater impediments to effective reasoning than those that derive from a confusion between reasoning and rationalizing, or, to make the same distinction in other terms, between weighing evidence on the one hand and defending a position or making a case on the other. This is the problem of our frequent failure, perhaps our inability, to assess evidence objectively and without bias when we have a vested interest in the outcome of a debate.

Many writers have addressed this problem. Here is a sampling of what a few of them have said:

> The human understanding when it has once adopted an opinion (either as being the received opinion or as being agreeable to itself) draws all things else to support and agree with it. And though there be a greater number and weight of instances to be found on the other side, yet these it either neglects and despises, or else by some distinction sets aside and rejects; in order that by this great and pernicious predetermination the authority of its former conclusions may remain inviolate. (Bacon, 1620/ 1939, p.36).

> For human nature is such that if A and B are engaged in thinking in common, and are communicating their opinions to one another on any subject, so long as it is not

a mere fact of history, and A perceives that B's thoughts on one and the same subject are not the same as his own, he does not begin by revising his own process of thinking, so as to discover any mistake which he may have made, but he assumes that the mistake has occurred in B's. (Schopenhauer, undated, p. 3)

> If we have nothing personally at stake in a dispute between people who are strangers to us, we are remarkably intelligent about weighing the evidence and in reaching a rational conclusion. We can be convinced in favor of either of the fighting parties on the basis of good evidence. But let the fight be our own, or let our own friends, relatives, fraternity brothers, be parties to the fight, and we lose our ability to see any other side of the issue than our own. . . . The more urgent the impulse, or the closer it comes to the maintenance of our own selves, the more difficult it becomes to be rational and intelligent. (Thurstone, 1924/1960, p. 101)

> It is not in the nature of the assertion, but in the manner of assertiveness that everyday thinking seeks to attain necessity. Its commonest introductory phrases, when it is expressed in words, are "of course", "beyond a doubt", and—especially perhaps in political circles—"I am (or "we are") confident that". The source of the compulsion being now within the thinker, and particularly in his social group, it is possible, and indeed common, for completely contradictory issues to claim the same necessity. Then the only way either side has of enforcing its claim is yet more violent assertiveness. It is partly on account of this that many people have said that everyday thinking is largely emotional thinking. (Bartlett, 1958, p. 1181)

Ellis (1973a, 1973b) has hypothesized that people who hold irrational beliefs are particularly likely to hold them dogmatically and that such beliefs interfere with their ability to reason effectively. In one attempt to test this hypothesis, Tobacyk and Milford (1982) had college students complete both the Rokeach Dogmatism scale and the Uncritical Inference Test and found correlations consistent with the idea that the greater the tendency to endorse irrational beliefs (as indicated by scores on the Rokeach scale), the greater the degree of dogmatism and the weaker the ability for critical inferencing.

The problem is a particularly insidious one, however, and it is not restricted to people who hold extreme views. Essentially everyone pays lip service to the idea that evidence should be assessed objectively. Who of us would not profess to desire that disputes in which we find ourselves engaged be settled in the interest of truth? However, such evidence as we have suggests that our behavior, when we are engaged in disputes, is anything but unbiased and objective.

The pervasiveness of this problem was impressed upon me recently by a demonstration of a project the objective of which was to teach secondary school students to think more effectively. The students had been trained in the application of a certain method to the analysis and evaluation of ideas. They were given specific ideas, typically in the form of aphorisms (e.g., "things are not always as they appear," "peace is more than the absence of war") and asked to assess them. The method required the students to think about (work with) the ideas, to ask specific questions about them, to consider the meanings of the words used to express them, and to compare them with similar and dissimilar ideas. Students worked in groups and then selected a spokesperson to report the results of their analysis and evaluation.

The method clearly worked in that it stimulated the students to think about the ideas and it gave them a structure in terms of which to do so. The spokespersons in the demonstrations were able to articulate the results of their group deliberations quite impressively. My misgivings about the demonstration arose during the question period following the spokespersons' presentations. Members of the audience questioned some of the conclusions that had been drawn. Students responded to the questioning enthusiastically and articulately. What impressed me most, however, was the fact that the responses were invariably defenses of the conclusions that had originally been drawn. In no case was there an acknowledgment by a student that one of these conclusions should perhaps be reconsidered and possibly modified. In short, the students had become effective debaters and could certainly hold their own in a dispute. They were poised, confident, and thoroughly enjoying themselves. They were not at all intimidated by the fact that the conclusions they had drawn were being challenged by adults. However, once having stated a conclusion or having taken a position on an issue, they saw their task from then on as that of defending the conclusion they had drawn or the position they had taken.

It would be unfair to blame this aspect of the students' behavior on the training program in which they had participated. The fact that they defended positions they had taken and failed to consider the possibility of modifying those positions in no way distinguished them from almost everyone else; they did precisely what most of us would do in similar circumstances, except that perhaps they did it more effectively. The training experience apparently did nothing to modify this behavior, except perhaps to reinforce it. I do not know of any program in existence that is demonstrably effective in modifying this kind of behavior. Indeed, I am unaware of any training program that has this as an explicit objective.

In my view, the importance of this problem is difficult to overstate. It undoubtedly is at the root of many reasoning difficulties in a wide variety of contexts ranging from interpersonal disagreements to disputes among nations. Is it too much to say that this is *the* fundamental cause of irrational behavior? The challenge the problem poses for education is not so much that of teaching people how to weigh evidence objectively, but that of instilling in them not only the willingness but also the desire to do so consistently.

VI. THE TEACHING OF REASONING

If our goal is to produce better reasoners, what might we try to teach? If the comments in Section V regarding the impediments to effective reasoning have any merit, they suggest that the teaching might have three major foci: natural limitations, knowledge, and attitudes.

A. Natural Limitations

I will not deal with the question of natural limitations here except to make two points. First, it is important to recognize that what can appear to be a natural limitation may be an artificial one deriving from inadequate learning experiences. Such unnatural limitations may be removed through appropriate remedial training. Second, those natural limitations that do exist seldom are the factors that limit the intellectual performance of individuals. That is to say, given that all of us have certain natural limitations, seldom do we perform at the maximum levels that those limitations would permit. The challenge is that of coming closer to maximizing our potential, whatever that potential may be.

B. Knowledge

In Section V,B, three types of knowledge that can be useful for reasoning were distinguished: knowledge of the topic about which reasoning is being done, knowledge of methods and procedures that can be used in the service of reasoning, and knowledge about human reasoning and about oneself as a reasoner. If, as I have claimed, an individual who is very knowledgeable about a given subject is better prepared to reason about that subject than one who is less knowledgeable about it, a primary objective of one who would reason well about a given subject should be to become knowledgeable about that subject. So much is obvious.

The problem with topical knowledge impediments is that they are not "fixable" quickly in any general way. Mere mortals cannot hope to know enough to be able to evaluate all the informal arguments they encounter on the basis of their knowledge of the topics those arguments address. However, it is within the realm of the possible to be aware of one's limitations in this regard, to realize when an argument relates to a subject about which one knows little, and to be willing to reserve judgment in such cases. When the subject of an argument is important to an individual, then his first objective should be to acquire the knowledge that would make an objective evaluation possible.

In contrast to topical knowledge, knowledge of methods and procedures that can be used to aid reasoning should be useful independently of subject area. Procedural knowledge is how-to knowledge. Examples of such knowledge that can be useful in reasoning are knowledge of:

How to represent class relationships with a diagram.
How to construct a contingency matrix.
How to determine logical equivalence.
How to use a truth table.
How to evaluate an argument.

Basic to such procedural knowledge is some understanding of logic and rules of deductive inference, a grasp of certain fundamental concepts (e.g., implication, falsifiability, weight of evidence), an appreciation of some basic distinctions (e.g., between truth and validity, between reasoning and rationalizing), and a variety of ways of explicating implicative relationships so as to help determine the validity or invalidity of argument forms (truth tables, Euler circles, Venn diagrams).

There can be little doubt that such knowledge is useful. Moreover, an advantage in teaching formal reasoning is the fact that there are some objective procedures that can be taught and there are objective criteria in terms of which to evaluate a student's performance. An argument in syllogistic form is either valid or not, and it is a relatively straightforward task to determine whether a student knows how to distinguish valid from invalid forms.

But, as we have noted, there is much more to reasoning than the construction or evaluation of formal arguments. Most of the arguments that we encounter in everyday life are neither formal nor precise. They are collections of assertions (not always explicit or direct) that are constructed for the purpose of persuading someone to believe or do specific things. Seldom can such arguments be determined to be valid or invalid. The most that one can say for them is that they are more or less convincing. In evaluating such arguments, one must decide whether, or the extent to which, one believes the assertions of which they are composed; one must judge how relevant those assertions are and weigh them accordingly. One must also be sensitive to relevant information that is not included in any given argument, and one must be willing to consider the merits of the argument relative to counterarguments that might be made.

The teaching of such things presents some problems. There are no methods for evaluating informal arguments that are comparable to those that are available for evaluating formal arguments. Indeed, there are no generally agreed upon criteria for judging the soundness of such arguments. Constructing them and evaluating them are both creative processes in which the role of domain-specific knowledge is critical.

Given the goal of improving the ability of students to evaluate informal arguments critically, how should one proceed? What specifically, by way of a procedure, might one try to teach? One attempt (Nickerson, 1983) to answer this question is represented by some lesson material that I developed for an experimental course designed to teach thinking skills to seventh-grade students in Venezuela. The concept of an informal (or plausible) argument is introduced in this material after some attention is given to formal (or logical) arguments. The concept of an argument is itself introduced only after several lessons focused on assertions.

An informal argument is defined as a set of assertions, one of which (the key assertion) is made more plausible by the others (the supporting assertions). The purpose of an informal argument is identified as that of convincing someone to believe or do something by giving reasons why he should. The material then engages the students in analyzing several simple informal arguments, distinguishing between the key assertion and the supporting assertions in each case. A procedure for evaluating informal arguments is gradually developed, containing the following steps:

- Understand the argument. Identify the key assertion you are being asked to believe and the supporting assertions. To understand an argument requires recognizing what one is being asked to believe and what is being claimed in support of that belief. Some of these claims may be made indirectly or implicitly, so it may be difficult to explicate them in some cases, but it should be done. If the argument cannot be made explicit, it probably cannot be evaluated.

- Consider whether you believe the supporting assertions to be true. Any supporting assertions that you consider to be false do not increase the credibility of the key assertion.

- Consider whether (or the degree to which) each supporting assertion that you believe to be true does in fact support the key assertion. An assertion must be true *and* truly supportive of the key assertion in order to enhance its credibility. An important aspect of evaluating informal arguments is being able to identify and discount claims that really are irrelevant to the point of argument.

- Try to construct a counterargument. A counterargument is an argument whose key assertion is contradictory to the key assertion of the original argument. In trying to construct a counterargument, one is naturally led to consider whether some facts that are relevant but detrimental to the original argument have been left unstated. Trying to think of counterarguments is an especially important aspect of evaluating arguments, because in deciding whether or not to believe a particular assertion (e.g., a key assertion of an informal argument), one really wants to weigh all the evidence at one's command, pro and con. Arguments typically present only pro information because their purpose is to convince. An important aspect of evaluating an argument therefore is that of filling in, to the best of one's ability, the cons. The ability to generate counterarguments depends heavily on knowledge of the subject. The more one knows that is relevant to the subject, the more likely one is to be able to produce legitimate counterarguments if there are any to be produced.

* Consider the relative plausibility of the original argument and the counterargument. This must be done, of course, in light of whatever reservations one may have about the supporting assertions as a result of applying the first three steps.

The procedure may be summarized succinctly as follows: Understand the argument. Identify the key assertion that is made and the assertions that are offered in its support. Consider whether the supporting assertions are true, and if they are, whether they really make the key assertion more believable. Consider what true assertions can be made that tend to make the key assertion less believable. Decide whether the weight of the evidence favors the key assertion or its denial.

The ability to use this procedure effectively obviously depends not only on some knowledge of the subject of the argument, but also on some knowledge about arguments per se. When the procedure is introduced, considerable attention is given to such things as the distinction between formal and informal arguments, the concepts of implication and contradiction, the concept of a counterargument, and the special difficulty of evaluating one's own arguments objectively and fairly. Whether this approach will be successful in improving the ability of students to reason effectively about arguments remains to be seen.

The third type of knowledge the lack of which was mentioned as possibly being an impediment to effective reasoning was self-knowledge: knowledge about human reasoning in general and about one's own strengths and weaknesses as an individual in particular. Of the impediments we have considered, lack of knowledge about human reasoning is perhaps among the easiest to address. Research has yielded a considerable body of knowledge about various ways in which we frequently reason fallaciously or suboptimally. To the extent that these problems are documented, it would seem to make sense to teach about them explicitly.

To be sure, teaching *about* reasoning, and about how reasoning goes astray in particular, is not necessarily the same as getting students *to reason* more effectively. But it seems unlikely that these are completely independent things. I strongly suspect that teaching students about reasoning helps to make them better reasoners, at least in some instances. On the other hand, I suspect also that teaching students about reasoning is not really enough. If reasoning skills are truly skills in the usual sense of the word, they are probably improved most effectively by practice.

Addressing the problem of individuals' lack of knowledge about their individual idiosyncrasies as reasoners is a more difficult task than that of teaching about human reasoning in general. However, the teaching about reasoning in general should provide some help in that regard, because it would give the individual a perspective in terms of which to view his own reasoning performance. Assuring that the individual develops a realistic view of his own strengths and weaknesses as a reasoner will be a challenge to the individual teacher.

C. Attitudes

The teaching of attitudes conducive to effective reasoning is probably the most important objective and at the same time the most problematic one. In the absence of a strong desire to be rational (which is different from a desire to appear to be rational), it is highly unlikely that one will reason effectively (which is not to say that one will never win disputes). But how does one instill in a student a commitment to the truth, an open-mindedness in evaluating evidence, a willingness (indeed a desire) to be proven wrong when one is wrong, a greater desire to arrive at conclusions that are most consistent with all the available evidence than to win disputes, a recognition of one's own fallibility and of the fact that even one's most strongly held beliefs could be wrong? I take it as apparent that such attitudes are important to rationality. It also is obvious that they are not universally held. If they were, the world would be a very different place.

How to instill such attitudes in students? I do not believe we know the answer to that question. One thing does seem clear, however; attitudes are probably more effectively projected than overtly taught. It seems a safe conjecture that teachers who consistently display such attitudes are more likely to see them appropriated by their students than those who talk about them but fail to live them.

VII. A COMMENT ON LOGISTICS

A logistics question pertaining to curricula for the teaching of reasoning skills is the question of whether such skills are better taught in the context of traditional content courses or by means of specially designed courses that are relatively content free. Each approach has its advocates and both are being tried. Representative of the arguments made in favor of the special-course, content-free approach are those made by Feuerstein in connection with his Instrumental Enrichment Program (Feuerstein, Rand, Hoffman, & Miller, 1980). Feuerstein and his colleagues argued that the use of traditional curricular content can meet with several "resistances," especially if the student has a history of failure with such material. Moreover, the assumption is made that the use of content-free material helps the student attend more directly to the objectives of the instruction vis-à-vis the development of cognitive abilities rather than concentrating on the content itself.

Representative of the integrated approach are the several community college programs that have grown out of the "learning cycle" approach to the teaching of thinking skills described by Karplus (1974). In these programs, teachers of traditional subjects such as physics, mathematics, and English have redesigned their courses with a view to facilitating the development of reasoning and other thinking skills in the process of studying the subject matter of the course. Descriptions of several of these programs may be found in Fuller (1980).

There are not sufficient evaluative data to support a firm conclusion that either of these approaches is better than the other. There is no compelling reason to view them as mutually exclusive alternatives. A recent report from the Task Force on the Teaching of Learning Strategies and Thinking Skills (1985) opted not to take a stand on the question of whether such things are better taught through special courses or in the context of the traditional curriculum. It recognized the possibility that both approaches could work, but did urge a close coupling of the teaching of these higher mental skills with the teaching of conventional content. Thus, when such things are taught in special courses, care should be taken to ensure that students are made aware of their relevance to traditional courses; conversely, when they are taught in the context of traditional courses, there is a need to highlight the higher order skills per se and their applicability to contexts other than that in which they are initially encountered.

ACKNOWLEDGMENTS

This chapter is based on BBN Report No. 5577 which was prepared for the U. S. Department of Education, Office of Educational Research and Improvement, National Institute of Education, under contract 400-80-0031.

REFERENCES

Bacon, F. (1939). *Novum organum*. In Burtt, E. (Ed.), *The English philosophers from Bacon to Mill*. New York: Random House. (Original work published 1620)
Bartlett, F. B. (1958). *Thinking: An experimental and social study*. New York: Basic.

Braine, M. D. S. (1978). On the relation between the natural logic of reasoning and standard logic. *Psychological Review, 85*, 1–21.

Caramazza, A., McCloskey, M., & Green, B. (1981). Naive beliefs in "sophisticated" subjects: Misconceptions about trajectories of objects. *Cognition, 9*, 117–123.

Carpenter, E. T. (1980). Piagetian interviews of college students. In R. G. Fuller (Director), *Piagetian programs in higher education*, (pp. 15–21). Lincoln: University of Nebraska–Lincoln, ADAPT Program.

Clark, H. H. (1969). Linguistic processes in deductive reasoning. *Psychological Review, 76*, 387–404.

Clement, J. (1982). Students' preconceptions in introductory mechanics. *American Journal of Physics, 50*, 66–71.

Cohen, L. J. (1981). Can human rationality be experimentally demonstrated? *The Behavioral and Brain Sciences, 4*, 317–331.

Einhorn, H. J., & Hogarth, R. M. (1981). Behavioral decision theory: Processes of judgment and choice. *Annual Review of Psychology, 32*, 53–88.

Ellis, A. (1973a). *Humanistic psychotherapy: The rational-emotive approach*. New York: Julian.

Ellis, A. (1973b). *Reason and emotion in psychotherapy*. New York: Julian.

English, H. B., & English, A. C. (1958). *A comprehensive dictionary of psychological and psychoanalytical terms*. New York: MacKay.

Evans, C. (1973). *Cults of unreason*. New York: Farrar.

Feuerstein, R., Rand, Y, Hoffman, M. B., & Miller, R. (1980). *Instrumental enrichment: An intervention program for cognitive modifiability*. Baltimore: University Park.

Fuller, R. G. (Director). (1980). *Piagetian programs in higher education*. Lincoln: University of Nebraska-Lincoln, ADAPT Program.

Gardner, M. (1957). *Fads and fallacies in the name of science*. New York: Dover.

Henle, M. (1962). On the relation between logic and thinking. *Psychological Review, 69*, 366–378.

Janis, I., & Frick, P. (1943). The relationship between attitudes toward conclusions and errors in judging logical validity of syllogisms. *Journal of Experimental Psychology, 33*, 73–77.

Johnson-Laird, P. N. (1977). Reasoning with quantifiers. In P. N. Johnson-Laird & P. C. Wason (Eds.), *Thinking*. New York: Cambridge University Press.

Johnson-Laird, P. N. (1985). Logical thinking: Does it occur in daily life? Can it be taught? In S. F. Chipman, J. Segal, & R. Glaser (Eds.), *Thinking and learning skills: Vol. 2. Research and open questions*, (pp. 293–318). Hillsdale, NJ: Erlbaum.

Johnson-Laird, P. N. (1986). Reasoning without logic. In T. Myers (Ed.), *Reasoning and discourse processes*. London: Academic Press.

Karplus, R. (1974). *Science curriculum improvement study: Teachers handbook*. Berkeley: University of California, Berkeley.

Kaufman, H., & Goldstein, S. (1967). The effects of emotional value of conclusions upon distortions in syllogistic reason. *Psychonomic Science, 7*, 367–368.

Kinkade, R. G. (Ed.). (1974). *Thesaurus of psychological index terms*. Washington DC: American Psychological Association.

Kyburg, H. E., Jr. (1983). Rational belief. *The Behavioral and Brain Sciences, 6*, 231–273.

MacKay, C. (1842). *Memoirs of extraordinary popular delusions and madness of crowds*, (2nd ed.). London: Bentley.

McCloskey, M. (1983). Intuitive physics. *Scientific American, 248*(4), 122–130.

Medawar, P. (1979). A bouquet of fallacies from medicine and medical science with a sideways glance at mathematics and logic. In R. Duncan & M. Weston-Smith (Eds.), *The encyclopedia of delusions*, (pp. 96–106). New York: Simon & Schuster.

Midwest Publications. (1981). *Thinking Skills* (Materials catalogue). Pacific Grove, CA: Midwest Publications.

Morgan, J., & Morton, J. (!944). The distortion of syllogistic reasoning produced by personal convictions. *Journal of Social Psychology, 20*, 39–59.

National Commission on Excellence in Education. (1983). *A nation at risk: The imperative for educational reform*. Washington, DC: U.S. Government Printing Office.

Nickerson, R. S. (1983). Verbal reasoning: Lesson series III. In *Project intelligence teacher's manual*, submitted to the Government of Venezuela, 1983.

Nickerson, R. S. (1984). Kinds of thinking taught in current programs. *Educational Leadership, 42* (1), 26–36.

Nickerson, R. S. (1986). *Reflections on reasoning*. Hillsdale, NJ: Erlbaum.

Nickerson, R. S., Perkins, D., & Smith, E. E. (1985). *The teaching of thinking*. Hillsdale, NJ: Erlbaum.

Nisbett, R., & Ross, L. (1980). *Human inference: Strategies and shortcomings of social judgment*. Englewood Cliffs, NJ: Prentice-Hall.

O'Brien, T. C. (1973). Logical thinking in college students. *Educational Studies in Mathematics, 5*, 71–79.

Perkins, D. N. (1982). *Difficulties in everyday reasoning and their change with education*. Final report to the Spencer Foundation, Project Zero, Graduate School of Education, Harvard University, Cambridge, MA.

Renner, J. W., & Lawson, A. E. (1973). Promoting intellectual development through science teaching. *The Physics Teacher, II*, 273–276.

Revlin, R., & Leirer V. O. (1978). The effect of personal biases on syllogistic reasoning: Rational decisions from personalized representations. In R. Revlin & R. E. Mayer (Eds.), *Human reasoning*. New York: Wiley.

Revlis, R. (1975). Syllogistic reasoning: Logical decisions from a complex data base. In R. Falmagne (Ed.), *Reasoning: Representation and process*. Hillsdale, NJ: Erlbaum.

Schopenhauer, A. (undated). The art of controversy. In T. B. Saunders (Trans.), *The essays of Arthur Schopenhauer*. New York: Willey.

Should the death penalty be allowed in Massachusetts? (1982, October 26). *Boston Globe.* pp. 1–2.

Slovic, P., Fischhoff, B., & Lichtenstein, S. (1977). Behavioral decision theory. *Annual Review of Psychology. 28*, 1–39.

Snyder, M., & Swann, W. B. (1978). Behavioral confirmation in social interaction: From social perception to social reality. *Journal of Experimental Social Psychology. 14*, 148–162.

Soelberg, P. O. (1967). Unprogrammed decision making. *Industrial Management Review, 8*, 19–29.

Sternberg, R. J. (1982). Reasoning, problem solving, and intelligence. In R. J. Sternberg (Ed.), *Handbook of human intelligence* (pp. 225–307). New York: Cambridge University Press.

Task Force on the Teaching of Learning Strategies and Thinking Skills. (1985). Curriculum reform and instructional strategies related to learning strategies and thinking. In *Excellence in our schools: Making it happen*. New York: College Entrance Examination Board.

Thomas, L. (1979). *The medusa and the snail*. New York: Viking.

Thornton, M. C. (1980). Piaget and mathematics students. In R. C. Fuller (Director), *Piagetian programs in higher education*, (pp.67–73). Lincoln: University of Nebraska, ADAPT Program.

Thurstone, L. L. (1960). In C. K. Ogden (Ed.), *The nature of intelligence*. Patterson, NJ: Littlefield, Adams. (Original work published 1924)

Tobacyk, J., & Milford, G. (1982). Criterion validity for Ellis' irrational beliefs: Dogmatism and uncritical inferences. *Journal of Clinical Psychology, 38*, 605–607.

Tomlinson-Keasey, C. (1972). Formal operations in females aged 11 to 54 years of age. *Developmental Psychology, 6*, 364.

Tversky, A., & Kahneman, D. (1974). Judgement under uncertainty: Heuristics and biases. *Science, 185*, 1124–1131.

Wason, P. C. (1974). The psychology of deceptive problems. *New Scientist, 63*, 382–385.

Wason, P. C. (1977). Self-contradictions. In P. N. Johnson-Laird & P. C. Wason (Eds.), *Thinking*. New York: Cambridge University Press.

Wason, P. C. & Johnson-Laird, P. N. (Eds.). (1972). *Psychology of reasoning: Structure and content*. London: Batsford.

EPILOGUE

Cognition and Instruction: Why the Marriage Sometimes Ends in Divorce

ROBERT J. STERNBERG
Department of Psychology
Yale University
New Haven, Connecticut 06520

I. INTRODUCTION

The marriage between cognition and instruction, like so many other marriages, can lead to divorce. The possibility of this unhappy ending to the relationship would not, perhaps, be apparent from a reading of the chapters in this book, which present an optimistic portrait of the marriage. Yet those who have actually attempted to apply cognitive principles to instruction know that the relationship between cognition and instruction is not an untroubled one. With the belief that an ounce of prevention is worth a pound of cure and that awareness of potential trouble spots in a relationship can often help mitigate their consequences, I describe here what I believe the main trouble spots to be. Table 1 presents a summary of them.

The main trouble spots I perceive are of three kinds: trouble spots at the level of theory, at the level of ability, and at the level of motivation. Each of these kinds of potential trouble spots is considered in turn.

II. THEORY

The marriage between cognition and instruction requires two theories, one of cognition and one of instruction. Moreover, these theories must apply both at the level of the classroom unit and at the level of the individual.

375

TABLE 1

Potential Trouble Spots in the Linkage between
Cognitive Theory and Educational Practice

	Theory	
	Nomothetic	Idiographic
Cognitive	1	2
Instructional	3	4
	Ability	
	Domain-general	Domain-specific
Student	1	2
Teacher	3	4
	Motivation	
	Intrinsic	Extrinsic
Student	1	2
Teacher	3	4

A. Cognitive Theory

1. Nomothetic

The nomothetic aspect of a cognitive theory is that aspect of the theory that applies to the group—to the classroom unit as a whole. Cognitive theories differ in a number of respects that are directly relevant to their application in instructional settings.

a. Completeness. Does the theory deal with the whole body of the relevant cognitive phenomena or with just a part of them? For example, a theory of mathematical learning will not be very useful in a classroom setting if it deals only with how children add or with how they subtract. Moreover, a full theory should specify both the processes that lead to correct answers and those that lead to errors.

b. Account of and Distinction between Competence and Performance. There is a big difference between cognitive competence and the student's use of that competence in his or her performance. Both are of key importance in the application of cognitive theory to instruction. A competence theory specifies what students could do under ideal circumstances. A performance theory specifies what students actually do, given both dispositional and situational constraints. Use of just a competence theory places unrealistic demands upon the student. For example, many teachers who have attempted to apply Piagetian theory to classroom teaching have ended up being sorely disappointed because the students did not behave in the ways that the theory indicated they should. Much of the problem was probably due to the fact that Piaget's theory is one of competence rather than of performance. Neither the theory nor the teachers made the necessary bridge to students' performance. At the opposite end, use of a theory that specifies only student performance may fail to do justice to the higher levels of competence of which students may be capable.

c. **Empirical Validity.** Refereed psychological journals usually set high standards for the empirical validation of theories that investigators propose. But there is nothing to stop educators from drawing upon cognitive theories that have little or no empirical validity at all. Indeed, some of the fads in contemporary education, especially those based on "brain theory," draw on theories that are considered to be very questionable by most psychologists. High visibility of a theory is no substitute for lack of theory verification.

d. **Instructional Relevance.** A cognitive theory may be largely correct and yet be instuctionally irrelevant. There are any number of reasons why a cognitive theory may be of little or no instructional relevance. For example, the theory may not specify the processes used in learning (although it specifies how that learning is used), or it may specify the processes of learning or performance, but at a level of analysis (too macroscopic or too microscopic) that is inappropriate for instuction.

2. *Idiographic.*

An instructionally useful cognitive theory should be able to deal with individual differences as well as with population commonalities. In other words, the theory should specify sources of individual differences, and what to do about them. For example, individual differences in learning and performance might be due to differences in component processes, the strategies into which these processes combine, the mental representations upon which the processes and strategies act, or the ways in which individuals allocate their attentional resources. Cognitive research indicates that in most instructionally relevant cognitive tasks, substantial individual differences do exist in these and other aspects of information processing. A cognitive theory that does not take into account individual differences may predict classroom performance based on a hypothetical average individual who does not actually exist.

B. Instructional Theory

1. Nomothetic

Perhaps the single greatest source of disappointment in the application of cognitive principles to educational practice is the absence of an instructional theory to mediate the link between cognitive theory, on the one hand, and educational practice, on the other. Cognitive psychologists who have not had a substantial amount of experience in elementary and secondary school classrooms (most of them have had no such experience) may not even realize that this is a problem. The instructional theory should specify the means by which instructional material that draws upon cognitive principles is to be conveyed. For example, the elaborated notions that make up our total framework for instantiating mastery learning or discovery learning provide bases for two different instructional theories. There are several questions that ought to be asked about a proposed instructional theory.

1. *Specification*. Is the instructional theory well specified in the sense of providing a clear and complete specification of what the teacher should do to apply it?

2. *Content relevance*. Is the instructional theory appropriate for the particular content to which it is being applied?

3. *Age relevance*. Is the instuctional theory appropriate for the ages of the children being taught?

4. *Fit with psychological theory*. Does the instructional theory fit, or mesh with the psychological theory?

Consider, for example, teaching of a mathematical skill, such as subtraction. There exist various alternative psychological theories for how children do subtraction (see Chapter 5 by Mayer). Once the teacher decides upon an appropriate (perhaps optimal) strategy to teach, he or she must decide how to teach that strategy, taking into account the variables above. Given the content and the probable age of the students, for example, discovery learning would probably be inappropriate for teaching students, say, how to borrow in subtraction.

2. Idiographic

There now is extensive documentation for the existence of student ability-by-strategy interactions. For example, discovery learning tends to be more successful for brighter than for less bright subjects (Egan & Greeno, 1973). The instructional theory thus needs to take into account individual differences in optimal learning styles. A practical problem for teachers is that it is usually not possible to individualize instruction fully when teaching to a large group. However, it is not impossible to present the same material in two alternative ways in the hope that some students will profit from both methods of instruction and that all students will profit from at least one method.

III. ABILITY

The extent to which the marriage of cognition and instruction succeeds will depend in part on the abilities of both students and teachers. In the case of the students, the most relevant abilities are learning abilities, whereas in the case of the teachers, the most relevant abilities are teaching abilities. These abilities may be either domain-general or domain-specific.

A. Student Ability

There are differences in applicability of both cognitive and instructional theories as a function of the abilities of the individuals to whom the theory is applied. It was noted earlier that the applicability of an instructional theory can depend upon student ability. Similarly, there are differences in cognitive strategies as a function of both levels and patterns of ability. For example, MacLeod, Hunt, and Mathews (1978) found that their subjects' inclination to use a spatial strategy in comparing sentences against pictures was a function of their level of spatial ability. On a more informal basis, I have found in my graduate multivariate data analysis class differential preferences for geometric versus algebraic representations of the same material (e.g., factor-analytic concepts) as a function of students' respective abilities in mentally manipulating abstract forms versus alphanumeric symbols. The very same concepts, therefore, can be understood in two completely different (although isomorphic) ways. A single cognitive model would not suffice for all students.

Interactions of task performance with abilities can be with respect either to domain-general or to domain-specific abilities. Although one might expect most interactions to be with the latter kinds of abilities (Egan & Greeno, 1973), most of the interactions that have been found to date have been with domain-general abilities (Cronbach & Snow, 1977). This may be because domain-general abilities are more easily measured in a reliable or valid way or because such abilities genuinely tend to interact more with instructional treatments.

B. Teacher Ability

Teacher ability, like student ability, can be either domain-general or domain-specific. *Domain-general teaching ability* refers to the sheer ability of an individual to teach without regard to subject matter, given the requisite knowledge. *Domain-specific teaching ability* refers to a teacher's specialized skill in teaching in a given area of subject matter. The effectiveness of the application of either cognitive or instructional theory to teaching depends dramatically on the ability of the teacher effectively to implement these theories.

Nowhere has this fact been illustrated so dramatically to me as in the teacher training I did for implementation of my program *Intelligence Applied: Understanding and Increasing Your Intellectual Skills* in Venezuela (R. Sternberg, 1986). Some individuals caught on quickly and proved to be excellent teachers, almost from the start. Others caught on, but more slowly. Still others never really fully caught on, although for a variety of different reasons. Some did not understand the material well. Others understood it but were unable to acquire a sense of how to convey it. Still others understood the material and were able to convey it, but only to a small handful of students whose cognitive predispositions matched their own. In short, for whatever strengths and weaknesses the program may have had, the teacher's ability to implement it was a key variable in its ultimate success—or failure—within a given classroom.

IV. MOTIVATION

We implemented closely related training programs for teaching learning-to-learn skills in two different school systems—one an inner-city school catering primarily to lower- to lower-middle-class students, the other a suburban school catering primarily to upper-middle-class students. In the inner-city implementation, the program was successful only to the most modest degree. In the suburban implementation, the program was successful almost to a spectacular degree. There were any number of differences between the two sites and implementations, but it was clear from the start that one difference overshadowed all the others—motivation, both on the part of the students and on the part of the teachers.

A. Student Motivation

It is a commonplace, but nonetheless important observation that no instructional program will truly succeed in the absence of student motivation. If the students do not care to learn, they won't. And often they don't. In most settings, one cannot simply count on students' being motivated. Hence, one must build motivational aids into one's program of instruction. This is true for any instruction, but it is especially true for instruction based upon cognitive theories, because such theories, in themselves, are usually *wholly* cognitive and hence contain no direct implications for how students can be motivated to learn their principles, or according to their principles. The most successful training programs of any sort are those that take the issue of student motivation seriously. For example, Feuerstein's (1980) Instrumental Enrichment Program seems to be most effective in its raising of student self-esteem and motivation to succeed (John Bransford, personal communication). The extremely effective motivational aids built into the program are probably even more important than the cognitive theory underlying it.

Student motivation may be either intrinsic, extrinsic, or a combination of both. In some cases, extrinsic rewards will need to be built into a program in order to motivate students to perform at all (B. Sternberg, 1977). However, it is important to take into account the fact that extrinsic reinforcers tend to undermine intrinsic motivation. What is worse, when the extrinsic rewards are taken away, as inevitably they are at some point during a student's career, the student may be left with no motivation at all to perform well on the tasks that were formerly extrinsically reinforced (Greene, B. Sternberg, & Lepper, 1976).

B. Teacher Motivation

Our unsuccessful foray into the inner-city school district mentioned earlier was marred by lack of student motivation, but part of this lack of student motivation was almost certainly a direct result of lack of teacher motivation. Almost from the first day, the teachers made it clear to us that they had little and in some cases no interest in the project. It would be convenient, but unfair, to blame the teachers. For one thing, teachers received no benefits from the school for participation in the program. To the contrary, the program took time away from their being able to teach the students what they saw as the primary subject matter of their course—subject matter on which the students, and hence the teachers, would be evaluated. For another thing, there was only the most minimal opportunity to inform the teachers as to just what was being done and why. As a result, their involvement tended to decrease as time went on, and they became increasingly uncertain as to just what it was they were supposed to be accomplishing. The main point to be made is a simple one: Without teacher motivation, very little will follow from any instructional program based on cognitive theory. To get teacher support we need full administrative support. In our own program, we lacked the latter and hence lost the former.

V. CONCLUSION

If this chapter has tempered the optimism one might experience after reading the chapters that precede it, then the chapter has accomplished one of its two goals. We have all had enough of starry-eyed marriages between cognitive theory and educational practice that end in painful, and sometimes bitter divorce. Matters of cognitive and instructional theory, student and teacher ability, and student and teacher motivation intervene between cognitive theory and its application. However, this brief epilogue has a second and more important goal than that of tempering optimism. This second goal is to make both theorists and practitioners aware that a successful marriage between cognitive theory and instructional practice may well be possible if only certain potential stumbling blocks are taken into account. It is better to take these things into account and to attempt to deal with them before the program is implemented than to wait until a later postmortem that seeks to discover just what went wrong in the implementation of a program. Thus, I believe, with the other authors in this book, that guarded optimism is both reasonable and desirable, because the time is certainly at hand to effect and maintain a successful and long-lasting marriage between cognition and instruction.

ACKNOWLEDGMENT

Preparation of this chapter was supported by Contract N0001483K0013 from the Office of Naval Research and Army Research Institute.

REFERENCES

Cronbach, L. J., & Snow, R. E. (1977). *Aptitudes and instructional methods.* New York: Irvington.

Egan, D. E., & Greeno, J. G. (1973). Acquiring cognitive structure by discovery and rule learning. *Journal of Educational Psychology, 64,* 85–97.

Feuerstein, R. (1980). *Instrumental enrichment: An intervention program for cognitive modifiability.* Baltimore: University Park.

Greene, D., Sternberg, B., & Lepper, M. (1976). Overjustification in a token economy. *Journal of Personality and Social Psychology, 34,* 1219–1234.

MacLeod, C. M., Hunt, E. B., & Mathews, N. N. (1978). Individual differences in the verification of sentence-picture relationships. *Journal of Verbal Learning and Verbal Behavior, 17,* 493–507.

Sternberg, B. J. (1977). *What do tokens and trophies teach?* Unpublished doctoral dissertation, Stanford University, School of Education, Stanford, CA.

Sternberg, R. J. (1986). *Intelligence applied: Understanding and increasing your intellectual skills.* San Diego: Harcourt Brace Jovanovich.

Index

Page numbers followed by *(t)* refer to a table, and those followed by *(f)* refer to a figure.

A

Ability of student, 9
  science education and, 189–190
  social studies and, 221
Abstract processes in music, 323, 324–326, 336
Achievement test, musical, 304–305
Acquisition–learning distinction in second language learning, 91–93
Adult musical cognition, 315–319
Aggregative processes, procedural knowledge and, 3–4
Algebraic application problems, 150–152, *see also* Mathematics
Algebraic computation, 147–150, *see also* Mathematics
Alphabetic system for reading acquisition, 35
  obstacles to, 35–37
Alternating procedures in written composition, 68
Alternative generation, 179
Analogy formation, 169
Aptitude hypothesis in second language learning, 98–100
Argument, 353
  informal, 353–358
  impediments to effective evaluation, 358–364
Arithmetic application, 145–147, *see also* Mathematics
Arithmetic computation, 139–145, *see also* Mathematics

B

Belief systems and reasoning skills, 351–353
Bloomfield, Leonard, 85–87
Bottom-up theories of word perception, 19

C

California Assessment Program, 139, 142–143, 150–151
Changing-note melodies, 318
Checking procedures in written composition, 68

Art, *see also* Children's drawings
  adult's ability to copy, 249–251
Artistic style in children's drawings, 242, 246–247
Associative-learning phase in reading, 40
Atomistic theory of musical aptitude, 303, 304
Attitude hypothesis in second language learning, 98
Attitudinal impediments to reasoning, 362–365, 369
Audio-lingual method of teaching foreign language, 86, 89
Automatic versus deliberate inferencing, 346–348
Automaticity
  in lexical access, 23
  and reading, 32–33
Automatization and second language learning, 107–108